++++++++++++++++++++++++++++++++

THE HEBREW NOVEL

++++++++++++++++++++++++++++++++

in C*z*arist Russia

☝

D1519695

THE HEBREW NOVEL

in Czarist Russia

A Portrait of Jewish Life in the Nineteenth Century

DAVID PATTERSON

ROWMAN & LITTLEFIELD PUBLISHERS, INC.
Lanham • Boulder • New York • Oxford

in association with the European Jewish Publication Society

ejps

ROWMAN & LITTLEFIELD PUBLISHERS, INC.

Published in the United States of America
by Rowman & Littlefield Publishers, Inc.
4720 Boston Way, Lanham, Maryland 20706

ISBN 0-8476-9338-4 (cloth : alk. paper)
ISBN 0-8476-9339-2 (pbk : alk. paper)

Printed in the United States of America

∞ ™ The paper used in this publication meets the minimum
requirements of American National Standard for Information
Sciences—Permanence of Paper for Printed Library Materials, ANSI
Z39.48–1984.

The European Jewish Publication Society is a registered charity which
gives grants to assist in the publication and distribution of books relevant
to Jewish literature, history, religion philosophy, politics and culture.
EJPS, 1st Floor, 37-43 Sackville Street, London W1X 2DL

In Memory of
Louis and Sarah Patterson

Contents

List of Illustrations

Preface to the
Second Printing

The first printing of *The Hebrew Novel in Czarist Russia* appeared in 1964 as number 13 in the Language and Literature series published by Edinburgh University Press. Shortly after its publication, one half of the total edition was destroyed in a warehouse fire. Consequently, the volume has been out of print for almost thirty years. A new title, *The Hebrew Novel in Czarist Russia: A Portrait of Jewish Life in the Nineteenth Century*, seemed more appropriate at the present time.

When the volume originally appeared, modern Jewish studies at university level in the English-speaking world scarcely existed beyond a handful of universities and Jewish seminaries in the United States. On the continent of Europe, the utter devastation inflicted by Nazi Germany during World War II was relieved only by the first faint stirrings of revival. The sole university in Israel, the Hebrew University of Jerusalem, was the only flagship of modern Jewish studies, which were further stimulated by the World Congresses of Jewish Studies meeting once every four years in Jerusalem.

In the last three decades the whole spectrum of Jewish studies at university level has changed dramatically. New universities in Israel, notably Tel Aviv University, Haifa University, Bar Ilan University, Ben Gurion University of the Negev, and the Open University of Israel, have all developed Jewish studies to an impressive extent. So much so, that many university teachers of Jewish studies throughout the world either come from Israel or have spent part of their higher education at an Israeli university.

In the spring of 1966, when I was invited to tour the United States as a B'nai Brith Lecturer, I had the privilege of speaking in the course of two months in some forty places around the United States, including many colleges and universities. Although there were few academic posts in Jewish studies in that year, it was my distinct impression that the time was ripe for great expansion in that field. In fact, the next twenty-five years witnessed a veritable explosion of Jewish studies in North American universities with the creation of literally hundreds of new academic posts and courses, reaching a peak of more than sixty thousand students enrolled in at least one course in Jewish studies at undergraduate level. Although student numbers have fallen, the creation of academic positions continues, and almost every week some new post in one or other of the many branches of Jewish studies is advertised and attracts candidates of high calibre.

Most gratifying, perhaps, is the resurgence of Jewish studies at university level in western, central, and eastern Europe, in the latter case particularly since the collapse of the Soviet Union in 1991. I vividly recall a visit to Moscow with my wife in December 1976, following a clandestine invitation to address Professor Azbel's Sunday morning seminar on the development of Hebrew literature in Czarist Russia. Some forty people sat crowded on the floor of a small apartment, listening with rapt attention for several hours. Because the study of Hebrew had been strictly forbidden in the Soviet Union for more than half a century—the only language to suffer such a prohibition—the subject matter was entirely unknown to most of the audience. Later that day we attended another gathering where young men were learning clandestinely to become Hebrew teachers, and where the conversation was conducted in Hebrew. The determination and sheer courage of these refuseniks made an indelible impression in our minds.

Since then, Jewish studies at university level have continued to grow in France, Italy, Spain, the Netherlands, the Scandinavian countries, and particularly in Germany, as well as in Hungary, Romania, and, more problematically, Poland. Most interesting, perhaps, is the resurgence of these studies in Russia, where despite the vast emigration of Jews to Israel and the United States, Jewish studies at university level are establishing a recognised place. In Great Britain, too, there has been considerable growth of interest in the field, particularly since the founding of the Oxford Centre for Hebrew and Jewish Studies in 1972.

In the second half of the nineteenth and the first decades of the twentieth centuries, the growth of Hebrew literature helped nurture the Jewish national movement. The conversational elements found particularly in the novels of the period may be discerned in the extraordinary revival of Hebrew as a spoken language in Palestine, which in turn stimulated conversational elements in Hebrew literature. The impact on Jewish cultural life under the British Mandate and then particularly following the creation of the State of Israel in 1948 makes the study of this early modern period most rewarding. It is for that reason that the reappearance of the present volume on the fiftieth anniversary of the creation of the State of Israel seems so appropriate.

Although the text and notes have not been altered, apart from two minor corrections, a select supplementary bibliography has been added for the benefit of the serious student. Particular attention should be drawn to the bibliographical works of Professor S. Werses and the volumes in the *Dorot* series devoted to the works of Reuben Asher Braudes and Peretz Smolenskin featured in the additional bibliography.

Sincere thanks are due to the members of the Committee of the Editorial Board of the European Jewish Publication Society and to Matthew Held of Rowman & Littlefield for making the reprinting of this volume possible.

David Patterson
Oxford, 1998

Preface

With the Partitions of Poland at the end of the eighteenth century, a substantial Jewish community was incorporated into the Russian Empire. The Czarist administration was henceforth confronted with the spectacle of a numerous, self-contained and undeniably exotic population living just inside the country's western borders. The Czar's new subjects clung tenaciously to their own distinctive religion, rituals, dietary laws, sartorial quirks, social conventions and system of education. Moreover, as Yiddish was the Jewish vernacular and Hebrew the written language, communication between Jews and Russians was at best tortuous and halting. To their neighbours the Jews appeared an inbred, self-contained and unintelligible community of highly doubtful loyalties.

The wave of nationalism which swept across Russia in the wake of the Napoleonic wars, sharpened the feeling of hostility towards what was considered an alien and hence suspect people living so close to a strategic frontier. As a result, the Czarist administration embarked upon a policy aimed at the 'russification' of its Jewish subjects, and tried throughout the nineteenth century to undermine their separateness, whether by coaxing and blandishment or, as was more frequently the case, by naked and unashamed oppression. Ruthless governmental persecution was aggravated, moreover, and rendered still more painful, by a phenomenal growth in the Jewish population.

The consequent deterioration of an economic situation already desperate occasioned a number of attempts on the part of the Jews to alleviate their plight. Indeed, the waves of emigration to western Europe and America, and the rise of the Zionist movement in the last decades of the century may be regarded in great measure as by-products of Russian nationalism. Certainly the remarkable growth of modern Hebrew literature, as well as the no less spectacular rise of Yiddish literature in Russia in the second half of the last century, reflect a vivid sharpening of Jewish self-consciousness. A like intensity of feeling may be observed in the considerable Jewish literature written in Russian in this period.

This volume comprises a preliminary and tentative endeavour to examine one section of that literature, namely the Hebrew novel in the two decades following the death in 1867 of the first Hebrew novelist, Abraham Mapu, to whom the present author has already devoted a monograph. The twenty years covered by this study roughly correspond with the final period of the Hebrew movement of Enlightenment known as *Haskalah*; although some of the authors under review had by then despaired of the efficacy of that movement as a panacea for Jewish ills, and were already casting about for other solutions.

Of the Hebrew novels published during those two decades the overwhelming majority are concerned with contemporary Jewish life in the *Pale of Settlement*, the area to which the Jews of Russia were confined. Because of the strict rules of censorship prevailing in Russia, however, many of the novels were written and published beyond the frontiers of the Russian Empire, while pseudonyms were frequently employed to disguise the reference to Russian towns. Such stratagems were familiar to the initiated and served to add a pleasurable spice of mild conspiracy to the enjoyment of reading works of fiction.

Compounded of a strange blend of fantasy and realism, these novels remain important for the light they shed on the development of modern Hebrew language and literature, for the influence they exerted on at least one generation of Russian Jewry, and for the considerable information which they yield relative to the social, cultural and religious conditions of Jewish life in Czarist Russia at a most formative period in Jewish history.

In view of the unfamiliarity of the novels under review, summaries of the plots and, wherever possible, brief biographies of the authors have been included in the Introduction.

Except in the case of familiar names the following system of transliteration has been adopted:

א	ʾ	ב	b	בּ	bh	ג	g	גּ	gh
ד	d	ד	dh	ה	h	ו	w	ז	z
ח	ḥ	ט	ṭ	י	y	כ	k	כּ	kh
ל	l	מ	m	נ	n	ס	s	ע	ʿ
פ	p	פּ	ph	צ	ṣ	ק	q	ר	r
שׁ	s	שׁ	š	ת	t	ת	th		

David Patterson
Oxford 1964

Acknowledgments

At every stage in the preparation of this book the author has benefited from the generous advice and help of numerous friends and colleagues. More particularly, he would like to acknowledge his indebtedness to Dr. G. T. Hughes, Emeritus Professor H. H. Rowley, Professor E. Ullendorff, Dr. M. Tyson and especially Dr. M. Wallenstein of the University of Manchester, Mr. I. Wartski of London, Mrs. M. Riley and Mr. R. May of Oxford, Professor C. Rabin and Professor S. Halkin of the Hebrew University of Jerusalem, Dr. G. Elkoshi of the University of Tel-Aviv, and Dr. I. Leef, city librarian of Tel-Aviv for their encouragement, assistance and advice. Publication has been greatly facilitated by the kindness of Professor D. Daube of All Souls College, Oxford. Finally the author wishes to thank his wife for her assistance in the preparation of the manuscript and for a number of helpful suggestions.

David Patterson
Oxford 1964

ONE

Introduction

The purpose of this study is to examine the Hebrew novel written in eastern Europe between the years 1868-1888. This period embraces the final stages of Jewish exclusivity in Europe, before the barriers were largely swept aside by the powerful forces and ideas of the outside world. Of all the cataclysmic events which have since changed the face of Jewish history—the vast migrations westwards to America, the strangulation of Judaism in the Soviet Union, the holocaust caused by antisemitism in Europe and the creation of the Jewish State—these novels reflect only the earliest presentiments. The magnitude of the achievements and catastrophes to come could not then be foreseen. And yet their writers demonstrate a striking awareness of their own society and they are singularly alive to the many pressing and immediate difficulties facing it. Their importance, indeed, stems largely from the fact that they succeeded in arousing a similar self-consciousness in the minds of an increasing circle of readers, and at the same time served as a channel through which the ideas fermenting in the outside world could begin to penetrate Jewish life. By promoting an awareness of contemporary Jewish society and by throwing light upon a number of its darker facets, the novelists helped to foster a growing dissatisfaction with the old order and a search for new forms and possibilities of living. Hence, they played a not insignificant role in the revolutionary changes which were destined to sweep across Jewish life in eastern Europe even prior to the outbreak of the First World War.

The following chapters are devoted to a survey of the Hebrew novel during the last two decades of the period of *Enlightenment* in Hebrew literature, usually termed *Haskalah*,[1] from two points of view. In the first place, an attempt will be made to evaluate the literary qualities of these novels with respect to such features as the manner of construction, the authenticity of characterization and the style of composition, with the aim of assessing their contribution to the development of modern Hebrew literature. Secondly, the novels will be reviewed in the light of the portraits of the social, cultural and religious conditions of Jewish life in eastern Europe, and particularly in Russia, in the nineteenth century which they reflect.

Neither aspect of these stories is entirely satisfactory. The twenty years following the death of the first Hebrew novelist, Abraham Mapu[2] (1808-67), represent a transitional period in modern Hebrew literature, during which the Hebrew author was confronted with a variety of complex and difficult problems, calculated to inhibit his artistic creativity in no uncertain manner.[3] The principal source of these particular problems may be discerned in the attempt to express the values of European civilisation in Hebrew garb. Not only were those values often insufficiently digested, but the chosen linguistic medium also proved a clumsy and inadequate instrument for their expression. Indeed, throughout the nineteenth century, modern Hebrew literature was severely handicapped by this twofold disability.[4] Again, the history of the Jews in Russia during the nineteenth century was characterized by periods of violent oppression on the part of the Czarist government on the one hand,[5] and by bitter strife and internal dissension within the Jewish community on the other. As all the novelists under review participated in that struggle in greater measure or in less, their writings are necessarily tendentious, and the portraits of their environment which they offer must, in consequence, be viewed with caution.[6] Nevertheless, both the literary and the social aspects of the novels of the period may be made to yield considerable information for the historian of literature and the sociologist alike.

The twenty years which form the subject of this study, open with the publication of S. J. Abramowitz's novel *Fathers and Sons* in 1868 and close with the appearance in 1888 of R. A. Braudes' *The Two Extremes*. It must be remembered that prior to this period the only original novels of any significance to have been composed in Hebrew were two historical romances, *The Love of Zion* and *The Guilt of Samaria* by Abraham Mapu, and a social novel *The Hypocrite* by the same author, only the first three parts of which had been published prior to his death in 1867.[7] The present state of Hebrew bibliography makes it impossible to ascertain the total number of original Hebrew novels published during the period under review with any certainty, while the dividing line separating the short novel from the long short-story must, of necessity, remain arbitrary to some extent. Nevertheless, the number of Hebrew novels published during these twenty years is certainly very limited, and can scarcely have averaged very much more than one a year.

The eighteen novels which have been selected for study in the present instance, therefore, may well approximate far more closely to the total number of novels published during the period than to a mere representative selection of them. Ten of the stories are by major writers such as P. Smolenskin, R. A. Braudes, S. J. Abramowitz and A. S. Rabinowitz, while the remaining eight are by minor authors, ranging from the well-known literary personality N. M. Sheikewitz on the one hand to such unknown figures as J. Leinwand, Sarah Feige Meinkin, B. I. Zobeizensky, M. Manassewitz, I. J. Sirkis and I. Weisbrem on the other. The novels of the minor authors have suffered so complete, and in most cases so well-deserved an oblivion that even the various histories of literature do not mention them, while the very names of their authors have, for the most part, been overlooked completely. Many of their novels have become as rare as manuscripts, so that recourse to microfilm has sometimes proved the only practicable method of reading them at all.

The following list comprises all the novels utilized in the present study. The Hebrew titles in transliteration appear in brackets, as do the original places and dates of publication in those cases where later, and more easily accessible editions have been employed:

1. S. J. Abramowitz, *Fathers and Sons* (*Ha-'Abhoth we-ha-Banim*), Odessa, 1868.
2. P. Smolenskin, *The Wanderer in the Paths of Life* (*Ha-To'eh be-Dharekhê ha-Ḥayyim*), Warsaw, 1905 (parts 1-3, Vienna, 1868-70; all 4 parts, Vienna, 1876).
3. P. Smolenskin, *The Joy of the Godless* (*Simḥath Ḥaneph*), Warsaw, 1905 (Vienna, 1872).
4. P. Smolenskin, *A Donkey's Burial* (*Qebhurath Ḥamor*), Warsaw, 1905 (Vienna, 1874).

5. P. Smolenskin, *Pride and Fall (Ga'on we-Šebher)*, Warsaw, 1905 (Vienna, 1874).
6. P. Smolenskin, *The Reward of the Righteous (Gemul Yešarim)*, Vilna, 1903 (Vienna, 1876).
7. P. Smolenskin, *The Inheritance (Ha-Yerušah)*, Peterburg, 1898 (Vienna, 1878-84).
8. R. A. Braudes, *Religion and Life (Ha-Dath we-ha-Ḥayyim)*, Lemberg, 1885 (1876-7).
9. R. A. Braudes, *The Two Extremes (Šetê ha-Qeṣawoth)*, Warsaw, 1888.
10. J. Leinwand, *The Artful Villain ('Oseh Mezimmoth)*, Lemberg, pt. 1, 1875, pt. 2, 1876.
11. S. F. Meinkin, *The Love of the Righteous ('Ahabhath Yešarim)* pt. 1, Vilna, 1881.[8]
12. B. I. Zobeizensky, *For Love of Ṣaddiqim*[9] *('Ahabhath Ṣaddiqim)*, Warsaw, 1881.
13. M. Manassewitz, *The Parents' Sin (Ḥaṭṭa'th Horim)*, Warsaw, 1884.
14. N. M. Sheikewitz, *The Outcast (Ha-Niddaḥath)*, Vilna, 1886.
15. A. S. Rabinowitz, *At the Crossroads, ('Al ha-Pereq)*, Warsaw, 1887.
16. I. J. Sirkis, *Esther ('Ester)*, Warsaw, 1887.
17. I. Weisbrem, *Between the Times (Bên ha-Zemannim)*, Warsaw, 1888.
18. I. Weisbrem, *18 Coins (Ḥay 'Aghoroth)*, Warsaw, 1888.

In the following biographical notes and brief summaries of the respective plots the same order of presentation has been maintained.

Shalom Jacob Abramowitz (1835/6-1917), better known by his pseudonym *Mendele Mokher Sepharim* (Mendele the Bookseller), was born in Kopyl, Lithuania, during the reign of terror introduced by Czar Nicholas I.[10] A diligent and receptive student, he received a traditional Jewish education[11] until the age of 17, after which he set forth with a professional beggar, Abraham the Lame, to wander through the towns and villages of the *Pale of Settlement*[12] in a covered wagon drawn by an old, broken-down mare. In spite of the degradation of that adventure, Abramowitz's wanderings furnished him with an almost unrivalled insight into the Jewish life of the period, which he was subsequently to utilize with such success in his later stories.

In 1853 he escaped from the clutches of his impecunious

patron by fleeing to Kamenets-Podolsk, where he was befriended by the Hebrew and Yiddish poet, Abraham Baer Gottlober, who introduced him to the ideas of the movement of *Haskalah*. From Gottlober's daughters, Abramowitz learned sufficient Russian, German and arithmetic to secure a post in 1856 as a teacher in a local government school. Two years later he went to Berdichev to devote himself to literary work, where he remained for a further eleven years. In 1863 he published a Hebrew story *Lim-medhu Hêṭebh*, which was later expanded into his novel *Fathers and Sons*.[13] In the following year, however, he abandoned Hebrew in order to devote himself to Yiddish, and during the next twenty years published a series of stories under the pseudonym of Mendele the Bookseller, which virtually revolutionized Yiddish literature.

In 1881 Mendele was appointed head of the *Talmudh Torah*[14] in Odessa, which city was then a major centre of Hebrew literature; and in 1886 he returned once again to Hebrew as his primary language of composition. In the course of nearly two decades he gradually recast almost all his major Yiddish stories into Hebrew; but so subtle was the process that the Hebrew versions must be regarded more as transmutations than as translations of the originals. His contribution to modern Hebrew literature during that period can scarcely be overestimated, and the affectionate title of 'the grandfather of Hebrew literature', by which he was known in his later years, bears adequate testimony to his literary importance.

The complex plot of *Fathers and Sons*, which is unfolded in a tortuous manner most difficult to follow, may be summarised as follows:[15]

Isaac, the tenth and unwanted son of poor parents, is committed to the service of an itinerant wonder-worker, and almost beaten to death by his hypocritical master who suspects him of having stolen his money. The money has, in fact, been appropriated by Aryeh's henchmen, and is used to support the wretched Isaac until his education is complete.

This Aryeh, whose real name is Elkanah, was born of rich parents, but so badly educated by his teacher, Isaac's father, that his mind was merely stuffed with superstitions and Ḥasidic tales of miracles and wonders. In consequence, on his father's death he was rapidly cheated out of his wealth, and thereafter lost his faith in the *Ṣaddiq*, or holy man, who failed to support him in his hour of need. Later, on the death of his only daughter, he despatched his son abroad to escape the press-gangs of Nicholas I.[16] Shortly afterwards, his wife and two remaining sons also expire. Wandering about poverty-stricken and in anguish, Aryeh becomes the leader of a band of thieves who, in the manner of Robin Hood, extort money from wealthy scoundrels in order to aid their poor victims.[17]

Now Aryeh has a step-sister, Sarah, married to a rich fanatical *Ḥasidh*, Ephraim Karmoli, who is anxious to rear his son Simon in their faith. But Simon's teacher, David, introduces him to the ideas of *Haskalah*, which so infuriates Ephraim that he beats his son, who forthwith leaves home. While staying at an inn, Simon's luggage is stolen by Aryeh's men, and in pursuing them Simon meets Aryeh, who befriends him, furnishes him with the means to study further, and eventually reveals himself as Simon's uncle.

David, meanwhile, has fallen in love with Ephraim's beautiful daughter, Rachel, whom he also endeavours to educate along the lines of *Haskalah*. But Ephraim's *Ṣaddiq*, who plans to marry Rachel to the son of one of his hypocritical henchmen, Peretz, advises Ephraim to expel David from his house for propagating heresy.[18] As a result David is compelled to flee the town. Fortunately, however, he is also befriended by Aryeh, who eventually identifies David as his long lost son! David waxes rich in trade, but Rachel has meanwhile been betrothed against her will to Peretz's son. Aryeh's men, however, find a document incriminating Peretz, which enables Aryeh—in a dramatic midnight encounter—to force the latter to abrogate the betrothal.

Ephraim, meanwhile, has fallen ill after the collapse of a business venture undertaken in his name by his agent Eleazar. His faith, too, has been shaken by the news that the *Ṣaddiq*, who had recommended the venture, had done so out of private interest. David rescues Ephraim from bankruptcy, but, on his death bed, the latter insists that he cannot break the contract of betrothal between his daughter and Peretz's son. Just at that moment, however, a letter arrives from Peretz abrogating the contract, so that Ephraim and Sarah are able to give their blessing to the union of Rachel and David.

An epilogue, dated five years later, informs the reader that Aryeh has died of remorse for his nefarious activities; that Rachel has given birth to two sons, named after their two grandfathers, while Sarah lives happily with her daughter and son-in-law, and

has come to learn that enlightenment is not synonymous with wickedness and sin!
The moral of the tale scarcely requires further elucidation.

Peretz Smolenskin (1842-85), by far the most prolific Hebrew novelist during the period under review, was born in Monastyr-stchina, in the province of Mohilev, in White Russia, into a life of privation, hardship and sickness.[19] As a child he saw his elder brother press-ganged into the army of Czar Nicholas I, never to be heard of again,[20] while his father, who had been forced to flee because of false accusations, died when Peretz was barely ten. A year later Smolenskin left home to study at the *Yešibhah* in Shklov, keeping himself alive by 'eating days'[21]—in the manner of poor *Yešibhah* students. Introduced by his brother to the ideas of *Haskalah* he began to learn Russian and read secular books, for which nefarious practices he was so persecuted that he fled to the Hasidic centre of Lubavitch, where he spent the years 1858-60/1. Later he wandered first to Vitebsk and then to Mohilev, supporting himself the while by singing in choirs and preaching in various synagogues. Reaching Odessa in 1862, he spent five years there studying music and languages, while earning a living as a Hebrew teacher. In Odessa, too, Smolenskin embarked upon his literary career by publishing a number of articles in the Hebrew journal *Ha-Meliṣ*.

Leaving Odessa in 1867, he spent a year travelling through Bohemia and Germany before finally settling in Vienna where he worked as a proof-reader and Hebrew teacher. Realizing that his plan to study at the university was quite impracticable, he abandoned hope of obtaining a systematic secular education and, with the aid of Solomon Rubin, founded the monthly *Ha-Šaḥar* (*The Dawn*), which was destined to become the most effective platform in Hebrew literature for *Haskalah* in its later period, and for the nationalist movement in its early stages. From 1868-85, with short interruptions, Smolenskin published, edited and managed *The Dawn*, while serving simultaneously as one of its principal contributors.[22] His literary activities yielded no financial profit, and he was even compelled to embark upon two long and tiring journeys in search of support for his journal, which he continued to publish until shortly before his death. In order to meet the additional obligation arising from his marriage in 1875, he undertook the management of a printing house, while in 1878 he launched a weekly magazine *Ha-Mabbiṭ* (*The Spec-tator*), which survived, however, for no more than nine months. In addition to all his various literary activities, Smolenskin also devoted much time and energy to public affairs. In 1874 he travelled to Roumania on behalf of the Alliance Israélite Universelle following the wave of pogroms suffered by the Jews of Roumania. As one of the leaders of the Zionist movement which arose in the 1880's, he also conducted negotiations with Sir Laurence Oliphant to obtain support for Jewish Settlement in Palestine. But finally his health broke down under the strain of so strenuous a life. Stricken with pulmonary tuberculosis, he died in harness at the age of forty-three.

The plot of *The Wanderer in the Paths of Life*, which clearly contains many autobiographical elements, is again extremely complicated. The hero, Josef, has no recollection of his father, and remembers only that, when he was a child of five, his mother, on her death-bed, gave him a letter for his uncle. After six months with a kind neighbour, his rich uncle takes him home, but his wicked aunt embitters his life, which is further saddened by his first experience of schooling in a *Ḥedher*.[23] Intent on returning to the kind neighbour who has meanwhile gone to Palestine, he is induced by a young man to take whatever valuables he can from his uncle's house, while his evil mentor promises to lead him to his goal. On the way, however, the young man takes the valuables and disappears leaving Josef to await his return! The lad is discovered by a band of travelling beggars and befriended by an old man, who, before his death, gives him a letter and some money, at the same time assuring Josef that someone will come for him. A few days later Josef is collected by an itinerant wonder-worker, and becomes his assistant. Later, however, Josef runs away from the wonder-worker taking the latter's pack which contains money and letters, because his master had appropriated the money bequeathed to Josef by the old man.

The young vagrant reaches Ma'aphelia[24] (Berdichev), where he witnesses the public humiliation of a young woman, Shulammit, accused of immorality.[25] He learns from his companion, Dan, that her father, Abinadab, a rich and generous man, had once befriended a young villain, Manasseh, to whom he had entrusted the education of his son Absalom. By dint of deep cunning, Manasseh had not only alienated father and son,[26] but had even managed to involve Absalom with the Polish revolutionaries, as a result of which Absalom had been sent into exile. Abinadab had died of shock, leaving his property to Manasseh with the instruction that he should marry Shulammit. The latter, however, had spurned him and married her father's agent. In revenge, Manasseh, by now the head of the community,[27] had trumped up a charge against the agent, who had been forced to flee. The villain is finally responsible for Shulammit's humiliation. Josef discovers that it was Manasseh, too, who had induced him to steal his uncle's valuables! From Dan, the hero learns how his uncle and his wicked aunt had brought about the downfall of Josef's wealthy father by planting forged banknotes in his house, because of the latter's hatred of the *Hasidhim*. Condemned to death, Josef's father had bribed his guards to allow him to escape and commit suicide, six weeks before Josef's birth. Josef's mother, meanwhile, had been left in dire straits, but had refused all help from her husband's wicked brother.

The second part of the novel describes the hero's experiences in the *Yešibhah* in Šekhulah[28] (Shklov), where Gideon, Dan's friend, takes him under his wing and introduces him to the ideas of *Haskalah*. Because of his secular studies he is forced to leave the *Yešibhah*, and is then press-ganged into military service.[29] In the detention centre, he once again meets Gideon, who has suffered a similar fate; but fortunately both of them are rescued, after learning more of Manasseh's villainies from the other hapless inmates.

In part three Josef is portrayed at the court of the *Ṣaddiq* of Ṣebhu'a'el[30] among the *Hasidhim*. Later he falls into the clutches of the wicked Jehoiarib, who employs him as a tool in his fight against the *Mithnaggedhim*,[31] and has Josef, himself, imprisoned. Rescued fortuitously, Josef returns to Šekhulah, where he had previously fallen in love with a lovely young girl called Shiphrah, and becomes her grandfather's agent. Shiphrah's mother, however, who is very ill, is advised by her doctor to travel abroad, and takes her daughter for company and Josef as an interpreter. Josef, who has meanwhile recognised Shiphrah's mother as his own wicked aunt, reveals his identity to her during a storm at sea, with the result that she relaxes her grip on the rail and is washed overboard! Shiphrah, who has previously witnessed the downfall of her father and brothers, loses her reason and dies shortly afterwards.

Josef proceeds to Hamburg, where he wins a fortune in a

lottery and loses it again as quickly. For some time he joins a troupe of travelling entertainers and, during his wanderings meets his old master the wonder-worker, who tells him of Manasseh's disastrous fate. From the wonder-worker the hero also learns that his father's attempt to commit suicide had failed, and that he had escaped to America, where he has since waxed rich. In consequence, Josef travels to London in search of news of his father. After suffering great hardship in the metropolis, Josef is befriended by a wealthy young lady, with whom he falls in love. Her haughty brother, however, so insults the vagabond suitor that Josef challenges him to a duel, in which he kills his opponent but is himself grievously wounded. On recovering some months later, he learns to his horror that he has shot his own step-brother and that his father has died of shock! To forget his misery Josef once again wanders abroad.

In the final part of the story, which largely consists of letters from the hero to his step-sister, Josef describes political and social conditions in the various countries through which he wanders. His final letters from Russia are full of despair, which stems from his bitter disappointment at the results of *Haskalah*. His sole comfort derives from the establishment of Jewish schools which combine traditional Jewish values with a systematic secular education. The hero finally dies defending his people against a bloodthirsty mob, but not before learning that his step-sister has decided to marry his old friend Gideon, now a university professor in Switzerland.

Even so brief a survey of a novel which exceeds a thousand pages is sufficient to reveal the kaleidoscopic nature of the work, which presents a vivid if tendentious portrait of Jewish life in eastern Europe in almost all its facets.

By contrast, the plot of *The Joy of the Godless* is comparatively straightforward. The story revolves upon the love of two teachers, David and Simon, for the same young lady, Shiphrah, who lives in the great city of 'Ašedoth (Odessa). David, who is a native of Šebhurah[32] (Warsaw), was married at 17; but as a result of his participation in the Polish conspiracy against Russia, he was forced to leave his pregnant wife and flee to Odessa, where he mixes in frivolous circles. Handsome and attractive, he conceals the fact that he is a married man, in his desire to win the hand of Shiphrah, the pupil of his friend and benefactor, Simon. The latter, in spite of the great hardships of his youth, is a fine Talmudist and has also acquired considerable secular learning; but he is neither over-handsome nor particularly polished. Previously disappointed in love, he devotes himself sincerely to the education of his pupils. Although secretly in love with Shiphrah, he overcomes his jealousy of David even to the extent of recommending him, against his better judgment, to Shiphrah's father as a potential son-in-law.[33] All the members of Shiphrah's family are partial to David's suit, except her more discerning grandfather. His view is overruled, however, and all arrangements for the wedding are set in motion.

Meanwhile David's deserted wife, searching for her husband with her little son, chances to meet Shiphrah in a wayside inn, and is invited to the ceremony. Husband and wife recognise each other in embarrassing circumstances and disappear in the ensuing confusion—leaving the field clear for Simon. The situation is complicated, however, by the fact that Simon had previously pretended to be a married man, in order to escape the designs of his landlady's love-sick daughter. In consequence, the landlady conveys the information to Shiphrah's parents, and only the intervention of a pious teacher from Simon's native town is able to save the day.[34] Meanwhile, a letter arrives from David with the news that he intends to commit suicide for love of Shiphrah. The whole plot, however, which is very slight, serves only as a framework for the long discussions on such topics as literature and love, which comprise the central core of the story.

The plot of Smolenskin's third novel, *A Donkey's Burial*, is far more original. It concerns the exploits of a practical joker, Jacob Hayyim, who, as the son of a grave-digger, has been brought up without any fear of evil spirits, in a superstitious environment.[35] In his youth he would habitually frighten his fellow-citizens by hiding in the cemetery at night and emitting piercing shrieks, while on one occasion he terrified the overseer of the *Yešibhah*, in which he was known as a gifted student, by appearing to him one night disguised as a ghost and prophesying his imminent death. His most serious prank, however, consisted of stealing the cakes prepared for the annual feast of the burial society in Kešulah;[36] the crime is inscribed in the society's records, so that the thief, if discovered, shall be given 'a donkey's burial'.[37]

Some years later Jacob Hayyim is married to Esther, the granddaughter of Gitzil-Shemariah, the president of the burial society, and reveals his prank to his wife who in turn tells her grandfather. As a result the hero is forced to flee the town, leaving Esther behind. He is then engaged as secretary to a government official because of his unusual facility in Russian[38], and accompanies the latter on his travels for some years. Eventually the official is appointed governor of Jacob Hayyim's native province, and the hero resorts to his former device of frightening Esther's grandfather out of his wits by appearing to him as the ghost of his own father, and demanding that Esther be reunited with his 'son'. The stratagem succeeds, and the hero is warmly welcomed back into the community, whose secretary he becomes.

Meanwhile Zebadiah, a rich, shrewd and influential widower, who also has designs on Esther, worms his way into the hero's confidence, learns of the trick he played on Esther's grandfather, and immediately denounces him. As a result Jacob Hayyim is removed from his post, while Esther's grandfather changes his will, entrusting his wealth to the community leaders. In revenge, the hero informs the authorities that the leading merchants are importing goods without paying the requisite duties, which leads to their imprisonment. Incensed, the community leaders excommunicate Jacob Hayyim,[39] and even when the hero, under pressure from his wife, reluctantly begs their pardon, Zebadiah frustrates his hopes by decreeing that Esther will not receive her inheritance unless the hero first divorces her.

Reduced to extremes of poverty, the hero plans revenge by joining a conspiracy with certain other disaffected members of the community. Zebadiah, however, learns of the plot, and hires a peasant to murder Jacob Hayyim and throw his corpse into the river. Anxiety for her husband's safety induces Esther to seek the help of the provincial governor, but without avail. Moreover, even after her husband's body is eventually recovered by fishermen and given 'a donkey's burial', Zebadiah is still able to prevent Esther from claiming her rightful inheritance. In disgust, Esther converts to Christianity,[40] and has her little daughter baptized.

So horrifying are some of Smolenskin's portraits of the darker sides of Jewish life that in his preface to the fourth edition of the novel in 1883 he confesses that he has introduced a number of changes and additions before allowing the work to be translated into any European language. It is indicative of the author's overall constructive approach to Judaism that he should have been so reluctant to allow his biting criticism to be known, as it were, 'outside the family'.[41]

Smolenskin's fourth novel, *Pride and Fall*, is not a continuous narrative but consists rather of a number of short stories loosely connected within a single framework. The collapse of the Viennese stock-exchange in 1873 caused widespread bankruptcy, and drove hundreds of merchants to seek refuge in America. In Smolenskin's novel, ten such fugitives meet fortuitously in a hotel in Hamburg and strike up an acquaintance. Later, on board ship, they decide to while away the journey by relating, each in turn, their respective histories. These stories, together with the discussions and arguments which they generate, comprise the remainder of the novel. Although each story is self-contained, a number of them have connecting links and, on occasion, supply the sequel of one or other of the previous narratives. The common theme, however, which endows the novel with a certain homogeneity, lies in the picaresque character of each narrative, with the respective heroes torn by fate from the traditional background of Jewish life in eastern Europe and swept like flotsam over the surface of an alien environment, without ever really striking fresh roots. The most successful individual stories are those that describe traditional Jewish life as Smolenskin had done in his earlier novels, with which these stories bear some striking affinities.[42] The novel is loosely wound up with a brief reference to the ultimate destinies of the respective travellers.

Of very different calibre is the plot of *The Reward of the Righteous*, which is outlined against the backcloth of the second Polish rebellion during the years 1861-4.[43] The story revolves upon the adventures of its two principal heroes, Emil and Isaiah. The former is the son of an orthodox but enlightened Jew, Shemaiah, who symbolises the ideal combination of traditional and secular learning, and who earns a dignified and comfortable livelihood as the chief agent of an important Polish lord. Emil, however, feels much more drawn to Polish than to Jewish society, and falls in love with Elisheba, the sister of the local Polish governor. Isaiah, on the other hand, is a brilliant Talmudic student to whom Shemaiah has secretly undertaken to teach languages and other secular subjects, but he is also devoted to his other teacher Gabriel, the principal of the *Yeshibhah*, formerly a *Maskil* and revolutionary, who has decided that Jewish traditional values are more important than secular ideas.[44]

Shemaiah engages Isaiah to instruct Emil in Jewish subjects;
but the latter, in spite of loyally defending his people against
abuse, becomes more and more involved with the Polish revolutionaries. Isaiah, on the other hand, sees only the greed, cupidity
and moral degradation of the Polish rebels, and after the seduction of two Jewish girls, Miriam and Bathsheba, by degenerate
Polish officers, he informs the Russian authorities that a certain
monastery is being used as a centre for the revolt. Smolenskin's
utter contempt and loathing for the Poles involved in the rebellion are apparently responsible for his complete failure to
censure Isaiah's disloyalty to the Polish cause.

Of the two young Jewish heroines who are in love with Emil,
Bathsheba contrives the downfall of Miriam her rival, and finally
dies full of remorse for the sorrow she has engineered. Miriam,
on the other hand, elopes with a Pole, who leaves her pregnant
and in such reduced circumstances that she eventually becomes
a washerwoman. Some years later, Isaiah who has meanwhile
studied law at St Petersburg and become a famous lawyer—
without, however, abandoning his piety or loyalty to his people
—is called upon to defend a poor woman who has lost her reason
out of fear that the Russian priest will punish her because she
still recalls her parents and her people with affection, and recognises in his client the hapless Miriam, whom he had, himself,
once loved so hopelessly.

Emil, meanwhile, in spite of his staunch loyalty to the rebels'
cause, encounters only bitter hostility and anti-semitism from his
Polish comrades, one of whom even makes an attempt on the
hero's life, because the latter has discovered him embezzling
the patriots' funds. Even Emil's heroic valour during the revolt
itself can save neither his father nor his sister, Zipporah, from the
misfortunes they suffer at the hands of the Polish revolutionaries.
With the collapse of the revolt, Emil flees to Vienna, whither
he brings his father and sister, and is also reunited with Elisheba and her brother. With Isaiah's appearance the picture is
once again complete, and the story ends happily in a double
wedding. Emil marries Elisheba who embraces Judaism, while
Isaiah is wedded to Zipporah who has meanwhile grown into a
beautiful and highly educated young lady.

Smolenskin's last novel, *The Inheritance*, is exceeded in length
only by *The Wanderer in the Paths of Life*, and is again remarkable
for the complexities of its plot.[45] Zerahiah ben Ezekiel, whose

family had originally migrated from Galicia to Roumania, and whose father had been killed defending his people in a pogrom, forsakes his native town to seek a livelihood and enlightenment in 'Ašedoth (Odessa), leaving behind his mother and his sister, Peninnah.[46] In Odessa he is engaged as a teacher in the household of the rich Jonah ben Amittai, with whose daughter, Naomi, he gradually falls in love. Jonah's brother Dov, however, who has designs on Naomi for his feckless son Zabdi, contrives to enrage Zerahiah to such a degree, that the latter forthwith returns to Roumania. On the way, however, the carriage overturns, with the result that Zerahiah is thrown out and breaks his leg. Fortunately, a kind-hearted local resident, David, brings him home, where he is nursed by David's daughter, Bithiah, and tended by a skilled physician, Eliakim, who also widens his patient's mental horizons. When Zerahiah is sufficiently recovered, Eliakim enrols him as a member of a secret society, pledged to the amelioration of Jewish social conditions,[47] from whose deliberations the hero becomes acquainted with many of the most pressing problems besetting Jewish life.[48]

When Zerahiah finally arrives home he finds the house has been sold to strangers. Having received no word from him for months, his mother and sister had sold their possessions in order to travel to Odessa in search of him. Ironically, they had spent the night in the same inn as Zerahiah without meeting him.[49] Zerahiah then decides to enrol himself as a student in the university of Vienna.

Meanwhile his mother and sister reach Odessa, where they fall into the hands of a band of scoundrels who attempt to procure Peninnah for a rich old profligate,[50] with the aid of fabrications concerning Zerahiah's whereabouts, and machinations of great complexity. After many perilous adventures mother and daughter travel to Vienna in the company of Jonah, who is seeking a cure from a prolonged illness, and his daughter Naomi. In Vienna, however, they are confronted with fresh difficulties.

Zerahiah's late father, Ezekiel, had a rich neighbour Simon, whose son Palti had previously sought Peninnah's hand without success. A series of misfortunes impoverish Simon and lead to his imprisonment, but he is still regarded as the head of the community. In consequence, a letter is sent to his address from a Jewish friendly society in Vienna with the information that Ezekiel's brother has become very rich in America, and is anxious to trace his brother's family who will become his heirs. The letter falls into Palti's hands, who forthwith forges a passport in the name of Zerahiah ben Ezekiel and sets out for Vienna in search of the inheritance. After meeting Zerahiah there by chance, Palti disposes of his rival by informing the police that Zerahiah is a revolutionary using a false passport. Zerahiah is consequently arrested and imprisoned. Fortunately, a young Christian seamstress, Miriam, in whose house Zerahiah had rented a room, is acquainted with the police-inspector investigating the case. Thanks to their combined efforts Palti's villainy is unmasked, while Zerahiah is released and united with his family. The story ends happily with the union of Zerahiah and his beloved Naomi.

Written during Smolenskin's last illness, the final section of the plot is clearly unsatisfactory. The main theme of the inheritance is left hanging in mid-air, while the denouement is premature and forced. Nevertheless, much of the plot is handled with a skill which affords ample proof of Smolenskin's considerable dramatic ability. It is unfortunate that he was unable to develop his theme to its logical conclusion.

Reuben Asher Braudes[51] (1851-1902), the third major novelist during the period under review, was born in Vilna and quickly established a reputation as a brilliant young student of the Talmud. On the death of his father in the lad's thirteenth year, Braudes wandered through southern Russia, residing in Kiev for some time, and then settled in Warsaw from 1875-82. During his stay in Warsaw he embarked upon a literary career, publishing numerous essays, critical articles and short stories in various Hebrew periodicals. After a brief sojourn in Lemberg, where he served as assistant editor to the journal *Ha-Boqer 'Or*, Braudes took up residence in Bucharest, fostering the idea of Jewish nationalism and publishing a Yiddish magazine called *Yehudhith*, which advocated the Jewish colonization of Palestine. In 1884, however, after his expulsion from Roumania as an alien Jew, Braudes returned to Lemberg, where he published a number of short-lived journals and contributed to both Hebrew and Yiddish periodicals. In 1891 he published the journal *Ha-Zeman* for some nine months, and from 1893-5 a Yiddish weekly, *Wecker*, which afterwards became the official Zionist organ in eastern Galicia under the title of *Jüdisches Wochenblatt*. An ardent Zionist from the moment of the first World Zionist Congress in 1897,

Braudes was appointed by Herzl in 1900 to serve as editor of the
Yiddish edition of the Zionist weekly, *Die Welt*. Moving to Vienna in 1896, he remained there until his death in 1902, publishing numerous *feuilletons*, sketches and stories. As an author, however, his fame rests primarily on the two novels published during
the period under review, namely *Religion and Life*, and *The Two
Extremes*.

The plot of *Religion and Life* is simple and straightforward, and
merely serves as a framework for a description of the fierce controversy over religious reform which raged in Lithuania between
the years 1869-71. In order to illustrate the harsh and over-
stringent attitudes adopted by the Rabbis in the interpretation
of Jewish religious law, the author selects three typical examples
around which to weave his story.[52] The first concerns the tendency
of the local Rabbi to take the negative view in cases where the
ritual fitness of a slaughtered animal is subject to the slightest
shadow of doubt. The story opens with a complaint that the
Rabbi has condemned three cows one after the other in a single
day, even though the butcher argues that in his opinion, based
on forty years of experience, the third was fit for consumption.
As a result the whole community is left without food for the
Sabbath, while the butcher sustains a ruinous loss. Next day in
synagogue the butcher dramatically interrupts the service before the reading of the *Torah* to raise the point once again, while
the hero, Samuel, a great Talmudic scholar with more than a
smattering of secular education, takes his side against the Rabbi,
denouncing the latter's tyranny. Samuel proves his point from
the Talmud, while the Rabbi supports his own case from the
Šulḥan 'Arukh,[53] the code of Jewish law. Meanwhile the congregation is astounded to find that two such authoritative works
can contradict each other! The Rabbi, however, stands his
ground, and accuses Samuel of heresy; while Samuel, who has
conceived an affection for the Rabbi's step-daughter, Hannah,
and does not wish to sever their relationship, breaks off the
argument.

The second example, too, is directed against the financial
loss caused to the innocent victims of excessively rigid interpretation. A child dies in a house adjoining the courtyard of that
occupied by Samuel's mother. As she and her neighbours have
neglected to throw away all the water standing in their houses
immediately after the death, all the food in every house is pro-

B

nounced unfit for consumption and, moreover, they are ordered to throw away all their cooking utensils and purchase new ones in their stead. Once more Samuel attacks the decision on the basis of his own profound knowledge of the sources of Jewish law, and once more without success.

The third example is far more germane to the plot and revolves upon the question of the *Yabham*.[54] Rachel, the second heroine of the story, has recently become a widow. Her father-in-law, Todros, had divorced his first wife under pressure from her relatives some thirty years previously, and left her pregnant. Since that time he has become so degenerate a drunkard that he cannot even remember the village in which his first wife lived. He is unaware whether she gave birth to a son or daughter, or whether the child is still alive. As the possibility exists, however, that the child is male and has survived, Rachel is refused permission to re-marry until her late husband's hypothetical stepbrother has first waived his prior claim to her hand.

Hearing of Samuel's growing reputation as a reformer, Rachel comes to the same town, where her brother Isaac Ephrat has just been appointed as a government teacher. It transpires that Isaac and Hannah were previously in love in Vilna, a relationship which they quickly resume. Disappointed in Hannah, Samuel becomes more and more attracted by Rachel and takes up her cause. As a private teacher, however, his livelihood has been undermined by his recently-acquired reputation as a heretic.[55] In consequence, he accepts an invitation from Isaac and Rachel to become a teacher in a private, progressive school which they decide to found.

A final complication is introduced in the shape of a student at the *Yešibhah* known as Ha-Birzi, who is also attracted to Hannah. As the circumstances of his own birth bear some resemblance to those described by the old Todros who befriends him, he imagines that he, himself, may be Rachel's step-brother, and therefore advances a claim to marry her, although she cannot tolerate the proposal. The remainder of the novel is devoted to a description of the intense preparations for battle undertaken by the orthodox and reform parties respectively.

The novel remains unfinished. From a letter written by M. L. Lilienblum—on whom the hero Samuel was modelled—to Braudes, however, it appears that the plot was to have been resolved as follows. It was to be revealed that Todros' first wife

gave birth to a girl, who died one month after birth. But as a result
of years of vexation over the issue, Rachel gradually wastes away,
and when the news is finally brought to her that she could have
married all the time, it only proves to be the last straw, and she
dies a few weeks later. This final blow sends Samuel out of his
mind, so that even ten years later Ha-Birzi finds him still in an
asylum.[56] It is, perhaps a blessing that the story was left in an
unfinished state!

Braudes' second novel *The Two Extremes*, which has something of the flavour of Goethe's *Die Wahlverwandtschaften*, depicts
the strikingly different types of Jewish life obtaining in the great
city of Odessa on the one hand, and a tiny Hasidic town, symbolically called Sukkoth (Tabernacles), on the other. The plot revolves upon the remarkable effect which each of these two entirely different environments can exert upon an individual who
has grown up in the other.

Jacob Hetzron, a rich inhabitant of Sukkoth, but uncharacteristic of that town by virtue of his aesthetic leanings, visits Odessa
on business and is introduced to Gabriel Ahitub and his family.
Gabriel's daughter, Lisa, so attracts him by her beauty, cultivated manners and musical accomplishments that he loses all desire
to return to the squalor of his native town. Captivated by the
lavish attractions of Odessa on the one hand and by Lisa on the
other, Jacob makes a bid for the young lady's affection, omit-
ting to mention that he already has a wife and children! Gabriel,
meanwhile, whose splendid household masks the fact that he is
in imminent danger of bankruptcy, is advised by his friend, Yurab—a lawyer by profession—to accept the rich Jacob as a son-
in-law in order to bolster his flagging fortunes. Lisa, however, is
also sought by a young student, Barzillai, who, hearing of Jacob's
marital status, informs Gabriel of the true position—with the result that the hapless Jacob is banished from the house.[57]

Nevertheless, Yurab again persuades Gabriel that such a match
is vital for his business interests, and advises Jacob to divorce
Sarah, his wife. With that in mind, Yurab journeys to Sukkoth,
but Sarah flatly refuses to contemplate the suggestion of divorce.
Moreover, in the course of time, Jacob finds himself becoming
less impressed by the external glitter of life in Odessa, while his
conscience begins to prick him over his desertion of his wife and
children.

During all this time Lisa's brother Solomon has been supervising a government building contract in Sukkoth, lodging the while in the home of Sarah's parents. He is deeply impressed by the peaceful atmosphere and devout piety which he encounters in the little town, and compares, most favourably, the quiet domesticity of the household in which he lives with the emptiness and frivolity of Jewish life in Odessa. In particular, the simple dignity which marks the Sabbath makes a deep impression on him. But he is no less attracted by Sarah's younger sister, Shiphrah, an unspoiled and lovely girl, who has secretly acquired some secular education from Benjamin, a clandestine exponent of Enlightenment who has fallen in love with her. So natural does Shiphrah seem to Solomon in contrast to his own spoiled and sophisticated wife, Rosalie, that he gradually finds himself devoured with love for her—a feeling which she readily returns. In an agony of conflicting emotions, Solomon confides his dilemma to Benjamin, who at once divulges his secret to Shiphrah. Although deeply in love with Solomon, she drives him from the house and refuses to see him further. Although bitterly disappointed, Solomon gradually discovers the darker sides of life in Sukkoth—the hypocrisy, pettiness, and particularly the fanatical obscurantism which culminates in a violent persecution of Benjamin who has been discovered reading a Russian book!

The denouement of the plot is engineered by a *deus ex machina* in the shape of an old long-lost grandfather from Vilna, who symbolises in his own person a happy fusion of orthodox Judaism and secular enlightenment. This pleasing combination is presented to both heroes as a healthier subject for emulation than either of the two extremes which have captured their imagination hitherto. By persuading Sarah to pay attention to her external appearance, he effects a reconciliation between her and her erring husband, Jacob. As the old man is, in addition, extraordinarily wealthy, not only is he able to solve the spiritual problems of his grandchildren—as both the heroes turn out to be—but he can also rescue them from their material dilemmas! By a further coincidence, Benjamin also discovers his long-lost father, whom the old man had supported throughout his medical studies. With both heroes safely restored to their respective wives, Lisa is wedded to Barzilai, and Shiphrah is married to Benjamin, whom she respects even though she feels she can never love him as she once loved Samuel! It may readily be imagined that the issues are portrayed with far greater conviction than the solution.

Biographical information in the case of a number of the minor writers of the period is scanty in the extreme. Little is known of Judah Isaac Leinwand, for example, beyond the fact that he was born in Lemberg on the 22nd March 1850, that he received a traditional Jewish education and that he published a number of poems and articles in various Hebrew journals in addition to his novel 'Oseh Mezimmoth (The Artful Villain) in Lemberg, 1875/6.[58]

The plot of The Artful Villain is complex and highly melodramatic.[59] The story is concerned with the machinations of a gang of criminals to ruin a rich old miser Abihail, whose second wife Jochebed, a young and beautiful but evil woman, is the paramour of the gang's villainous leader, Nabal. Four years previously Nabal, with Jochebed's aid, had ingeniously tricked the old man's eldest son Absalom into admitting to the ownership of forged banknotes, for which crime Absalom had been sentenced to five years imprisonment. More recently, one of the gang in the disguise of a Polish nobleman has sold the old man a gold icon stolen from a church. In his distress Abihail turns to his old friend Gershom, a famous lawyer whose daughter Zipporah is secretly in love with the imprisoned Absalom. Gershom undertakes to beat the villains at their own game, and receives considerable help from Absalom, who has learned many details of Nabal's wicked past from the revelations of a fellow prisoner Tobiah, who has also been falsely imprisoned at the villain's instigation. Meanwhile, the gang succeeds in kidnapping Abihail's second son, Eleazar—who has been endeavouring without success to warn his father of his step-mother's iniquities—and in imprisoning him in a lunatic asylum! Simultaneously, other members of the gang disguised as policemen terrify the old man into surrendering the gold icon, which has to be returned to the church.

Gershom, however, has meanwhile succeeded in planting one of his own agents Yannai, who was once, himself, a victim of Jochebed's wicked schemes, into Nabal's gang. Moreover, a fortuitous meeting with Jonathan, a young man from England who has been searching for the murderer of his father for some years, greatly eases the lawyer's task. From a photograph in Jonathan's possession, it becomes clear that the villain who ruined his father's household is none other than Nabal! Once Yannai has assembled sufficient incriminating evidence to convince even Abihail of his young wife's treachery, the old man bursts in on her while she is revealing her true self, with the result that she dies of fright! Eleazar is rescued from the lunatic asylum, while Absalom and Tobiah are released from prison and exonerated. Finally, in a lengthy court scene—during which the whole plot is virtually repeated—all the members of the gang receive their just deserts. In spite of a brave attempt to bluff his way out of the charges, Nabal is sentenced to fifteen years imprisonment with hard labour, after which he is to be handed over to the British authorities, who had already condemned him to death! For the 'good' characters, the story ends happily with the union of Absalom and Zipporah, while Eleazar, too, is wed to Tobiah's eldest daughter, Shiphrah.

In view of the extremely small number of women writers in Hebrew literature, it is all the more unfortunate that it has not proved possible to locate even the most elementary biographical information in the case of Sarah Feige Foner-Meinkin beyond the fact that she was born in Riga,[60] that she spent a number of years in Dvinsk during her childhood, and that her family was to be reckoned among the descendants of Elijah, Gaon of Vilna.[61]

Her novel, *The Love of the Righteous*, is permeated with an atmosphere of 'cloak and dagger' mystery, and yet contains elements of serious social criticism, particularly against the Jewish custom of arranging marriages regardless of the wishes of the bride and bridegroom.[62] The action, most of which takes place in Italy in 1861, is concerned with the adventures of Finalia, the daughter of an impoverished French baron, Meir Adelberg, who is being hunted by the French authorities as a Republican leader, and her lover Victor, whose father has disappeared as a result of a dispute with the Jesuits, and whose young sister has been kidnapped into a nunnery.[63] Finalia's hand, however, is also being sought by Jahdiel, a rich but villainous *Ḥasidh* from Galicia who is determined to possess her at all costs. Her natural prejudice against Jahdiel is strengthened by the fact that her friend Henrietta has been made by her parents to marry another *Ḥasidh* of a similar type, and is so unhappy that she eventually makes an attempt upon her own life scarcely a month after the wedding. Fortunately, the heroine's father is determined to respect his daughter's wishes.

Now the Baron, who is in danger of being kidnapped by French spies, is befriended by the local governor who invites the Baron to stay with him until the danger is past. Meanwhile, the governor also invites the whole family to a sumptuous ball, and himself falls in love with Finalia—much to Victor's chagrin. Although the young lovers are later reconciled, Victor is warned that his life is in danger and leaves for Rome; but during the ensuing six months most of their letters to each other are intercepted. In a mood of great depression, the heroine is suddenly confronted by two villainous looking men, who force her to sign three letters —one to her parents saying that she has left home for love of Victor, one to Victor to the effect that she is going to marry the governor, and a third to the governor purporting to have been written by the heroine from Rome. In the event, however, the governor shrewdly decides that all three are forgeries. She is then carried away unconscious, and driven in a carriage for several days until she finally arrives in Brody in Galicia. There she finds herself imprisoned in the house of the wicked Jahdiel; but with the help of a servant she manages to escape one stormy night and boards a train for Vienna. With that, the first part of the story is concluded.[64]

Baer Isser Zobeizensky[65] (1860-1900) was born in Velizh near Vitebsk in White Russia. During the eighties of the nineteenth century he contributed articles and *feuilletons* in Yiddish, Hebrew and Russian to the Judaeo-Russian press, including a history of Vitebsk compiled from archive-material. Apart from the Hebrew novel under review, Zobeizensky also published in Warsaw in 1887 a Yiddish novel, *Die Schwere Zeit (Hard Times)*, in four parts, which describes the effects of the pogroms in Russia after 1881. A second edition of the work appeared in 1901.[66] His Hebrew novel. *For Love of Ṣaddiqim* was criticised by Alexander Zederbaum because of its air of unreality, its poor style and its linguistic mistakes—although less severely, perhaps, than it deserves. Zederbaum, who refers to Zobeizensky as an unknown author, ends his review on an encouraging note, at the same time lamenting that the year's crop of Hebrew books has been very thin and the number of buyers pitifully small.[67]

The plot of his novel *For Love of Ṣaddiqim* is both tortuous and fantastic and mainly constitutes an attack on the blind allegiance to the Ḥasidic holy men displayed by the rich and pious Sarah Bath Tobhim. The mother of a son and two daughters, Sarah was left a widow when her husband died of grief after their son had sold himself into military service at the age of eighteen. Subsequently, but still ten years prior to the opening of the story, she had married her elder daughter Zipporah to Naphtali the son of a *Ṣaddiq*; but shortly after the wedding Naphtali had robbed them and disappeared without trace. Sarah then married her late husband's former agent Gemalli, a common man who had become rich, and the father of a boorish son Peretz, born to his first wife eighteen years after their marriage. Sarah's younger daughter, Hadassah—an educated and beautiful young lady— is in love with her teacher, Israel, who supports his poor widowed mother out of his salary, and who, as a youth, had been persecuted for his enlightened views. Sarah, however, angrily rejects the young hero's plea for her daughter's hand and drives him from the house. Israel is then drafted for military service,[68] where he subsequently distinguishes himself in battle and becomes an officer. In spite of the fact that all correspondence between the young lovers is intercepted by Sarah, they remain faithful to each other. Finally, however, Sarah insists that Hadassah be married to a *Ṣaddiq* who has just arrived in town. At the ceremony Zipporah screams and faints; the *Ṣaddiq* puts a phial to her lips and she dies forthwith. It transpires that the *Ṣaddiq* is Zipporah's husband, Naphtali, who deserted her fifteen years previously! He is arrested for murder while Hadassah suffers a fit.

Some time later, Gemalli's son, Peretz, consults the *Ṣaddiq* of another town because he has learned of his father's plan to disinherit him in favour of Sarah and Hadassah. The *Ṣaddiq*—who turns out to be the same Naphtali in disguise, after a dramatic escape from prison!—reveals that he is Peretz's real father, and advises him to kill Gemalli and the old servant who is his real mother, and then burn the house and marry Hadassah! In consequence, after Gemalli's sudden death in mysterious circumstances, a will is found leaving Peretz everything. Because Hadassah refuses to marry him, Peretz drives her and her mother from the house. But the fire which consumes his property also devours the room they have rented nearby, so that they are left penniless and homeless.

Compelled to seek employment, Hadassah is engaged as a servant in the household of a Jewish officer who turns out to be none other than Israel! The young lovers are joyfully reunited, and the chief guest at the wedding ceremony, Israel's superior officer, Samson, turns out to be Hadassah's long-lost brother!

Peretz is subsequently arrested, charged with the murder of Gemalli and the servant (his mother), and the will is proved a forgery. The villainous *Ṣaddiq*, too, is brought to justice, while Sarah,
with her children and her property restored, completely loses
her faith in *Ṣaddiqim*. The most blatantly crude and grotesque of
all the novels under review, even Zobeizensky's *For Love of Ṣaddiqim*, nevertheless contains more than a grain of serious social
criticism.

Marcus Manassewitz (1858-1928) was born in Lithuania, but
received his education in Latvia and spent the greater part of his
life in Libau where he founded a school which lasted for 38 years.
Although his first literary steps were in the field of *belles-lettres*,
including stories, poems and fables published in a number of
Hebrew periodicals,[69] the bulk of his writing was connected with
pedagogy and comprises a whole series of text-books for the study
of Hebrew.[70] In 1920 he left Latvia for America, where he continued his educational activities and his work for the Zionist
movement. Even his novel, *The Parents' Sin*, was composed with
a didactic purpose, as is clearly stated in the foreword.[71]

The heroine of *The Parents' Sin*, Miriam, was born into a large
family whose pride in genealogy far outstripped its means. Constantly at loggerheads with her father because of his desire to wed
her to a student of the *Yešibhah* instead of to a craftsman who
could earn a livelihood, her wish to marry Benjamin, an enlightened young silversmith, is frustrated by her father's machinations which result in Benjamin's imprisonment on a trumped-up
charge of theft. Meanwhile her father induces a young Talmudist, Gershon, to marry his daughter by promising him a large
dowry which after the wedding he is unable to honour. In consequence, Gershon disappears a month after the wedding, while
her father's creditors, who have lost confidence in his financial
position, conspire to ruin him. In the resulting hardship, both
parents and six of their nine children die, while Miriam is left
to eke out the meagrest of livelihoods to support herself and her
twin sons by working as a seamstress for some years.

Finally, her poverty grows so acute that she sets out in search
of her husband together with her children, one of whom dies on
the journey. After wandering as a beggar for a year, she learns
from a passing traveller that the plot against Benjamin has finally come to light, and that he has recently been released from

prison after five years. Eventually, Miriam reaches the home of her aunt, where she finds her sister, who had also been deserted by her husband two weeks after the wedding ceremony. Her aunt relates how her only son had disappeared twenty-seven years previously, and from the description of the circumstances Hannah realises that it must be Benjamin. So once again they all set out in search of Benjamin and the two erring husbands.

Some six months later they come across a man whom both sisters claim to be their husband! He, however, denies the accusation, and advises them to visit the local Rabbi to whom he bears an astonishing resemblance. The Rabbi does, indeed, turn out to be husband of them both; but as he has remarried in the meantime, he generously consents to grant them both a bill of divorce! Meanwhile Miriam's aunt discovers her son Benjamin worn out with sickness, and Miriam arrives just in time to witness a harrowing death-bed scene. A year later her aunt expires, and although her sister finally remarries, the heroine, sick of life, prefers to live alone[72] and write her history to expose the stupidity of parents in forcing their children to marry against their will, especially when the motive is one of family pride.

The prolific Yiddish writer Nahum Meir Sheikewitz[73] (1847-1905) was born in Nesvizh, Lithuania, into a family which had once been wealthy, but whose fortunes were then in decline.[74] Although an able pupil with a prodigious memory, his childhood was embittered by the vicious beatings of a series of sadistic teachers.[75] Even at an early age, however, he displayed all the signs of a gifted storyteller. After studying at the great *Yešibhoth* at Mir and Volozhin, he became acquainted with the ideas of *Haskalah*, and at the suggestion of S. J. Fünn, whom he met in Vilna in 1872, he began to write popular stories in Yiddish. Henceforward his output was prodigious, amounting to upwards of two hundred novels, as well as some forty dramas and comedies which he wrote for the Yiddish theatre after moving to Odessa in 1878. Although his novels are all of a romantic, melodramatic kind,—he was able to write a story of over a hundred pages in a day or two!—he performed an important service by attracting a wide circle of Yiddish readers, which encouraged his more gifted successors to create a serious Yiddish literature. Because of the mounting criticism directed against him,[76] however, and the ban on the Yiddish theatre imposed by the Russian government,

Sheikewitz emigrated to America in 1889. Once in New York he immediately resumed his prolific activity, both as a novelist and playwright, at the same time contributing numerous articles to the Yiddish press.

One of the comparatively few novels written by Sheikewitz in Hebrew, *The Outcast*, again describes the disastrous results arising from the attempt to force a young girl to marry against her will, and once again places the entire responsibility firmly on the shoulders of the parents. Hannah, the heroine and narrator of the story, describes herself as the child of observant but unscrupulous parents, who are determined to marry her to a student of the Talmud, Jacob Parhi—a sickly youth, who is the younger son of the fanatical Asher Parhi. She, however, falls in love with Jacob Rimmon, an enlightened teacher in the local government school, and a close friend of Abraham Parhi, the talented elder brother of her intended bridegroom. In a series of midnight visits, Jacob tells Hannah the story of his life.

Although grandsons of a very wealthy man, Jacob and his brothers had been swindled out of their inheritance, after their father's death, by the machinations of his rich uncle Abraham Rimmon.[77] After leaving the *Yešibhah* at 18, Jacob had fallen madly in love with the daughter of a successful card-sharp,[78] but on learning of her indifferent morals he had left his native town to seek employment in his uncle's business. The latter had received him kindly and found employment for him with one of his agents, Gitzil Roš-Kelebh.[79] The latter's daughter was in love with Abraham Parhi, who had befriended Jacob Rimon and introduced him to the ideas of *Haskalah*. After some months, however, Gitzil had managed to trick Jacob into signing a document waiving all claim to his share of his grandfather's inheritance. Unable to prove his uncle's villainy, Jacob had gone to Vilna to study in the Rabbinical Seminary established by the government,[80] and subsequently obtained his present teaching post.

At this point the story is picked up once again by Hannah. Their midnight meetings discovered, Jacob Rimmon is made to flee the town, while the preparations for her marriage to the sickly Jacob Parhi proceed apace. Unable to face the prospect, however, Hannah flees on her wedding day with the aid of the local Polish governor. After four days in the latter's house she realises that he is plotting her conversion to Christianity.[81] So Hannah flees once more and makes her way by train to Kiev, where she is forced to eke out a miserable existence as a seamstress. Finally she is befriended by her cousin Samson, whose inheritance her parents had usurped when the lad was orphaned, and who had been Hannah's childhood friend. Samson had subsequently been brought up by a Polish guardian and converted to Christianity. He offers to marry Hannah if she, too, will agree to become a Christian. After much heart-searching Hannah is finally baptised. But overcome by remorse, she is on the point of committing suicide when Jacob Rimon, who has meanwhile succeeded in gaining his inheritance and has learned of Hannah's plight from Abraham Parhi, appears in the nick of time, and takes her off to Jerusalem where she becomes a Jewess once more. Jacob's wicked uncle and his accomplice, Gitzil, are sentenced to imprisonment, but are released at Jacob's request, while the story ends with the news that Hannah's father, whose obstinacy has been the cause of all her misfortunes, has lost his reason.

Among the major writers under review, Alexander Süsskind Rabinowitz (1854-1945) stands somewhat apart.[82] Born in Liady in the province of Mohilev to poor but strictly orthodox parents, Rabinowitz received a sound traditional education, and was introduced to the literature of *Haskalah* at the age of fifteen via Mapu's novel, *The Hypocrite*.[83] For some sixteen years after his marriage in 1872 he eked out the barest of livelihoods, mainly as a Hebrew teacher, and was compelled to wander from place to place in an attempt to support himself and his family. In 1888, however, he was appointed to a teaching job in the *Talmudh Torah*[84] at Poltava, which he occupied with great success for seventeen years, at the same time contributing stories to a number of Hebrew journals. In 1897, he was sent as the local delegate to the first World Zionist Congress at Basle, and nine years later settled with his family in Palestine, where he worked as a teacher and librarian in Jaffa. In 1917, however, he finally left teaching in order to concentrate on literary work, and throughout the remainder of his long life he devoted himself to the composition of biographical, historical and pedagogical works, as well as to a wide variety of editing and translation. A convinced socialist, Rabinowitz composed the first novels in Hebrew written in a real socialist vein. Nevertheless, throughout his life he remained faithful to orthodox Judaism.

Rabinowitz's first novel, *At the Crossroads*, is the story of a rake's progress, and differs radically in its point of view from all the Hebrew novels of the period. The hero, Jehiel, is introduced as a poor orphan with a taste for learning, who enthusiastically embarks upon the study of Jewish traditional sources at the comparatively advanced age of seventeen. In the course of three years he makes excellent progress, and after his marriage to Hannah, a beautiful and virtuous young woman, he continues his studies in her father's house for a similar period.[85] With the impoverishment of the bride's father, however, the young couple and their daughter Bathsheba move into separate quarters, while Hannah opens a shop to support her family.[86]

This peaceful existence comes to an abrupt end with the visit of a travelling book-seller, from whom Jehiel purchases some works written from the point of view of *Haskalah*, which start him on the slippery slope away from Judaism. He neglects his study of the Talmud in favour of secular books which he understands only in part and consorts more and more with loose companions, who lead him into bad habits. Next he turns his back on Judaism and Hebrew completely, concentrating instead on Russian literature and what he considers broader human problems—a process which amounts in practice to despising all things Jewish.

In the course of nine years his wife pines away and finally dies in childbirth; whereupon the hero succumbs to the fascination of an 'enlightened' young woman, Janet, who talks like a typical heroine of a 'love story'. After a brief but passionate romance, Jehiel marries her, only to find that she rapidly destroys the business which Hannah had built up so laboriously, at the same time completely neglecting the household. As poverty enters the home, love rapidly disappears through the window, and after a series of violent quarrels Janet returns to her father.

Reduced to dire financial straits, the hero moves to the capital in an attempt to earn a living as a journalist; but as the last of his money melts away he finds himself living in indescribable squalor, having plumbed the depths of degradation since his original departure from the straight and narrow path. The novel ends abruptly with the information that the hero, while working in a factory (with forged papers), has been murdered by a peasant, from whom he had stolen a trifling sum of money, and that his daughter Bathsheba—brought up in accordance with the hero's cosmopolitan principles—has finally married a gentile postman. From the standpoint of sustained and effective satire, Rabinowitz's novel has few rivals during the period under review.

Israel Joseph Sirkis (1860-1928) was born of extremely wealthy parents in Podolia, who provided him with both a traditional and secular education. Deeply interested in philosophy, particularly as applied to Judaism, and himself the author of a number of books on philosophical themes, Sirkis was also a patron of Hebrew literature, always willing to extend most generous support to any young writer of promise,[87] as well as to literary institutions. After the Russian Revolution he lost all his possessions and fled to Roumania, leaving his family behind in Russia. So reduced were his circumstances, that had it not been for the help extended to him by a number of *Maskilim* in America who remembered his former generosity, he would have starved to death.[88] A number of his letters to the philanthropist Israel Matz, which have fortunately been preserved, provide a pathetic illustration of the misery of his material position during his last years, made all the more poignant by contrast with his previous wealth and magnanimity.[89] Nevertheless, even during the period of his greatest poverty, his literary activity continued undiminished.

The plot of Sirkis' novel *Esther* is weak and formless to the point of absurdity. The heroine, who earns a meagre livelihood as a cook in her aunt's house, is admired by her cousin Solomon and a simpleton called Qalsi.[90] By a series of misunderstandings, however, Solomon becomes convinced that she prefers both Qalsi and the brother of a gentile servant, Marisi, to himself. For her part, Esther is primarily interested in saving sufficient money to buy a new dress,[91] which she never actually manages to obtain in spite of several 'near misses'. Her one love is for her aunt's little daughter, Shiphrah, whose subsequent death from diphtheria renders her wild with grief. In consequence she goes to live with Marisi in a village, from which Solomon unsuccessfully attempts to bring her back by force. Disowned by her family, who fear that she may turn to Christianity, Esther decides to seek a new life in America. After saving her passage-money by working as a seamstress, and being tormented by the other girls, she persuades Qalsi to accompany her, and the story closes with a final description of the emigrants about to set out upon their long journey. The novel, which abounds with philosophical reflections, is permeated with a deep sense of nationalism, and strongly advocates the emigration of Jews from Roumania, the country where the story is unfolded.

Israel Weisbrem, the last of the novelists under review, was born in Grodno in 1838 and later became a merchant in Warsaw. It would appear that his father, Benjamin Zarah Weisbrem, who died in Warsaw in 1896, was a wealthy and public-spirited man. Unfortunately, it has not proved possible to discover any further biographical information beyond these meagre details.[92]

The theme of *Between the Times* is concerned with Gershon, the shiftless son of Peretz and Hannah Rekin, who own a shop in a little town in Lithuania. Gershon irresponsibly takes their small store of capital and absconds with Tamar, the only surviving child of Nahum Tobiah, the local Rabbi. But almost at once Gershon abandons her in order to woo the rich former mistress of a deceased Polish noble, to whom Gershon discovers he bears an extraordinary likeness. The lady in question, Miriam, for her part is anxious to marry into a respectable Jewish family in order to appease her parents who have never been able to forgive her previous misconduct. Meanwhile, the abandoned Tamar falls into a decline and is taken to hospital, where she is befriended by a rich Polish noblewoman, Elenora, a devout Catholic, who takes her to her estate and nurses her back to health. One day Elenora introduces Tamar to her neighbour Miriam. The young women at once strike up a friendship, and Miriam invites Tamar to stay with her. Inevitably Miriam learns of Gershon's double dealings and reluctantly breaks off their betrothal. This misfortune has a sobering effect on Gershon, who decides to seek his fortune abroad.

Meanwhile, Rabbi Nahum's adopted son Jonathan, who has always loved Tamar, finds life intolerable without her presence and seeks his fortune in America, where all trace of him is lost. Gershon, too, sails for America, where after some five years of hardship, including two years in a coalmine, he is befriended by a rich man called Kanelly, who finds employment for him in Quebec. During all these years Tamar, who has returned to her parents' home, resists all proposals of marriage in the hope that Jonathan will one day return. Miriam, too, who has become reconciled to her parents, entertains similar aspirations with respect to Gershon.

Suddenly the little town is electrified by the news that Sir

Kanelly of Quebec is coming to open a factory nearby. Sir Kanelly eventually calls on Rabbi Nahum and turns out to be none other than Jonathan. After his engagement to the faithful Tamar, Jonathan journeys to Quebec to settle his affairs, returning five weeks later with his assistant—Gershon! A double wedding serves to round off the happy ending.

The improbabilities of *Between the Times* are closely rivalled by some of the more startling events woven into the plot of Weisbrem's second novel, *18 Coins*, which is more than twice the length of its predecessor, and divided into two parts.

The plot centres upon the efforts of Gedaliah and Malka Skopitzki, a very rich but miserly couple, to marry off their daughter, Eve, to Joseph, the son of the wealthy Simon Rebetzek. Both Gedaliah and Simon are pious *Ḥasidhim* and faithful supporters of the local holy man or *Ṣaddiq*—so much so that their belief in the latter's supernatural powers constitutes an important element in the plot. Indeed, when the fire-insurance companies raise their premiums, the tight-fisted Gedaliah—most of whose wealth is in the form of merchandise—decides to send a gift to the *Ṣaddiq* in exchange for the latter's protection, even though he is told explicitly that the *Ṣaddiq's* own property is insured! Simon's faith in the *Ṣaddiq's* powers rests on firmer foundations. He attributes his success to eighteen copper coins which the *Ṣaddiq* once gave him—in return for eighteen gold coins—at a time of dire hardship. The coins have proved so efficacious that Simon, rising from strength to strength, had finally become the sole agent of a wealthy Polish nobleman, an absentee landlord, whose entire estates he supervises, even dwelling in the ancestral mansion. Simon treasures his eighteen coins, which he considers to be the source of his extraordinary good fortune, and generously contributes to his *Ṣaddiq's* funds. For his part the *Ṣaddiq* is anxious to foster an alliance between his two wealthy supporters, and details Shemaiah, a rather dubious character, to be Simon's secretary in order to expedite the proceedings. The only obstacle is that Joseph, Simon's son, who has enjoyed a liberal education and moves in a circle of young Polish nobles, refuses even to consider the match proposed for him.

Now Joseph has a young friend, Michael, whose father David Rosen is a wealthy *Maskil*. Joseph falls in love with Michael's sister Elisheba, while Michael himself is attracted to Rebecca, the second of seven poor sisters, who earn a precarious living with the needle. As the prospect of such a double wedding is not likely to be to the *Ṣaddiq's* advantage, Shemaiah determines to put a spoke in the wheel, and prevails upon Azriel Romberg, a pseudo-*Maskil*, to further his plans. With the help of an expert forger they send slanderous letters to the young lovers and their parents, as a result of which Joseph's mother falls into a decline and dies.

In the course of time, however, the misunderstandings are resolved, and in Part Two of the novel Simon remarries, taking none other than Rebecca's older sister Sarah, who brings Rebecca along to live with them. Simon invites the Rosen family to spend a holiday on the estate, and goes so far as to write to the *Ṣaddiq* asking permission for Joseph to marry Elisheba. But this the *Ṣaddiq* indignantly refuses, demanding that Simon should either break off relations with the *Maskil*, David Rosen, or return his eighteen coins. Nor are Michael's marriage plans any more successful. His mother scornfully rejects his plan to marry a girl of such lowly origins, and to spare Rebecca further embarrassment Simon suggests she should spend some time at a lonely hunting lodge in the forest.

Meanwhile Azriel has been pressing Shemaiah for a reward for his herculean, though unsuccessful, attempts to divide the lovers. To be rid of him Shemaiah has him captured and imprisoned in a dungeon in that self-same hunting lodge. On hearing of this, the *Ṣaddiq* decides that it would be best to induce Azriel to emigrate to America, and when the latter's wife, Esther, arrives to ask the *Ṣaddiq* of her husband's whereabouts, he tells her to make ready to join her husband in America. Esther, vastly impressed by the *Ṣaddiq's* omniscience, sells up her possessions in preparation for the journey. In the hunting lodge, however, Rebecca is beginning to suspect that all is not well, and sends a message to Simon to that effect.

At this juncture the miserly Gedaliah reveals that he is about to pay off an old score against a minor Polish noble, Glupski. The latter has borrowed money from Gedaliah on the security of his estate, but Gedaliah is careful not to remind him of the expiry date. Instead he turns Glupski and his family out of their home with such callousness that the half-demented nobleman sets fire to the miser's entire property—which is not, of course, insured.

At the risk of their lives, Joseph and Michael rescue Glupski from the flames, and almost at once courageously rescue

C

Rebecca, who has been kidnapped by Shemaiah and his henchmen with the object of holding her to ransom. The young lovers
are reunited and their parents consent at last to the double union.
The *Ṣaddiq* despatches the villains to the holy land to repent,
while Azriel and Esther are reunited. But in her heart Esther
always believes in the *Ṣaddiq*, and Simon, too, continues to send
his contributions and maintains his faith in his eighteen coins.
Gedaliah, however, goes mad with grief and spends the rest of
his days running up and down his room in the asylum shouting
'Give me money! Give me money!'

From what precedes, the general outlines of the Hebrew novel
during the twenty years under review, and the broad literary
genre to which for the most part they belong, may be readily ap-
preciated. In the following chapters an attempt will be made to
estimate the literary qualities of these novels, their importance
in the history of the development of modern Hebrew literature,
and the overall picture of the social, cultural and religious conditions of Jewish life in eastern Europe, and particularly in Russia,
during the nineteenth century which they reflect. In assessing
their significance, however, one further aspect is worthy of note.
In the years when these novels were composed, Hebrew was still
almost exclusively a literary language, in the sense that the first
attempts to foster its employment as a living vernacular were
still embryonic.[93] For that reason, it is only fair to remember
that these writers entered the lists with one arm firmly tied
behind their backs. Whatever victories they won ought, therefore, to command considerable respect.

PART I

TWO

An Exercise in Structure

Of all the factors which illustrate the tentative, groping and experimental nature of the Hebrew novel during the twenty years following the death of the first Hebrew novelist, Abraham Mapu, in the autumn of the year 1867, the early attempts at plot construction remain, perhaps, the most illuminating. Not that the difficulty of weaving a convincing plot was either the sole or even necessarily the most formidable of the numerous obstacles lining the path of the Hebrew novelists. The many hazards confronting them in the spheres of characterization, style and language, on the one hand, and the absence of an informed and critical public with developed tastes and exacting aesthetic standards on the other, were equally severe. Each of the many ingredients that constitute a novel generated its own complex of intricate problems. Collectively they formed a barrier of sufficient magnitude to give even the bravest pause.

Admittedly, the trail had previously been blazed to some extent. In spite of the limitations of his stories, and their many serious shortcomings,[1] Mapu had accomplished the pioneer task of actually writing novels in Hebrew, and his influence may be discerned in the works of his successors time and time again.[2] But his long social novel, *The Hypocrite*, whose contemporary setting served as a model for almost all the novels written in Hebrew for more than half a century[3], had raised as many problems as it had solved, and merely emphasized the many pitfalls to be circumvented. Hebrew literature simply lacked a tradition for the writing of novels, and hence no yardstick had as yet been fashioned against which the various possible combinations of form and content might be measured.

Whereas the problems besetting style and characterization, however, were largely determined by linguistic considerations and remained, therefore, the more readily comprehensible,[4] the factors governing the choice of plot are not so immediately manifest. Novels might not, indeed, have existed to any extent in Hebrew but they abounded in the literatures of Europe, and were accessible either in the original, or in the two major languages with which the Jewish exponents of Enlightenment in eastern Europe were most familiar, namely Russian and German.[5] With the accumulated experience of European literature in the development of plot upon which to draw, and the existence of a wide variety of examples demonstrating the subtleties of construction and delicate artistry employed by many of the major European novelists at their disposal, the general ineptitude and lack of artistic restraint characteristic of most of the novels under review require some explanation. That the phenomenon is not always a result of the mere lack of any critical sense may be demonstrated—at least in the case of Smolenskin, one of the major offenders with regard to vagaries of plot— by the extremely discerning and sensitive discussions devoted to literary criticism, particularly in the analysis of *Hamlet* and of Goethe's *Faust* which constitute a substantial proportion of his early novel, *The Joy of the Godless*.[6]

Three principal reasons, then, may be regarded as responsible for the peculiarities of plot and construction which most of these novels display. In the first place, the structure of the novels is affected to a considerable degree by the differing purposes envisaged by their authors. All the novels display elements of social motivation in greater or lesser degree, although in some of them this aspect is dominant, while in others it is merely incidental. At the same time, they all necessarily attempt the literary task of unfolding a tale in a manner designed to hold the reader's interest, and are thereby subject to aesthetic considerations. Both these factors, however, tend to influence each other adversely. The social criticism and the propagation of reformist ideas permeating these novels constitute a didactic element which seriously affects their literary merit. Only too frequently the smooth flow of the narrative is violently interrupted to enable the author to hammer home some specific lesson or expound his own particular views.[7] That the structure of the novel frequently suffers in the process provides an interesting illustration of the transitional nature of Hebrew literature in the period under review. The Hebrew novelists had not yet learned to fuse their didactic and artistic aspirations into one harmonious unit.[8]

In this respect the Hebrew novels of the period may be roughly divided into three main categories, namely, those in which the social or didactic purpose is clearly of prime importance although the plot may also command considerable attention; those which were written first and foremost as romances or tales of adventure, but whose authors, too, were unable to resist the inclusion of didactic elements, sometimes with arresting effect; and those in which both literary and didactic considerations play an almost equally important role. To the first category belong the early novels of Smolenskin, *The Wanderer in the Paths of Life* and *The Joy of the Godless*, Braudes' first novel *Religion and Life*[9] and Rabinowitz's *At the Crossroads*.[10] The second category includes Leinwand's *The Artful Villain*, Sheikewitz's *The Outcast*, and Weisbrem's novels *Between the Times* and *18 Coins*. The third category, broadly speaking, covers all the rest, namely Smolenskin's *A Donkey's Burial, Pride and Fall, The Reward of the Righteous* and *The Inheritance*, Abramowitz's *Fathers and Sons*, Braudes' *The Two Extremes*, Meinkin's *The Love of the Righteous*, Zobeizensky's *For Love of Ṣaddiqim*, Manassewitz's *The Parents' Sin*, and Sirkis' *Esther*.

Such categorization, however, should not be regarded as a mark of quality. Zobeizensky's novel for example, although avowedly didactic in purpose,[11] is remarkable for the wild extravagances of its plot; conversely Braudes' *Religion and Life* and Rabinowitz's *At the Crossroads* display many signs of careful and deliberate construction, while Braudes' second novel *The Two Extremes* is distinguished by the consummate artistry of its structure. Any such classification, indeed, depends rather on the author's manifest intention than on his comparative dramatic skill, and should be regarded as a sign of emphasis rather than a criterion of achievement.

The second factor responsible for the structural peculiarities of many of these novels—and particularly in the case of those by Smolenskin—may be sought in the manner of their composition. As editor and general factotum of the journal *Ha-Šaḥar* (*The Dawn*),[12] Smolenskin was compelled to pursue all his activities at a furious pace,[13] and often against the pressure of imminent publication. The fact that his stories were published in his journal in serial form, therefore, provides an explanation of two of the most detrimental aspects of the structure of his novels.[14] Serialization naturally encourages a tendency to think in terms of a number of episodes rather than an overall unity. The mere fact that each instalment must in great measure be self-contained exerts a baneful influence on the general cohesion of the novel. Serialization, again, requires that each instalment end on a note of suspense in order to whet the reader's appetite and sustain his curiosity until the next issue of the journal. The subterfuges demanded by such an expedient, however, inevitably exact the price of unexpected twists and complications, sometimes of so confusing a nature that the author may feel constrained to re-capitulate his themes to make the plot comprehensible at all.[15] Again, the very nature of serialization lends itself to the inclusion of lengthy sections comprising completely extraneous material, which on occasion appears to have little purpose except to fill up space.[16]

A most revealing description of the manner in which Smolen-skin composed his novels may be found in his poignant preface to the second edition of *The Wanderer in the Paths of Life*, where the author discloses the harrowing conditions in which he was compelled to write:

The publication of *Ha-Šaḥar* imposed a heavy burden on my shoulders and involved me in enormous labour which devoured all my time without granting me a moment's respite. For dur-ing the first three years of its publication, far from bringing me any reward for my toil, *Ha-Šaḥar* compelled me to work like a slave in order to support myself and keep the journal alive, since the expenditure far exceeded its income. Like a doting mother, who shirks no task, however wearisome, for the sake of her offspring, I cared for it and nursed it, reared it, and kept it alive. I deprived myself of sleep and enjoyed no relaxation for many years merely in order to safeguard its exis-tence. During that time I acted as contributor-in-chief, proof-reader, accountant, office-boy, clerk and editor—performing all these functions alone without any assistance. And as the readers of *Ha-Šaḥar* are well aware, I did not fill its pages with news and matters of ephemeral interest which could be put into the press without scrutiny, but with a variety of serious academic and scientific works, all of which I had to read from beginning to end before allowing them to go to press, and which I had to annotate from time to time whenever the need arose. Under such circumstances one may readily understand that every minute of my time was occupied. Only at night (for the most part from 10 p.m. to 1 or 2 a.m.) was I able to compose my own contributions for *Ha-Šaḥar*. During those hours I wrote this novel, too, sometimes with my head spinning like a top so that I could scarcely see the paper in front of me. And on each occasion, far from being able to read over what I had written in search of mistakes, I was only too happy merely to succeed in finishing the section in time for printing. On each occasion I found myself compelled to send the manuscript to press the moment it was written. Is it surprising that I sometimes discovered later that whole lines and indeed entire conversations had been missed out? For due to the speed with which I wrote I failed to notice that my hand had not always faithfully reproduced the thoughts which I had intended. I was aware of all this without being able to do otherwise, and so I comforted myself with the hope that I would live to see a second edition which I would then be able to correct. It was, moreover, my original intention to divide the story into four parts; but when I saw how long it had become and that it had already extended over two full years, I decided not to include the fourth part for fear my readers might think that it was a deliberate plot on my part to induce them to subscribe to *Ha-Šaḥar* merely for the sake of the story. Indeed, I have always taken care, both then and subsequently, not to ensnare my readers into subscribing to *Ha-Šaḥar*. For that reason I confined the story to three parts, and reserved the fourth for the day when a second edition might appear.[17]

This illuminating confession furnishes an important key to the understanding of the construction of Smolenskin's plots. Novels written under such duress are not likely to exhibit the signs of careful planning or subtlety of form. Nor is it surprising that careless slips and, indeed, even serious errors sometimes occur. In the second part of *The Inheritance*, for example, the name of one of the heroines is suddenly changed from Peninnah to Zipporah because another character of the same name has meanwhile been introduced.[18] What is indeed remarkable, in such circumstances, is the author's overall grasp on the development of his plots, and his unusual success in tying up the many loose ends.[19]

The difficulties arising from the conditions under which Smolenskin was compelled to write were further aggravated by the complex types of plot which characterize his three major novels,

The Wanderer in the Paths of Life, *The Reward of the Righteous*, and
The Inheritance. The influence of Mapu's long and tortuous social
novel *The Hypocrite*, itself partly modelled on Eugène Sue's *Mystères de Paris*,[20] must clearly be held more than partly responsible
for the sometimes bewildering complications of these stories, as
even a superficial comparison of the incredible machinations of
Zadok, the arch-villain in *The Hypocrite*, with the gruesome villainies of Manasseh, his counterpart in *The Wanderer in the Paths
of Life*, will readily demonstrate. But both Mapu and Smolenskin must bear a joint responsibility for bequeathing the same
tortuous legacy to many of the minor novelists under review,[21]
a legacy shared by Abramowitz's influential novel *Fathers and
Sons*, whose plot is formless to the point of incomprehensibility.[22]

The third factor to play a part in conditioning the pattern
of plot which characterizes so many of these novels arises from
the nature of the public for whom they were intended. It is important to remember that traditional Jewish education in eastern Europe was exclusively restricted to the study of religious
texts, and in particular the Talmud, which demanded an inten-
sive and concentrated analysis of extremely intricate and subtle
legal arguments, frequently involving hair-splitting casuistry.[23]
Within such an intellectual climate there was no place for the
concept of literature as an instrument for the expression of
aesthetic or emotional attitudes.[24] But the narrow intellectual
horizons were paralleled by a mode of life which was similarly
circumscribed by poverty, circumstance and deliberate oppression.[25] A desire to break what they considered to be the intellectual and physical shackles of Jewish life, and acquaint the Jewish
people with the rich and variegated possibilities afforded by
European civilization, ranks among the leading aims of the exponents of Enlightenment, the *Maskilim*. That life must be lived
and felt as well as thought might almost be regarded as their
watchword.[26]

For the modern reader, therefore, the plots of most of the novels
under review may well appear unduly complicated, melodramatic and sometimes utterly fantastic and far-fetched. They
are frequently presented with a naïvety which to a more sophisticated reader seems crude, unpolished and, indeed, absurd. For
the contemporary generation of young eastern European Jews,
however, the plots of these novels constituted their most attractive
and fascinating aspect, partly because they represented a com-

pletely new and unimagined literary *genre,* and partly because the stirring events, the colourful adventures, the whole quick excitement of activity stood out in such sharp contrast to the drab and shabby sameness of their own lives. Into the poverty and squalor of a small town or village in the Russian *Pale of Settlement,*[27] for example, where the sum of intellectual activity was harnessed to the dry machine of Talmudic casuistry, these novels brought a vivid experience of activity and a refreshing sense of emotion. The more complex the plot, the more intricate the machinations, the more dramatic the vicissitudes and quirks of fortune, the more powerful and appealing was their effect upon young minds accustomed to complex and tortuous modes of thought but starved of heroism and colour.[28]

The fascination was all the greater because these novels dealt primarily with a familiar scene but one which was now endowed with a fresh dimension by virtue of exaggeration, satire and an acceleration of events which lent purpose and excitement to a humdrum and parochial environment. Through the prism of the novelist's mind their familiar world took on a different colouring, which emphasized the pettiness and follies of their little lives and faced them with a distressing portrait of their own society in decay. Although frequently read surreptitiously and in stealth[29] —a factor which only added a spice of danger to the excitement —these novels served to arouse a state of self-consciousness, and to foster an awareness of the forces of conflict and change at work in society. That this fresh and highly critical appraisal of a known environment was conveyed through such exciting channels as a complex plot, substantially increased its fascination.

One further consideration deserves attention in partial explanation of the weaknesses of construction apparent in the majority of these novels. The same widespread absence of any literary training or critical appreciation among their readers, in consequence of the prevailing system of education, applies in great measure to the novelists themselves, particularly in the case of the minor authors. Introduced to secular learning and the very concept of literature at a comparatively late stage, and then normally by haphazard and autodidactic means, their initial disadvantages were formidable. Untrained and untutored in any formal sense, their experiments in fiction often display an ignorance of basic literary principles. It is significant, for example, that one of the minor novels under review is written almost without punctuation of any kind.[30] It must be admitted, too, that the natural talents displayed by Leinwand, Meinkin, Zobeizensky, Manassewitz and Sirkis are severely limited.

Three of the novels under review, however—namely the two novels by Braudes, and Rabinowitz's *At the Crossroads*—are characterized by plots of a much less flamboyant and perplexing nature, while a fourth, Sirkis' *Esther*, can scarcely boast of any plot at all. Of all the novelists, Braudes displays the most developed sense of plot construction. This is particularly the case in his second novel, *The Two Extremes*, which displays all the signs of careful planning, and is remarkable for the skilful balance and harmonization of its themes. The same natural dramatic skill may also be discerned in the first two parts of Braudes' first novel, *Religion and Life*; but here the author's avowed social purpose[31] and the frequent interspersion of long passages of polemic detract considerably from the artistry, while the third part, which was never completed, devotes less and less attention to the plot, concentrating instead upon the social, cultural and particularly the religious problems which constitute the author's prime concern.[32] In similar vein the main emphasis in Smolenskin's *The Joy of the Godless* falls upon the lengthy dialogues devoted to love, literature and kindred topics,[33] for which the plot comprises a loose and comparatively unimportant framework.[34]

The fantastic ending to Rabinowitz's *At the Crossroads*, however, injects a puzzling note into what is otherwise a soberly constructed novel, whose plot displays many signs of careful planning and considerable artistic skill. The gradual demoralisation of the hero consequent upon a growing addiction to the ideas of a debased Enlightenment[35] is skilfully contrasted with the solid virtues of traditional Jewish life which one by one he has abandoned. The plot is simple, economical and refreshingly free from extraneous or superfluous matter. Once having made his point, however, the author seems suddenly to have lost all interest in his story, and without further ado proceeds to wind it up in an absurd manner within a single paragraph. Here, again, the initial lack of a literary training and an aesthetic discipline is only too painfully in evidence.

It may be readily imagined, therefore, that the plots of almost all these novels are characterized by an unevenness and jerkiness, and give the impression of developing in fits and starts. This effect is largely determined by the many interruptions to the narrative to which, for a variety of reasons most of them are subject. Many of these interruptions are virtually independent of the plot, or connected with it only in an incidental manner. All too frequently the authors break the smooth flow of the narrative in order to introduce passages or even whole chapters devoted to social criticism and satire, historical analysis, personal opinions or a wide variety of extraneous material.[36] Similarly, the strong didactic tendencies common to all these authors constantly interrupt the continuity of the plot, sometimes in unashamed and blatant form.[37] 'Indeed, the aim of this story is solely to open people's eyes. . . .' Sheikewitz deliberately affirms,[38] while elsewhere the hero of his novel, disgusted at the treatment meted out by his uncle to a Hebrew writer, decides that if he ever waxes rich he will support such authors generously, provided only that their writings be of service to their people![39]

The authors of these novels, indeed, regularly intervene in order to address their readers directly. Although usually a stylistic device,[40] such intervention may frequently constitute a deliberate interruption to the narrative for a specific purpose. On more than one occasion, for example, the plot of Smolenskin's *The Wanderer in the Paths of Life* is suspended while the author assures his readers that the characters and modes of behaviour which he is describing are really true to life, and that his main purpose is to relate an actual story rather than stand in judgment.[41] It is significant that he, himself, points out and justifies some unlikely aspects of his narrative, at the same time explaining his reasons for having composed a picaresque novel, instead of writing a story of love or adventure.[42] After stressing that he could, indeed, have written a love story—he appends a short example with a number of variations!—Smolenskin reaffirms that truth belongs to a different category, and although the light-minded reader may find it dull, future generations may draw a lesson from his tale.[43]

Braudes, too, frequently interrupts the course of his novel, *Religion and Life*, in order to give the reader the benefit of his personal predilections, sometimes in a highly impassioned and emotional form:

Alas, I write of these matters with my heart's blood. When I recall Israel's sorry plight due to the oppression of the Rabbis and their estrangement from the people, my blood boils. I know that the Rabbis have not caused these splits and factions out of malice. I know that it is merely because of their lack of understanding, their ignorance of the people and its way of life, their inability to see the real causes and their clouded vision that they have fashioned this *calf* for us. But the calf prances in our midst, the factions increase and the splits grow wider. Who knows whether we may still be able to repair the damage, and somehow save the fabric.[44] Yet they still remain silent, their minds are still unable to comprehend rightly, their eyes still do not see the real chain of cause and effect! . . . Alas, O Lord! Why have you struck the leaders of this people blind? Why are you so vexed with your flock that you have deprived its shepherds of their sight?. . .

Dear Reader! Come with me, and I shall lead you into the innermost conclaves of the *Law*. Let me open the doors of the Rabbis' houses for you, and bring you into the councils and assemblies of the community. I shall introduce you to all such as took part in this dispute; I shall reveal their weapons to you, read their letters to you, and spread out their motives at that time like an open book before you. So that you, yourself, may be able to reply to these questions, and clearly understand the nature of the men who led the people, the extent of their abilities, and the limits of their concern for the common people and its needs.[45]

Among the examples of personal intervention on the part of the minor writers, a number of instances are extremely revealing. Leinwand, for example, finds it necessary to explain to his readers how the villain, who is impersonating a nobleman, is able to produce tears at will. By way of illustration he points out that actors can display emotions quite different from their real feelings![46] Sheikewitz, again, frequently intervenes to justify the inclusion of certain elements such as dreams, passages of natural description, or even rows of dots on the grounds that all Hebrew writers do so! This technique affords him a series of opportunities to criticize a number of abuses in contemporary Hebrew literature—although his own novel is far from blameless in that regard.[47] In similar vein Weisbrem interrupts his story for a discourse on the modern fashion among authors to describe women as 'the fair sex' or 'the weaker sex'.[48] Sirkis, on the other hand, intervenes in order to contrast his treatment of the ending of his story with the method which a writer stemming from another people would adopt. His statement, incidentally, constitutes an interesting example of a national self-consciousness, which is inherent in all the novels under review:

A writer stemming from another people would adopt harsh measures at this juncture. . . Is it conceivable that after all the terrible happenings that befell Esther and ground her into the dust, they would resuscitate her and despatch her to another land?! Such a writer would choose to portray Esther committing suicide, or would himself assume the role of the angel of death and let his pen consign her to the grave.

But that is not my way! For I am a writer who stems from the people of life; and I am fully aware how that people will pursue life at all costs.

My people loves life, and whoever hates life, hates my people. That is an incontrovertible rule.[49]

Elsewhere the author addresses Salmon, one of his characters, in defence of Esther, expresses surprise that Salmon's stratagem has succeeded, and later—as though admitting the weakness of his plot—apologises for Salmon's renewed suspicions with respect to his heroine.[50]

More frequently, however, these interruptions to the narrative are deliberately introduced as an integral element of the plot, and as such comprise the author's method of unfolding and developing his theme. Of the many dramatic techniques adopted for such purposes, perhaps the most common and certainly the most successful is the use of the *Rahmengeschichte*, or 'Frame-Story', which constitutes a self-contained narrative inserted into the overall framework of the novel. During the nineteenth century the device was very much in vogue among German novelists, of whom the chief exponent was Theodor Storm (1817-1888). In view of the predilection for German literature displayed by the Hebrew exponents of Enlightenment, it is scarcely surprising that the device should have found its way into the Hebrew novel.

The technique is particularly favoured by Smolenskin. The first part of *The Wanderer in the Paths of Life*, for example, includes a lengthy frame-story outlining the history of the villainous Manasseh which extends—with some interruptions[51]—from chapter 11 to chapter 26, and virtually comprises a novel in itself.[52] Similarly, although on a far more modest scale, the

histories of a number of young men held in prison while await-
ing military service provide the material for further frame-stories
in the second part of the novel.[53] Smolenskin uses the same technique, only in a much grander manner, in his novel *Pride and
Fall*, in which a series of frame-stories, told by a group of prospective immigrants journeying to the United States of America
following the collapse of the Viennese stock-exchange, comprises
the entire novel.[54] That the form seriously affects the novel's cohesion may be readily imagined. Smolenskin's other novels, however, also resort to the device. The *Joy of the Godless* contains no
less than three such stories,[55] while in *A Donkey's Burial* chapters
2 to 6 constitute a kind of frame-story supplying the background
to the events described in the opening chapter. The second part
of *The Reward of the Righteous* includes a frame-story in the form
of a letter,[56] and *The Inheritance* also employs the device of the
frame-story.[57]

Abramowitz introduces a slight variation in technique by including a frame-story in *Fathers and Sons*, the first part of which
is recounted in letter form,[58] while the latter half is narrated by
one of the characters.[59] Braudes employs the device in order to
outline the childhood and education of his hero, Samuel,[60] while
Manassewitz finds the technique convenient for illustrating the
dire consequences which may follow an 'arranged' marriage.[61]
The most notable example, however, occurs in Sheikewitz's novel,
The Outcast, a considerable portion of which is cast in the shape
of a frame-story relating the story of the hero Jacob's life,[62] and
which itself contains another frame-story.[63] Again, it is of interest
that the author feels constrained to justify his employment of the
device through the mouth of his heroine, the narrator of the
tale:

'Thank God for that!'—I can imagine many of my readers
saying happily—'We are already weary of waiting to hear the
end of your romance. And now the glad time has come.'
Of course, you are right! I know the temperament and tastes
of people who like novels. If the author presumes to prolong
his tale by introducing subsidiary stories, no matter how attractive, they will merely be regarded as obstacles. But I did
warn you right at the beginning that I wasn't sure of the way
I should unfold this story to overcome the laziness you usually
display when reading about the truth. My tale is not a fairy
story; everything in it is true. For that reason I regarded it as

השחר

יאיר נתיב על דרכי בני ישראל בזמן העבר וההוה

אָז יִבָּקַע כַּשַּׁחַר אוֹרֶךָ וַאֲרֻכָתְךָ מְהֵרָה תִצְמָח. (ישעיה נח. ח)	**Dann wird anbrechen gleich dem Morgenroth dein Licht, und deine Heilung schnell gedeihen!** *Jesaia 58, 8*

בו יבואו

א) מאמרי חכמה, דברי הימים, תולדות אנשי השם, תולדות השיר והמליצה בשפת עבר.

ב) ספורים בדוים, שירים ומסעות, בקורת הספרים הכתובים בשפת עבר.

ג) באורים בכתבי הקדש, בתלמוד מדרשים ואגדות.

ד) חדשות הנעשות בארץ, חדשות הנעשות בקרב בית ישראל. ידיעת ספרים.

ה) מכתבי אנשי השם. דרשות אשר הטיפו המטיפים הנודעים בשם יעתקו לשפת הקדש.

יוצא לאור מדי חדש בחדשו

על ידי

פרץ בן משה סמאלענסקין

חלק ראשון

חוברת ראשונה לחודש תשרי

שנת תרכ״ט לפ״ק

ווין

בדפוס של יעקב הכהן שלאססבערג

Frontispiece of the first issue of Smolenskin's journal Ha-Šahar, Vienna 1868

my duty to relate everything which has bearing on my history; and Jacob's history is inextricably connected with my own, as you, yourselves, will see in the course of my story. Many of the characters mentioned by Jacob will soon reappear in person. Then you will admit my wisdom in recounting for you the complete history of my beloved. . . .[64]

Parallel to the use of the frame-story, the narrative is frequently interrupted in order to sketch events which took place prior to the opening of the story, or supply information relevant to the previous history or experiences of one or other of the characters.[65] The technique involved sometimes resembles the one used in the modern cinema known as a 'flash-back'[66] and on one occasion Smolenskin even employs a 'flash-forward'.[67] From time to time in Braudes' novels an oblique approach is employed, whereby a situation gains added significance when viewed from a different standpoint. Thus the conflict in *Religion and Life* between Samuel and the Rabbi receives a fresh colouring through Hannah's eyes.[68] In like manner, although the narrative of the first part of Smolenskin's *The Reward of the Righteous* is seemingly interrupted at one point for more than a chapter,[69] the intervening material must be regarded less as an interruption than as a different method of unfolding the plot. Again, the plot is frequently suspended at moments of high tension for dramatic effect. This is particularly the case in the novels of Smolenskin,[70] where the technique is a natural consequence of publication in serial form.[71] By its very nature, however, the method faced its author with the formidable problems of renewing the dramatic tension, picking up the threads of the narrative, and eventually tying up all the loose ends.[72]

In an attempt to overcome these difficulties Smolenskin often resorts to the common literary technique of engaging his reader's attention by dropping hints of what is likely to happen in the course of the plot. In the very first chapter of *The Wanderer in the Paths of Life*, for example, the letter given to Josef by his dying mother, her anger against his uncle, and the latter's distress, all serve as pointers to the eventual unravelling of the story. A little later another hint of the villainous role played by Josef's aunt is conveyed in the statement: 'The wicked woman embezzled his father's wealth and brought him to an early grave; and now she is depriving the son of a share of the fortune which is rightly

D

his.'[73] The reader is comforted, however, by occasional references to the hero's future prosperity.[74] But more frequently, in
Smolenskin's novels, such hints presage not happiness but misery
and misfortune.[75] Sometimes the intimation is presented to the
reader in the form of an aside: 'He looked to me like a hunter or
a spy (the reader will learn who these spies and hunters were in
the course of the story) and I was afraid of him. . .'[76] The first
part of the novel closes, moreover, with the frank admission that
the next part will contain a love story![77]

Braudes, Sirkis, Sheikewitz and particularly Leinwand resort
to the same device.[78] The latter, for example, confirms the suspicions of Gershom the lawyer with respect to the validity of a
court summons received by his client by adding in brackets:
('Nor was his fear ungrounded as the reader will see in the course
of the story').[79] A similar presentiment of evil is contained in the
following gloomy warning: '. . . But Eleazar was unaware of the
cloud as small as a man's hand coming up from the north to
darken his happiness. . . .'[80] Fortunately, however, the reader
has already been given to understand that the villains are all due
to get their deserts in the end![81] A further device of a similar
order employed, in particular, in Smolenskin's *The Reward of the
Righteous* consists in letting the reader know more about what is
going on than the characters in any particular scene, or alternatively in deliberately withholding information, already known
to the reader, from the character whom it most closely concerns.[82]
On occasion, too, he fills in gaps in the reader's knowledge of the
plot by supplying—sometimes at length—the motivations responsible for the behaviour of his characters.[83]

The complexities of plot, to which most of the novels are
subject, are responsible, too, for the many problems arising from
the time factor to be encountered in these stories.[84] Although
this factor is, on occasion, handled with considerable skill—particularly, for example, in the first part of Braudes' *Religion and Life*,
where the events of the story are cleverly integrated[85]—more
frequently the novelists flounder about in some distress as though
completely out of their depth. Sometimes years slip by in the
course of a few lines.[86] Elsewhere the problem of coordinating
parallel series of events is badly handled. In chapter 13 of Smolenskin's *The Joy of the Godless*, for example, although Eve is described as having run away two months previously, the statement
cannot easily be reconciled with the other events. In Sirkis' *Es-

ther, again, the action outlined in chapter 4 takes place on the day following that described in the opening scene of the book. It is difficult, however, to determine quite when the happenings of chapter 3 occurred. The sequence of events is certainly most confusing.[87] Indicative of the overall lack of subtlety is the frequency with which the lapse of three years is used as a convenient but rather haphazard measure of time. In *The Wanderer in the Paths of Life*, Josef serves the *Ba'al Šem* or wonder-worker for three years.[88] In *Fathers and Sons* Aryeh maintains Simon for a similar period.[89] In *The Love of the Righteous* the young lovers are separated for three years without even receiving a letter from each other,[90] while the heroine of *The Parents' Sin* supports her twin sons by sewing for an equivalent span.[91] In the course of three years the hero of *At the Crossroads* becomes a considerable scholar, and after his marriage pursues his studies for a further three years as the guest of his father-in-law.[92] As a result of such defects of structure most of the novels under review inevitably display a serious lack of cohesion.

An examination of the principal themes which comprise the plots of the majority of these novels,[93] however, provides an even clearer indication of their literary quality. Most of them are riddled with an extraordinary variety of villainy, conspiracy and intrigue, often of an extremely naïve and tortuous nature.[94] On numerous occasions the villains concoct base plots in order to ensnare their enemies, for example by planting incriminating evidence or bearing false witness against their innocent victims.[95] Such devices occasionally furnish interesting evidence of unashamed piracy. In chapter 25 of the first part of Smolenskin's *The Wanderer in the Paths of Life*, for example, the arch-villain plants stolen goods in his victim's house, including a gold icon taken from a church. The identical villainous device is used by Leinwand in *The Artful Villain*, where it becomes an important element in the plot.[96] Parallel to these contrived and tortuous machinations are the numerous instances of informers and spies,[97] with the concomitant lawsuits, suspect wills, court-summonses and trial-scenes.[98] Of the latter the most tedious, perhaps, is again to be found in Leinwand's novel, where the whole plot is virtually repeated in court.[99] In spite of the trying repetition, however, and the extraordinary complexities of the plot, which even include attempts to have innocent victims locked away in lunatic asylums,[100] the scene maintains a consistency of detail not always encountered in these novels.

The stories contain numerous examples of ambush and kidnapping, both attempted and actual.[101] The most serious is the account of a young girl kidnapped into an Italian nunnery in *The Love of the Righteous*, which is clearly modelled on the famous Mortara case at Bologna in 1858.[102] More melodramatic are the two abductions in Weisbrem's *18 Coins*, accomplished with considerable daring and adroitness.[103] But the brief kidnapping of the heroine of Sirkis' *Esther*, although one of the few positive actions in the entire novel, is pitifully weak.[104] In similar vein, arrest,[105] imprisonment of various kinds,[106] release,[107] rescue,[108] and escape[109] all constitute popular and over-worked themes in these novels. Smolenskin's characters are particularly prone to find themselves in prison, usually on trumped-up charges! On the other hand, the revelations of a fellow-prisoner may provide a convenient method of furthering the plot.[110]

Among the many nefarious practices, with which these novels abound, theft[111] and forgery[112] are by far the most common, and from time to time they are introduced with considerable dramatic effect. In *The Wanderer in the Paths of Life*, for example, the hero is lucky enough to win a fortune in the Hamburg lottery and hires a room in an expensive hotel. During the night, however, he hears cries for help coming from the next room, and rushes in to find a girl fighting for her life against an assailant. While Josef grapples with the man, the girl takes refuge in his room, and when the hero finally returns, it is only to find that she has stolen his entire fortune![113] At the other extreme the hero of Rabinowitz's *At the Crossroads* is murdered by a fellow workman, from whom he has stolen a few coppers![114] It is of interest that forgery represents almost the sole instance of deliberate villainy in Braudes' novels,[115] although for most of the authors it ranks only as one crime amongst many. The hero of Sheikewitz's novel, however, almost loses his inheritance as a result of a forged document, a matter of considerable importance for the plot.[116] The list of petty crimes includes such varied items as embezzlement,[117] smuggling,[118] pawning imitation jewels,[119] poison-pen letters,[120] impersonation and disguise.[121] The latter device again provides an excellent example of plagiarism. Abramowitz, Leinwand and Weisbrem all allow their villains to disguise themselves as policemen in order to commit a crime in strikingly similar manner.[122] In spite of the fact, however, that the many villainous exploits frequently add pace to these novels, the occasional attempts to sketch the underworld as such are painfully unconvincing.[123]

The novels also contain many examples of violence and physical assault, ranging from such milder manifestations as faceslapping,[124] attempted seduction[125] and rough and tumble[126] to extreme forms such as wounding,[127] hanging,[128] murder[129]— actual or attempted—rape[130] and arson.[131] The latter category contains a number of examples of house-burning,[132] a device probably borrowed, again, from Mapu's novels where the theme is used on several occasions.[133] Among the most remarkable examples of violent action, however, is the forcible release from a nunnery of one of the heroines of Smolenskin's *The Reward of the Righteous*, via the agency of a detachment of soldiers.[134] A similar anti-clerical attitude is clearly reflected in S. F. Meinkin's *The Love of the Righteous*.[135]

This catalogue of malevolence may be paralleled by an equally impressive list of human suffering and misfortune, to which the novelists constantly resort in the search for thematic material. Particularly noticeable is the heavy incidence of fainting, which affects a wide variety of characters, male as well as female, at every conceivable opportunity,[136] and which forms a convenient method of concluding a dramatic episode, or preventing revelations or actions which might otherwise prematurely unravel the plot. The prevalence of the device, however, seems to indicate that this propensity for fainting may reflect a fairly familiar pattern of contemporary social behaviour. Other forms of physical debility include a wide variety of sickness, insanity and raging fever,[137] all of which provide the authors with excellent opportunities for pathos or melodrama. On one occasion, however, Smolenskin endows the ravings of one of his heroes, who has fallen into a fever, with ingenious, if crude, psychological overtones—a technique which represents a significant advance in modern Hebrew literature.[138] The novels also contain six cases of suicide[139] and many instances of attempted or threatened suicide[140]—of which the most notable occurs in Sheikewitz's novel *The Outcast*, whose heroine opens the tale by assuring the reader in the very first chapter that he is bound to be interested because she intends to commit suicide on its completion. Happily,

however, by the final chapter she is able to change her mind
and frankly admits her indifference to the reader's disappointment! But even Braudes, for all his usual dramatic restraint,
allows the hero of his *The Two Extremes* to contemplate suicide, a
solution which he declares he has read in many stories and often
witnessed at the theatre![141] Death in more conventional forms
stalks the pages of these novels with monotonous regularity,[142]
while Smolenskin goes so far as to allow one of his heroes all-
unknowingly to kill his own step-brother in a duel.[143]

The colouring of these novels, however, is by no means uniformly sombre. Life and love provide at least as rich and copious
a supply of themes as suffering and death. Love, indeed, comprises a leading motif in almost all these novels, while Abramowitz's
Fathers and Sons and Sheikewitz's *The Outcast* go so far as to describe themselves unashamedly as love stories. Far from representing a common-place literary element, however, the very
notion of romantic love constituted a revolutionary development
within the framework of orthodox Jewish concepts, and its introduction into these novels must be regarded as a didactic no
less than a literary device.[144] Nevertheless, the employment of
love-themes represents an important ingredient in many of the
stories as such, and frequently serves as a powerful motivating
factor in the development of plot. Not only do the love-scenes
themselves furnish the authors with daring dramatic material,[145]
but they also provide a framework for the introduction of appropriately cognate themes, such as the many discussions on the
nature of love,[146] the strategy involved in arranging suitable
matches,[147] and the final culmination of a happy ending with the
heroes and heroines ultimately united beneath the wedding
canopy.[148] The darker side of marriage, however, is also represented in the not infrequent instances of divorce, desertion, bigamy
and deception.[149] The most blatant examples of marital infidelity
occur in Manassewitz's *The Parents' Sin*, in which both the heroine and her sister are unwittingly married to, and immediately
deserted by, the same man, whom they later discover firmly wedded to a third lady. Happily, however, he readily agrees to grant
the sisters bills of divorce![150]

Not unnaturally, the constant employment of such dramatic
themes as treachery, violence and love arouses heated passions
among the characters involved, which in turn give rise to fresh

themes and motivations of a more emotional nature. Of these, the most common is the desire for revenge, which on occasion finds expression in the most violent terms. In *The Wanderer in the Paths of Life*, for example, the evils perpetrated by the villainous Manasseh are outlined to the hero by his friend Dan, culminating in the following outburst:

> Even though your own parents were ruined by scoundrels as were mine, and even though your father's fortune was usurped by strangers without hope of redress, nevertheless you were ignorant of what had transpired because your oppressors struck before you were old enough to be aware of life, and you have only just learned from me by hearsay of the villains who robbed your father's wealth and stripped you of everything. But my case is different. I have witnessed each disaster with my own eyes as one misfortune after another swept across my father's house and laid it low. I have seen it both in its palmy days when fortune smiled, and in its final and complete collapse. I have known my sister both at the time when she dwelled virtuously in a prosperous home, and in the hour of her degradation!! But what's the use of talking!—he suddenly shouted, kicking his legs like a maniac—No! I won't go mad!! . . . . he cried again in a terrible voice, clutching his head between his hands—I must live! Don't leave me, sanity. I need you still! To take revenge! I shall be revenged!![151]

Later in the story the hero receives a letter written by the same Dan, outlining the final catastrophes that have devastated his father's household, and ending with a similar dramatic cry for revenge:

> What is left for me in life? What joy can await me in so bitter a life? Shall I ever know repose? Can my couch console me? Can I think of life after that terrible, terrible day? Can I find words dreadful enough to describe what befell us? My father, my father! Your image floats before my eyes, goading me to keep alive—to live for revenge! You, indeed, are in the grave, finished with all the pains that flesh is heir to; and even though you were not granted to die peacefully in bed, it makes no difference to you now. But my sister, my sister, my dear innocent sister. . . No! I cannot bring myself even to speak of it, my very hand refuses to set it down on paper. The blood pounds and thunders in my heart and courses through my veins. My sister, my sister, I shall not die until I have completed my plans. My father's words are now the sole remnant

of my inheritance. On his death he bequeathed me only an
angry heart unswervingly intent upon revenge. Revenge, revenge! I, too, shall take revenge! My sister, I shall drown the
blood of your shame in the blood of your betrayer. I shall not
die, nor lose my reason until I have exacted vengeance for us
both!!'[152]

By contrast, one of the most effective examples of the revenge
motif is described in a light-hearted and, indeed, humorous manner. In Weisbrem's *18 Coins*, the miserly Gedaliah is motivated
by a desire for revenge to disinherit the degenerate Polish noble
Glupski, while the latter in turn avenges himself on his oppres-
sor by setting fire to Gedaliah's property. Before doing so, however, Glupski first vents his wrath on the Jews in general by destroying the 'Sabbath Limits'[153] in the little town where Gedaliah
is staying overnight, with the result that the town is virtually
paralysed.[154] The scene also enabled the author to satirize the
striking contrast presented by extreme ritual piety side by side
with an utter ruthlessness and immorality in business.[155]

The natural desire for vengeance on the part of the heroes
against the perpetrators of the monstrous crimes so frequently
encountered in these novels is often gratified in accordance with
the rules of 'Poetic Justice'. The downfall of the arch-villain in
The Wanderer in the Paths of Life, for example, and his sentence to
imprisonment with hard labour for life are engineered by one of
his former dupes,[156] while the hero of the same story reveals his
identity to the wicked aunt, who has been the cause of all his
misfortune, during a violent storm at sea, with the result that she
relaxes her grip on the ship's rail and is conveniently washed
overboard.[157] But vengeance is not the only emotion employed
as a means of developing the plots. Jealousy and remorse serve
almost equally well as motivating factors, and both are introduced on numerous occasions.[158]

From what precedes, it will be evident how important a role
melodrama plays in the majority of these novels, while even the
stories of Braudes, Rabinowitz and Sirkis—who display, in general, a much more sober and restrained attitude in assembling
the material for their plots—cannot be entirely absolved from
an occasional resort to the device.[159] The use of melodrama, however, is not solely confined to situation or action, but may be
equally discerned in the patterns of behaviour or the modes of

speech which the novelists introduce from time to time. The mood may be gauged from even the shortest of passages: 'While speaking, his cheeks flushed scarlet and his eyes flashed fiery sparks';[160] or, '. . . My friend shouted angrily, grinding his teeth and stamping his feet like a madman',[161] or again, 'The Rabbi was in a furious rage, stamping his feet and biting the ends of his beard. . .'[162] More revealing still is the following passage from Smolenskin's *Pride and Fall*:

I entered his room and found him sitting on the ground facing the wall. I called him two or three times by name but he neither answered nor turned his head. But when I drew near and laid my hand on his shoulder a shudder passed through his body, and he fixed his eyes on me for a few moments. After recognising me, he plunged headlong to the ground tearing his clothes in fury, pulling at his hair, biting himself and beating his head on the wall until two policemen came hurrying to restrain him. He struggled with them like a maniac for several minutes until they overpowered him and made him sit on a chair. Then he grew calm and remained quite motionless.[163]

In like manner the novels include many examples of melodramatic expression, sometimes consisting of a single sentence,[164] occasionally with additional emphasis by way of italics,[165] or presented in the form of an emotional outburst in violent language.[166] Of these, perhaps the most glaring example appears in Leinwand's *The Artful Villain*, where the treacherous wife gloats over her wicked plans to destroy her aged husband in classical melodramatic fashion, and finally almost betrays herself by speaking her thoughts aloud:

'Vain hopes!' the words escaped the woman's lips, her eyes flashing anger and contempt. 'You might as well despair, old man,' she went on to herself; 'Summon all hell's demons to your aid, and see if they will save you from my hands. If only you knew that it is I who am responsible for all your misery and sorrow. . . . . Just a moment ago I pretended that it was my sincere desire to listen to your secrets and share your pain, so that you might believe the more firmly in my sincerity, and that it might never cross your mind that I am well aware of the reason why all this evil has afflicted you; even though I alone am responsible for urging Nabal, my lover, to bring it on your head. . . . But I will still make you suffer that which you propose to inflict upon my beloved, who is so much your

superior; I will yet destroy your rotten life, to stop you lingering on indefinitely to my own chagrin! Give thanks to God,
you hateful and loathsome old man, for saving you from my
hands thus far! For every day I long to see the angel of death
carry you away. But since the years drag by and my hope
remains unfulfilled, I shall be patient no longer, but take
revenge for my lost youth which I have wasted in your home,
unable to obtain my freedom because of your long life that
drags on without end. . .'[167]

The reader can scarcely be blamed for any lack of sympathy
when she eventually dies of fright![168]

Melodrama, however, is most frequently introduced as an
element of the plot, and usually in the form of violent and exciting
action. A number of the minor novels, indeed, are characterized
by an overall air of melodrama. Apart from Leinwand, whose
story represents the most crude and thoroughgoing example of
the *genre*, although closely rivalled in this respect by Zobeizensky,[169] the stories of Manassewitz and Sheikewitz, as well as Weisbrem's *18 Coins*, all blatantly resort to melodrama.[170] S. F. Meinkin's *The Love of the Righteous* differs only in the fact that its overall melodramatic flavour is of the 'cloak and dagger' type and
deliberately attempts to foster an air of mystery.[171] Abramowitz
too, relies on the device on a number of occasions, particularly
in his portrayal of a thieves' den—clearly modelled on the numerous examples in Mapu's novels[172]—in his resort to rogues
disguised as policemen,[173] and in the midnight meeting during
which the valiant Aryeh blackmails the wicked Peretz into
breaking off his son's engagement to the heroine![174]

The novels of Smolenskin, however, gain the laurels for the
greatest variety and certainly the most exciting examples of melodrama. Although by virtue of the sheer bulk of writing, the
melodramatic element plays only a limited role in Smolenskin's
stories, all of them partake of this device. In *The Wanderer in the
Paths of Life* the responsibility for melodramatic villainy may be
divided almost equally between the wicked Manasseh and the
unscrupulous *Ḥasidim*, described by Smolenskin in the most lurid
colours.[175] Sometimes the episodes are depicted in strikingly similar terms:

> . . . . On the first day of the festival of Passover when we had
> just taken our places for the midday meal, four armed soldiers
> suddenly burst into the house led by an officer of the law.

'Clap the traitor in irons!' the officer commanded, and the soldiers hastened to do his bidding. The fear of death descended on us all; my mother fainted and fell off the chair; my elder sister, who was then about eighteen, fell on her knees before the officer pleading for an explanation; while my younger sister and I wept bitterly but no one paid any heed to us.[176]

Later in the very same chapter the episode is virtually repeated:

. . . We were sitting at home together when four armed soldiers led by an officer suddenly burst into the house and put handcuffs on my father and my sister and led them away without a word. I was so tongue-tied with fear that I could not even ask of what crime they were being accused or whither they were being taken. My younger sister fainted and fell to the ground unconscious, at which Manasseh hastened to her aid to bring her back to life; so that he, too, neglected to ask the officer about my father and my sister. But a few minutes later I recovered sufficiently to try to overtake the prisoners in search of an explanation. I ran like a stag through the streets and alleys but could not find them. I searched the streets until midnight, but in vain! And so I returned home without knowing what had happened to them.[177]

Smolenskin's other novels, too, contain numerous examples of equally violent melodrama.[178]

A further dramatic device which occurs in most of the novels under review[179] is the frequent resort to coincidence for the development or denouement of the plots—a common convention in nineteenth-century European literature. Strangely enough, the most outrageous examples occur in Braudes' *The Two Extremes*, which otherwise displays the most consummate artistry of construction to be found in all these novels. The resolution of the plot devolves upon the striking coincidence that the *deus ex machina*—in the shape of a rich old man from Vilna, who represents an ideal combination of orthodox Judaism and secular enlightenment—turns out to be Judah, the long-lost grandfather of all the principal heroes and heroines![180] Almost in the same breath, the doctor whom Judah adopted as a youth is conveniently identified as the vanished father of a secondary hero.[181] Earlier in the plot, moreover, the chance visit of Rosalie's husband to the little town of Sukkoth engenders a coincidence which is of major importance to the plot.[182] In the latter case, however, the author does make a serious attempt to make the coincidence more credible.[183]

Similarly, in Abramowitz's *Fathers and Sons*, not only does David, the hero, turn out to be Aryeh's son, but his closest friend, Simon, discovers that his mother is Aryeh's step-sister.[184] Such coincidental relationships comprise a favourite device. In Zobeizensky's novel Hadassah learns that she is Samson's sister,[185] while Manassewitz allows his hero, Benjamin, to be recognised, by means of a birthmark, as the long-lost son of Miriam's aunt.[186] Sheikewitz, too, succumbs to a similar temptation, and identifies the policeman who befriends his heroine as her childhood friend,[187] while Weisbrem leans equally heavily on the device, in that Miriam is strongly attracted to Gershom because of the latter's amazing likeness to her late husband.[188]

Smolenskin, again, is no less prone to utilise coincidence in the development of his plots. This is especially the case in *The Wanderer in the Paths of Life* where, for example, the hero Josef discovers that his own mother and the mother of his close friend, Dan, are sisters.[189] On another occasion he finds that a fellow prisoner is his cousin,[190] while his childhood sweetheart disastrously turns out to be the daughter of his wicked aunt.[191] Similarly, the teacher in Switzerland with whom his step-sister falls in love is none other than his old friend Gideon.[192] Even more surprising, however, is the regularity with which the perpetrators of numerous crimes at widely differing times and places are all identified as the central villain of the piece, Manasseh.[193] The technique is highly reminiscent of that adopted by Mapu in his treatment of Zadok, the arch-villain in *The Hypocrite*.[194] Hardly less credible coincidences occur in the *Joy of the Godless, Pride and Fall* and *The Reward of the Righteous*.[195]

As a variant to the device, Smolenskin occasionally resorts to the stratagem of mistaken identity for similar effect. After shooting the arrogant brother of his beloved in a duel in which he, himself, is severely wounded, Josef later learns that he has killed his own step-brother in error, and that his sweetheart is, in fact, his step-sister.[196] In similar vein one of the heroines of *Pride and Fall* is driven to suicide because her fiancé mistakes her brother for her lover.[197] More successful, however, is an extremely humorous episode in *The Joy of the Godless* where Simon, soliloquizing over his passionate love for Shiphrah, is overheard by his landlady's daughter of the same name, who immediately concludes that she is the object of his affection and bursts into the room to fling herself into his arms. Simon is able to extricate himself only by pretending that he was speaking of his (non-existent) wife, a fabrication which later becomes an important element in the plot.[198]

An additional stratagem utilized by almost all the novelists,[199] in greater measure or in less, is the insertion of dreams and particularly nightmares—sometimes of a very vivid kind—into their stories. The dramatic potentialities of the device, as previously demonstrated in Mapu's novels,[200] were ideally suited to the melodramatic, episodic character of so many of these stories. The very frequency of such dreams[201] seems to emphasize Sheikewitz's satirical but highly significant remark in *The Outcast* that he has introduced a nightmare only because all Hebrew writers do so, and appends a footnote referring specifically to Mapu and Smolenskin![202] One of the most effective examples of the *genre* occurs in *The Parents' Sin* where the hero enters the heroine's room with a gun and threatens that if her father will not consent to their marriage he will either kill him or commit suicide. Rushing after her lover in panic, the heroine discovers him being throttled by another man (her father) in his own home. Whereupon she hits the assailant over the head with the gun, which goes off and kills both father and lover! Only then is it revealed that the whole episode was only a nightmare.[203] Meanwhile, however, the reader has been treated to a spectacular adventure without any necessity to shrug it off as mere fantasy. In like manner Smolenskin includes distorted fragments of his plots in nightmares and feverish dreams on a number of occasions.[204] Although somewhat forced and lacking in artistry, these nightmares are highly imaginative, and contain a number of clever psychological overtones.[205]

One of the most prominent characteristics of the great majority of the novels under review[206] is the large number of letters which they contain.[207] Here, again, the influence of Mapu's *The Hypocrite*, which itself includes more than sixty letters,[208] is very much in evidence—so much so, that almost the entire fourth part of *The Wanderer in the Paths of Life* is written in letter form, and contains features common to the class of epistolary novel exemplified by Richardson's *Pamela*. The letter represents a convenient instrument both for the advancement of the plot and for the purpose of outlining the previous history of one or other of the characters. Letters are used to supply the reader with information not previously known or, by virtue of interception,[209] they may give the villains access to private details of their enemies, or afford an opportunity for forgery, thereby furthering their plans for the slander, scandal or persecution which often comprise important factors in the plots.

Braudes, however, who is particularly prone to the device,[210] uses the letter form in *Religion and Life* as a vehicle for the propagation of his ideas in the struggle for religious reform.[211] He states categorically, moreover, that the despatch of letters was a factor of great importance in the bitter struggle between the orthodox and reform factions in Lithuania from 1868 onwards, which comprises the theme of his novel, and that both parties pursued a fiery campaign of letter-writing.[212] A not dissimilar motivation may be observed in the tendency of a number of novelists to satirize the crude, crabbed and, indeed, barbaric style of Rabbinic and, particularly, Ḥasidic correspondence. Abramowitz, indeed, in a footnote to such a letter, purporting to emanate from a religious bigot, declares that he has been compelled to correct the style and grammar for the benefit of the reader. Nevertheless, he is still compelled to add additional footnotes explaining its obscurities.[213]

Weisbrem adopts an even more devastating stratagem. In *18 Coins* he includes three examples of letters written in barbaric style as a satire of the type of Hebrew ascribed to *Ḥasidhim*. On each occasion, however, he includes them only as footnotes, prefacing each one with the satirical remark that he is presenting them for the benefit of readers who delight in polished Hebrew![214] While not original to Weisbrem,[215] the device constitutes an effective means of satire, although weakened by the many lapses in the author's own Hebrew style. Indeed some of the letters in these novels, written by enlightened heroes, and so, presumably, purporting to represent good epistolary style, are flowery to the point of absurdity.[216] Weisbrem, however, employs a more original and effective weapon of satire in his other novel, *Between the Times*, where an ignorant and bigoted Hebrew teacher who has undertaken to address correspondence in Latin script prior to its despatch abroad makes so many elementary mistakes that the letters never arrive—with almost fatal consequences for the love theme. In spite of all remonstrances the teacher obstinately clings to his misconceptions until finally the letters are returned with an official 'address unknown'.[217]

Many of the novels, too, are characterized by the frequent reference to vast sums of money which are woven into the plots. The romantic appeal of large fortunes is all the more readily comprehensible in view of the grinding poverty of the vast majority of the Jews of eastern Europe in the nineteenth century.[218] In *Pride and Fall*, for example, which is concerned with the consequences of the collapse of the Viennese stock-exchange, immense sums of money bob in and out of the narrative, varying from a hundred thousand shekels—the normal equivalent of roubles in these novels—to no less than fifteen million.[219] Elsewhere vast inheritances and bequests,[220] and on one occasion a fortune won in a lottery only to be lost almost as quickly,[221] severely strain the reader's credulity. Again, the introduction of large dowries amounting to ten and twenty thousand or even a million roubles must clearly have excited the imagination of the poverty-stricken young men who devoured these stories with such avidity.[222]

From what precedes, the many weaknesses of construction and plot, which mar the artistic unity of almost all the novels under review, may readily be conceded. Of all these stories only Braudes' *The Two Extremes*, and to a lesser degree Rabinowitz's *At the Crossroads*, display any real sense of cohesion, while even they tend to run wild in the closing stages.[223] For the rest, the lack of any adequate literary tradition or training, the absence of careful planning and subtle integration, the signs of over-hasty and slapdash composition, the deleterious consequences of serialization, the unevenness of writing for want of critical restraint, the inhibiting consequences of an all too obvious didacticism, and the frequent intrusion of crude melodrama in a wide variety of guise, all combine to undermine the aesthetic value of these stories. Above all, a number of the minor writers simply lack the talent necessary for the writing of a successful novel.

Nevertheless, it would be quite misleading to infer that these novels possess no literary merits. On the contrary, many of the authors—such as Smolenskin, Braudes, Abramowitz, Sheikewitz, Rabinowitz and Weisbrem—clearly display a genuine feeling for their craft, and their novels contain imaginative and very attractive elements. Their talents emerge, however, primarily in the episode rather than the completed work. For although these

novels suffer from the general inability of the authors to maintain cohesion, the individual chapters and episodes are frequently
powerful, moving and excitingly tense.[224] Many of the incidents excel in the rapidity of action and dramatic skill with which
they are outlined. Again, there are numerous examples of the
clever use of contrast, such as Braudes' most effective introduction of a song before a dramatic climax in *The Two Extremes*,[225]
or the dramatic pause in the tense court-room atmosphere of the
synagogue in *Religion and Life* when Samuel interrupts the service
to engage in fierce public debate with the autocratic Rabbi of
his community.[226]

One example, among many, of the very attractive episodes
which the novels contain occurs in the fourth part of *The Wanderer in the Paths of Life*.[227] In a letter to his step-sister from Berlin,
Josef recommends to her care a young musician Halfan, whose
story he proceeds to relate. Although extremely talented and encouraged by his teachers, the young man had fallen into disso-
lute company, from which he had been rescued by a rich 'Mae-
cenas' and his beautiful daughter, who had invited him to live
in their home while providing for all his needs. In the course of
a year of splendid treatment Halfan had become so conceited
that he had attempted to make love to his patron's daughter.
Although his suit is rejected by father and daughter alike, he
bombards them with offensive letters, protesting his worthiness
and demanding their consent. Finally his patron asks him to
leave, although generously offering to continue his allowance.
Halfan, however, simply refuses to go, so that his patron is compelled to take his daughter on a protracted visit to Paris, and
shuts his house completely. The young man, incensed, continues
to write to them daily, while squandering his allowance on disso-
lute living, and finally sinking into the direst poverty. A final
plea to his former benefactor, however, is rewarded with a sufficient grant to make his way to Berlin, where Josef had befriended
him.

Simple in form, the episode is narrated with such verve and
gusto, enlivened with sporadic touches of humour, that it exerts
a considerable appeal, and clearly illustrates the ability of the
more gifted of these writers to unfold an attractive tale. Elsewhere, they demonstrate a natural facility for dramatic irony,
which sometimes—as when a somewhat dubious character over-
hears a conversation in which he is described as being so foolish

Peretz Smolenskin

that he would not be able to understand even if he were listen-ing![228]—is undoubtedly of high order. Again, the imaginative handling of such varied material as, for example, the theft of the Burial Society's cakes in *A Donkey's Burial* or the Polish revolt in *The Reward of the Righteous* or the 'Rake's Progress' theme in *At the Crossroads* bears ample testimony to the inventive capacity so frequently encountered in these stories.

Essentially experimental in character, these novels constitute a tentative, groping, crude but indispensable bridge between the first, naïve attempts of Abraham Mapu to fashion a Hebrew novel and the more mature and satisfying works of the subse-quent period. For all their many weaknesses, their role in the development of modern Hebrew literature was of great impor-tance, for not only did they demonstrate, for later novelists, in un-mistakable fashion, the many pitfalls to be avoided, but—on the positive side—they served as the experimental proofs of dramatic techniques and modes of narration which might profitably be developed further. It is scarcely an exaggeration to maintain that any real understanding of the modern Hebrew novel in its later and, from the point of view of artistry, much more mature phases, requires some understanding of the literary merits and deficiencies of the novels published during the last decades of *Haskalah*, the twenty years under review.

E

THREE

In Search of People

The dual purpose motivating the novelists of this period, as outlined in the previous chapter, is partly responsible for the problems of characterization encountered in these stories, and offers
an interesting parallel to the difficulties of plot construction inherent in the attempt to fuse the two major but conflicting elements common, at least to some extent, to all the novels under
review. The dramatic devices and techniques required for the
unfolding of a story of adventure, where action, excitement and
romance constitute the primary means of engaging the attention
of the reader, are very different from the literary treatment
necessary for the exposition of didactic ideas and social criticism,
which largely depend upon the depiction of situation and environment. Similarly, the clumsy juxtaposition of action and situation, arising from the attempt to harmonize two such distinctive
literary media, is partly responsible for many of the problems of
characterization to be encountered in these novels.

Stories of adventure and romance depend for their appeal far
more upon the excitement of stirring events and rapid action
than upon any subtlety of characterization. On the contrary,
their purpose is, perhaps, best served by stereotyped heroes and
villains, whose emotional reactions may be readily prognosticated
no matter how involved or unexpected the intrigue or circumstance to which they are subjected. The virtues and sterling worth
of the heroes may be taken as equally for granted as the manifold villainies and unscrupulous practices of their opponents—
while the same applies to their female counterparts in either case.
So much so, that the potentialities of quick excitement and adventure vary in almost direct proportion to the exaggeration of

villainy and virtue exhibited by the respective parties. From the point of view of character, the most outstanding feature is predictability. The element of surprise stems not from the persons involved but from the plot. Hence the characters must be regarded as 'flat' rather than 'round', as facets of personality rather than complete characters, with no claim to any independent existence outside the particular set of circumstances in which they are temporarily involved.

It must be admitted that such characters also serve a certain didactic purpose. The inevitable triumph of the heroes and the well-deserved punishment finally meted out to the villains, which supply the natural conclusion to a novel of romance, obviously point the simple moral of the superiority of good over evil. An additional didactic significance may be added, moreover, by identifying the 'good' characters with a certain point of view and making them the advocates of certain specific ideas, at the same time portraying the 'villains' as the natural exponents of diametrically opposite views. Such didacticism, however, generally tends to be both shallow and superficial. In the first place, the exaggerated characteristics inherent in the very nature of such heroes and villains remove them from the realm of the reader's practical experience, so that their views are liable to be taken no more seriously than the fictitious events in which they are involved. Again, while the villains, at least of many of these novels, display a certain firmness of purpose and ready initiative throughout the greater part of the story until the final unmasking and defeat, and thereby command the respect and even the grudging admiration of the reader as people who know what they really want, the heroes often display an annoying helplessness in the face of the intrigues of their opponents, and frequently appear to triumph rather by good luck than by good management. Their exaggerated virtue and preoccupation with abstract ideals, moreover, tend to reduce them only too easily to the shadowy denizens of an unreal world, or—what is worse—may readily make them appear self-righteous prigs.

It is indicative of Smolenskin's perspicacity, in this respect, that he goes so far as to rebuke the hero of his novel, *The Joy of the Godless*, for that very fault. As though impatient with Simon's excessive piety which is preventing him from courting the heroine, Smolenskin deprecates such helplessness in no uncertain terms:

He (Simon) made the mistake common to many people who think they have suddenly discovered truth. He imagined quite wrongly that Shiphrah knew her own mind enough to be consistent, for he was unaware how difficult it is to fathom the thoughts of a young lady. Through an excess of righteousness he was led astray; and just when the time was ripe to act on the verse 'Be not righteous overmuch',[1] he neglected his own learning and so committed a great error. 'Be not righteous overmuch' is a lesson to be learned from everyday occurrences, and the misfortunes which dog our every step should teach us that sometimes righteous people go astray through trying to be over-righteous. Even the birds of the air and the fish of the sea confirm the lesson 'Be not righteous overmuch'—that one should not succumb to the waves of circumstance, but fight against them. Set your face against wind and storm, the birds declare, not merely in words but through action. The mere fact that birds always turn their faces into the storm, while the fish spread their fins to swim against the waves, is a sign that every living creature was created for struggle. And what is man that he should be over-righteous, offering his back to the blows of time and bending his head like a reed before his fellow who is borne aloft on fortune's chariot. God helps those who help themselves, and if you try to live in heaven while still in mortal flesh, you will only fall and break your neck, to the delight of all who behold you.[2]

This timely warning against over-idealization in the delineation of character is particularly apt in the light of the patterns of characterization laid down in Abraham Mapu's novels. Although, perhaps, less blatantly than most of the novelists under review, Mapu had also attempted to impose a strong didactic note into his stories of adventure. As a result, the great majority of his characters may be divided simply into 'black' and 'white', namely paragons of virtue or heinous villains.[3] In order to propagate his views, Mapu further endowed his heroes and heroines with all the ideal virtues favoured by the exponents of Enlightenment, while the villains are made to personify their very antithesis. That the great majority of his characters, the heroes and heroines in particular, are 'flat' and colourless is scarcely surprising. Indeed, only three of the very minor characters in his novels carry any real conviction.[4] However, Mapu's immediate successors, the minor novelists in particular, time and again resort to the same clear-cut division between 'black' and 'white', while the fascination exerted by Mapu's stories extends, in many cases, even to the names of the characters of the novels under review.[5] With the exception of Rabinowitz, Sirkis, and—to a lesser extent—Braudes, all the novelists resort in some degree to the introduction of stereotyped characters drawn in black and white. Whereas, however, in the novels by Abramowitz, Leinwand, Meinkin, Zobeizensky, Manassewitz, Sheikewitz and Weisbrem they represent the dominant pattern of characterization, Smolenskin's stories—like those of Braudes—include a wide variety of different types, frequently portrayed with far greater subtlety and insight. In this respect, Rabinowitz's novel is remarkable in that its hero personifies the negative consequences of the movement of Enlightenment,[6] thereby flatly contradicting the moral implied by so many of his counterparts.

This widening of the scope of characterization, which was to prove of great significance for the development of Hebrew literature, stems partly from the demands of the second important ingredient of these novels, namely the bitter social criticism and the serious educational purpose which permeate these stories.[7] The didactic element is expressed not in terms of action and excitement but in terms of situation and conflict. It represents the static as against the dynamic side of the stories, and as such necessarily induces characterization in greater depth. Whereas the adventurous aspect of these tales need only describe the interplay of deeds and action with little stress on character, social, cultural and religious conflict is dependent upon the clash of intellect and personality to a very much greater extent, and demands the delineation of 'round' characters with more flexibility, a greater range of personality, and the ability to develop under the influence of changing circumstances and ideas. The social purpose of the novelists even extends to the use of symbolic names (for towns as well as characters), usually of a satirical nature, such as the cantor called Genubhath, the match-maker Kozbi and the butcher Terephon, with their respective overtones of theft, deceit and ritual impurity.[8]

Whereas the social purpose of the novelists exerted so damaging an effect upon the plot-construction of these stories,[9] it is of interest to note that the same purpose proved of considerable benefit for certain aspects of characterization. Nevertheless, the fusion of adventure and social criticism within a single framework, each exerting its own particular influence upon the characters and each demanding different qualities from the *dramatis personae*, inevitably gives rise to serious incongruities which inhibit the delineation of integrated and satisfying personalities. This literary demerit is all the more regrettable since the more talented authors—Smolenskin and Braudes in particular—display considerable acuteness and sensitivity in many of their characterizations. In comparison with Mapu's creations, their characters frequently display a certain maturity and the power to convince; but even Smolenskin and Braudes lack the literary tradition, experience and equipment necessary to sustain a complete personality throughout an entire novel.

In the case of Smolenskin, in particular, the situation is aggravated by the very method of composition. Serialization is liable to impair the delineation of character almost as much as it may undermine the overall unity of the plot—particularly when each instalment is written under severe stress.[10] In English literature, Dickens' *Pickwick Papers* provides an admirable example of the changing role of Mr. Pickwick's companions as the story progresses. The same impression that the complete novel has either not been first thought out from beginning to end or has undergone radical changes in the course of serialization emerges not infrequently from Smolenskin's novels, particularly the longer ones.

An interesting illustration of the changing conception of a character's role occurs in *The Reward of The Righteous*, where the wife of a degenerate Polish officer, symbolically named Kalbi (Cur),[11] is first introduced in mildly satirical terms in the following very effective little sketch:

The bald gentleman with the long black side-whiskers and dark, flashing eyes was called Kalbi. He rarely spoke of his noble lineage, but constantly referred to his many noble friends, to great lords, their tables and their retinues. The beautiful lady carrying on a charming flirtatious conversation with the master of the house was his loyal spouse. They comprised an excellent partnership—in which she supplied money while he squandered it; and they constantly addressed each other in terms of the greatest endearment—in other people's homes.

In his youth he had sought an heiress like Ben-Susi[12] and the other nobles, while his wife had been a famous beauty, and had sought a husband who could set her in the lap of luxury. Aware, however, that many gentlemen despise mere beauty, and that only a rich heiress might justifiably be proud, she spread the mischievous rumour that she was due to inherit great wealth from her uncle, a veritable Croesus. She openly quarelled with her mother, insisting that she did not wish to know about her fortune, and that she would only choose a man who loved her for herself. If he were only interested in wealth, he could look elsewhere. Although reticent about his noble lineage, Kalbi constantly boasted of his fine horses and splendid dogs, while his friends declared him to be a man of untold wealth. When questioned directly, however, he always denied it, insisting that he had never mentioned a word to anyone about his wealth—a sure sign of riches. In Paris he became acquainted with the maiden who was so insistent that no one pay regard to her inheritance. They fell madly in love, and he swore to her that he had no interest at all in her great fortune. She took him at his word, promising that even if what his friends declared were not true, she would still choose him with all her heart. The priest blessed their union and they were happy—for a single day and night, until each realised that the other had spoken the truth, that her mother, like his friends, had spoken deceitfully, and that her inheritance had never existed any more than his riches.[13]

Although introduced early in the story, it is significant that the lady is referred to only as Kalbi's wife until almost the end of this long novel,[14] when the author finally endows her with the symbolic name of Delilah le-Beth Ramiel.[15] Meanwhile, however, she plays a more and more important role in the story, and turns out to be a woman of strong character, daring and resource, and one of the most lively personalities in the novel.[16] Yet, the reader is left with the strong impression that the author had not originally envisaged her role nor, for that matter, much of the detailed development of the third part of his tale.

Quite apart, however, from the problems of characterization arising from the content and mode of composition of these novels, the authors under review were faced with the much more serious difficulty of inadequate linguistic equipment.[17] A full realization of the obstacles lining the path of the early Hebrew novelists inevitably demands some understanding of the limitations of language—admittedly self-imposed to some extent—at the disposal of these writers.[18] It must be remembered that this period is one of experimentation from the point of view of language as well as of literary form. Indeed, both aspects are, in great measure, mutually dependent. Hebrew was still a literary language, and the first attempts to revive it as a spoken medium were still embryonic. While the contribution of these novelists to the revival of the language is of considerable importance, their efforts to forge Hebrew into a sufficiently flexible instrument for the expression of a wide range of ideas remain only partially successful.[19]

For the moment it may suffice to confine the discussion of this very important factor to the two most obvious ways in which it directly affects the problem of characterization. In the first place the projection of a character depends partly upon description. The more detailed and precise the information which the author is able to supply, the clearer and more vivid will be the picture in the reader's imagination. But this is one of the very points which demonstrate so clearly the linguistic deficiencies of the novels under review. The authors, time and again, are compelled to resort to tock descriptions and inexact modes of expression in the delineation of their characters. So much so that externally it is often difficult to differentiate between them.[20]

The following passage from Sheikewitz's novel, *The Outcast*, not only represents a typical example of the external description to be found within these novels, but also sheds some light on the author's reluctance even to embark upon the task—although the reason may well be that outlined above rather than the one he, himself, suggests:

My prospective father-in-law, Rabbi Asher, was about fifty, short and slight. A yellowish beard, in which streaks of white had begun to appear, surrounded his cheeks (if one may use the term cheeks, for instead of cheeks there were merely two hollows beneath two protruding bones covered with bronze-coloured skin). His long, thin nose sat, or stood, between two big green eyes. His head was very large, and nature seemed to have erred in placing it on so small and frail a body. His two long side-curls hung down to his shoulders. He was clad in a long, wide coat, tied about his loins with a silken girdle, to which was attached a red handkerchief, but so big that its ends touched the ground. His head was crowned with a hat with broad edges (*Streimal*).[21]

I resent writers who burden themselves and all novelists

with the yoke of describing to their readers the complete appearance of their characters. I cannot fathom what benefit accrues to their readers from such descriptions. What difference does it make whether my father-in-law was tall or short, whether his nose was long or snub, or whether he wore fine clothes or was dressed in rags? 'Then who laid you under any obligation to describe your father-in-law?' Should any reader ask me such a question, I swear I could not find an answer. I know all this is superfluous and silly, and yet I couldn't prevent myself giving the whole sordid picture. But why should I be surprised? Do we not constantly see people doing things against their will; and if you ask them why they do so, they cannot answer. But the wise man will understand that the real reason is because other people do the same. Darwin was right in deciding that men are descended from apes. Man is indeed an ape, and loves to imitate the actions of others. He will find pleasure only in such things as please other people, or which other people do. And even though he may realise that other people are making a mistake, he will, nevertheless, be unable to restrain himself from doing likewise. But let me return to my tale.[22]

Nevertheless, the novels contain a number of similar descriptions of a considerably higher standard, such as Smolenskin's portrait of a ragged Lithuanian with his toe peeping out of his shoe like a mouse through a hole,[23] or the grotesque *Hasidh* in *The Inheritance*,[24] or the hideous old woman in *The Wanderer in the Paths of Life*.[25] The same advance may be detected in Abramowitz's portrait of a stuttering teacher,[26] or Braudes' description of the drunken Todros,[27] or Leinwand's thumbnail sketches in *The Artful Villain*,[28] or Weisbrem's humorous portrait of Shemariahu the agent in *Between the Times*.[29] Here and there, it is even possible to see descriptive touches of high order,[30] which seem to foreshadow Abramowitz's later brilliant techniques in his novels written under the pseudonym *Mendele Mokher Sepharim*, which constitute the first aesthetically mature works in modern Hebrew literature.[31]

The second serious hindrance to the creation of convincing characters, stemming from the linguistic limitations which confronted the novelists, is inextricably bound up with the question of dialogue. Whereas in real life conversation is determined by the character of the speaker, who creates and moulds his speech, in the novel as also in the drama the reverse is true.[32] There, it is the dialogue, itself, which gives the characters life and determines their personality and temperament. For the writer in a living, spoken language with a long tradition there exists an abundant wealth of conversational material, including idioms, colloquialisms, terse, pithy phrases and a wide variety of colourful expressions, with which he will have been familiar from childhood, and which he may adopt or reject at will. He will have at his disposal, moreover, a wealth of short, idiomatic turns of phrase for the most common elements of conversation, which will freely serve in place of one another, and thereby obviate the resort to tedious repetition.

The Hebrew novelists of this period, however, were faced with a very different situation. In spite of the long literary tradition of Hebrew, and the conversational elements to be found in the Bible in some quantity,[33] it was precisely in the field of lively and universally accepted idiom that Hebrew was so painfully lacking. For that reason the authors under review were compelled to resort to all sorts of circumlocutions and forced and clumsy terminology in an attempt to create any sort of sustained and comprehensible dialogue. That they were able to compose such lengthy novels at all within so unlikely a linguistic framework constitutes a tribute to their tenacity, ingenuity and devotion to Hebrew, and must command the reader's admiration and respect. But it is hardly surprising that much of their dialogue, particularly in the short, rapid snatches of conversation where the idiomatic deficiencies proved most formidable, is laboured, artificial and unconvincing. Vagueness and approximation rather than exactness of expression are to be encountered all too frequently in these novels, with the writer attempting to foster a convention among his readers that when such and such a phrase is used, what is actually meant is something else. The injurious effect of such practice on the delineation of convincing characters scarcely requires elucidation.

The stilted and artificial conversation which permeates these novels—those of the minor and less talented writers in particular —may be gauged from the following passage from Leinwand's novel, which is typical of many:

> 'Why don't you tell me, Abihail?' the woman asked suddenly as though unwillingly. 'Why don't you tell me what is so troubling you that your mind can find no peace, and you have

been irritable all day? Ever since this morning I have been enquiring the reason for your rage and anguish, while you stubbornly reply: "There's nothing the matter!" But you cannot hide from me the signs which clearly attest to the fact that you are turning over plans how to be revenged on your enemies, and punish them sevenfold for their sins. It would appear that some new evil has befallen you of which I know nothing. So tell me! What have they done to you? Or what are the villains planning against you?'

'Nothing at all! Nothing at all!' the old man replied, continuing to pace up and down.

'But I can clearly see that there is something the matter, so why do you keep silent about it? Please tell me, so that I may know what has happened to you; perhaps I can help in some way. You know that I would sacrifice my flesh and blood on the altar of my love for you; I would pour out my soul rather than not come to your aid. So sit down here beside me and tell me everything about it while I listen attentively. If this evil has come by the agency of your enemy, Nabal, I am prepared to do for you on this occasion something that I have never done in my life before: I shall go to the law-court, kneel at the feet of the district governor and implore him to hasten and rescue you from that destroyer, and make him reap the reward of his deeds. For how long shall he remain a stumbling block to you?—How long shall he go on bringing gloom and despondency into our home?'[34]

The same novel later yields a classically stilted passage in the shape of an opening conversational gambit purporting to come from a child of seven:

'Hurray, mother!' the child shouted innocently. 'How lovely it is for us to live here together in this big room which is so superior to the dark, narrow room which we lived in previously. Nor will you scream any more because of your pain, for the doctor will remove your hurt and provide you with an excellent remedy for your illness, the cramp—Mother! Will the doctor be coming here today?'[35]

Even the more talented writers are sometimes guilty of almost equally stilted dialogue. The following passage from Smolenskin's *Pride and Fall*, in spite of its deliberately satirical purpose, is only a slightly exaggerated example of many passages of ordinary conversation:

'No sir, you are very much mistaken, for they will not think in that way. They know very well that I do not seek their company, and that it is they who seek mine; and they would not be guilty of such folly as to think that I would honour them to the extent of enjoying their company. No sir, you are wrong, very wrong.'

'Perhaps I am wrong, and have attributed a fault to them of which they are blameless. But be so good as to inform me of your experiences with the great ones of the land with whom you have kept company, for my soul longs to know the ways of the nobility, whom I have never seen, and whom I regard with veneration. Their manner of life surpasses my imagination and I presume that their thoughts are more exalted than those of mere ordinary mortals.'

'If that is your wish, I shall endeavour to instruct you', the little man answered haughtily, 'I shall gladly enlighten all who seek instruction from me.'

'You are very kind. But I should have thought that for a man of your good will and integrity it would only be right to give instruction not to one individual but to a complete audience, and expound your knowledge of high society in public so that many people may be grateful to you. May I make so bold, therefore, as to suggest that you save your instruction until tomorrow and let us all listen in one assembly. Then you could relate the story of your life and your experience of the nobility, so that everyone may know who you are and honour you accordingly, while even those who are in error may learn to value your real worth.'

'But they are so insensitive and unintelligent, and you can see for yourself that whenever I wish to tell them anything they rise against me and pour scorn on my words, for they are people without understanding.'

'For that reason I shall support you so that such noble wisdom may not be lost on them, and I shall persuade them to pay attention to your words from beginning to end. But be sure to relate the story of your life, for doubtless it will contain much wisdom and knowledge.'[36]

The constant resort to the third person singular in place of the second as a mode of polite address, although frequently found in the Bible and still in use in modern Hebrew, tends to add still further to the stilted nature of the dialogue.[37]

In spite of such serious obstacles, however, the more talented of the authors under review make many courageous and effective attempts to create a lively and convincing dialogue. Indeed, their efforts are not only highly ingenious but on numerous occasions surprisingly successful. The following passage from Rabinowitz's *At the Crossroads*, portraying an altercation between mistress and cook, may serve by way of illustration:

'I've warned you over and over again; over and over again I've warned you,' the woman shouted at the cook without taking her nose out of the basket. 'It's all the same to you whether I tell you or not. I talk and talk and talk, and you—Tphu!' With that she spat straight into the basket of meat. 'It's all right for him, confound him! . . . What difference does it make to him if there's nothing to put on the table? Every time he sends a breast, and nothing else. But you should know better. How many times have I told you that I can't abide the taste of a breast of meat?'

'But when I brought a shoulder, you told me that a shoulder was not to your palate,' replied the cook.

'That's a lie, you wicked girl! I didn't say any such thing. God forbid that I should. A shoulder of meat is my favourite dish. The day before yesterday the soup that came from a shoulder was simply heavenly. And now you bring me a breast —only a breast!' The mistress broke into a wail, as though some terrible and irrevocable disaster had suddenly befallen her.

'The day before yesterday you weren't here; you were out riding with Mr. David,' the cook replied.

'It's not true. The day before yesterday I was at home; I didn't go anywhere. And I still have the taste of that soup in my mouth,' the mistress retorted, licking her lips as though to taste the soup which was still cooking in her imagination.[38]

Almost twenty years previously Abramowitz had enlivened his novel with a number of similar and equally colourful arguments between mistress and maid, which constitute one of the most attractive features of *Fathers and Sons*. In the following passage the maid discovers an important letter which Sarah has mislaid:

'Mistress! Mistress!' the maid shouted at the top of her voice, suddenly opening the door and poking her head into the room.

'What are you shouting about?' Sarah rebuked the maid. 'You'll have the whole town here in a minute if you shout like that.'

'I think,' the maid said, handing a letter to Sarah, her mistress—'I think that's the letter you have been searching for today. I found it among the dry willow branches that were thrown under the stove. I found it, and so may I always find good luck. You must have left it when you were cooking the willow leaves for the prescription.³⁹ And look! I've found it. May I find my lover in the same way!'

'Look at her opening her mouth again!' Sarah grumbled at the maid, whose talk was not to her liking. 'Get on with your work and stop talking nonsense.'⁴⁰

Smolenskin, too, succeeds in creating many passages of lively conversation within his novels, such as in the quarrel between the teacher and his wife, or the spirited conversation of the *Yeŝi-bhah*⁴¹ students, or the argument between Josef and the beadle in *The Wanderer in the Paths of Life*.⁴² Equally fetching are the exchanges between a Rabbi and a woman whose husband wishes to divorce her, and between Simon's landlady and her two love-sick daughters⁴³ in *The Joy of the Godless*;⁴⁴ while *A Donkey's Burial*, *Pride and Fall* and *The Reward of the Righteous* all contain good examples of lively dialogue and repartee.⁴⁵ But the most mature attempts to create a colloquial, idiomatic type of conversation occur in Smolenskin's last novel, *The Inheritance* where, for example, the splendid exchanges between husbands and wives and the grotesque dialogue between the crooked lawyer and two rival *Ḥasidim*, intent on having each other banished or imprisoned, represent a marked advance in this essential element in the writing of convincing novels.⁴⁶ For clarity and directness of expression, however, Braudes' novels contain a number of still more impressive examples,⁴⁷ which bear the same testimony to his innate literary sense, as may be seen in the construction of his plots.⁴⁸ These occasional flashes of genuinely lively and even racy dialogue and repartee serve to illustrate the importance of these novels as an essential, transitional stage in the development of modern Hebrew literature.

The sheer technical difficulty of sustaining conversation in such an artificial and laboured medium partly accounts for the frequent resort to the long speeches⁴⁹ and soliloquies⁵⁰ which many of these novels contain. The monologue, which is far less dependent on the brief and idiomatic phrases of the kind that add spice and colour to conversation, proved a considerably easier and more suitable instrument of expression. It accorded well, moreover, with the social and didactic purposes so manifest in these novels, providing an admirable vehicle for the expression of the author's particular views. Soliloquy, too, may serve as a dramatic device, and is particularly well adapted for creating an atmosphere of melodrama, or—as the following example shows—for sustaining a state of suspense:

'How dreadful fate can be. It can crush a person completely. This must be a punishment from God! A sweet, innocent girl of honest and kind-hearted parents, my own benefactors, and gone to the bad! How she has sinned! But what a terrible punishment she has suffered. I shall treat her kindly. Who knows what may have happened to her parents? Perhaps they, too, are wandering about in search of bread. Otherwise they would surely not have allowed their only daughter to sink into the mire, even after going astray. What could have delayed my servant? Is he searching for her in vain? Or could she have recognised me, too, and feel too ashamed to return to see me? No, she didn't recognise me, and if she is ashamed, I shall insist on her accepting my help for her parents' sake. I shall certainly reward her. But perhaps my eyes deceived me and I am making myself a laughing stock. No! My eyes couldn't have deceived me, and even if they did—far, far better that I should be a laughing-stock than a hard-hearted ingrate.[51]

One further interesting attempt to overcome the problem of direct speech is worthy of remark. In his novel, *18 Coins*, Weisbrem attempts to indicate the characteristic speech of a poor woodcutter by the regular introduction of the *waw* consecutive —in spite of the fact that elsewhere its usage is comparatively restricted in his novels. This appears to be a deliberate device to mark the inferior speech of an ignorant labourer. Although clearly unsuccessful the attempt in itself is significant as an indication of the author's awareness of the problem.[52] Elsewhere, there are endeavours to project specific idiosyncrasies of character by the repeated introduction of certain particular phrases into a person's conversation.[53] This device was destined to become one of the highly successful features of Mendele's later novels.

Any analysis of the success or failure of the authors under review in the delineation of character must properly be viewed in the light of all the factors mentioned above. As previously stated, the major characters presented the authors with the most formidable difficulties, and it is not surprising that many of the heroes and heroines, especially those drawn in 'black' and 'white' and personifying respectively the opponents and exponents of the ideals of Enlightenment, should be virtually indistinguishable each from the other. Nevertheless, the novels of Smolenskin and particularly Braudes include major characters drawn with considerable clarity and insight.

Of these the most effective, perhaps, is Samuel the hero of Braudes' *Religion and Life*. Braudes' success in characterization stems partly from the fact that he modelled Samuel on an extraordinarily forceful and dramatic personality, Moses Leib Lilienblum,[54] so that his hero bears the impress of reality and conviction. But the reason lies equally implicitly in Braudes' superior literary talents. Were it not for the fact that the author deliberately concentrates less and less on the artistic aspects of his novel in the interests of his declared didactic purpose,[55] the hero, Samuel, might well have emerged as a rounded and completely satisfying character. But the novel also contains two additional major characterizations of importance, not to speak of a number of minor portraits drawn with great skill. The degenerate drunkard, Todros, with his extraordinary flair for *Gemaṭria*,[56] but his complete inability to remember the name of the village in which he was first married—a crucial point involving all the major characters in the plot—and the young *Yešibhah* student, known as Ha-Birzi, who falls in love with Todros' widowed daughter-in-law, and hopes against hope that Todros may turn out to be his long-lost father, which would automatically give him first claim to her hand in Jewish law, are drawn with a high degree of sensitivity and sympathetic insight. Indeed, more than any other of the novelists under review, Braudes appears to be able to get inside the skins and minds of such of his characters as interest him primarily, portraying the hopes and fears, the strengths and weaknesses of each of them in turn with delicate restraint. The principal hero of his second novel, *The Two Extremes*, although less credible a character than Samuel, is also portrayed with considerable skill, although in this instance his sensitivity is somewhat exaggerated.[57]

Smolenskin's novels, too, contain a number of well delineated heroes. Most important of these is Josef, the central character of his longest novel, *The Wanderer in the Paths of Life*, which describes the harsh vicissitudes of its hero's life from beginning to

האבות והבנים

ספור־אֲהָבִים

מֵאֵת

שָׁלוֹם יעקב בן־חיים מֹשה אַבְּרַאמָאוִיץ.

————————⋅►-0-◄⋅————————

אדעסא

בדפוס מ. א. בעלינסאן.

תרכ״ח

Дозволено Цензурою, Одесса 4 Марта 1868 г.

Title-page of the first edition of Abramowitz's
Fathers and Sons, *published in Odessa,* 1868

end. Although a picaresque hero, Josef not merely reflects the social patterns which confront him during his wanderings, but is equally affected by them, so that far from remaining static his character changes and develops throughout the novel. The author has endowed his hero with a wide range of facets of personality and mood. At various stages in the novel Josef displays deep introspection,[58] courage,[59] modesty,[60] deceitfulness,[61] imagination,[62] remorse,[63] pessimism,[64] loyalty[65] and a curiously ambivalent attitude towards his people,[66] a kind of love-hate relationship, which reflects the attitude not only of Smolenskin, himself, but of many of the novelists under review. Indeed, not only does this novel contain many autobiographical[67] elements, but to some extent it might almost be regarded as the mirror of an entire generation, in which all the writers are reflected in some measure. It is significant that the Josef of the fourth part of the novel, written some years after the rest, has really become quite a different character,[68] thereby probably reflecting Smolenskin's own change of outlook.

Two other heroes of Smolenskin's novels are also worthy of remark. The central character of *A Donkey's Burial*, Jacob Hayyim,[69] is an alive and original creation, with his love of practical jokes and disrespect for persons,[70] coupled with the irresistible urge to boast of his mischievous deeds which finally betrays him,[71] his unscrupulousness[72] and humility,[73] despair and hatred,[74] and his fatal facility in language.[75] Zerahiah, the hero of *The Inheritance*, again represents an interesting study. At the start of the novel the hero is portrayed as a pleasant and enlightened young man with high ideals, but rather obsessed with his own importance, and in consequence prone to hasty and unwise action.[76] He is also unwilling to receive instruction, for which the author criticizes him severely![77] A series of misfortunes, during which he is horrified to hear himself dismissed contemptuously as only 'half-educated' by men who have really made their mark in life,[78] gradually induce him to change his ideas,[79] until he finally achieves a greater maturity of outlook.[80] Although Smolenskin is clearly using Zerahiah as a weapon against the half-digested Enlightenment dangerously prevalent amongst the young generation of his day,[81] the real development of character and the widening range of ideas experienced by his hero are proof of a genuine attempt at characterization.[82]

In the treatment of his villains, too, Smolenskin displays

F

considerable skill. Even the black-hearted Manasseh, whose
hideous crimes permeate *The Wanderer in the Paths of Life* and
are responsible for much of its highly melodramatic flavour, is
described as a subtle if treacherous man, capable of ingratiating
himself firmly in the good graces of a benefactor whose entire
household he plans to destroy. Entrusted with the education of
the youthful Absalom by his father Abinadab, Manasseh first
leads the young man into bad habits and then deliberately attempts to alienate father and son. Before slandering Absalom to
his father, however, in the most dreadful manner, Manasseh
first simulates deep distress and extreme hesitancy:

'What's wrong, Manasseh, my friend?' Abinadab enquired
good-humouredly. Manasseh replied not a word, but continued to sigh in a heart-broken manner.
'What's wrong? Why don't you come in?' the old man asked in astonishment.
'Forgive me, Sir,' Manasseh spoke up in a trembling voice.
'Forgive my dreadful sin. Alas! I have committed a sin for
which there is no atoning, and I have become a burden to
myself. I can no longer look upon your face, for my sin is too
great to bear!'
'What do I hear?!' the old man exclaimed in confusion—
'Tell me your sin. Perhaps it is not so very great?'
'No, Sir; it weighs upon me! Only one thing do I ask. Show
me the same kindness now as you have always shown me in
the past—'
'What is your request? I am listening.'
'My sole request is that you should send me away. Send me
away and I shall depart. I shall wander about the earth, dwelling alone in the wilderness and the forest. But I can dwell
in your house no longer!' he said bitterly, clapping his hands
and weeping copious tears.
'But tell me what is your sin. You are so upset that I cannot
make head or tail of what you say. Tell me in what way you
have erred, so that I may judge whether you are right in saying that you can no longer dwell in my house. Perhaps you
are exaggerating, and if you tell me I may be able to forgive
you.'
'I know you won't be able to forgive me, for my sin is dreadful. Send me away to hunger and sickness. I can no longer
stay in your house, for my sin burns like fire within me.'
'What do I hear?' the old man cried in terror. 'Manasseh,
whom I look upon as pure and upright, has committed so

grave a sin! A sin that he is afraid to confess! I don't know what to think. Can it be . . . is it perhaps . . . Shulammit,' the old man shouted suddenly, his eyes flashing as he rose from his chair in terrible wrath like a leopard that has caught the scent of prey. Shulammit, who was sitting in a corner of the room embroidering silk, thought her father was calling her, and rising at once she came over to him and asked:

'What do you want, father dear?'

'Are you in the room?' the old man asked in dismay. 'Would you mind leaving until we have finished our conversation?'

The girl went out, and Manasseh, who had been embarrassed at seeing her, being unaware of her presence, recovered his composure and replied:

'I don't understand what you mean? How does Shulammit concern me?'

'Pardon an old man's mistake. I know your thoughts are pure. But stop talking in riddles. Speak plainly, so that I may know what answer to make.'

'Alas!' Manasseh began contritely. 'Woe is me! I have not proved worthy of the trust you placed in me. I only took my eyes off him for a moment, and alas . . .'

'Now I begin to catch your drift,' the old man said, resuming his seat. 'I suppose you have caught my son up to something, eh? Tell me, don't deny it!'

'Quite so, sir! Only today has it dawned upon me that he has strayed from the straight and narrow path. Up to now he has hoodwinked me, for he seemed to be going along the right lines, and I was taken in. Alas! it's all my fault, Sir!'[83]

The same novel contains another villain of some character in the personality of the malignant Jehoiarib, the hunchback, who is responsible for Josef's first adventure in treachery and deceit.[84] More interesting still, however, is the portrait of a villain in *The Inheritance*, Palti by name, who differs from the more usual *genre* in that his villainy develops only gradually due to his growing entanglement in a web of difficult circumstances.[85] His obsession with the desire to gain an inheritance to which he has no claim, and his passion for money eventually make him talk to himself and—a clever psychological touch—even affect his gestures.[86] Although even blacker villains of the type common to classical melodrama may be found in the novels of Leinwand, Meinkin and Zobeizensky, while Sheikewitz and Weisbrem are also prone to introduce scarcely less malignant schemers, it is significant that apart from a character who bears the satirically symbolic name of 'Ebhen Ḥen,[87] in *Religion and Life*, Braudes' novels are singularly free from melodramatic villains. Minor intrigue and hypocrisy are frequently encountered, but all within a reasonable framework which makes no undue demands on the reader's credulity.

Perhaps the principal weakness in characterization common to all these novelists lies in the portrayal of the major heroines, particularly the romantic heroines within these stories. Although most of the writers under review were staunch advocates of the concept of romantic love,[88] the environment in which their formative years were spent was so inhibiting that their descriptions of romance reflect an intellectual approach in far greater measure than any personal, deeply emotional experience.[89] In consequence, their youthful heroines in particular are colourless and unconvincing, displaying few signs of individuality or real spirit. Apart from the previously mentioned Kalbi's wife,[90] who in any case can scarcely be considered in this category, the only young heroines that command any measure of respect are in the first place Miriam, the vivacious gentile girl who finally converts to Judaism'[91] in Smolenskin's *The Inheritance*, and who is portrayed as a real character of flesh and blood,[92] and secondly Rachel, the widowed heroine of Braudes' *Religion and Life*, who, although not pretty,[93] is endowed with a fine mind and character and makes a serious attempt to come to terms with life.[94] Like Samuel, the hero of the tale, she unfortunately suffers from Braudes' blatant neglect of his story in the third part of the novel.[95]

As in the case of the plots, however, it would be quite misleading to deny these novelists the ability to portray character. On the contrary, within the linguistic limitations outlined previously, they display considerable insight and literary talent. But just as their plots are far more remarkable for the skill with which single episodes are handled rather than any success in overall construction, so in the same way their minor characterizations, and especially the thumb-nail sketches which abound within these novels, are frequently of high order. Smolenskin, in particular, is a master of the art, as may be seen from the following satirical portrait of an egotist:

> 'What's the matter, dear? With whom are you angry?' the woman asked nervously.

'The insolent fellow dared to put on airs! He seems to think that he, too, is head of the community, and that he, too, has the authority to beat and curse. But I showed him that it is I who am the head of the community, I alone, and that without me nobody may move hand or foot. Let him go to the devil. Let them all go to the devil—all that live on charity. We don't want them; we want upright men to eat of our bread, so that our charity may be regarded as real righteousness.'

'Who has dared to give himself airs?' the woman enquired in a faltering voice.

'Who? Ze'ebh!'

'But if Ze'ebh is to blame, why are you angry with all the rest to the point of driving them away?'

'Be quiet! Don't open your mouth! I am head of the community and master of this house. I have built this house by my own efforts. The house is mine and everything in it belongs to me. Did your father give me a large dowry? All my position of honour is the result of my own work and I've told you a thousand times to hold your tongue when I'm talking! Do you hear me?!'

'I have heard that only too often,' the woman answered with a sigh.

'Hold your tongue!!' the master of the house roared at her. 'This house belongs to me, and everything you see in it belongs to me, and you belong to me. I am the master of this house, and the president of the synagogue, and let nobody dare to defy me! Bring the bread!'

The woman got up and quietly set the table with bread, salt and wooden spoons. Before the master of the house she placed a large knife and a bottle of brandy. After the ceremonial washing of the hands, the master of the house took his place, with his wife, who had come to him without a dowry, on his right. On his left sat a little boy, whom his wife had produced to make up for the missing dowry, while his nephew, whom Ze'ebh had dubbed a girl, and myself sat opposite them. The master, who had provided the house and all its contents, and who also owned the bottle of brandy, poured himself out a glass, and then a second and a third. Perhaps to demonstrate that he was master and could do anything he wished without let or hindrance, he gave each of us a glass as well; and after the meal he repeated the performance and tossed off three glasses before we said grace. For a few moments he sat in silence, while all the rest of us were frightened to utter a sound for fear of his wrath. Suddenly a peal of laughter burst

from his mouth, reverberating for several minutes. Then he turned to the spouse who had come without a dowry and did not, therefore, dare to ask the reason for his laughter. But he took the initiative and asked:
'Wasn't I right, my dear? You know that I am a good man with a kindly nature, and that I only fly into a rage occasionally, don't you, my dear?'
'Yes, dear,' the woman replied, 'only occasionally.'[96]

The same novel, *The Wanderer in the Paths of Life*, also contains the following amusing portrait of a studious little lady:

The Rabbi introduced me to his wife, saying: 'Miriam, here's a lad who knows as much of Holy Writ as an old man!'
The woman, who was sitting at a table reading a book called *Re'šith Ḥokhmah*[97] stood, and looked at me through tiny eyes deep-set behind yellow eyelids, which radiated sparks of joy, and said: 'You are welcome. With all my heart I cherish all who are learned in Holy Writ and cleave to it. I'm a woman, and yet my soul thirsts for Holy Writ, which I study day and night. For that is a person's only passport through this world. No object however precious, including even royal dainties or splendid raiment, can compare in my sight with Holy Writ. That alone sustains my spirit, and I give thanks to God, my Creator, seven times a day for gracing me with understanding.'
I was astounded at what she said, for I had never heard a woman speaking in this wise. But on closer observation, I realised that she must be speaking the truth, for her clothes and all the household effects and the two children squatting on the floor all bore witness to the fact that the mistress of the house spent night and day studying Holy Writ. Her husband, too, hastened to confirm what she had said:
'You must realise that my wife has sufficient understanding to grasp the words of the sages, and she is familiar with many of the laws of the *Šulḥan 'Arukh*;[98] and for that reason everyone in town refers to her as the "Half-Rabbi".' On hearing herself praised by the 'Whole-Rabbi', the 'Half-Rabbi's' face lit up, and she nodded her tiny head which reached her husband's navel (it was also, perhaps, because she was just half her husband's height that the townsfolk called her the 'Half-Rabbi') and her curved nose, on which the traces of boils could be seen, turned red with pleasure.[99]

In spite of the lady's malicious attitude to her more domesticated neighbour, the latter confirms that she is sincerely charitable and devoted to good works.[100]

A more substantial portrait of a minor character may be seen in the Lithuanian teacher, upon whose testimony that the hero, Simon, is a bachelor[101] devolves the denouement of *The Joy of the Godless*. For all the man's unworldliness and unprepossessing exterior, it is apparent that Smolenskin attaches more weight to the traditional values and ethical worth that the pious teacher represents than to the frivolous 'enlightened' young men, whom the novel pillories. It is significant, for example, that the Lithuanian's word is accepted without question.[102] Here, again, Smolenskin endeavours to pinpoint the man's character by a recurrent use of phraseology, once more reminiscent of the artistic use of that device so frequently to be encountered in Abramowitz's later stories:[103]

'I'm a truthful man,' the teacher cried, quivering in every limb. 'Did you imagine I would tell lies? Do I not fear the Lord? Am I not familiar with the words of our sages of blessed memory who declare that the liar delays the coming of the holy spirit, and that the seal of God is truth? Do you think that I am affected by the heresy of this lewd city? I shall preserve my integrity as taught me by my fathers and forefathers. I shall not curry any man's favour, not even Simon's—even though he has been very generous to me. For in an impious place one may not even show respect to a Rabbi, even if he has conferred a major blessing on us by sheltering us under the shadow of the holy spirit—how much less, then, to a man who has done me a mere passing favour in this transient world . . .'

'In what way has he strayed from the right path?' the old man broke in, seeing no end to the torrent of words.

'How? Has he not abandoned his study of the Talmud in his desire to study in a government Rabbinical seminary?[104] That a student from the *Yešibhah* in Dungtown[105] should want to study at a government Rabbinical seminary! Isn't that sin enough?'

'Is that the only sin you hold against him?'

'Even apart from that there are others in plenty. Even though he has done me a very great favour, I can't deny it. It grieves me to think that a native of my town should spend all his days reading secular books. I have admonished him to his face to abandon such practices, for with all my heart I wanted to save him. As truly as I want God to let me see my wife and children again, I wanted to save him, for he is a kind-hearted man, and did me a great favour.'

'What answer did he give you?'

'He just laughed and didn't answer anything, as truly as I want God to let me witness the comforting of Zion and Jerusalem. Amen.'

'But surely there is no great sin in all this?'

'No great sin? You astonish me! No great sin? Then what would you call a great sin? But even supposing you were right, I might even forgive him myself, were he not guilty of another terrible sin, because of which the curse of God is laid upon him.'

The whole company eyed each other in dismay.

'What sin is that?' the old man enquired.

'Eight years have passed since his eighteenth birthday and he is still not married. Yet it is stated explicitly in the Talmud that every man who is still unmarried at twenty bears the curse of God,' the teacher exclaimed, gesticulating with head, hands and feet.

As everyone exchanged glances, the old man went on. 'How do you know he isn't married? Supposing he has actually fulfilled the commandment and you are accusing him unjustly.'

'How do I know? If I were not positive, I wouldn't have said so. I know that the man who suspects the innocent can only expect to be punished. If I were not positive, I wouldn't have slandered him or reproved him for his sin. But his own mother is inconsolable because he is still a bachelor. She is a woman and loves him still, just as though he had remained a pious man and not become an 'Apiqores.'[106]

'Indeed, she claims that were it not for the fact that her husband, the tailor, is at loggerheads with him, he could have become a great Rabbi in Israel. But her husband made him leave the Yešibhah so that he fell in with bad company and learned their habits. Now all the other women mock her, and declare that no one would marry his daughter to such an 'Apiqores. She is heart-broken and implored me to persuade him to get married, but he wouldn't answer me. As truly as I want God to let me see my wife and children soon, I speak the truth.'

At this, Shiphrah brightened visibly, while the old man, too, became more cheerful. Nevertheless, he enquired further: 'But how do you know that he hasn't married without telling his mother?'

'No! He wouldn't do that. She is always imploring him in

her letters to take a wife, and had he done so, he would have told her the good news. Moreover, I have known him since he was born, and I know that he left Dungtown when he was thirteen, and he was a bachelor then. Then he remained unmarried in Darkville for five years—unlike his father of blessed memory who stood beneath the wedding canopy at fourteen.[107] And ever since he left Darkville he has been here.'

'Yet this woman insists that he has a wife at home', the old man replied, pointing at the widow.

'It's a lie! How right our sages were in saying: One may not take evidence from a woman!' the teacher shouted angrily. 'Would I make false accusation against any man? Am I not aware that slander is a great sin? Had I not known for certain that he is guilty, I would have remained silent. If he had taken a wife, I would have forgiven his other sins and made my peace with him. But everything I have said is true—as truly as I want the God of truth to let me witness the redemption of Israel and the comforting of Zion!' the man cried fervently, raising his eyes to heaven.[108]

Even more amusing is Smolenskin's satirical portrait of an example of a shallow but brazen young man, purporting to be a teacher without any knowledge or qualification.[109] Without a word of French, the impertinent young Kozbi[110] defeats a native Frenchman in a contest to decide which of the two would make the more suitable teacher:

He (Kozbi) arrived at Solomon's house seeking employment as a teacher of French to his son. Solomon was taken with the idea, but his wife, who had already chosen a native Frenchman to teach her son, wouldn't hear of it. After arguing the matter, they decided to summon both the Frenchman and Kozbi to a contest in French before making a final choice. Kozbi was not at all put out by the suggestion, even though he couldn't speak a single word of French; and as soon as the Frenchman arrived he shouted a number of queer-sounding words at him, at which the astonished Frenchman shook his head as a sign of incomprehension. At that Kozbi burst out in Yiddish: 'You can see for yourselves that the man is an impostor. He cannot understand a single word of French, and yet he makes himself out to be a Frenchman. In my opinion the man's a thief, and has only come to spy out the land.' The master of the house, who was as totally ignorant of French as his wife, flew into a rage and stormed at the Frenchman: 'Get out of here, you scoundrel, before I throw you out neck and crop.' The astounded Frenchman, who had not understood a single word of what had happened, hurriedly left the house, and Kozbi was engaged as the teacher.[111]

Subsequently, by playing on the sympathies of his employer, Kozbi cunningly succeeds in extracting payment without even giving a single lesson! The instances cited may be paralleled by many equally successful thumb-nail sketches, all testifying to the author's innate literary skill.[112] It is of interest, however, that many of his most successful portraits in miniature bear generic, not individual titles, such as the Pole, the Lithuanian, the deserted wife or the *Ḥasidh*.[113]

Braudes, too, displays great facility in the skilful characterization of minor characters, in which respect he is certainly the equal of Smolenskin, if not his superior. His flair for straightforward description is sometimes strengthened by the introduction of a tiny episode by way of illustration, which adds a third dimension to his sketches:

The short silence was broken by the sound of a door opening, and a man stepped into the house. He was a tall, thin man of about forty, with bowed shoulders and shrivelled cheeks.[114] His hair and long, narrow beard were coarse and sandy. He wore no collar, and his clothes were shabby and unkempt—the personification of a *Melammedh*.[115] The man was, in fact, a *Melammedh*, and known as 'The *Melammedh* from Minsk'—an honourable name in the town Pelaguth,[116] for he occupied the foremost place in his profession by virtue of his immense knowledge of the Talmud with all its relevant decisions, opinions and hair-splitting arguments. The students of the *Bêth ha-Midhraš*[117] could bring any difficulty to the *Melammedh* of Minsk and be sure to receive an authoritative answer. He was also well versed in medieval philosophy, having read the *Guide to the Perplexed*, the *Kuzari*, the *Duties of the Heart*, the *Principles*,[118] and other philosophical texts of that period; and their ideas appealed to him. Continually wrapped in thought, he neglected his clothes and combed his hair only on Friday evenings. For that reason, the other *Melammedhim*, who regarded him with disfavour, had nicknamed him 'The Philosopher' —in the sense of good-for-nothing.[119]
Genuinely pious and upright, he shunned all hypocrisy and cant, and abhorred dishonesty. He was content with his lot and generous to the poor, so that many praised him for his

righteousness. When the commentary on the *Guide to the Perplexed* called *Sepher ha-Narboni*[120] came into his hands, he declared that it contained many suspect ideas, and should not be taught to Jewish pupils. 'Then why don't you condemn it to be burned, like all heretical works?'[121] he was asked. 'Should I usurp God's function in judging a man's works?' he replied. 'Do you not know the statement in the Talmud: Let the owner of the vineyard come and destroy the thorns himself?' This was his usual reply to anyone who came complaining that such and such a youth was becoming a heretic. Although much upset, he would only reply, 'It is not for us mortals to interfere in God's affairs. Let the owner of the vineyard come and destroy the thorns himself.'[122]

Although of a very different kind, the following passage from Braudes' other novel, *The Two Extremes*, illustrates in like measure the author's ability to endow even his very minor characters with an attractive individuality, which bears witness, once again, to his literary skill. A young student in Odessa, Levi Suravin, nicknamed 'The Englishman' because of his undemonstrative temperament, cultivates an original approach to courtship:

Detachment and indifference characterized all his actions, which were performed punctiliously, calmly and unhurriedly. He was very sparing with his time, and so punctual that his watch was scarcely ever out of his hand. His thoughts and ideas were equally exact and strictly defined. Poetry and rhetoric exerted no appeal for him, nor had he any sympathy for them. Unimaginative and unemotional, he kept aloof from the things of the spirit, neither ecstasy nor exaltation playing any part in his life. The words 'cool and calculated action' were continually on his lips, and he boasted to his friends as follows: 'I am never attracted by mere empty rhetoric. My stomach will never get full on poetry, nor am I likely to sustain my spirit with high-flown, meaningless phrases. . . .'

Levi Suravin, however, enjoyed life and was fond of company. He was no hermit, and was often to be found in the houses of his friends. Nor did he spurn female society. But here, too, he comported himself as in everything else, and kept their company after his own fashion. The girls of Odessa were divided in their opinions about him. While one declared him to be a boor, and affirmed that she could not abide him because of his neglect of the rules of 'good society', the other maintained that he was a thoroughly enlightened man, who organized his life intelligently and was possessed of sound views. . . .

On one occasion Suravin took a fancy to a young lady, and
wanted to take her into his confidence and enjoy her company.
A few days later he approached her and said:
'My dear young lady! Imagine that I have already whispered
sweet nothings into your ear, that I have already spoken of
the scattered sunbeams, the lovely flowers and roses, the
majestic moon floating through the night, the shining stars,
the verdant fields and the chirping of the birds, and that I have
already recited poems about them all—after all, the purpose
of such things is only to please you. And so I declare: Let's not
bother with all such poetic fancies. Let the sun shine and the
flowers bloom, let the moon and stars illumine the darkness
of the night—that is what they were created for—and allow
me to state plainly that I have taken a fancy to you, and I
hope you will like me, too—Do I make myself clear? . . .'
    The reader may well imagine that the young lady, brought
up on the principles of 'correct etiquette' favoured by the
modern generation, turned aside from him contemptuously,
declaring that he had insulted and embarrassed her . . .
    Suravin, too, turned away from her, remarking that she was
silly, and never bothered to speak to her again.[123]

In more serious vein, *Religion and Life* contains an extremely
shrewd characterization of a young man,'Ebhen-Ḥen,[124] who is
gradually forced to adopt hypocritical and deceitful practices
because of his father's desire to identify himself with the extreme
orthodox faction and yet still remain an 'enlightened' man.[125]
The impossible attempt to run with the hare and hunt with the
hounds exerts such conflicting pressures on the son, that he
finally descends to the only real villainy to be found in Braudes'
novels.[126] The author's deep concern for so tragic a situation is
expressed with great power. The hypocritical Wolfe, the Preacher,
and his son Dov are also drawn with no mean skill.[127]

The lesser-known authors, too, occasionally demonstrate a
similar facility for the delineation of minor characters. In
Weisbrem's *18 Coins*, for example, when the miserly Gedaliah
is advised to provide a dowry of ten thousand roubles for his
daughter, he displays considerable firmness of character:

    Ten thousand roubles, apart from the clothes and presents,
    and the rich wedding-feast that I will have to supply to fill
    the bellies of a lot of parasites—the bill will go on mounting
    until it consumes all the wealth I have acquired with the sweat

of my brow; and as my money disappears, so will my status decline, and with it the respect afforded me in the synagogue and the community council. I regard my money highly, because it is responsible for all the dignity, wisdom, and understanding which the whole congregation attributes to me. Nor did I acquire my wealth without any effort, but by hard work and sweat. How many days have I toiled along the roads, and how many nights have I laboured in my lifetime? For when everyone else was sleeping sweetly in bed, I was still awake, trudging from town to town and village to village, never relaxing, toiling with might and main to store up wealth. I paid no heed to the people who referred to me contemptuously as a usurer; nor was I moved by all the oaths and curses when I came to collect my debts from those to whom I had lent money on interest but who refused to pay. I sent the bailiffs after their bedding, pillows, clothes and whatever else they had in the house—and all of that only to increase my wealth. And from that money you expect me to give the best part to a man who has done nothing to earn it. No, Jekutiel, I won't do it. Five thousand roubles is more than enough for my daughter's dowry.[128]

In spite of the poor quality of its construction, and the almost complete absence of plot, Sirkis' novel, *Esther*, contains two original characterizations, which have no parallel in all the novels under review, and which display a considerable imaginative insight on the part of the author:

Qalsi was a young man of about 25, but to look at him one would guess his age to be only 16 or 17. In stature he was dwarf-like, with broad shoulders, short, fat arms and legs, and a proportionate frame. His expression bore witness to the fact that his mind had not developed, and was unlikely ever to do so. When he wasn't speaking he seemed to be sunk in lofty speculation. His eyes, which were inclined to be bloodshot, appeared always to be focussed on some distant object. His temperament was unstable; one moment he would be weeping bitterly, and the next bursting into disturbing peals of laughter. Qalsi was one of Isaac's friends, and for that reason the latter treated him kindly and supplied him with ample work of the sort which required little intelligence but only good faith. Isaac had discovered that whenever he was performing a mission for him, Qalsi would guard his property carefully and allow no-one to steal it. When Isaac bought wine or corn, he would send Qalsi to the distillery, and Qalsi would watch it like a faithful dog. Whenever he purchased wheat, he would send him to the granaries, and on no occasion had Isaac cause to complain that Qalsi had stooped to embezzlement or fraud.[129]

The author then proceeds to outline Qalsi's pretensions and conceit, and the sport the other workers have with him. No less interesting is the portrait of the strange, unsympathetic Kemuel, the father of the novel's heroine, with his odd mixture of hypocrisy and faith and the strange dualism of his personality:

> Kemuel had never studied Kabbalah, and knew nothing of its method (although he was famous as a Kabbalist). But being cunning and deceitful, he stored up kabbalistic dicta in his memory and pretended to be well-versed in its secrets. . . . If anyone made so bold as to enquire what was the difference between the various systems, he would fly into a rage and give the person to understand that not everyone was fit to hear from his lips of such exalted matters. In his heart he really believed that he alone was acquainted with many lofty concepts, but that he had no time to raise them from the abyss of oblivion, and that all periods were not equally suitable for the pursuit of the knowledge of God. . . .
>
> The large measure of respect shown to Kemuel, and his own astonishing concepts, served to induce remarkable modes of behaviour in order to attest the loftiness of the holy spirit within him. He adopted strange practices and became a by-word amongst his fellows. He afflicted himself with prolonged fasts, and renounced all pleasures. But all this was done less for sincere reasons than because he enjoyed his reputation as 'an unusual man'.
>
> A man of Kemuel's type will adopt such practices and behave oddly in order to attract attention. He would fast on days when he knew of no reason for fasting; and on the days when he wasn't fasting, he resorted to strange habits of eating and drinking: one day he would eat only milk dishes, and on another only meat dishes; one day he would drink only mead, and the next spirits. If anyone asked him the reason, he would make no reply, but merely grimace with his eyes and lips, to suggest that not everyone was fit to know the secret. . . .[130]

One additional figure worthy of note is that of the marriage-broker or *Šadhekhan*. The very nature of the profession demanded a lively character, capable of flattery, boldness, intrigue, deceit and quick decision. But, above all, success or failure would often depend upon the marriage-broker's sheer willpower and tenacity of purpose. As a result the marriage-brokers depicted in these novels are colourful personalities, and in their presence the stories come to life.[131] This is particularly the case, for example, in Weisbrem's *18 Coins*, in which Jekutiel plays a by no means inconsiderable role.[132] By far the most convincing member of the profession, however, appears in Braudes' *Religion and Life*; Zalman Yentis, with his love of mischief, intrigue and practical jokes, and his cunning techniques and unscrupulous determination, must undoubtedly be ranked amongst the most successful characterizations to be found within the novels under review.[133]

From what precedes, it may be inferred that in spite of the many serious difficulties arising from the conflicting purposes, the lack of any adequate literary tradition, the inattention paid to detail,[134] and above all the linguistic limitations from which all these novels suffer, a number of the authors display no mean skill in the delineation of character. While the principal heroes, heroines and villains emerge, for the most part, as unfinished and unsatisfying personalities, whose unreality frequently contrasts starkly with the intense realism of much of the writing, the minor characters are frequently portrayed with such insight and verve that they represent a marked advance over their counterparts in Mapu's novels. In the realm of characterization, as in construction, these novels serve as a transitional stage towards the greater artistic maturity of the succeeding period. In this respect, at least, their contribution to the development of Hebrew literature should not be underestimated.

FOUR

Expression and Experiment

That the Hebrew novel in the twenty years under review represents a transitional stage in the development of modern Hebrew literature may be readily conceded in the light of the many incongruities of plot and characterization encountered in the preceding chapters. For all its elusive quality, an examination of the style in which these stories are written furnishes equally convincing evidence for that conclusion. Of all the various ingredients which comprise a novel, style is, perhaps, the one most difficult to define. So inextricably is style bound up with content, that it is virtually impossible to view it in isolation or treat it as a separate entity. Bearing the same relationship to content as form to matter, it cannot be conceived in terms of an independent existence; and yet it sets its imprint upon all the other elements of a literary work in the shape of presentation, arrangement and cohesion. But whereas plot, characterization and language may be regarded almost as concrete factors, capable of individual treatment, style is something of an abstract quality, ready to vanish before any attempt at definition. Whether apparently simple or complex, it remains a highly individual phenomenon, as difficult to imitate as a signature.

The elusive nature of style is emphasized by its dual character. For the author it represents the particular mode in which his attitude towards his own experience is expressed. As such it constitutes a deliberately chosen instrument for his artistic creativity. For the reader, style is rather the channel through which the impact of the author's ideas may be conveyed, but one whose conductivity varies directly with the measure of sympathetic appreciation which the reader is prepared to extend. As both

Shalom Jacob Abramowitz

these factors are highly subjective, it is little wonder that individual opinions concerning the appeal exerted by any particular author's style may differ so widely.

Nevertheless, in spite of the subjective aspect, certain criteria may, perhaps, be postulated to serve as fixatives for an appreciation of stylistic qualities, at least in some measure. In the first place, the relative attraction of a particular style would seem to depend upon the suitability of form to content. The greater the harmony which exists between the matter and its mode of expression, and the more complete the fusion of both elements into one harmonious union, from which neither element violently obtrudes, or distorts the other's shape, the more likely is the style to be regarded as artistically satisfying and mature. Secondly, the natural rhythms and cadences of any particular language, which result from long usage and familiarity, and thereby exert a deep emotional appeal, play an important role in determining the shapes and patterns of expression most likely to meet with approval. The most impressive stylists are those who appear to be able to put their finger on the magic spring of language—that is, the writers who are able to string words together in a way that strikes a familiar chord in the emotions, thereby engendering a satisfaction which even the same words in different order are unable to evoke. This choice and arrangement of words, which holds the key to an author's style, is at once complex and elusive in the extreme. It contains the secret of all great writing, poetry and prose alike and, for all the apparent simplicity which may characterize the final result, it derives from a conscious or unconscious process of selection and rejection on the author's part most difficult to fathom, in which both instinct and experience play a decisive role.

In the third place, the efficiency of an author's style may be evaluated with reference to the purpose of his writing. Different objectives are best served by various modes of expression. For the moment it may suffice to mention, with reference to this study of the Hebrew novel, that a particular style adopted as admirably suitable for the unfolding of a romantic, melodramatic adventure story may prove a far less effective instrument for the propagation of serious ideas, for social criticism or for the advocacy of various types of reform. A variety of aims is scarcely calculated, however, to produce the uniform and cohesive style which comprises such an important factor in mature, artistic composition.

G

98 THE HEBREW NOVEL

Fourthly, what may be described as the more mechanical aspects of style, which are largely responsible for the colouring and flavour of a literary work, must be taken into consideration. These aspects are more susceptible to examination and analysis, whether they fall under the category of literary devices such as, for example, description, imagery, simile, and metaphor, by means of which the author attempts to widen the connotation of his ideas and strengthen their impact on the reader, or whether they signify the author's approach to his material by resorting to satire, irony, pathos, humour, hyperbole, understatement or any comparable method, again designed to heighten the reader's awareness of the particular nuance which the writer is anxious to convey.

An appreciation of the stylistic qualities of the novels under review must take account of all these factors, which may be cautiously accepted as criteria of some validity in estimating their literary worth. It is also essential to bear in mind, however, that all these novels suffer from the severe linguistic limitations, to which some reference has already been made.[1] A fair evaluation of the achievements of these novelists, therefore, must take relative as well as absolute standards into consideration. In other words, they should properly be viewed not solely from the standpoint of literature as such, but also as the product of a particular stage in the history of Hebrew literature. Just as it is scarcely fair to criticize a craftsman for his inability to fashion an object which demands instruments of greater precision than those at his disposal, so is it equally unfair to condemn a novelist for literary imperfections, which stem inevitably from the inferior quality of the linguistic resources at his disposal. On the other hand, while we recognize a writer's achievement in the face of a severe linguistic handicap, the real aesthetic validity of his work must be measured against more rigid and universally acceptable standards.

If, for the purposes of this study, the movement of Enlightenment known as *Haskalah*,[2] which arose in Berlin during the last decades of the eighteenth century, be regarded as the starting point for the rise of modern Hebrew literature,[3] it may be argued that for rather more than the century extending approximately from 1790 to 1890, Hebrew literature is characterized by two features of great importance which divide it sharply from the preceding period. These two features are responsible in great measure for the immature and unsatisfactory nature of almost all the Hebrew literature produced during the first century of its modern phase; they also help to explain many of the stylistic deficiencies of the novels under review, especially when measured against the first two of the criteria mentioned above—namely, the suitability of form to content, and the relative attraction exerted by any particular choice and arrangement of words.

The first great change in Hebrew literature, stemming from the movement of *Haskalah*, is one of spirit.[4] By far the greater part of the Hebrew literature composed during the previous epochs reflects one or other of the manifold aspects of Judaism. There is, therefore, an organic connection between the subject-matter and the vehicle for its expression, namely Hebrew, with the result that the form and content suit each other admirably. But from the end of the eighteenth century almost the entire literary productivity of the exponents of Enlightenment, the *Maskilim*, is devoted to a deliberate endeavour to express the values of western European civilization in Hebrew garb. Although fully comprehensible as a serious attempt to facilitate the transition of the Jews of western Europe from the medieval to the modern world, and thereby assist their adaptation to the intellectual and cultural environment of modern life with the aid of the principal, if not the sole, literary medium at their disposal, the compelling urge to express a wide variety of concepts and ideas, and convey the detailed information necessary for an understanding of the whole range of modern knowledge, subjected Hebrew to severe stresses and strains which the language was ill-equipped to bear.

In using Hebrew as the vehicle for translated or original works devoted to philosophy, science, history, geography, politics and economics—to mention but a few subjects out of many—the *Maskilim* were faced not only by a serious lack of vocabulary and terminology for the purposes of exact definition and by insufficiently flexible modes of expression, but also by the absence of a literary tradition and the generally accepted conventions necessary to convey such varied information in clear, precise and economical terms. As such ideas were often alien to Hebrew moulds, the language had to be stretched, pulled and grotesquely distorted in the attempt to adapt it to new purposes. Far from there being any harmony between form and content, the matter was violently thrust into unsuitable linguistic patterns, which bulged and sagged as pathetically as a grossly ill-tailored garment.

This sorry state was further emphasized by the second great change in the Hebrew literature of the period. As an essential feature of their programme for the reform of the Jewish educational system to meet the demands of modern life, the *Maskilim* staunchly advocated the pursuit of higher standards of aesthetic appreciation, which were to be attained by the cultivation of more refined modes of expression.[5] They were convinced that only by such means could the growing generation be prepared for an eventual full participation in the cultural life of western Europe. To that end the *Maskilim* deliberately abandoned the somewhat crude and crabbed style of Rabbinical composition then generally in vogue, in favour of a return to the language of the Bible. Their choice was determined by two principal factors. In the first place, they believed that by directing the students' attention to the Bible as a whole—in contrast to the traditional system of education which limited such Biblical study as was permitted to the Pentateuch, while concentrating almost exclusively on a rigorous training in Rabbinical sources[6]—they would help to foster a sympathetic appreciation of a more heroic age in Jewish history with its emphasis on political freedom, so important psychologically in their struggle for emancipation. Secondly, they felt that a study of the superb poetry of the Bible would inculcate an aesthetic appreciation of literature, and so encourage the development of a more cultivated outlook.

In accordance with these aims, the exponents of Enlightenment chose to imitate the language of the Bible in their own writings, deliberately attempting to limit their vocabulary to that found in the Bible, and adopting its phraseology at every possible opportunity. Their obsession with the refinements of literary composition—although initially a most commendable attempt to improve the aesthetic qualities of Hebrew literature—gradually degenerated into a highflown rhetorical, euphuistic style, generally known as *Meliṣah*, which is all too frequently characterized by a mediocrity of subject-matter shrouded in over-ambitious phraseology.[7] While the sincerity of their intentions was undoubtedly genuine, the application of such methods adversely affected the development of modern Hebrew literature for more than a hundred years. Indeed, the striking feature of most of the *belles-lettres* produced during that period is the marked contrast between a theory of literature designed to produce works of high aesthetic value and the poor quality of the great majority of the literary compositions actually produced.

In terms of the Hebrew novel, the resort to the language of the Bible is most clearly illustrated in the stories of the first Hebrew novelist, Abraham Mapu.[8] Mapu's historical novels set in ancient Palestine in the time of Isaiah, represent the most thorough-going and sustained attempt in modern Hebrew literature to compose a major work in the style and language of the Bible. Although Mapu was betrayed into frequent lapses from Biblical vocabulary and structure by his own traditional education and the semantic changes which had occurred in Hebrew vocabu-lary—especially as they appear in Yiddish, Mapu's spoken lan-guage—his narratives, nevertheless, constitute a remarkably consistent attempt to employ the elements of Biblical language for the purposes of the novel. His success stems not only from a most skilful fusion of the various Biblical materials into a smooth and relatively consistent style, but also from the fact that in de-scribing a Biblical setting in the language of the Bible, the form of his novels was admirably suited to the content. Even though Mapu projects the ideals of the movement of *Haskalah* back through the centuries to the period of the Prophets, there is no obvious dichotomy between the style and subject-matter of his stories.

In his novel of contemporary life, however, the case is very different. For all his valiant efforts to apply similar linguistic tech-niques to the composition of *The Hypocrite*, Mapu was confron-ted by the far more formidable problem of portraying a contem-porary scene in archaic language. It is significant that the in-congruity of form and matter became so obvious even to Mapu himself, that in the preface to his fragment *The Visionary*, the author actually states his belief that he has exhausted the possibi-lities of writing novels in the restricted language of the Bible, and urges his successors to avail themselves of the rich linguistic strata of post-Biblical Hebrew.

So powerful was the impact of Mapu's novels, however, that not only did *The Hypocrite* direct the main stream of the Hebrew novel into social channels for several decades, but even the author's warning concerning language was largely disregarded during

the twenty years following Mapu's death, namely the period
under review. Admittedly no subsequent novelist attempted so
thoroughgoing an imitation of the language of the Bible. Nevertheless, Mapu's immediate successors still clung to the principle
of using Biblical vocabulary, although the post-Biblical element
does, indeed, become gradually more conspicuous. The most significant change, however, during the two decades under discussion is the increasing departure from Biblical sentence-structure and syntax—including a far less frequent resort to the *waw*
consecutive, which towards the end of the period is used quite
sparingly, and sometimes for deliberate effect,[9] and a tendency to
introduce much longer and more complicated types of sentences
constructed more loosely and with greater flexibility.

The transitional aspect of these novels, therefore, stands out
most clearly by comparison with Mapu's more faithful allegiance
to Biblical forms on the one hand and the subsequent novels by
Mendele, in which all strata of Hebrew—and a considerable
admixture of Aramaic—are welded into a supple and highly artistic mode of expression on the other. Stylistically, they are inferior to both Mapu's historical novels and the novels of Mendele, even though the more important writers far outstripped
Mapu in clarity, vividness, dialogue and the ability to formu-
late complex ideas. This inferiority may be the more readily
acceded in the light of the criteria previously suggested.[10] The overall adherence of the novelists under review to the vocabulary and
phraseology of the Bible for the depiction of the contemporary
scene in eastern Europe during the nineteenth century gave rise
to that incompatibility of form and content which is so detrimental to an author's style. Again the retention of Biblical phraseology within a sentence-structure, only Biblical in part, created
new and unfamiliar rhythms, in which the choice of words frequently appears out of harmony with their arrangement.

In amplification of these charges it may be well to begin by illustrating some of the clumsy circumlocutions and imprecise descriptions to which the novelists were frequently compelled to
resort in the absence of more exact and universally accepted terminology.[11] The following examples are presented in literal translation in order to conjure up the same sense of awkwardness inherent in the Hebrew originals. To express the term 'museums',
Smolenskin produces 'houses for the collection of things ancient

of days';[12] a 'tuning fork' becomes 'an iron fork with two teeth that emits a sound';[13] a 'sledge' is described as 'a winter cart that has no wheels';[14] an 'invalid chair', on the other hand, is 'a long chair which has wheels';[15] the phrase 'a shooting stick with six little mouths'[16] must surely represent a 'six-shooter', while there is an even more ambitious 'shooting stick with twelve little mouths';[17] a 'gambling den' is described as 'a house for the gathering of the joyful who play cards until the light of morning'.[18]

A further aspect of the problem may be recognised in the fluid state of the terminology employed in the attempt to find Hebrew equivalents for modern concepts. As the subsequent development of Hebrew into a modern language containing a vocabulary sufficiently wide and varied to cope with the entire range of objects and ideas has depended upon an extremely complex process of word-coinage, the early attempts to overcome such difficulties assume a particular significance. At the same time, it poignantly reflects the severe linguistic handicap suffered by the novelists in the period under review. In this instance, again, only a small number of representative examples have been chosen by way of illustration. In attempting a literal translation of the phrases employed, it is difficult to convey the exact shade of meaning where the terms are very similar. For that reason each general term is followed by the various Hebrew equivalents in transliteration.

To express the idea of 'post' or 'post-office' the following Hebrew phrases are employed—*Bêth ha-Raṣim*[19] (house of runners), *Bêth ha-Mikhtabhim*[20] (house of letters), *Bêth Mišloah Mikhtabhim*[21] (house of despatch of letters), *Taḥanath Bêth ha-Raṣim*[22] (the stage of the house of runners), *Ha-Post*,[23] *Do'ar*,[24] *Bêth ha-Do'ar*[25] (house of the post), *Batté-Do'ar*[26] (houses of post). Similarly, postmen are designated as *Raṣé ha-Melekh*[27] (king's runners), *Nose' ha-Mikhtabhim*[28] (bearer of letters), *Nose' ha-'Iggeroth*[29] (bearer of epistles). As may be seen from the notes, different terms are frequently employed by the same author, even within the same novel—an interesting illustration of the fluidity of terminology.

A similar variety of terms is used to express the idea of 'train' or 'railway'—*Markebhoth' Eš*[30] (chariots of fire), *Merkebheth ha-Qiṭṭor*[31] (chariot of steam), *Markebhoth ha-Barzel*[32] (chariots of iron), *'Eghlath ha-Qiṭṭor*[33] (carriage of steam), *Mesilloth ha-Barzel*[34] (paths of iron), *Ha-Massa'*.[35] The term 'newspaper' is also well represented by a variety of different phrases, mainly conveying the idea of 'news-letter', or 'leaves which make new things known'. The following are among the most common, although occasionally they can be longer and more complicated[36]—*Mikhtabh 'Itti*,[37] *Ha-Mikhtabh 'Itti*,[38] *Ha-Mikhtabh ha-'Itti*,[39] *Mikhtebhê 'Eth*,[40] *'Alê ha-'Ittim*,[41] *'Aleh Mikhtebhê ha-'Ittim*,[42] *'Alim ha-Mašmi'im Ḥadhašoth*.[43]

The terminology for the idea of 'smoking' includes a number of interesting variants, apart from the use of European terms such as *Sigharettah*[44] or *Papiros*.[45] The straightforward *'Alê Ṭabaq*[46] (tobacco leaves) pales somewhat before such colourful phrases as *'Alê Merorim*[47] (bitter leaves), *'Abhaq 'Alê Merorim*[48] (the dust of bitter leaves), *'Ašan 'Alê ha-Qiṭṭor*[49] (the smoke of leaves of steam), and the splendid *'Alê Merorim be-Thakhrikh Neyar*[50] (bitter leaves in a paper shroud)! The phrases used to describe a kitchen, however, are simpler and only three in number—*Bêth ha-Mebhaššelim*,[51] *Bêth ha-Mebhaššeloth*[52] and *Ḥadhar ha-Mebhaššeloth*.[53] In this case, too, as so frequently elsewhere, all three have since been superseded by the more convenient term *Miṭbaḥ*. Again, only two phrases are found for the term 'library', namely, *Ḥadhar ha-Sepharim*,[54] and *Bêth 'Oseph ha-Sepharim*[55] (connoting respectively 'the room of books' and 'the house of collection of books'). Both have since yielded pride of place to the shorter *Siphriyyah*.

The lack of confidence displayed by the novelists in much of the modern terminology to which they make resort may be gauged from their frequent habit of supplying an explanatory word or phrase, in brackets, in Hebrew, Roman or Russian characters, giving their intended meaning in Yiddish or a major European language.[56] By such means they presumably hoped to establish a conventional meaning for the particular usage. On occasion, they even append a footnote explaining or justifying the particular connotation attached to the word in question. The following examples are typical of numerous similar instances—*Lo'-Hu'* (Nihil),[57] *Bêth ha-Taḥanoth* (Bahnhof),[58] *Ha-Parwar* (Boulevard),[59] *Ha-Minnim* (Klavier, with an explanatory footnote),[60] *Ṣayyar ha-Luḥoth* (Schilder Mahler),[61] *Temunoth Šonoth* (Statuen),[62] *Netiyyatham ha-Ṭibh'ith* (Instinkt).[63] No less frequently the term adopted is a straightforward transliteration from European languages. The range of terminology demanding such treatment may be inferred from the following examples—'electricity',[64] 'magnet',[65] 'civilization',[66] 'romanticism',[67] 'ceremonial',[68] 'coffee',[69] 'telegraph'[70] and 'gendarmes'.[71] It is indicative of the fluid state of the language at the time, as well as of the novelists' carelessness, that the latter two terms are differently spelled within the same novel, while the transliteration of 'coffee' appears in two quite different versions on the same page! From all the examples quoted above, the measure of incompatibility between form and matter, which affects the style of these novels so adversely, may readily be conceded.

A further disability arising from the extreme limitations of the vocabulary at the disposal of these novelists may be observed in the recurring phraseology which abounds within these novels.[72] It is as though the novelist, once having lighted upon a phrase which appears felicitous, feels compelled to employ it over and over again, whenever the opportunity arises. This phraseology, most of which is derived directly from the Bible, is partly a legacy of Mapu's novels, which are also characterized by the device.[73] It may be traced through all these novels with remarkable consistency. Some of the phrases, such as *Ṭubh Ṭaʿam wa-Dhaʿath* in the sense of 'cultivated taste'[74] or *Daʿath la-Nabhon Naqel* (the intelligent man will easily understand) or *Niphqeḥu ʿÊnaw Lirʾoth* (his eyes were opened and he became aware), reflect the ideas of Enlightenment, which the authors, for the most part, were anxious to disseminate.[75] The great majority of such phrases, however, appear to have been employed partly for aesthetic reasons, because they appeared felicitous and sufficiently 'literary', and partly because it had become the convention to employ them. Departure, for example, is frequently described with the phrase 'he set his steps to the way', while to denote amusement, or even amused contempt, the novelists turn naturally to the expression 'a light smile appeared on (or hovered or passed over) his lips'. Guilt is normally described by means of the phrase 'the expression on his countenance bore witness against him', and dejection conjures up the image 'with his head bent like a reed' or alternatively 'with a sigh rent from his loins'. Similarly, caution is usually enjoined with the advice 'to put a muzzle on one's lips', while injured innocence resorts to the phrase 'what evil have you found in me?'

Again, recourse is sometimes made to a particular conjunctive phrase, which appears to catch the author's fancy and is then employed over and over again. In chapter 6 of the third part of *Religion and Life*, for example, Braudes suddenly resorts to the phrase *'Ephes Ki* (only that), which subsequently appears at least

on every second or third page, and sometimes even more frequently. In *The Two Extremes* he returns to it with even greater
enthusiasm, so that the phrase occurs no less than two hundred
times in the course of the novel—an average of more than once in
every two pages! On the other hand, the same author displays
considerable skill in his use of *Ha-'Umnam* (Can it really be?) in
the tenth chapter of the second part of *Religion and Life*, in order
to reflect the doubts of each of the major characters in turn. The
word is further emphasized by its employment as the chapter
heading.

The second of the above-mentioned factors which seriously im-
pedes the stylistic quality of these novels, namely the retention of
Biblical phraseology within a sentence-structure only Biblical in
part, is equally demonstrable. Although the number of phrases
either lifted directly from the Bible, or closely modelled on Biblical passages, goes far beyond the possibility of any detailed
enumeration and, indeed, permeates the novels from beginning
to end, a number of examples drawn from different stories
almost at random may serve to illustrate this aspect of the style.
For the purposes of simplification, only such passages as are most
immediately recognizable have been selected:

> . . . And as he increases his pain so shall he increase his
> knowledge.[76]
> . . . From his shoulder and upwards taller than all the
> people.[77]
> . . . Send, I pray thee, by the hand of him whom thou wilt
> send. . . .[78]
> . . . So we have chosen a broken reed for our support.[79]
> . . . And his sitting in the house was a little. . . .[80]
> . . . And his tongue clave to his palate. . .[81]
> . . . His eye cannot see enough, nor his ear have its fill of
> hearing.[82]
> . . . For the Lord has dealt bitterly with me. And it came to
> pass on the next day when I went out to the city gate that the
> whole town was astir, saying: Is this David ben Elkanah![83]
> . . . He remembered the redness of his eyes from weeping,
> and the whiteness of his cheeks from poverty.[84]
> . . . And behold Nahum the butcher came to meet them[85]
> . . . . And it came to pass that the voice was heard in the city,
> saying. . . .[86]
> . . . . Do you not know, have you not heard? . . . .[87]

... Is my master, too, among the musicians? ...[88]
.... To seek the one whom my soul loves, but I sought him and did not find him.[89]
.... This is an evil thing which God has given to the sons of men to afflict them, namely 'money'.[90]

The mock-Biblical style of this latter example is particularly prevalent in Abramowitz's *Fathers and Sons*, as in the following passage:

Salmonah is a great city, in which there are more than two hundred thousand inhabitants, who cannot distinguish their left hand from their right hand, and much cattle.[91]

It is important to emphasize that these examples could be multiplied by hundreds, if not thousands, if the part played by Biblical phraseology within these novels is rightly to be understood. It is equally important to remember, however, that these phrases constitute isolated fragments embedded in prose which, although largely compounded of Biblical vocabulary, is far from remaining Biblical in syntax and structure. In consequence, no matter how skilful the individual use of such fragments may be, they tend to leap out of the text, and sometimes obtrude as uncomfortably as a sore thumb. More significantly, in the present context, the natural rhythms of the Biblical passages, which possess the magic of long familiarity and deep emotional appeal, are not in harmony with such rhythms as may be found in the rest of the prose in which they are embedded, and which naturally account for by far the greater part of the stories. This uncomfortable fusion must bear considerable responsibility for the unevenness of style. Instead of flowing smoothly, the prose is constantly interrupted by snatches of Biblical phrase, so that the total effect is one of patchwork, rather than a smooth and even surface. Instead of striking a chord in the emotions, the overall choice and arrangement of words and phrases is equally likely to produce a discord. No other element, perhaps, within these novels, bears greater witness to the transitional nature of these novels, and their want of an established literary tradition, than this aspect of the style.

Closely linked with this only half-digested Biblical phraseology is the constant resort to *Meliṣah*, the high-flown, euphuistic mode of composition previously mentioned.[92] Although this style is highly praised on a number of occasions within the novels[93] and was for long considered the hall-mark of an 'enlightened' man, it can scarcely be considered an asset to the literary qualities of these stories. In practice, the desire for refinement and beauty of expression which underlies the attachment to *Meliṣah* so enthusiastically displayed by the exponents of Enlightenment, degenerates all too easily into a pretentious and highly florid mode of writing, frequently masking concepts of a very mediocre kind. The irritating discrepancy between common-place matter and the exaggerated manner in which it is expressed obtrudes only too frequently within these novels, and exerts an adverse influence upon the smoothness of the style.

Here, again, a few examples out of many must suffice by way of illustration. Instead of the simple form 'I wept', adherence to *Meliṣah* produces 'the windows of my eyes were opened'.[94] A phrase such as 'the man was snoring' is rendered 'a sound as though of flutes was heard escaping from his two nostrils'.[95] Instead of such an expression as 'I am not inventing the matter', the prose becomes 'no bird of heaven has brought the sound to me';[96] A similar approach may be discerned in such expressions as: '. . . And the fruits of love sprouted up like the grass of the earth'.[97] '. . . For then I would have chosen strangling for my soul rather than become a target for time's arrows which pierce my bowels anew each moment';[98] '. . . Nevertheless the opening of her lips was sweetness';[99] '. . . Stronger than lions were these young men, as though carved out of sapphire';[100] '. . . Who suddenly became a den of vipers and a tongue of adders';[101] '. . . And his lips dripped myrrh';[102] '. . . My heart raged like a turbulent sea';[103] '. . . Because death was already flashing its eyes at me;'[104] '. . . They took their places in the carriages attached to horses of fire and smoke of wind'.[105]

As an illustration of one of the more sustained passages written in similar style which abound in these novels, the letter left by Jonathan, one of the heroes of Weisbrem's *Between the Times*, before fleeing the house of the Rabbi, his guide and mentor, may serve as a typical example. It is of interest that many of the letters in these stories are deliberately written in similar florid style, as though designed to serve as models of the epistolary art, and demonstrate the cultivated manner of their authors:

My honoured father[106] and benefactor!
Since the day your daughter left your house and vanished, your home has become too narrow for me, and light has turned

to darkness in your habitation. Therefore have I fled from before you, and I have decided to escape to the ends of the earth, where I shall hide myself in the crevices of the rocks, or wander afar to the distant isles and dwell at the furthest end of the sea. Perhaps there I shall be comforted—I know that I have acted perversely, and my sin is black before you, O my friend and benefactor. But forgive me, sir, in your great mercy, for this day I am as an unfortunate and dejected soul. My only remaining hope rests with God who has given me life, that I shall again return and look upon your countenance. Jonathan.[107]

It must be admitted, however, that some of the minor writers, such as Manassewitz, Zobeizensky, Meinkin and particularly Leinwand, are the worst offenders in resorting time and again to long sequences of florid, overloaded and sometimes meaningless phrases.[108] The major writers, on the other hand, are far less prone to lapse into passages overloaded with *Meliṣah* for its own sake, and it is significant that Abramowitz—in a long and important discussion in *Fathers and Sons* on the purpose of literature[109] —strongly attacks the uncritical use of *Meliṣah*, arguing that it is only justifiable when combined with positive and constructive ideas aimed at improving social conditions and raising the general standard of critical appreciation. One of the heroes, Jonathan, for example expressed this view as follows:

> ... I am sick and tired of empty, useless *Meliṣah*, and meaningless words that have nothing constructive to say. I cannot deny that even I, who prefer our holy tongue above all other languages, nevertheless scarcely read any books or articles written by our modern authors. . . .[110]

Later in the same chapter the following revealing exchange takes place between Nahum, a Hebrew author, who is powerfully satirized because his book lacks serious content, and David, the idealized exponent of Enlightenment:

> 'According to what you say, one should write or translate only serious or scientific works. Then what about *Meliṣah*, the daughter of heaven,[111] which is accorded a place of honour in the literature of all nations.'
>
> 'Indeed,' David replied, '*Meliṣah* performs an important function, if the daughter of heaven is also the daughter of nature and life, and if she is infused with the spirit of under-

standing. The glory of *Meliṣah* is only the recognition of the beautiful, the exalted, the wonders of the mind, and their correct presentation in good taste and in a reasoned manner; it is the recognition of nature and life, which are portrayed *via* its agency. But its worth is bound up with them alone, and only they can endow it with real value.'[112]

David then proceeds to affirm that fine phrases in themselves without real content are valueless; but that unfortunately the majority of Hebrew writers are interested only in stringing beautiful words together without turning their attention to nature or the problems of society, which would in turn exert some influence on their readers. Such writers claim that they should compose only to please themselves, without any obligation to the reading public. David insists, however, that if such writers were to adopt a fine style and simultaneously deal with important topics, including Jewish problems, then they would attract a much wider reading public. Finally, he advises Nahum to present his readers with matter which has real bearing on their lives. It is significant that some, at least, of the novelists under review clearly recognised the unsatisfactory nature of an exaggerated concern with *Meliṣah*, even when they were unable to emancipate themselves from its dominion.

From what precedes, the factors working against the creation of a unified and cohesive style may readily be imagined. Indeed, stylistically—as in so many other respects—the scales were heavily weighted against the authors under review from first to last. So heavy and rigid were the linguistic shackles and the literary conventions to which they were subjected, that the mere writing of a novel at all under such limiting conditions demanded courage and tenacity of high order. The very achievement must command respect. But when, to such initial setbacks to cohesion, the dual purpose of these novelists is added, namely their attempt to combine an adventurous story of romance with social criticism and stern didacticism, each with its own particular demands on style,[113] it is scarcely surprising to find that, far from maintaining any overall unity of style, the quality of writing is fluctuating and uneven, so that the style as well as the plots[114] frequently appears to be progressing in fits and starts, almost independently of the writer's wishes. It is as though the material were almost as much in control of the writer as the writer of the material.

It is within these limitations that the success or failure of the novelists must be estimated; and if such relative rather than any absolute criteria be accepted, the achievements of the more important writers are remarkable. Although all the novels suffer from the stylistic disabilities outlined above in greater measure or in less, many of them include numerous, substantial passages written with great power and persuasiveness, representing an important advance in the process of development towards a mature Hebrew novel. Just as with the plots, where the main strength of the novelists may be discerned in their skilful handling of the individual episode,[115] while in characterization the minor characters are delineated with far greater success than the principal heroes and heroines,[116] so in the case of style, the impact exerted by the individual passage is often far more convincing than that arising from the novel as a whole.

Among the most striking passages are those devoted to the criticism of social abuses, with which these novels abound. Here, the sincerity and indignation of the authors tend to strip their writing of the unnecessary verbiage which mars their style when they are deliberately pursuing a mere literary effect. Once their foremost concern becomes the exposure of some evil in society, or a fulmination against the ridiculous consequences of human stupidity, the writing often becomes much more straightforward and direct—and correspondingly more effective. Unlikely as it might at first appear, the strong didactic element in these stories, in direct contrast to its effect on plot and characterization, frequently serves as a beneficial influence upon the style. In *Fathers and Sons*, for example, Abramowitz describes the virulent opposition of the Jews, and particularly the Ḥasidic faction,[117] to the governmental decree founding compulsory elementary schools for Jewish children,[118] that were to supersede the *Ḥedher*,[119] the traditional institution for Jewish education. After outlining how the large Jewish community bribed the gentile headmaster to let them know the date on which the government inspector was due to appear, so that the school was packed with children on that day—much to the inspector's satisfaction—although otherwise it remained empty, Abramowitz proceeds to outline the headmaster's own attitude as follows:

The headmaster justified his action on two counts. In the first place, even if he had taken issue with his fellow citizens, it would have been of no avail. He, himself, was an old hand in the evasion of the law, and the word of a single individual was never accepted. 'If two people tell you that you are drunk', to quote the old proverb, 'go and lie down.' In the second place, he was not of their faith, nor were his ancestors of the faith of their ancestors. So why should he be interested in improving them, or sacrificing himself on the altar of Enlightenment for the Jews?! Why should he put himself out for people in whom he had not the slightest interest? It was all the same to him whether they had *Melammedhim*[120] or teachers, or whether they studied in *Hedher* or an elementary school. He didn't hold with any of them! Was it for this that he had acquired wisdom and knowledge in the upper division of the theological college—to educate the Jews? . . . Even without it, he told himself, the Jews are cunning, and can get the better of us by guile. Admittedly, they have bribed me with their own money, but won't they get it back from me again? Yesterday, Moses the pedlar squeezed money out of me. Today Samuel got the better of the bargain, and tomorrow some other Jew will relieve me of whatever little money I have left. . . . The Jews have given, and the Jews have taken away, the Devil take them! In this way the headmaster constantly justified himself and granted himself a pardon. He would repeat the phrase 'Go to the Devil! Go to the Devil!' a few times, and then stretch out his palm for a secret bribe.[121]

The passage is significantly free of the flowery, euphuistic phraseology which mars so much of the story; it might almost indeed serve as a model of clear, direct and unpretentious writing.

In Smolenskin's novels, too, the sections devoted to social criticism contain some of the most powerful examples of his writing. *The Wanderer in the Paths of Life*, for example, contains the very moving description of the abduction of Jewish children for twenty-five years of service in the Russian army[122] which is scarcely inferior to an even more harrowing scene of a similar kind in A. Koestler's *Arrival and Departure*. A similar power of expression may also be detected in his portrait of life in the Jewish quarter of Odessa,[123] or in his defence of Israel against the calumnies levelled at her by her enemies,[124] or in Josef's first experiences at the *Yešibhah*[125] or among the *Hasidim*.[126] *The Joy of the Godless* also contains a number of effective passages, such as the moving exposition of the plight of a divorced woman[127]—Smolenskin is always at his best with the underdog. Elsewhere in the same novel he describes a number of his characters in a manner calculated to outline certain social ideas. Here, too, his style is straightforward and admirably suited to his theme.[128] In *A Donkey's Burial*, the terrible social criticism inherent in the case of the young couple, who are tarred and feathered because it is alleged that they have been seen kissing, is made all the more effective by virtue of the light satire in which the grotesque horror of the situation is veiled.[129] Again, in *The Inheritance*, Smolenskin's horrifying description of the plight of the Jews in Roumania[130] is further enhanced because of the callousness of the narration.[131] The same story contains an almost lyrical description of the manner in which a man is thrown into prison for possessing a Talmud without a royal seal.[132] Equally powerful is the indictment of the Jewish community of Vienna, and, in particular, of the bitter experiences liable to occur to any poverty-stricken Jew who becomes dependent upon that city's 'philanthropists'.[133] *The Inheritance*, too, bears witness to Smolenskin's great skill in developing arguments, relevant to the Jewish problems of his day, in clear and lucid Hebrew.[134]

A similar power of expression may be discerned in Braudes' novels, particularly in *Religion and Life*, so much of which is devoted to the exposition of serious religious and social problems. Much of the novel is written in a forceful and decisive style which stems, perhaps, from the author's avowed didactic purpose. Certainly, the episodes flow more smoothly, with little exaggerated searching after effect, while the overall presentation is more natural and convincing than is the case with most of the novels under review. The scene in which the hero Samuel outlines his views on Judaism and the problems facing the Jewish people is particularly noteworthy for its clear, direct and forceful style. The changes in the conditions of Jewish life which, in Samuel's opinion, require parallel modifications in the *Šulḥan 'Arukh*, the great codification of Jewish religious law, are outlined by the hero as follows:

Take a man lying in prison, shut up in a dungeon or a dark cell and never allowed outside—such a man would not notice that times change. It would make no difference to him what time it was. Day and night, winter and summer, cold season and warm would merge together and all appear the same to him. Were we to trust his judgement, we would find no need to change our way of life to meet the changes of nature and

H

the seasons. We would never need to change our clothing, or the running of our households or our habits. Nevertheless, we who are free are well aware that we feel such changes, we are very conscious of the fact that as the seasons change we, too, change our mode of life. Our habits in summer are different from those we pursue in winter. But the same applies to the problems of life; for life, too, changes like the seasons, assuming many different shapes and guises. In the wake of changing events, or the growth of scientific knowledge, or the change of law and custom, the necessities of life assume new forms from time to time. Both the necessities of life, and the manner of earning a livelihood are different now from what they were in former times. But we—you and I—are not aware of the change, for we are far removed from the main currents of life, because we do not earn a living from trade, nor do we engage in business. We spend our days shut away in our *rooms*, while the little money that we earn is brought to us at home. So we are like a prisoner in a dungeon, who has no means of distinguishing between day and night or summer and winter. If we, ourselves, feel no contradiction between the precepts of the *Šulḥan ʿArukh* and our mode of life—that is because our life is different from that of the normal man. Indeed, the life we lead would not conflict with even the severest Rabbinical stringencies nor with the entire range of their prescriptions and ordinances; just as formerly there was no conflict between them and the life of Israel in general, for the simple reason that *the whole people* lived then as we live now, imprisoned in their houses. Tyrannical governments oppressed them, forbidding them entry into the schools, and the pursuit of science and knowledge, and forbidding them to till the earth. They were not allowed to reside in a *city* or to enter human society. Our forefathers were always prisoners of the government, and for that reason never felt the demands of life. Therefore they quietly bore the heavy yoke which the Rabbis placed on their necks. But today the position is very different, now that our fellow Israelites have gained freedom and have woken up to life. Since the powers are treating Jews kindly, and breathing the spirit of life into their nostrils, we can now see very clearly that the ways of the *Šulḥan ʿArukh* are too restricted. Today both *Religion* and *Life* cry out for reform in no uncertain terms. And if we do not go out now to the aid of *Religion* and *Life*, disaster will overtake us. . . .[135]

Even the minor writers occasionally demonstrate their ability to write in forceful style where the subject-matter is sufficiently serious. Again, it is of interest to contrast the comparatively clear and straightforward writing of such passages with the many lapses into a more pretentious, laboured and artificial style. It is as though the matter prevents the author from concentrating too deliberately upon the manner, with equal benefit to both. The following passage from the final chapter of Sheikewitz's *The Outcast* may serve by way of illustration:

Why has Israel remained in Exile for thousands of years? Why has the end not yet come for its distress? Are we to believe that in the course of so many years not a single opportunity could be found to depart from slavery to freedom? Are we to believe that in the course of so many years the sun of fortune has never once appeared to point the way to Zion? Yet we know that every man has his destined hour. The orthodox reply that Israel will not be redeemed until the Messiah comes riding on his donkey, while the *Maskilim* hold a variety of opinions. Some maintain that Israel is isolated among the nations, and no government will concern itself with finding a solution. Others reply that nature[136] has dispersed the Israelites among all peoples in order that the barbarians may learn wisdom and understanding from them. (How fortunate for you, Israel, to have merited so great a task!) Others, again, declare that the time of grace has not yet come, but in the end it will be well. For my own part, I believe that the reason lies in the continual differences of opinion which have always beset Israel. The believers failed to respond to any salvation by natural means which may have appeared, in the belief that without the Messiah and without the white donkey Judah would never be saved while the 'enlightened' assimilated to the nations, delighted with their temporary respite, without worrying about what would happen in the end of days. And so Israel has not been redeemed until this day; and it is difficult to imagine that it ever will be saved in the future if it continues along the path it has travelled up to now.

. . . I realise that my words will be in vain. I know that neither the orthodox nor the enlightened will read what I have written. The former regard the reading of love-stories as sinful, while the latter are ashamed or unable to read a story in Hebrew. And the few who do read what I have written will pay no heed to it, and as soon as they have finished the story, they will cast it aside and forget about it for ever. Nevertheless, I could not restrain myself. There is a spirit within man, which sometimes compels him to speak even to sticks and stones. . .[137]

This compulsive urge to give vent to fervently-held opinions on a variety of subjects is by no means confined to Sheikewitz. Smolenskin and Braudes, in particular, are prone to use their stories as vehicles for the determined expression of their personal views.[138] This tendency is partly responsible for the marked element of realism to be found in these novels—frequently side by side with wildly improbable adventure and romance. As illustrations of this realism, which tends to exert a sobering influence on the style, it may suffice, perhaps, to mention Smolenskin's shrewd political reflections[139] and his grave warning to young Jews not to become involved in the Polish revolts against Russia.[140] Equally urgent is his advice to young men to acquire the sort of knowledge which can help them to earn a dignified livelihood rather than waste their time and energy in the dilettante pursuit of a fragmentary 'enlightenment'.[141] His brutal description of the hardship facing any penniless young man who attempts to win a university education falls under a similar category.[142] In like manner, Smolenskin deliberately sets out to destroy any romantic illusions about emigration to America, presumably as a warning to his young readers not to embark too lightly on such an adventure.[143] In this respect his views stand in marked contrast to those expressed by Sirkis in *Esther*, where the encouragement of emigration to America seems to be one of the primary purposes of the story.[144] Between the publication of *Pride and Fall*, however, in 1874 and that of *Esther* in 1887, the plight of the Jews in eastern Europe had worsened considerably, and emigration had begun to reach vast proportions.

Braudes' *Religion and Life* is characterized by equally marked tendencies towards realism, even to the inclusion of extracts of an anonymous pamphlet circulated in Vilna during the battle for religious reform in the years 1869-71, and which constitutes the main theme of this story.[145] As in the case of Smolenskin, the element of realism exerts a generally beneficial effect on the author's style in terms of clarity and precision. On the other hand, however, the same motivation is responsible for the numerous footnotes which are scattered throughout many of these stories. While increasing the range of information to be derived from these tales, it can scarcely be claimed that they enhance their aesthetic qualities. The footnotes serve, however, to demonstrate the strength of the didactic element inherent in these novels.[146] It is of interest that although Abramowitz,

Braudes, Meinkin, Sheikewitz, Rabinowitz, and Weisbrem all favour the device, Smolenskin does not resort to the use of footnotes in his stories.

In compensation, however, Smolenskin's realism may be clearly discerned in the frequent reference to the *Milḥemeth Ḥayyim* or 'battle of life', which occurs in almost all his novels. Referring, for example, to the sheltered life of the heroine of *The Joy of the Godless*, the author writes: '. . . She had never known want, and understood nothing of the battle of life. . .'[147] The same idea occurs again in such phrases as: 'Why should I not gird up my strength to wage the battle of life like everybody else?'[148] or '. . . I am continually preparing my body for the battle, the battle of life'.[149] Or again '. . . For he wearied of the battle of life, seeing that the misfortunes were too great for him to bear. And he hastened to put an end to the dreadful battle, the battle of life.'[150] The same concept is also to be found on a number of occasions in both the novels by Braudes. In *The Two Extremes*, for example, one of the heroines declares that '. . . Love is only a weapon for us young women with which to fight the battle of life. . .'[151]

Realism, again, may be seen in the many references to literature as a force in life, and the role it is destined to play in society.[152] Of particular interest is Braudes' description of the effect of Russian literature on Shiphrah, one of the heroines of *The Two Extremes*,[153] and—even more importantly—on Samuel, the hero of *Religion and Life*. In the latter instance Samuel's introduction to Russian literature is deliberately engineered by the heroine of the story, Rachel:

Rachel had brought her books with her from Naharayim, the latest Russian books at that time, devoted to questions of *community life*, a word then in vogue, and of reform in social life in general; questions of 'bread and butter', work and money, the people and its rulers, men and women, and many similar matters. They also probed into the question of faith and religion in general, subjecting them to searching criticism in the light of natural science—'matter and force', Darwin's theory of the Origin of Species, the ideas of materialist philosophy, and the theories of determinism in nature and history. All such ideas were brought together and treated at length in these books, which aroused great interest among the youth. Rachel, too, had read and thought about them a lot, and had

become a devotee of their ideas. She always kept a selection of
them near at hand, and had brought them to Pelaguth with
her. Now she had handed them over for Samuel to read, to
learn his opinion of them. . . .

Rachel was very well aware that these books would give rise
to a conflict in Samuel's mind. She knew that he would then
turn his attention away from reforms for the Jewish people
in particular, and concern himself with the reform of religion
and society in general. She knew that in the wake of these new
ideas he would again be plunged into doubt, not merely about
the sanctity of the *later* codifiers, and their place in Judaism,
not merely on the score of the Rabbis and their writings, not
merely about religious stringencies and their heavy yoke—
Samuel would now be assailed by doubts concerning even the
sanctity of the *earlier* codifiers, the law-givers themselves, religion in general. . . . Rachel knew very well that a new creature
would be created, that Samuel would become something he
had never yet been and never wanted to be—a heretic in the
full sense, denying the validity of the whole *Torah* . . . She knew
that she was deliberately wresting from him his main aim;
she knew he could no longer seek a reform of Judaism, and
that he would abandon his hope of becoming a reforming
Rabbi. . . .[154]

Such passages are written in a refreshingly clear and straightforward style, largely unspoiled by unnecessary verbiage or too
much deliberate striving after effect.

A similar phenomenon may be observed in the considerable
quantity of philosophic speculation which these novels contain.
Once again, Smolenskin is the most prone to introduce reflections of a speculative nature into his writings,[155] very frequently
as a convenient method of opening a chapter. On occasion, these
reflections are written in a most pleasing manner, with frequent
recourse to striking similes.[156] Although very different in flavour
from the simple, narrative style, which Smolenskin often employs with considerable skill, particularly in the unfolding of individual episodes,[157] they frequently exert an equally attractive
appeal. To a much lesser degree passages of philosophic speculation and reflection also occur in the stories of Braudes, Rabinowitz and—in by far the most self-conscious form—Sirkis.[158]

On the other hand the novels contain an equal number of
passages written in a highly emotional and frequently quite

effective style. Love, happiness, excitement, anger, jealousy, sorrow, or the desire for revenge, as well as a passionate concern with intellectual, social or religious problems, are reflected in turn as the mood of the stories changes.[159] Although often melodramatic in flavour, the emotional outbursts are frequently colourful and sometimes portrayed with considerable skill. When, for example, the hero of *The Two Extremes* is severely reprimanded by his beloved for having concealed from her the fact of his being a married man, Jacob replies as follows:

> 'You are right, darling Lisa, when you say: "If I had only opened my heart to you". . . . . Alas, Lisa, Lisa! If only I could open my heart to you; if only God would grant me the power to open your pretty eyes so that you might see right into my heart; if only I had the means to tear aside the veil from my heart in order that you might see with your own eyes and comprehend what lies therein; if I could only teach you the *language of hearts*; if only one heart could talk directly to another, and one soul express its feelings to the other; if only we were speaking now not with our *mouth* and *tongue*, not with *lips of flesh*, but with our spirit, with our very breath of life, with the feelings of the soul and the emotions of the heart—then you would really know how guilty you are of rubbing salt into my wounded heart; then you would know that *I have no wife* . . . . Lisa! You have won my wounded heart completely, without leaving the smallest space for anyone but you; you have filled my whole soul, and no one else has the slightest claim on it. . . . You, and you alone are the centre of all my thoughts—then how can I lie by saying that I have another wife? How can I pretend that any other soul has a place in my heart? . . . I have no wife now! I have no wife, when I look upon your lovely face! I have no wife, for I belong to you, body and soul! . . . . Whether I have already sent her away, or already given her a bill of divorce, whether she has already received the document or not, it makes no difference to us: she is already gone, expelled from the recesses of my heart; she is a stranger to me, a stranger to my spirit and to my life, and to everything I have —then how could I have told you that I have a wife? How, even now, can I deceive you by telling you something that isn't true? . . .'[160]

Quite effective in its portrayal of the hero's agitation, the above passage also provides an illustration of the fondness for the rhetorical question encountered very frequently in Braudes' stories and the later novels of Smolenskin.[161] More emotional, still, are the numerous examples of genuine pathos to be found throughout the stories,[162] of which the most moving, perhaps, occur in the novels by Manassewitz and Sirkis describing the fatal illness and tragic death of a young child.[163]

The emotional quality of the writing is frequently bolstered by the resort to a wide variety of simile and metaphor, often of an imaginative kind. A frustrated desire, for example, is likened to 'a bird whose wings have been clipped, so that it no longer has the strength to raise itself, but wastes away and dies';[164] while a life without love is compared to a 'sunless rainy day, or a dark house without even the light of a candle'.[165] A marriage for money is likened to a sick child who will take its medicine only if bribed.[166] Again, the warriors of the Viennese stock-exchange are described in terms of Greek heroes,[167] while financial vicissitudes become '. . . messengers of the gods of gold and silver ascending and descending the ladder of chance'.[168] In order to describe the conflict between the orthodox and reform factions in *Religion and Life*, Braudes makes skilful use of metaphors and similes drawn from the battlefield,[169] while Smolenskin, on one occasion, turns to nature for an equally sustained metaphorical passage.[170] As is only to be expected, however, the greater part of the imagery is necessarily drawn from the Bible side by side with the Biblical phraseology in which it is largely expressed. As such, it all too often bears a familiar rather than an original stamp. In this respect too, the circumscribed literary value of these novels is all too obvious.

Much the same applies to the passages of natural description included in these stories. It is of interest that while the first Hebrew novelist, Abraham Mapu, makes extensive use of natural description in his novels,[171] skilfully drawing upon the whole range of suitable language to be derived from the Bible, and while Abramowitz in his later novels raised the art of natural description to a masterly level, the examples to be found in the novels under review are comparatively few in number and of inferior quality. With one modest exception,[172] the rare passages of natural description in Smolenskin's stories[173] are short, stereotyped and display clear traces of Mapu's influence.[174] On only one occasion does Smolenskin pay lip service to the idea of nature as a teacher so favoured by the exponents of Enlightenment,[175] while his real attitude may well be reflected in the remark of Josef, the hero of *The Wanderer in the Paths of Life*, that he is attracted not by nature but by society.[176]

Braudes, however, takes the question of natural description more seriously, and although the descriptive passages which he includes in his novels are fragmentary,[177] he is at pains to emphasize the impact nature exerts on enlightened minds, and its soothing effect upon the spirit.[178] The minor novelists occasionally introduce a passage of natural description, usually displaying the influence of Mapu, and apparently out of a sense of duty.[179] It is significant, for example, that Sheikewitz's heroine expresses the following sentiment after a short passage of natural description:

> I have followed the pattern laid down by writers who describe for their readers the beauties of nature on every occasion when they talk of love. But I must confess that I find no satisfaction or pleasure in such descriptions (which only conform to current fashion). I know that all the time when I was deeply in love, I paid no heed to the beauties of nature.[180]

Later in the story the heroine apologises again for having fallen into the trap of natural description for a second time![181]

The one important exception to the general neglect of natural description in these novels may be found in Abramowitz's *Fathers and Sons*.[182] In this respect, at least, it is possible to discern the first glimmerings of the great artist Abramowitz was destined to become. His natural descriptions excel all those of his contemporaries not only in their positive approach, especially as expressed by the author's determination to find the correct terminology, even at the expense of having to explain his terms in footnotes,[183] but also in his skilful weaving of the descriptive passages into his narrative so as to provide a subtle contrast to a neighbouring episode, or maintain dramatic tension.[184] Moreover, his descriptions of animals have no parallel in any of the novels under review,[185] and constitute an equally important contribution to the development of modern Hebrew literature.

Seeds of the future artist may also be discerned in the touches of humour scattered throughout Abramowitz's novel.[186] In this instance, *Fathers and Sons* is far from being an exception to the rule. On the contrary, Smolenskin's novels contain a far greater number of humorous touches and episodes which, although sometimes a little heavy-handed, rough, coarse or even cruel, add a

vivacious element to the stories.[187] One short example of Smolenskin's biting wit may serve by way of illustration:

On her left sat a maiden of about eighteen, whose expression declared that even though she was aware of the great
compliment paid to her that day in having been selected as a
bridesmaid, she would nevertheless have agreed wholeheart-
edly to relinquish that position to the bride, if only the latter
would relinquish her own position to her in exchange. . . . .[188]

Although Braudes' stories are virtually devoid of humour,
some of the other novelists display occasional humorous touches.
When, for example, the heroine of Manassewitz's *The Parents' Sin*
begs a gravedigger to bury her son for nothing, he replies: 'If
the rich men of our town came to know about it, they would all
fall dead at once in order to be buried for nothing. . . .'[189]

Rabinowitz, too, enlivens his story with occasional flashes of
humour reminiscent of Abramowitz,[190] while Sirkis' *Esther* includes one or two examples of rough humour.[191] More successful still are the humorous episodes which occur in Weisbrem's
novels, where they are portrayed with an amusing ingenuity.[192]

Far more effective than the humour, however, are the numerous passages of satire and irony to be found in many of these
novels, but particularly in those of Smolenskin. As one of the
principal weapons in the armoury of the social reformer, satire
is employed time and again to ridicule the various abuses in society which the author makes the target for his shafts, whether
the evil consists in the use of power and wealth for nefarious purposes, such as bribery, corruption, or the perversion of justice on
the one hand, or human foibles, patterns of behaviour, mental
attitudes and base superstitions on the other.[193] Particularly
virulent are Smolenskin's satirical attacks on German Jews who endeavour to hide their Jewishness by pretending to be German,[194]
and on the behaviour of the degenerate Polish nobility especially
during the revolt against Russia.[195] Satire and irony are also employed with considerable skill by Braudes, Abramowitz and Weisbrem.[196] The latter, for example, portrays the defection of the
members of a small community from a fast, which they have imposed upon themselves because the inclement weather has made
it impossible to recite the blessing over the new moon, as follows:

How surprised and mortified the Rabbi was at the time of
the *Minḥah* prayer to find that there were not ten men who

had fasted until evening; for of the people who had roared like lions for the imposition of a fast on all the congregation, not more than six or seven had actually fasted, while the rest had gorged themselves. Peretz Reikin had forgotten it was a fast-day, and had sipped a glass of spirits, which had put a sparkle into his eyes and so appealed to him that he had eaten and drunk as usual. Reuben the wine-merchant had been invited to a friend's house to take part in a circumcision ceremony, and had put the fast aside in order to fulfil another command-ment, namely that of partaking in the accompanying feast—a commandment which he had always fulfilled most scrupu-lously throughout his life. Reb Phinehas, who was old and ail-ing, had been afraid to fast lest it finish him off, and had been granted a dispensation by the Rabbi. Of all the people who had gathered the previous evening in the Rabbi's house, and whom we have enumerated by name, the only ones to fast were Reb Solomon who had sat from morning to night in the *Béth ha-Midhraš*, studying God's *Torah*, and Azriel the money-lender and Zebulun the *Melammedh*. The local wits mocked them by saying that if Azriel had been offered a meal without payment, he would have eaten his fill without taking any notice of his vow; while they slandered Zebulun the *Melammedh* by suggesting that his wife, who supported him in his old age with what she earned in the market, had given him nothing to eat after hearing of his vow; but that when she left the house Zebulun had stolen two or three pastries and some cheese. . . .[197]

Although less forceful than Smolenskin's satire, Weisbrem's gentle style is not without its own appeal.

One further aspect of style is worthy of note. All these novels are bedevilled, in greater measure or in less, by a literary device which once exercised an hypnotic influence on the European novel and was imported wholesale into Hebrew literature, name-ly the ingenuous intrusion of the author in the first person, with or without an accompanying exhortation to the reader. Some form of: 'And now, dear reader, let us transport you. . .' is as common in the Hebrew novel during the period under review as in contemporary European literature. Although the device is subject to so wide a variety of form and treatment that a com-plete study might well be devoted to its analysis, in the present instance a numerical assessment, aimed solely at indicating the comparative frequency of its use, must suffice. As three novels,

Smolenskin's *The Wanderer in the Paths of Life*, Manassewitz's *The Parents' Sin* and Sheikewitz's *The Outcast*, are written in the first person, they have been excluded from the present analysis. In the other novels, the number of occasions when the author resorts to the first person are given as follows:[198]

In Smolenskin's *The Joy of the Godless* the device is used in 20 passages;[199] in *A Donkey's Burial* in 17 passages;[200] in *Pride and Fall* in 10 passages;[201] in *The Reward of the Righteous* in 33 passages;[202] in *The Inheritance* in 53 passages;[203] Abramowitz's *Fathers and Sons* contains 17 such passages.[204] In Braudes' *Religion and Life* the device occurs in 69 passages,[205] and in *The Two Extremes* in 18 passages.[206] Of the remaining novelists, Leinwand uses the device in 24 passages;[207] Meinkin resorts to it in 11 passages,[208] Zobeizensky in the same number,[209] Rabinowitz in 9 passages[210] and Sirkis in 24.[211] Weisbrem, however, uses the device more sparingly, introducing it into *Between the Times* in only 4 passages and into the longer *18 Coins* in 10 passages.[212]

In like manner the authors address their readers directly as follows:

In *The Wanderer in the Paths of Life*, Smolenskin exhorts the reader in 22 passages[213]—although in long sections of the story he dispenses with the device; in *The Joy of the Godless* in 15 passages;[214] in *A Donkey's Burial* in 13 passages;[215] in *Pride and Fall* in only 2 passages;[216] in *The Reward of the Righteous* in 10 passages[217] and in *The Inheritance* in 8 passages, mainly in the second part of the novel.[218] Abramowitz is a little more prone to the device, which appears in 16 passages in *Fathers and Sons*.[219] Braudes' *Religion and Life* is permeated with exhortations to the reader to the number of 45 passages.[220] By comparison, *The Two Extremes* contains only a modest number, 13 in all.[221] Of the minor novelists, Leinwand's story contains no less than 34 such passages,[222] while Meinkin's novel introduces the device in 10 passages.[223] Zobeizensky addresses his readers directly in 8 passages,[224] and Manassewitz in only 3.[225] Sheikewitz, however, returns enthusiastically to the device, which appears in 37 passages in his novel.[226] Rabinowitz, on the other hand, confines his exhortations to 5 such passages, mainly towards the end of his novel.[227] Sirkis, however, is more prone to the device, which he uses in 20 passages.[228] Weisbrem's novels are commendably free from the device. The reader is addressed 4 times in *18 Coins*, and in *Between the Times* on only 2 occasions.[229]

Of all the novelists under review only Smolenskin and Braudes were able to overcome to any significant degree the severe stylistic difficulties arising from the serious linguistic limitations which hinder their stories at every turn. Braudes deserves considerable praise for his valiant effort to create a relatively consistent, if somewhat heavy style—a fact which, in the circumstances, pays tribute to his highly developed artistic sense. By a skilful use of the resources at his disposal, a natural sense of economy and restraint, and by keeping the more flamboyant tendencies in contemporary Hebrew prose under a measure of control, Braudes succeeded in imposing a certain homogeneity on the various styles dictated by the different types of subject-matter which his novels contain.

Smolenskin, on the other hand, although unable to give the various elements in his stories any sort of stylistic unity, managed to create a number of more lively and readable styles to cater for the various ingredients of his novels. Although the overall impression conveyed by his writing is something of a patchwork, the individual segments, whether consisting of social criticism, philosophical reflection, sober realism, wild adventure or simple narrative, remain relatively faithful to themselves. The story of the villainous Manasseh, for example, in *The Wanderer in the Paths of Life*, is unfolded in its own characteristic style, to which the author reverts whenever the character is reintroduced. Although his prose is insufficiently tight or economical of phrase, Smolenskin's writings are enlivened by his verve, his flashes of enthusiasm, his sudden changes of mood and his highly developed sense of drama. His style is most successful in the swinging narrative, in the passages devoted to fierce social criticism and in the harsh realism which exerts a compelling fascination upon the reader. It is weakest in the love themes, which are stilted and unnatural, and in the dialogue, for the reasons outlined in the previous chapter.

Among the other novelists, Abramowitz, Sheikewitz, Rabinowitz and Weisbrem displayed some feeling for style and language, and their stories are enlivened with many pleasing passages. None of them, however, succeeded in any real measure in overcoming the linguistic difficulties sufficiently to create a consistent or convincing style. Even Abramowitz's *Fathers and Sons* gives only occasional glimpses of the splendid artistry which was to grace the writer's later novels. Indeed, in the absence of any great intrinsic merit, the most interesting aspect of the story is the service it renders as a yardstick for measuring the author's subsequent literary development. The remaining novels by Leinwand, Meinkin, Zobeizensky, Manassewitz and Sirkis have little to recommend them as far as style is concerned. They are written in so deliberately a flowery manner, and are so replete with *Meliṣah*, that at times they read almost like parodies of the elevated and highly self-conscious style so favoured by the *Maskilim*, at which the authors are obviously aiming. Stylistically, however, as in so many other respects, they serve at least to illustrate the achievements of the more gifted novelists of the period, and provide a valuable standard of comparison for gauging the formidable problems which faced the Hebrew writer during the second half of the nineteenth century.

PART II

FIVE

Social Reform

The literary inadequacy which mars the Hebrew novels during the period under review inevitably relegates them to a secondary status. As works of art they exhibit a number of glaring deficiencies, so that their interest depends in part upon the light they shed on the development of modern Hebrew literature. In that respect, however, they provide both valuable and eloquent testimony to the many pitfalls lining the path of the Hebrew writer in the second half of the nineteenth century, and to the serious problems to be overcome before the Hebrew novel could reach aesthetic maturity. In the absence of any such evaluation, it would be impossible to appreciate the achievements of later Hebrew novelists in an adequate manner.

The Hebrew novel of this period, however, possesses another dimension of equal validity. The aesthetic failings are partly compensated by the variety of information relative to contemporary Jewish life in eastern Europe which these novels afford in abundance. This aspect is all the more significant because the patterns of Jewish social life in eastern Europe have meanwhile been so violently disrupted that little if anything remains of the close-knit, virtually self-contained society reflected in these novels. The information to be gleaned, therefore, is no less germane to the social history than to the literary history of the period, and offers many an illuminating glimpse into a world that has vanished utterly, but one which formerly represented the most important and creative centre in Jewish life.

The efficacy of the Hebrew novels under review in this respect is determined by their social character. Largely written with the object of reform, the social element contained in these novels is

I

sometimes primary and sometimes incidental, but rarely is it entirely lacking. Although broadly embracing the ideas of the Hebrew movement of Enlightenment or *Haskalah*, the writers display considerable differences of opinion with respect to the objects of their reforming zeal and the methods for the achievement of their aims. So complex were the internal and external pressures at work in Jewish society, that the earnest desire of the novelists to alleviate Jewish distress and stem the tide of disintegration is frequently more convincing than the validity of the measures they advocate. Indeed, far from displaying any unified plan, the ideas propagated vary considerably not only from one author to the next, but on occasion even within different novels by the same author.

Underlying all these novels, however, including even the more extravagant and fantastic, there may be discerned a serious awareness of the many evils besetting Jewish life, which reflects a strong social conscience and a deep conviction of the specific role of literature as a remedial factor in society.[1] Almost without exception they advocate the unfettered pursuit of secular learning in addition to the traditional religious education, and the acquisition of such knowledge as will help alleviate the all-pervading poverty, and enable Jews to earn a dignified and reasonably assured livelihood. In consequence such mental attitudes as obscurantism, religious fanaticism, prejudice and superstition become the special targets of their attack, for in a mental climate compounded of such elements they recognized the principal obstacle to the spread of their own views.

As the most effective weapon in the armoury at their disposal, the novelists constantly resorted to irony and satire in order to ridicule many of the prevailing Jewish attitudes and patterns of behaviour. Not infrequently their satire becomes so biting and virulent that their portraits of society degenerate into crude caricature and on occasion present a distorted and sometimes very misleading picture. The information relative to social conditions yielded by these novels, therefore, falls into two broad categories, and may be utilized accordingly. Whenever the polemic, didactic or satirical note is dominant, the information should be viewed with caution, and often serves rather to illuminate the mental outlook and emotional attitude of the authors themselves, and their estimate of the evils prevailing in society, than to provide a trustworthy guide for the evaluation of the phenomena as such. On the other hand, wherever the descriptive element is dominant, and the details furnished may be regarded as incidental rather than deliberate, far more reliance may be placed on the information obtainable, certainly as far as the external features of society are concerned.

The profoundly serious attitude of many of the novelists is stated explicitly on a number of occasions both in the prefaces to the novels and in the body of the novels themselves, where the narrative is completely interrupted for the purpose. The most illuminating confession of intent may be found in the prefaces to R. A. Braudes' *Religion and Life*. In his preface to the first part of this novel Braudes declares that his book depicts the religious struggle which raged between the exponents of *Haskalah* and the Rabbis in Lithuania between the years 1869-71, that he has chosen the form of a novel because of its suitability for the chronicling of such events, and that future historians will find all the necessary facts within the framework of his story.

The author's preface to the third part of his novel is even more explicit. Here Braudes states emphatically that the purpose of literature should not be the amusement of the leisured classes in the form of tales of wonder far removed from reality, but rather a deepening of the reader's awareness of life and its problems. Life itself, Braudes declares, is a gigantic novel. But whereas it is always difficult to see our own actions in correct perspective, it is comparatively easy to evaluate the behaviour of other people, and this applies particularly to the characters of a novel, whose actions may be judged dispassionately. Partly for that reason, and partly to sugar a somewhat distasteful pill he has chosen to couch his chronicle in novel form. He warns the reader, however, that while he has allowed the plot to dominate the foreground of the first two parts of the novel, in the third part he intends to lay the main emphasis on his depiction of the actual course of the struggle, so that frequent diversions from the story are to be expected. But why, he asks, should his readers evince so great an interest in mere figments of the imagination, when the events and ideas outlined are of such greater importance? It is, perhaps, a little strange that Braudes, who of all the writers under review displays the most developed artistic sense, should have underestimated its importance so dramatically.

The final chapter of the first part of Smolenskin's *The Wanderer*

in the Paths of Life illustrates the author's social purpose with
equal clarity. Smolenskin, too, declares that he has deliberately
chosen not to write a romance or adventure story, but to depict
the actual circumstances of the Jewish people through the eyes
of his hero in his wanderings from town to town. In the belief
that this portrait of prevailing conditions, no matter how distasteful, may serve to instruct future generations, he emphasises that
he is concerned not with fiction but with fact. Similarly, the eighteenth chapter of the second part of the novel is entirely devoted
to an outline of the social conditions of the Jews in Russia, resulting in a complete interruption to the narrative, while the twenty-
fourth chapter opens with a restatement of the author's
purpose, which is to reveal the full horror of the Jewish situation during the reign of Czar Nicholas I.

The minor writers, too, occasionally declare a deliberate social
purpose. Sarah F. Meinkin, for example, prefaces her romantic
novel *The Love of the Righteous* with the remark that the story constitutes an attack on the evils besetting Enlightenment that arise
from stupidity and fanaticism. In similar vein, Manassewitz declares, in a foreword to his novel, *The Parents' Sin*, that as long as
certain stupid conventions prevail, and as long as the older generation continues to demand blind obedience from the younger,
the Hebrew reader will derive advantage from stories such as
his! It is of interest that even the poorest of these novels—cheap
and badly written cloak-and-dagger romances though they be
—usually display from time to time some disturbingly serious
social element, although normally without specifying any deliberate purpose. Certainly the overall impression arising from
these novels is that the Hebrew writer possessed so strong a social
conscience that a story written simply for its own sake was
scarcely conceivable.[2]

It is not surprising therefore that these works abound with
passages relative to the social background of Jewish life in all its
facets. In spite of the wide range covered by the novels, whose
plots embrace conditions in villages, small towns and great cities
in a variety of countries, the overall picture that emerges is one
of crushing and ever-increasing poverty.[3] Time and again the
novelists describe the wretched struggle to wrest the meagrest
of livelihoods from a hostile environment; and although they are
only too ready to castigate the darker sides of Jewish life, towards

the victims of extreme poverty they usually display considerable sympathy:

Is it their fault that their condition is so abject? Do they not seek work and some means of livelihood? Can you blame the pedlar tramping with his pack from one village to the next, or the shopkeeper lingering in his shop till midnight with the cold freezing the very marrow in his bones, or the craftsman who toils night and day to earn a few coppers, all of them working themselves to death to earn a crust of bread for themselves and their children. . . .?[4]

On occasion, however, the sympathy may be tinged with irritation, where the author feels that the particular cause of poverty is mere ineptitude. Such, for example, is the case in Smolenskin's *The Joy of the Godless*, where the author is sketching the life of his hero who was born in a town

. . . the majority of whose Jewish inhabitants were wretchedly poor, as are most of the Jews of that whole province. They have to hire themselves into the service of wastrels, while the tax-farmers grind them into the dust—and worst of all the mayor, who flays the very skin off their bones when the taxes are due, to extort ground rents for their houses, which might as well be their graves. His father was born of wealthy parents, but grew up in poverty, for the family fortunes suddenly collapsed—an everyday occurrence in these parts where the merchants are ignorant of mathematics and have no understanding of business. They trade as long as they have wares at home, and when their stocks are all used up, their money disappears, and with it all their dignity and status. . . .[5]

Even in such conditions of universal poverty, the economic plight of Lithuanian Jewry is portrayed as extreme.[6] But there, at least, the misery is partly relieved by the piety and devotion to study exhibited by a substantial proportion of the Jewish population:

That land is steeped in poverty, and the Jews who dwell there are paupers. The earth gives little yield, business is poor and foreign trade unknown. There are no important rivers and no large factories. So the Jews who depend on petty trade know only poverty and want. Rye bread with sorrow and water with tears is all their portion, while white bread and meat grace their table on Sabbath only. But take heed of those paupers, for the *Torah* goes forth from them! The Lithuanian

Jews have the greatest regard for study. There is not a town whose house of learning is not crammed with scholars young and old, nor is there a man, no matter how poor, who will not contribute to their maintenance, sharing his crust with them and hurrying to their aid. For they are all scrupulously pious, cherishing the traditions of their fathers and clinging to their old customs with unyielding tenacity.[7]

In striking contrast Smolenskin portrays the demoralization which extreme poverty can engender, in his description of a troupe of professional beggars who live by wandering in covered wagons through the villages of the Pale of Settlement in search of alms. In order to arouse pity and so increase their begging prospects, they pretend all sorts of physical infirmities, carefully disguising themselves as cripples:

> When I opened my eyes I saw the entire troupe sitting on the ground, all of them industriously at work. One was tracing out wounds on the skin of his leg; a second was putting a patch over a perfectly good eye; a third was tying his arm in a sling, while a fourth, who had been running about like a colt only a moment previously, was supporting himself on a crutch. All the others followed suit.[8]

The portrait of general poverty, however, for all its wretchedness, pales before the description of the deliberately inflicted poverty suffered by the Jews of Roumania. The bitter plight of the many unfortunates robbed of their livelihood by the decree forbidding Jews to serve as innkeepers is portrayed by Smolenskin in a particularly harrowing scene:

> Some thirty men, women and young children stood barefooted and dressed in rags, with hands and feet so filthy as to be scarcely recognizable, and with hair and beards clogged with the mud and dust of a long journey; their thin, haggard faces were seemingly plastered with filth, for the dust and sand had mixed with their sweat to form a sort of plaster. The eyes of each of them reflected sorrow and dreadful suffering. Once Zerahiah had finally recognized them to be Jews, he determined to enquire of what terrible crime they were guilty, that they were dragged about like captured wild beasts. He was informed that they were all guilty of the same crime, namely that they were all innkeepers, but had failed to leave their inns quickly enough after the decree. For that reason they had been taken captive and plundered. They had not been allowed to

take any of their possessions with them, and had been forced to abandon all their property. They had already been driven along on foot for thirty days, without knowing where they were being taken . . . .[9]

The dire poverty and oppression suffered by the Jewish communities in Poland,[10] Galicia[11] and Austria[12] as well as those of Lithuania and the Russian Pale of Settlement are portrayed in vivid detail. Very frequently the picture is painted with deliberate intent and the colouring tinged with the author's righteous indignation. But sometimes an incidental remark such as '. . . . and she gave her five kopeks, a sum great enough to support my family and myself for a whole day',[13] or 'This answer revealed to Simon the real poverty of a man who could regard ten roubles as an immense fortune',[14] can be equally illuminating.

That the almost universal poverty was aggravated by ferocious taxation is a constant source of complaint, particularly in the novels of Smolenskin and Braudes.

'What can we do? The taxes increase from day to day, and weigh three times more heavily upon us than upon the rest of the population, nor have we any redress. We have no alternative but to starve to death, together with our wives and children . . .'[15] Oppressive as were the taxes on wine, candles, flour and salt[16] —all essential commodities for Jewish ritual purposes—the tax on meat was particularly burdensome.[17] The tax-farmers, whose duty it was to ensure a supply of meat in return for the privilege,[18] are constantly described as rapacious, pandering to the rich, and cheating the poor of their rightful share:

> 'What's the use of asking?' one of the women shouted. 'Don't you know that we are not supposed to eat meat even on the Sabbath?. . . Only the rich are allowed to gorge themselves with meat like animals, while we are grudged even the very bread in our mouths—yet you still ask for meat! . . . They make sure that all the rich wives have a good supply, but for us even the weekly ration of bones, which we pay for through the nose, is not forthcoming today. Why should we be silent? Isn't our money as good as anybody's?'[19]

The general economic hardship is illustrated, too, by the many descriptions of unwholesome living conditions, and the general squalor resulting from such stringent poverty. Smolenskin, for example, gives the following portrait of a teacher's hovel as seen through the eyes of the young Josef in *The Wanderer in the Paths of Life*:

> ... When I say a house, let not the reader imagine that I saw a stone house. On the contrary! From outside it appeared as small as a dog's kennel, built of thin, rotting planks. The straw which served as a thatched-roof reached the ground, and was useless as a shelter against anything but the lightest rain, because all the goats from roundabout had set upon it, and so eaten their fill, that half of it had been consumed. Inside, the house consisted of a simple room, murky and filled with soot, with cobwebs filling all four corners from floor to ceiling. The floor was simply a layer of clay. ... A large stove occupied fully a quarter of the room. Between the stove and the right-hand wall stood a bed made up ready, and on the other side—a smaller bed strewn with hay and straw, but without any covering. Facing the stove there was a large unpolished table, whose surface was pitted with marks engraved by the teacher, during his instruction, with the little knife that was never out of his hand. ...[20]

Admittedly, the Hebrew teacher occupied a lowly status in society, but according to Manassewitz even the Rabbi frequently fared little better: 'The Rabbi's house—like all the Rabbis' houses in the small towns—was small and humble, and built of thin wooden planks.'[21]

On a number of occasions, however, the novelists portray living conditions which are inferior still, and fall within the category of the worst type of slum. Braudes, for example, describes how thirty poor families live in hovels leading off a single courtyard,[22] while Rabinowitz gives the following picture of the quarters occupied by poor Jews in a large Russian city, designated by the letter N:[23]

> 'Be careful you don't fall here,' the guide said as they reached a dark, narrow corridor reeking of slime. ...
> 'Why doesn't anyone clean it up?'
> 'Who would bother to clean it? The people who live here are the poorest of the poor, who have grown up all their lives in filth without ever knowing good, clean air; and out of sheer laziness they even pour their slops into the corridor. The landlord is only interested in getting the rent for his rotten, mouldy rooms, not keeping them clean. .....'
> With that they came to another room, with two windows opening on to a cesspool. All round the walls were beds,

blackened with filth and grime, and laid with mattresses, through whose torn covers the rotting straw could be seen....[24]

More harrowing still is Smolenskin's description of slum conditions in 'Ašcdoth, the pseudonym frequently employed to designate Odessa. The following passage recounts the squalor from which one of his heroes has been rescued:

> ...He remembered the loathsome cellar in the street known as 'The Sheepfold', whose stench was renowned throughout the city, and infested the neighbouring streets in all directions. Yet the occupants of Samuel the Lithuanian's house were grateful for such a treasure, both those who lived in the topmost attic, where vermin swarmed over the floor and over the walls which remained as damp in the summer as in winter, and those whose rooms lay in the bowels of the earth without any sort of flooring, and which even the sunlight was too terrified to approach, so that whenever the occupants conceived the odd desire for light, they were compelled to burn candles even at noon. These rooms were not separated by walls and doors. Only the pillars which supported the roof of the cellar marked the boundaries dividing one family from the next. Some twenty families resided in this dungeon; nor were all of them mere beggars, for the number included tradesmen and petty dealers. Many of the families even hired out a portion of their rooms to a lodger to ease the burden of the rent which was considerable. The landlord was always putting pressure on them to pay in advance, for fear lest it might not be forthcoming on the date due, and a week's rent be lost.[25]

No wonder then that the novelists, in their role of social reformers, were anxious to reveal the worst features of poverty in all their stark horror. For the same reason they are at pains to show how cleanliness and tidiness can do much to alleviate the general misery, and that poverty need not necessarily be accompanied by squalor. Many of the characters depicted in laudatory spirit temper their poverty with a neat orderliness that invests them with a quiet dignity. The following is Rabinowitz's description of a cobbler's house:

> The house they entered contained three rooms, separated by thin partitions. The first room served as a combined kitchen and workshop, with a polished stove standing in the corner. Opposite the stove near the window there was a low square table, on which lay the cobbler's tools. The second room con-

tained a red table and red chairs, with bowls of flowers at both windows, a mirror on the wall, and everything neat and tidy. The floor was scrubbed and polished to perfection, and the lamp hanging from the ceiling cast a glow over the whole room.[26]

The same virtues are applauded even among the more prosperous sections of the community, where—contrary, perhaps to expectation—they are still described as rare:

The house was not large, but then neither was the family that occupied it, consisting only of Shemaiah, his wife, son and daughter, one servant and a serving girl. But its aspect was pleasing both outside and in. There were no expensive ornaments, but everything was perfectly clean and tidy—an unusual sight in all that town. Nor did the house resound with the noise of merriment and song, but peace and quiet reigned.[27].

Such passages illustrate one of the aims frequently encountered in these novels, namely the raising of the general standards of behaviour and taste towards a more refined and graceful mode of life.

The prevailing poverty is naturally closely linked with the occupations pursued by the Jews of eastern Europe and the novels shed considerable light in this respect. Most interesting, perhaps, are Smolenskin's bitter attacks upon the theories propounded by the *Maskilim* of western Europe to the effect that the Jews of eastern Europe should alleviate their miserable economic plight by forsaking petty trade and business, and educating themselves instead to become craftsmen and farmers. Admittedly, great numbers of Jews did scrape the meagrest of livelihoods from peddling, petty trading and peripheral occupations, as will be seen; while manual work commanded scant esteem and was frequently regarded with contempt. Smolenskin, however, argues vehemently that the Jews in Russia, and Roumania in particular, do, in fact, pursue all manual trades and crafts, and include large numbers of tailors, cobblers, agricultural workers, woodcutters, charcoal-burners, porters and carters—to mention but a few of many. Far from too many Jews being employed in such occupations, the root trouble arises from the large number of Jews so occupied in proportion to the amount of work available.[28]

As a result—such occupations offer only the most slender of livelihoods and those who pursue them border on starvation, no matter how strenuously they work.

Reference has already been made to the livelihood to be gained from tax farming,[29] which was frequently of a very lucrative order, in spite of the ill-feeling it was liable to arouse. Other profitable occupations described in the novels include, for example, the carrying out of government contracts, such as building roads[30] or barracks;[31] lending money on interest—frequently in conjunction with other business activities;[32] merchandising of various kinds, particularly in agricultural and kindred products such as grain,[33] spirits,[34] sacks,[35] wool[36] and cattle skins.[37] Indeed, one of the characters is described in the following terms:'. . . His whole appearance and characteristics were reminiscent of the dealers in sheep and cattle to be found in the little towns of our land, Galicia.'[38] A further occupation, which could prove very lucrative, was that of agent, factor or middleman to a rich landowner or merchant. Such a position often lent itself to bribery and corruption, and is duly censured in the novels.[39]

The vast majority of occupations, however, were very far from being lucrative. Many Jews, particularly in the Russian Pale of Settlement, earned a meagre livelihood as innkeepers. 'My mother', says the heroine of Manassewitz's *The Parents' Sin*, 'managed the inn, which was the only one in our town.'[40] This occupation suffered a severe blow, however, when the railway was introduced into Russia.[41] But a single regular method of earning a livelihood, no matter how meagre, was comparatively desirable. The most serious disadvantage suffered by large numbers of Jews was the absence of a fixed permanent occupation, which necessitated the pursuit of a variety of peripheral or seasonal activities, all equally unsatisfactory:

> Since Zebulun had ceased to be a *Melammedh*,[42] he had resorted to selling books and ritual fringes throughout the year, which he supplemented with the sale of ritual wine for Passover, and citrons for the Feast of Tabernacles. But in spite of all his business activities he could not have supported his household in even the most frugal manner, were it not for his wife who diligently bought all kinds of foodstuffs that were brought to the market, and resold them to the rich. . . .[43]

A similar diversity of occupation is described by Rabinowitz in his novel *At the Crossroads*:

His livelihood was derived from a variety of sources. In summer he was in charge of the brick-kiln belonging to the mayor, for which efforts he received ten roubles and a measure of flour per month. During the rainy season he worked for a woodcutter, and made little windows for the peasants, while in winter he extracted oil from hemp.[44]

No less unpleasant than the lack of any stable occupation was the illegality of method, which many Jews were compelled to employ in order to earn a livelihood. Such were the disabilities suffered by Jews in Czarist Russia[45] that they were frequently forced to live not by the law but against it. In a very moving passage Smolenskin reveals the plight of a Jewish community, whose main economic activities—the manufacture of synthetic tea, and trading in beaver skins—have been forbidden by the government, and who are reluctantly compelled to adopt the expedient of forging government seals in order to earn a livelihood.[46] Elsewhere he refers to wine-smuggling as a Jewish occupation,[47] while Weisbrem, too, writes of Jews who live by smuggling goods across the frontier.[48]

Of all occupations,[49] the wretched one of the *Melammedh* is described most vividly. In spite of traditional Jewish veneration for learning, the teaching of children was regarded as the lowliest of professions, and frequently adopted only after all other economic avenues had been tried without success. As a result, the teacher was often a bitterly frustrated man who vented his spleen upon his pupils, in the shape of vicious beatings, which occasionally resulted in permanent injury.[50] Even for the youngest children, lessons were normally continued from dawn until dusk, and were usually conducted in the teacher's home in a room which frequently served also as the living room.[51] Remuneration was as wretched as the status and condemned the teacher to a life of direst penury. Not infrequently a *Melammedh* was compelled to find employment as a private tutor in another town, and was able to visit his wife and family only at the festivals.[52] The situation is portrayed by one of Smolenskin's characters who is made to remark:

I have chosen the most despised profession of all—that of a teacher to Jewish boys! A profession which begins in shame and degradation, and ends in sickness and want. How often have I witnessed the fate of those whose substance and whose very flesh it has consumed, and who have perished at last in poverty and unnoticed.[53]

A similar impression is conveyed by Braudes on numerous occasions:

Now that we have learned that the man is a *Melammedh* it is enough to visualise his appearance, mode of life, financial position, thoughts and habits. That one small word contains the magic power to tell us explicitly all we need to know. At the mere sound of the name *Melammedh* (especially in a little town in Lithuania), we conjure up the picture of a poor, downtrodden man with a drooping head, crushed beneath the burden of a constant struggle barely to support his family, a man ignorant of all the ways of the world.[54]

Braudes, however, is equally careful to differentiate between the wretched status of the *Melammedh* and the much more fortunate position of the Jewish teacher in a government school, who commanded a relatively good salary and dignified status, whose livelihood was regular and assured and, most importantly, not dependent on the whims of his pupils' parents, their frequent inability to pay his fee, or their displeasure should he voice any unorthodox view.[55] Smolenskin, on the other hand, is far less impressed by many of the so-called 'modern' teachers, and castigates them on a number of occasions in no uncertain terms.[56]

An equally ubiquitous figure, a step above the *Melammedh* in status,[57] was the marriage-broker or *Šadhekhan*, who performed an indispensable function in a society, where marriages were arranged by the parents without normally consulting the wishes of their children. The qualities necessary for success in such a profession were clearly very different from those required by a *Melammedh*. The latter needed no nore than a smattering of traditional learning in order to practise, whereas the former was largely dependent on his personality, which had to include the ability to secure the attention of his intended client, whether by flattery, *bonhomie* or sheer impudence. In consequence, the marriage-brokers—certainly as depicted in these novels[58]—were often colourful characters with considerable charm. They were usually male, but the function might be performed by women, although more likely in an amateur capacity.[59] The fact however, that the *Šadhekhan* depended for his livelihood on the percentage of the dowry[60] which was his due, naturally led to serious abuses of the system by its practitioners, which the novels frequently point out.[61]

The 'Golden Rules' of match-making, from the point of view of the *Šadhekhan*, are pithily summarised as follows:

It is a firm rule to match a rich old man with a poor virgin of good family (and which family isn't good in their parlance?). It is also a firm rule that the daughter of a *Naghidh*[62] with some physical infirmity—blind in one eye, flat-nosed, lame or hunch-backed—be wedded to a poor but clever student, who will be described as an outstanding genius. But under no circumstances may one arrange a match between two well-connected families, or two families of scholars. Learning must remain the prerogative of the poor, who must also reserve the sole right to be of good family. For what profit could a match-maker derive from arranging such marriages? When a match is arranged between two poor families, the brokerage will not exceed five roubles, in spite of the immense effort required. For that reason they rigidly insist that a young man of good family be wedded to a rich girl of humble family; and a young scholar be mated with the daughter of an unlettered *Naghidh*. In that way 'the wolf may be sated and yet the lamb remain whole'.[63]

Another professional to derive a livelihood from marriages was the jester or *Badhehan*, whose duty it was to amuse the guests, sometimes with the aid of doggerel verses composed for the occasion, and who might also give a moral discourse before the ceremony. This institution is subjected to devastating satire in Sheikewitz's novel, *The Outcast*.[64] Weddings, too, provided a livelihood of sorts for Jewish musicians,[65] who otherwise enjoyed few opportunities to earn money from the practice of their art. One additional professional class, who earned a livelihood in Lithuania and Poland from betrothals, weddings and similar celebrations in the houses of the rich, comprised the male cooks, who were known as *Servers*.[66]

Among the miscellaneous occupations mentioned in the novels, Braudes describes a man who earns a livelihood by making boot polish

...whose manufacture and sale was then not so widespread as latterly. He had learned the trade from a German who had been passing through his home town—and he had fashioned a little wooden box which he filled with the polish he made, and carried on his shoulder for sale. This box assured him an entry into the houses of the town's most prominent citizens (for the common run of people who wore shoes or sandals, were not accustomed to use such a product)....[67]

Pawnbrokers,[68] itinerant booksellers,[69] quack doctors[70] and lawyers,[71] clerks and book-keepers[72] all play a part in these stories. Particularly poignant are the remarks by Sheikewitz—no doubt based on bitter experience—on the hard lot of the Hebrew author,[73] and Weisbrem's description of a man, part of whose occupation consists of addressing letters, in Roman characters, written by women whose husbands have been forced to emigrate.[74] Equally sad are the references to the miserable lives of young girls employed as servants[75] or seamstresses[76] compelled to work long hours for the barest pittance. On the other hand, a more flamboyant note may be detected in the reference to Jewish card-sharps,[77] and in the shape of a character who is employed to play cards, billiards and dice with the guests at a night club, and win their money whether by fair means or foul! It must be admitted, however, that the latter scene carries with it scant conviction.[78]

The relationship between the individual and the community on the one hand and the state on the other are treated on numerous occasions. Of particular significance are the frequent and vehement attacks launched against the leaders of the local Jewish communities and the alleged abuses of their powers. Such portions of the novels as deal with the conditions of Jewish life during the repression of Czar Nicholas I (1825-55)[79] constantly denounce the evils perpetrated by the community leaders in carrying out the Czar's decrees, especially in the conscription of young men for military service.[80] But quite apart from the terrifying power bestowed upon them by that authority, they are portrayed as abusing their privilege of granting or withholding a necessary travel permit;[81] as inflicting corporal punishment— in one case on a woman unjustly accused of adultery who is beaten so ferociously that finally she confesses to the crime;[82] as handing over victims to the civil authorities for imprisonment,[83] and as using the stocks for punishment of minor religious infringements.[84] They are also accused of misappropriating monies entrusted to them for safekeeping, often the property of widows and orphans.[85]

The power of the community to punish erring individuals is portrayed by Smolenskin in the form of a public humiliation inflicted upon a young man and woman who are alleged to have been seen kissing. The culprits are led with great pomp and circumstance to the courtyard of the principal synagogue as follows:

> . . . His whole body was clad in a sack smeared with tar and covered with feathers, while a tall hat similarly treated was placed upon his head. His hands were tied with a rope, whose ends were firmly grasped by the two beadles . . . and he was dragged along followed by hundreds of boys shouting 'Sinner! Sinner!' For in honour of the occasion all the teachers had released the children from school so that they might witness the punishment and learn a lesson from it . . . And as they shouted, they threw dust and stones at the culprit. The girl was treated in like fashion. She, too, was dressed in similar finery—her 'bridal robes' as the citizens had it. Once in the synagogue courtyard the older boys spread a piece of matting over four staves and placed the sinners under the 'wedding canopy', shouting and singing at the top of their voices, and pronouncing a mock wedding service, while all the spectators shouted 'Bad luck to you! Bad luck to you!'[86]

In contrast, the novels provide equal illustration of the positive sides of Jewish communal life, particularly in the provision of education[87] and in the charitable work of many individuals and societies.[88] With respect to the latter, Smolenskin gives a most interesting account of the work of a society for the care of orphans, including the details of its organization:

> Everyone who wishes to be considered a member of the society . . . pays an annual subscription of not less than a rouble, and provides a meal for one of the orphans once a week. Membership of the society has already reached two thousand. . . . Each orphan, or child whose father has died and whose mother cannot provide for him, is admitted to the orphanage at the age of two, cared for by a nurse until he is five, and then sent to school. The society maintains many schools just for orphans, and the officers of the society keep a close watch on the children to see they don't go off the rails, and on the teachers to ensure that they do their job properly. The children study at these schools until the age of thirteen, when they are examined, and the bright ones sent to continue their education at a *Yešibhah*,[89] while the others are apprenticed to a trade which will support them. The society pays for the apprentice-

ship until the lad has become a craftsman. After that it buys him the tools and equipment necessary to ply his trade, and continues to help him until he has married and set up house. In turn he must bind himself to teach his trade gratis to the society's orphans, and help the society to the best of his means . . . . But the most important service which the society does for the orphans is to protect them from being summoned for military service . . . .[90]

Relationships between the individual and the state are illustrated by the many references to various governmental decrees affecting the Jews, issued during the reign of Czar Nicholas I and subsequently. In the early years following the accession of the more liberally minded Alexander II in 1855, the position of the Jews improved considerably; but even then the censorship demanded extreme caution in the expression of any criticism of the government, however mild. Smolenskin, for example, in outlining the horrors perpetrated by Nicholas I against the Jews, confines himself to a mere statement of the various decrees, and ironically blames the Jews for bringing down such coals of fire upon their own heads![91]

The decree founding governmental elementary schools for Jewish children—bitterly resented by the orthodox, who not without reason feared they would encourage conversion to Christianity[92]—is mentioned on a number of occasions.[93] Smolenskin roundly condemns the subsequent wave of child-marriages contracted in a desperate attempt to evade the decree.[94] In similar vein, in order to circumvent the decree prescribing the teaching of Russian in the *Yeŝibhah* for one hour each day, resort was made sometimes to bribery, and sometimes to limiting this instruction to such boys as were considered too stupid to learn Talmud![95]

Further decrees concerning the Jews mentioned in the novels include those prohibiting the possession of a Talmud without the royal seal,[96] the teaching of Talmud,[97] and the gathering of a quorum of ten males for divine service in a private house.[98] Abramowitz also refers to the copies of the Bible with Mendelssohn's German commentary printed by the government for the use of Jewish pupils, although he alleges that the *Melammedhim* were extremely opposed to using them, and sold them wherever possible![99] Legislation affecting personal status may be discerned in the reference to the laws that Jews must adopt surnames,[100] abandon their traditional garb[101] and cut their side-locks short.[102]

K

More relevant to the internal cohesion of the community is the governmental prohibition of the use by the Rabbis of the *Ḥerem*, or excommunication.[103]

The alleviation of some of the worst features of the repression following the accession of Alexander II is naturally welcomed with enthusiasm. The new privileges afforded the Jews in the spheres of education, trade, and residence, under certain conditions, outside the Pale of Settlement, seemed to augur a happier future.[104] But above all, the rescinding of Nicholas's ferocious decrees governing military service was regarded as a veritable act of salvation.[105] The exponents of Enlightenment, in particular, viewed the government's educational measures with satisfaction. The government is portrayed as siding with them in their struggle against what they regarded as the stubborn obscurantism of their orthodox opponents;[106] while the Jewish teacher in government employ—in his green uniform with yellow buttons![107]—enjoyed a dignity of status, which stood out in striking contrast to the humiliating position of the *Melammedh*.[108] The general relaxation of repressive measures is poignantly illustrated, too, by a printer's footnote in Abramowitz's novel, *Fathers and Sons*, which reads: 'In its mercifulness, the government granted us permission in the year 1862 to establish printing presses in all areas of Jewish settlement.'[109]

The reforms of Alexander II, however, were only partial. Residence outside the Pale of Settlement required a special licence and was subject to stringent regulations. Such Jews as were forced by poverty to seek a livelihood in the cities of the interior without the necessary documents, walked in constant fear of arrest and deportation.[110] In such cases Jews were often content to live in appalling conditions of squalor, provided only that a blind eye was turned upon their mere existence:

> The government police do not scrutinise every Jewish lodger here so carefully as is the case with other houses which fall under the jurisdiction of different squads. You will find many people who have been living here for fifteen years, although their documents are stamped *en route*,[111] to show that they are not resident. . . .[112]

In the face of a legal system devised primarily for their oppression, the Jews of Russia were continually forced to resort to bribery in order to live against the law. The corruption and venality of the Russian administration afforded the sole means of avoiding the full weight of a crushing and intolerable burden. The method, however, was expensive, for the cupidity of an official had to be aroused sufficiently to outweigh his fear of the government inspector! The approach, moreover, might require such tact that it was often left in the hands of a professional agent.[113] The following example is typical of many in the novels:

I wasn't born yesterday, and I know how to handle these officials. Even his predecessor, who was prepared to whitewash any crime and even allow patent murderers to go scot free provided only that they gave him a sufficient bribe, even he would have thrown me out, if I had mentioned the word 'bribe' openly. An official in his high capacity doesn't accept bribes. But if I were forgetful enough to leave a jewelled ring on his table, for which I had paid a thousand roubles, or a fine carriage and pair in his courtyard, he never reminded me to collect whatever I had forgotten, but in turn forgot the affair in question just as I had forgotten the valuables, and released the prisoners whom I described as relatives or members of my household, promising to guarantee their future good behaviour. . . .[114]

The novels allege wide-spread bribery among the judiciary,[115] among teachers in governmental schools,[116] and particularly among gaolers.[117]

'There (in prison) he found many other Jews who, like himself, had been arrested during the night. But they were familiar with the prison ropes and bribed the gaoler, who provided them with a clean room all to themselves.'[118]

Although Smolenskin on occasion defends bribery as the only possible means by which Jews can exist at all,[119] he bitingly satirises its misuse for personal gain by underhand means.

'. . . For whoever heard of anyone winning a big claim for his house and property from an (insurance) company, without giving a share to anyone, not the police, nor the town-clerks, nor the fire-brigade, nor even the company's officials . . . .?'[120] Nevertheless, so widespread, apparently, was the practice of bribery that even 'good' characters can regard it as perfectly natural.[121] It is significant, however, that in the case of one government official, at least, an attempt to bribe proves fruitless, because the man concerned is described as 'a Jew-hater and a German, who despised bribery'.[122]

Of all the miseries inflicted by the Russian government on its Jewish subjects, however, the conscription for twenty-five years of military service imposed by Nicholas I was undoubtedly the most horrifying, and in consequence provides a constant theme in these novels. According to the decree,[123] ten Jews out of every hundred were to be conscripted each year by lot. But the Jews, who regarded such military service as a virtual death-sentence —as very frequently it was—resorted to every possible device to evade conscription: by flight, bribery, self-mutilation and even suicide. Braudes describes the first impact of the decree as fol- lows:

> Three months later the Czar's decree concerning conscrip- tion was announced. This was quite an unprecedented de- cree for Jews, and it is not surprising that people were terri- fied by it. They regarded it as a tragedy, fasted continually, and even resorted to evil practices to escape its burden. Many people deliberately cut off a finger, or blinded themselves in one eye, until a man who had been born with some physical imperfection was regarded with envy. Those who could not bring themselves to do such a thing fled the town, and went into hiding in the villages, or in caves or forests, until only old men, women and infants were left in the town.[124]

Young men disguised themselves as girls,[125] and officials were bribed to alter the details of age, place of birth and family cir- cumstances[126]—for an only child was normally exempt. An ex- ample is instanced of a man callously adopting an orphan solely for the purpose of sending him to military service in place of his own son.[127] But the most common device for evading the decree consisted in bribing the official registrars not to register the birth of a son.[128] So widespread did this practice become that finally the Czar decreed that any young man without a birth certificate could be conscribed, or might be sent as a substitute for a recruit. The law was applied even to mere children of eight or ten, who were first sent to 'pre-military training establishments' until they were eighteen, from which time their twenty-five years service began![129]

This cruel decree touched off a veritable reign of terror. Hence- forth no child was safe—certainly no child of poor parents.[130] The community-leaders, who were invested with authority to muster recruits,[131] and whose responsibility it was to see that the correct quota was supplied, hired kidnappers to press-gang young children on the streets, in the schools and from the *Yešibhah*.[132] Children were kidnapped in broad daylight and sold as substitutes for the sons of the rich,[133] so that the poor lived in a state of perpetual terror. It is little wonder that the community was rent by bitterness and hatreds, whose scars took more than a generation to heal.

The full horror of that terrible epoch is most vividly described by Smolenskin, who as a child had himself witnessed the kidnapping of his elder brother, a lad of about ten. Like so many of these 'Cantonists'—as they were called[134]—the boy was never seen again. Smolenskin never forgot the episode, and poured out all his pent-up bitterness in the following account:

Let the reader imagine twenty or thirty wagons full of human sheep passing before him. Each wagon contains about twenty boys with cruel fetters on their legs, overcrowded and sprawling on top of one another. One is crying bitterly—My leg!—Another is screaming—My arm's broken! A third wails desperately—My head, my head!—A fourth groans—I'm sick! Mother, mother come and help your only son! I'm dying. And a fifth—moans quietly. And the mothers? They accompany the procession with sweet delightful songs. Listen, reader, while I sing you some of those I heard with my own ears, when I witnessed such a scene on recruitment day, so that you will know that I speak the truth:

Oh! If only I were in my grave. That would be my only consolation!

If only I had had a miscarriage, and so not seen you in such a plight!

If only I had died before you were born! . . .

Curse the man that kidnapped you. Curse the father that sired you. Curse myself for bearing you for such misfortune. Is there no God in Heaven?! Why doesn't He rise and save us from these fiends? My son, my son! Give me back my son. He's my only one. Give him to me. I carried him, bore him. He's my son. I won't leave him to those blackguards. I'll save him if it kills me. . . .

Now try to imagine the emotions felt by those who have witnessed scenes like these, and heard the songs with their own ears, sung by the bereaved women in the very moment of their anguish.

. . . What's all the fuss about. Why do they weep? Are they any better than all the other women in the land? I don't

understand! Every country has its conscription, yet they don't
go shouting and screaming in the streets.

You might well ask, reader, if you have never travelled
abroad, nor seen the terrible things that went on there at
that time . . . . Have you heard where they were taken? Where
these poor lost sheep lay down? Do you know that these were
children of ten or twelve, who had never before set foot outside
the city wall, and that they were sent to the remotest exile—
to a land of dreadful piercing cold, whose inhabitants are like
wild men of the wilderness, merciless with one another, never
mind with strangers of another faith; a land where previously
no Jew had ever set foot, a land whose mere mention is enough
to terrify us in the safety of our homes? To such a land these
Jewish lads were sent, straight from the home, from school or
synagogue . . . . to pasture sheep and pigs, to suffer beatings
and cruel insults, to hear their ancestral name reviled all day,
to be forced to eat swine's flesh, which they have always regarded as an abomination; and at the end of every sorrow-
laden day, to rest from toil in a byre together with the cattle,
with the cold biting into their very bones. Yet I have still not
told you more than the merest fraction of all the terrible evils
that befell them, for I have no more strength to utter them;
and even while I write the tears flow from my eyes, and the
blood pounds in my temples. So tell me reader: What's all the
fuss about? Why does the whole people weep? Why has joy
vanished from their midst? Why do they cry even when cele-
brating? For even their festivities are overlaid with bitter tears
when they recall their cruel fate . . . . Even at weddings they
remember that they have borne sons in vain. For how can they
enjoy their offspring, when they are dragged away to another
land, never to return alive? . . .[135]

One novelist, alone, displays a totally different attitude to
military service, and even then only after the abrogation of the
twenty-five year term. With glowing patriotism Zobeizensky
outlines the advantages to be derived from service in the army,
particularly in the improvement of physique.[136] He is at pains to
point out that since military service now lasts no more than three
or four years, it should be welcomed rather than evaded.[137] It is
significant that when his hero is drafted into the army, he is not
worried at the thought of serving his country, but only for the
sake of his poor mother, who depends upon him for her support.[138]
His subsequent heroism and promotion, and the important
part played by Jewish soldiers in the Russo-Turkish war, are

clearly designed to bolster patriotic feelings.[139] In similar vein, the gallant commanding officer, appropriately named Samson, turns out to be a Jew, who had converted to Christianity only in order to qualify for a commission.[140] It is, perhaps, unfortunate that the novel's publication in 1881 should have coincided with the wave of government-sponsored pogroms that ravaged the Jewish communities of Russia!

One further aspect of social life reflected on numerous occasions within these novels is the position and status of the woman. The picture which emerges, however, is complicated partly by the traditional ambivalent attitude maintained in respect of woman, and partly because the novels portray a period of transition in Jewish society, during which the scope of activities available for the woman, and in consequence the male attitude adopted towards her, changed radically. Almost all the novelists display a serious concern for the dignity and status of womanhood; but the opinions expressed regarding her traditional role and the desirability of altering it vary considerably. Many features of the old position are roundly condemned; but so are a number of innovations. Conversely, while certain aspects of the trend towards the emancipation of women are welcomed, the disappearance of some of the older virtues is equally deplored.

To the general inferiority of women's status, however, the novels bear ample testimony. Traditionally denied the religious education provided for the male, they remained almost entirely ignorant of the only sort of knowledge which constituted the criterion of intellectual capacity. Ignorance was so easily equated with stupidity, that womenfolk were normally regarded as mentally inferior, and themselves subscribed to the prevailing opinion. Sheikewitz offers the following perceptive review of the position:

> In the towns of Lithuania most men held the common fallacy that a woman's opinion was to be despised, and that woman was simply not endowed with intellect. For that reason whatever a woman said was regarded by her husband as stupid. Not infrequently one would hear women making such statements as 'I'm only a dumb brute', or 'What can I say? I'm only a stupid, foolish woman' or 'What can a silly woman like me do?'—only because these women hear their clever husbands reviling them every day. They learn that they are mere

animals in human guise, and that they cannot properly see or understand what goes on in front of them. No sooner does a woman venture an opinion than her husband rebukes her: 'Be quiet, you stupid brute!' or 'How dare a silly, senseless woman interfere in matters that don't concern her'. Many a woman has struggled to show her husband that she isn't a dumb brute, but on the contrary a rational being. Finally, however, they yield, and admit that they are only ignorant women after all. In many towns the term 'woman' is used to denote stupidity and ignorance; and when a man wants to dub his neighbour ignorant and stupid, he will say: 'You're talking like a woman . . . .'[141]

The same contemptuous attitude is apparent in the question that the marriage broker, Nahum, puts to the heroine in *Fathers and Sons*: 'Can you actually *write*? . . . show me a sample of your writing, and I will find you a nice husband.'[142] The frivolity, light-mindedness and inability to see beyond external appearances, attributed to women, are reflected in the importance they attach to clothes, trinkets, and the outward trappings of life.[143]

The conservative attitude demands that young ladies remain modestly at home, in innocence of all the ways of the world. They are not to be schooled, nor even encouraged to frequent the society of other young ladies. To speak to a strange man or even look at him is quite unthinkable. Their one ambition should be marriage, ideally to a Rabbi, in the hope of bearing sons who will themselves turn out to be great scholars, and daughters who will marry Rabbis in their turn.[144] Yet these same women are expected after marriage not only to rear a family, but frequently to make a livelihood too, by opening a shop or keeping an inn, so that their husbands may be able to devote themselves to study.[145] Such women, at least, command a well-earned respect as a reward for their efforts, and personify the ideal type of womanhood.

As the only conceivable course for a young lady, the thought of marriage dominates her own mind, and that of her parents.[146] In seeking a prospective son-in-law, the father is primarily motivated by two factors—in the first place that the boy should be a gifted young student of the Talmud, and secondly that he should be a scion of a famous family.[147] Such factors as age, compatibility or even the bridegroom's ability to earn a livelihood play no part in the procedure. In consequence, many of the novelists stress the tragic results which may well ensue from such a union, and criticize the usual methods of selection in no uncertain terms.[148] The bride and bridegroom, themselves, are not consulted, nor are their wishes taken into consideration in the slightest. The following scene from Abramowitz's novel *Fathers and Sons* may serve by way of illustration:

Sarah—Ephraim exclaimed as he hurried into the room— Be quick now, Sarah, and prepare a celebration, for this evening we are going to fix the terms of the marriage contract. I have just this moment come from the bridegroom's parents. Everything has been properly arranged.—Your daughter doesn't think so,—Sarah replied bitterly.—What doesn't she think? —Ephraim asked, glancing alternately from his wife to his daughter.—Your daughter says, Sarah replied, that she doesn't want to be betrothed unless she can see the prospective bridegroom first. That's what Rachel says.—But who is asking her whether she wants to or not? Ephraim addressed his wife without looking at Rachel.—She can sit in her room while we fix the terms.—It's all very well to talk, Ephraim—Sarah replied, sighing and shaking her head. You ought to be ashamed of yourself! Ephraim hotly reproved his daughter, and spat straight in her face.—You ought to be ashamed to say any such thing. It's not nice for a young girl; it's wrong for a young girl to interfere in these matters! . . . You ought to be ashamed! . . . It's not nice; it's just not nice! . . . What concern have you got with the bridegroom? . . . Shame on you! . . . What are things coming to? . . . How times have changed! . . . What terrible times we live in! . . .[149]

It was quite usual for the young couple to meet for the first time only on their wedding day, and even the groom's father might have seen his prospective daughter-in-law only once prior to that date. For that purpose it was a common custom for an eligible young lady to serve wine to the marriage-broker and her prospective father-in-law, in order that they might have at least one glimpse of her.[150] One instance in which a father considers that he should consult his daughter's wishes with respect to marriage is portrayed as most unusual.[151]

Early marriage was accepted as normal,[152] and a young man still single beyond the age of eighteen was regarded with surprise and, indeed, suspicion.[153] Even Smolenskin, in spite of his severe criticism of so many facets of Jewish life, argues that early marriage is well suited to the prevailing Jewish conditions.[154] Very different, however, is the attitude to child-marriage, a practice which enjoyed much favour as an attempt to evade the decrees of Nicholas I.[155] The misguided nature of that institution, and the tragic and frequently disastrous results which ensued are pointed out with great bitterness on a number of occasions.[156]

In consequence of the system of early marriage and the preference shown to young Talmudic students, the question of the dowry assumed great significance, and its terms were committed to writing at the betrothal ceremony.[157] As the bridegroom was usually unable to provide for himself, let alone his wife and family, the dowry normally included an undertaking by the bride's father to provide board and lodgings for the young couple for a specified number of years. At the end of that period they would have to start fending for themselves, frequently with the additional burden of a young family. Meanwhile the full weight of maintenance was borne by the bride's father, often at the price of considerable self-sacrifice.[158] In addition, a sum in cash was normally expected, which would vary enormously according to the circumstances of the bride's parents.[159] This sum was often placed in the hands of a third party for safe-keeping, from the time of the betrothal until the wedding ceremony.[160] It would appear that even the bridegroom was sometimes expected to provide a dowry in order to marry a girl of good family.[161]

The forces of change, however, are very much in evidence within the novels, and from time to time it is possible to detect the scent of rebellion. The *modern* generation of young women is portrayed as learning to read and write, and as studying languages.[162] To the horror of the older generation, they begin to seek each other's company instead of remaining modestly at home. Worse, they dress their hair, eagerly follow the latest fashion, pad themselves on occasion, fore and aft, and even dare to revolt against the marriage-broker![163] Upon marriage, the Jewish woman cut her hair short, and covered her head with a kerchief in order to avoid attracting other men. But on occasion they are portrayed as substituting a wig for the kerchief—in the case of one woman in order, at least, to attract her own husband![164] While applauding the effect of certain innovations, the novelists also record the negative results.[165] Most noticeable, however, is the prominence they give to the concept of romantic love.

In their endeavour to foster the concept of western European

civilization as a necessary step along the road to Jewish emancipation, the exponents of Enlightenment laid great stress upon
the emotional aspect of personality. Life, they insisted, must be
felt as well as thought, if it was to be a rich and meaningful experience. Time and again they emphasize the importance of a
free expression of emotion; and it is partly for that reason that
love plays so prominent a role within these novels.[166] Their intention, however, is seriously handicapped by their own limited
experience—a necessary consequence of their own upbringing
and environment. Hence their approach to love is largely intellectual, and the force of their appeal is dulled in its passage
through a barrier of non-participation. But of the sincerity of
their intent there can be little doubt.

It is difficult to realize quite how revolutionary was the introduction of the concept of romantic love into the traditional
framework of Jewish life in eastern Europe.[167] Again and again
the novels reveal the fact that the idea of young Jews marrying
for love has hitherto been inconceivable.[168] Now, however,
the idea is propagated with full force. Passage after passage is
devoted to a panegyric of pure love, and its ability to exalt and
inspire, to quicken the senses and deepen the lover's awareness
of life, so that the whole gamut of emotion is revealed from
ecstasy to black despair.[169] There are long discussions—particularly in Smolenskin's *The Joy of the Godless*, where they arise out
of an analysis of Goethe's *Werther*—on the difference between
love and desire,[170] and also on the difference between love and
friendship.[171]

More interesting, still, are the passages written in the language of love, which employ a variety of expressions of endearment and affectionate phrases.[172] For the most part they are
hopelessly artificial and unconvincing, and are deservedly satirized by Rabinowitz in his novel, *At the Crossroads*, in particularly
caustic terms.[173] More daring still is the portrayal of a love scene,
even including a kiss.[174] On occasion a character will languish
out of love,[175] while another even hangs himself because his love
is rejected.[176] No wonder, therefore, that Rabinowitz staunchly
defends the traditional methods and values of Jewish marriage,
contrasting them with the debased concepts of romantic love,
and bitterly criticizing modern writers 'who pour scorn and contempt on all the customs of their fathers, and ridicule any marriage not preceded by love. . . .'[177] In lighter vein, Smolenskin

sketches a humorous and satirical picture of a landlady and her two daughters whose lives revolve entirely on the twin axes of love and marriage, and who interpret every remark and action, no matter how unlikely, in that twin light.[178]

From the examples outlined above, it will be evident that these novelists have concentrated in great measure on the darker aspects of Jewish life, and such features of society as they regard as harmful and debasing. Such an attitude is naturally conditioned by their social purpose, and for that reason it is as well to repeat the earlier warning that the picture which arises from their descriptions should be viewed with caution. It would be wrong however, to imagine that their attitude to Jewish life is entirely negative. On the contrary, these writers display a sincere and affectionate regard for Judaism, while their deep sympathy for their fellow Jews and passionate concern for their welfare is beyond all doubt. Although they never spare the rod, the chastisement is delivered with a loving hand; and for all the ferocity of their attack, the balm of consolation is usually forthcoming in equal measure. For their own generation they served the dual function of signpost and social conscience; for subsequent generations they shed much light on contemporary Jewish society in eastern Europe, and provide a series of fascinating glimpses into a vanished world.

SIX

The Cultural Dilemma

Of all the information relevant to the social conditions of Jewish life in eastern Europe during the nineteenth century, which these novels yield so liberally, no aspect is better served than the description of the cultural and educational background. Here, again, it is no mere accident that these stories furnish so many glimpses into Jewish cultural life. The period, which they portray, witnessed a process of radical transition from the old traditional, orthodox outlook to a new, largely secular, more liberal position, which is generally designated by the broad and somewhat loose term, *Haskalah*, or Enlightenment.[1] Whereas the old view demanded a rigid and unquestioning adherence to the patterns of a self-contained, unyielding Jewish life, hostile to all encroachment by, or contact with, the external, Gentile environment, the exponents of Enlightenment advocated Jewish participation in the main stream of European culture, and enthusiastically championed the cause of emancipation as a necessary step towards the ultimate fulfilment of that aim.

Of necessity, therefore, the *Maskilim* propounded significant changes in the syllabus and methodology of the Jewish educational system, with the aim of introducing secular subjects in addition to the study of the religious sources which hitherto comprised the entire curriculum. They favoured, moreover, radical changes in the methods of instruction as well as the establishment of proper schools to replace the private *Hedher*.[2] Ideally, they envisaged a harmonious balance of religious and secular education, such as would help to rear a generation of young Jews loyal to their ancestral traditions, yet equally at ease with the intellectual concepts of European civilization. Indeed, these ideal characteristics to be embodied in a new type of Jew are time and again personified in the heroes and heroines of the novels under review.

The staunch defenders of the old orthodoxy, for their part, bitterly opposed all such changes. In the proposed reforms to the educational system they suspected a direct threat to traditional Judaism, and feared that a generation reared on such ideas might well be prone to abandon the old ways entirely in a passionate pursuit of the new. The experience of German Jewry half a century earlier had shown only too clearly how the desire for emancipation encouraged a process first of assimilation and then of wholesale conversion to Christianity. Any breach, however slight, in the ancient bulwark guarding the distinctiveness of Jewish life was liable to allow a tide of change to sweep away the protective scaffolding of Judaism and endanger the entire edifice. Such fears prompted them to oppose the ideology of the exponents of Enlightenment with an adamant and, indeed, fanatical obstinacy, which frequently expressed itself in blank obscurantism. In the event, their premonitions proved to have been amply justified, although it is highly doubtful whether they ever understood the full complexity of the forces mounting steadily against the maintenance of their position. In the meanwhile, the exponents of Enlightenment readily took up the challenge, the radicalism of their demands increasing in direct proportion to the growing ferocity displayed by their opponents.

The period, therefore, was heir to a *Kulturkampf* in the fullest sense of the word. The battle was waged with great bitterness and with little regard for the niceties of conduct. The opponents of the new trends attempted not merely to outlaw what they regarded as rank heresy, but to isolate its protagonists from the community by ostracism and open condemnation. Wherever possible they applied economic as well as social sanctions, so that many an enthusiastic reformer was rapidly faced with the sobering and cogent argument of loss of livelihood. The exponents of Enlightenment, in return, intensified the propagation of their ideals by means of the spoken, and particularly the written, word, castigating the narrowness and obscurantism of their opponents, and exposing them to the lash of their satire and invective. Gradually the battle came to be regarded as a struggle between the generations—an open conflict between fathers and sons. Quite how clearly divided this particular struggle was in actual practice is difficult to estimate with any accuracy. That it served as a convenient literary convention, however, and as such provides a constant theme in contemporary Hebrew literature, is indisputable.[3] For the *Maskilim*, the picture of youthful idealism and unselfishness triumphing over senile ignorance and selfish bigotry exercised a fascinating appeal. The novels, indeed, abound with confrontations of this sort, frequently presented as integral elements in the plots, but arising no less often out of the many serious discussions which intersperse the stories, and which contain many of the particular author's most serious reflections.

The general attitude which the authors display towards the movement of *Haskalah* is, however, by no means clear cut. On the contrary, opinions vary considerably as to the efficacy of that movement. Although all the novelists, in greater measure or in less, are advocates of Enlightenment and social and educational reform, while some of them also champion minor religious reform, the novels contain many bitter attacks upon the negative features of *Haskalah*, while even the ideals of that movement are on occasion subjected to scathing criticism. *Haskalah*, in fact, clearly signified a number of different things to different men. In its original form, as developed by the disciples of Moses Mendelssohn and referred to in the novels as the 'Berlin-*Haskalah*',[4] it had advocated the widening of Jewish horizons to embrace western European culture, and the integration of the Jewish community into European society. To effect these ends, its supporters endeavoured to encourage the study of secular subjects, and particularly European languages. They were equally anxious to develop an aesthetic appreciation among Jews, and raise their level of taste, especially in the fields of language and literature— hence their emphasis on a correct knowledge of grammar, and the employment of a refined speech.[5] Again, they advocated the acquisition of professional skills and crafts in order to alleviate the Jewish economic situation.[6]

These measures continued to be regarded as the ideals of *Haskalah* for almost a century, even though the centre of activity soon shifted from Germany to eastern Europe, where the conditions of Jewish life were radically different. Little by little, even the basic theories of such *Haskalah* in terms of eastern European Jewry were called into question, while the unsatisfactory results of a widespread but frequently debased application of those theories rapidly became all too evident. A mere smattering of a foreign language, a little ill-digested secular knowledge coupled with the adoption of western European style clothing, was only too often regarded as the mark of an 'enlightened' man, and adequate reason for abandoning the traditional practices of Jewish orthodoxy. Even Abraham Mapu, for all his devotion to the ideals of *Haskalah*, had recognised some of the negative consequences of that movement, and embodied them in the person of Emil in his long social novel, *The Hypocrite*.[7] Many of his successors, Smolenskin and Rabinowitz in particular, bitterly attacked not merely the less desirable features of *Haskalah* as illustrated by the shallow and shiftless young men who were attracted by its outward trappings and superficial appeal, but even some of its basic assumptions. Yet they, too, were equally convinced of the importance of secular learning—provided only that it were serious and properly applied.

Within the novels, therefore, the movement of Enlightenment is both passionately defended and passionately attacked. Its ideals are presented sometimes naïvely, sometimes with considerable subtlety, and sometimes in terms of bitter scepticism. In evaluating the various aspects of the mental climate of Jewish life in eastern Europe which these novels portray, therefore, it is as well to remember—as was equally the case in their depiction of social conditions—that the views of the different authors are heavily weighted, and allowance must be made for consequent exaggeration. Here again, however, much of the relevant information may be derived from incidental rather than deliberate description, and is the more likely to be closer to life-size. With regard to certain features of the cultural scene, moreover, both the positive and negative features are sometimes outlined by the same author, so that it becomes easier to gain a more balanced impression.

The conflict between the old generation and the new, so frequently encountered in these novels,[8] is also subject to a variety of treatment. Sometimes it is the young generation that is blamed for rebelliousness, frivolity and indifference,[9] while elsewhere, and more frequently, the old generation is accused of obscurantism, intolerance and obstinacy. A typical example of the latter may be discerned in a scene from Braudes' novel *Religion and Life*, where the young hero Samuel, who has recently been introduced to *Haskalah*, is discovered reading a secular book by his father-in-law Issachar and the latter's eldest son, Isaac:

On entering the house they found Samuel sitting in his room reading a Russian book.

'That I should live to see this!' Issachar groaned bitterly.

Samuel, who had been engrossed in his book and had not noticed them come in, was so startled at suddenly hearing his father-in-law's voice that the book fell out of his hand. But he pulled himself together at once, and picked it up from the floor. 'Why are you shouting at me?' he calmly asked his father-in-law.

'How can you have the impertinence to ask, you heretic?' Issachar roared at the top of his voice. 'Was it for this that I brought you here without a shirt to your back, so that you could spend the whole day reading heresies? Was it for this that I clothed your nakedness and married my daughter to you, so that you could turn out to be a sinner and a scoundrel'?

'What's all this?' Leah and Deborah enquired simultaneously, brought to the room by Issachar's shouting.

'Just look what your son-in-law's up to. That will make you happy . . . .' Issachar replied angrily. 'Here I am at the age of fifty, and just when I was getting old and expected to see some joy from my offspring, the Lord has brought this on my house . . . . I had to bring a *heretic* here. . . .'

'A heteric? . . . .' Leah faltered after her husband.

A smile, albeit tinged with both sadness and anger, flickered across Samuel's lips, but Leah didn't notice.

'I don't want a her-tic. . . . What did you call him?'

'Heretic,' Issachar and his son quietly corrected her.

'I don't want such a scoundrel to be my son-in-law or my daughter's husband.'

'And I don't want to be a heretic's wife'—Deborah chimed in loudly.

'All right then.' Samuel replied fiercely, assuming a cold expression. 'In that case let's go to the Rabbi and get a divorce.'

'Did you hear that'? Leah shouted—'it's a mere nothing for him to go to the Rabbi and divorce my daughter, and they haven't been married a year. . . . .'

'What do you want me to do, then?'

'Listen, Samuel,' Isaac said in calmer tones. 'You're not such a fool as to believe you can get away with that when you know very well how much money has been spent on you . . . . The best thing for you to do is to apologise, beg their pardon,

L

and henceforward stop reading those filthy corrupting books. They will forgive you if you mend your ways.'

'I will not mend my ways, because I haven't done anything wrong,' Samuel answered equally calmly. 'We live down here on earth, not up in heaven, and so we ought to understand the people we live among, and their language. And so I have started to learn to understand the language of this country,[10] and I have begun to read books which explain how people in this land live. I intend to pursue them, and I won't budge one inch...'

'How dare you say such things in my presence,' Issachar roared, beside himself with rage. 'I can't believe my own ears. You won't give up your heresies? And do you think I shall allow you to carry out your evil designs in my house?'

The reader may easily imagine the insults and curses that followed.[11]

The conflict, however, is occasionally outlined in more subtle and less crudely antagonistic terms. Smolenskin, for example, attributes part of the malaise which affects so many of the younger generation to the fact that their fathers have so effectively insulated them from all contact with modern ideas during their formative years that when they are finally confronted by the new concepts, they are already too old to come to grips with them, or even to derive any real benefit from the attempt.[12] The consequences of allowing children a little secular education, on the other hand, can be equally unfortunate:

As long as the children are small most parents accede to their requests without too many scruples. Sometimes they even allow them to study things which the children demand merely out of envy of their companions. It frequently happens that fathers ask for their sons to be instructed in Talmud before they can even understand the Bible, only to humour a child's desire to emulate his friends. Similarly, many parents have allowed their sons and daughters to study secular subjects and languages, not from any conviction that such knowledge graces its possessor, and may even on occasion prove valuable, but solely because their sons and daughters have complained that the children of some relative or neighbour are learning them, and taunting them for not taking part. So the fathers consent, and allow them to learn what they want, under the impression that it is only a waste of money. In the course of years their children change completely. The fathers imagine that their children are the same as before; but the children start thinking: Are you really our fathers? Surely the ideas and habits of ten generations divide us. Once the children have become conscious of their own spirit, they want to live by it— and that's where the trouble breaks out. The parents have allowed their children to study, but not to live accordingly. What happens then? If the children cannot remain loyal to their parents, either they will rebel against them openly, or they will search out like-minded companions in secret and un- burden their hearts to them. Thus the children will become more and more estranged from their parents, by frequenting houses which their fathers despise or where they are not allowed to set foot; and there they will learn the ways of their new friends. But, since they have to act stealthily for fear of their parents' disapproval, they begin to regard their parents as a stumbling block and a cause of annoyance. Almost im- perceptibly they develop an antipathy towards their parents, submitting only because they are not strong enough to oppose them, but nursing the resentment inside them. This is the fate that befalls many of the youngsters in our communities here; and their parents are to blame, either for allowing them to study, or—once having so permitted them—for trying to cramp their spirit.[13]

In the same novel, *The Reward of the Righteous*, Smolenskin re- views the problem on a still more serious plane. The spiritual conflict facing the thinking young men of that generation is per- sonified in the figure of the young hero, Isaiah, who is torn be- tween two loyalties—his profound knowledge of and deep regard for the ancient traditional learning, which he is anxious to pur- sue in order to be of service to his fellow Jews, and his ardent desire to deepen his already considerable secular learning and thereby equip himself to earn a dignified livelihood. 'I am con- fronted by two generations, and I cannot make up my mind where my real place lies.'[14] Nor can he even decide to which of his two masters he should turn for advice:

I have two teachers, and I love them both. Each of them is sincere, yet each regards the teaching of the other as poisonous .... The advice they offer and their plans are as different from each other as north from south, or earth from heaven. But what of me? I cannot obey them both. One wants to put my legs in fetters, so that I could no more leave this place than a block of wood, while the other would have me sprout wings and soar away to heights, which I cannot nor do I wish to attain. Such is the fate of all who are not at peace with themselves. I feel like some creature, half beast half bird, which in time of conflict tears itself to pieces. That is my present fate, and who knows whether it will not always be so, unless I can summon up sufficient strength to take my stand upon the one side or the other.[15]

The conflict, however, finds its most serious expression in a long discussion in the same novel between Isaiah's teachers, Shemaiah and Gabriel, who respectively personify the finest qualities of the new ideal and the old.[16] To Shemaiah's contention that the young generation must be allowed to satisfy its thirst for knowledge, and that fathers have no right to expect their children to sacrifice all their wishes merely to please their parents, Gabriel replies that the preservation of the ancient tradition is far more important:

> ... We regard the inheritance from our fathers as the most precious thing in life. The *Torah*, bequeathed to us by our ancestors, is the elixir which quickens our spirit. Only by virtue of the *Torah* are we fully alive, and were we to allow ourselves to be robbed of it, we might just as well be dead. For then our life would perish and our memory would fade; for we would then be responsible for the deaths not merely of ourselves, but of hundreds of generations, of four thousand years of our existence. At one stroke we would erase ourselves from the pages of history, as though we had never been. And it is for that that we fight with our heart's blood and consider no sacrifice too dear. We are prepared to offer ourselves and our children completely on the altar of that love, the love of our ancestral faith, the *Torah* of our fathers and their memory . . . .[17]

The significance of this passage lies in the fact that it represents the conflict not as the normal reaction of a young generation against its parents, but as a breach in a long tradition. In other words, the problem is not of a general nature, recurring every generation and hence not unduly worrying, but constitutes a special and particular situation of fundamental significance. Such an interpretation is very different from the view propounded later in the same novel that the opposition shown by the older generation to the new ideas stems from a normal paternal desire to prevent a son from stumbling into wrong paths, and that the present 'enlightened' generation will react to their own children's deviations in similar fashion.[18] For Gabriel the spread of *Haskalah* to the detriment of the old loyalties can only spell disaster. He is quite unmoved by Shemaiah's contention that many of the greatest Jewish sages—Maimonides in particular—were also masters of secular learning. Without the iron discipline of traditional Jewish study and practice, Gabriel contends, the lad who plunges into the icy waters of modern knowledge will be inevitably lost to Judaism:

> For a youth whose mind is lacking in both piety and the knowledge of *Torah*, who has not yet trod the ancient ancestral path, who has not yet discovered the original fount of inspiration of his fathers, who has not yet seen the light which guided his ancestors for thousands of years when darkness covered the earth—for such a youth to be plunged into a strange and hostile well! When he stretches out his arms to swim, and dives to the bottom in search of pearls, he will either never emerge from the depths, or the currents will sweep him into the mighty ocean that swallows all that enter it. Do you know what mighty ocean that is? It is the ocean in which we have been an island for four thousand years, a refuge for every soul that seeks the light of life. It is the ocean which has swallowed whole peoples and countries like a monster—whole peoples, together with their gods, their wisdom and their very memory. Only this little island rises boldly from its midst, unharmed by the fury of the waves, blunting the monster's teeth and standing firm. And now our sons, our pride and joy, to whom the island naturally belongs, but whose fathers wish them to be as Maimonides, are being carried out into the mighty ocean to perish for ever in its depths.[19]

These passages serve to illustrate the nature of the struggle at its most significant level, and shed considerable light on the cultural conditions of eastern European Jewry. It would clearly be a distortion to present the opposition of the orthodox to the *Maskilim* naïvely as a conflict between obscurantism and enlightenment in terms of black and white. Again, it would be equally misleading to view the situation as a struggle between ignorance and knowledge. The exponents of Enlightenment were not confronted by an uneducated populace. Had that been the case, their task would have proved much more formidable. On the contrary, a large section of the Jewish population was highly literate with many great centres of scholarship.[20] Many of the staunchest advocates of orthodoxy were men of high intelligence and profound erudition; and although admittedly, such scholars comprised only a very small fraction of the population, it must be remembered that the number of *Maskilim* of comparable character was probably smaller still. The champions of orthodoxy, moreover, commanded the respect and allegiance of the vast majority of the Jews, who naturally tended to adopt the attitudes towards *Haskalah* promoted by their leaders.

The conflict must be considered, therefore, in terms of emphasis. For orthodox and *Maskilim* alike, education occupied a position of prime importance. For the orthodox, however, education was focussed on the study of religious texts, particularly the Talmud, and its main object was the preservation and understanding of traditional Judaism. Except for occupations of a religious character, such as the Rabbi, ritual slaughterer or cantor, it could have no professional significance; although in traditional circles it represented the only kind of learning which commanded respect. It was, moreover, confined almost exclusively to the male.[21] The *Maskilim*, on the other hand, were more concerned with the problem of introducing secular education into Jewish life, partly to foster an appreciation of European culture as a step towards emancipation, and partly to facilitate professional activity. They were equally concerned with the principles of pedagogy—in which respect the justice of their cause can scarcely be denied[22]—and they also advocated education for the female.[23]

Before further examination of the main traditional cultural institutions and the activities of the *Maskilim* reflected in these novels, one additional factor demands consideration. The steadfast devotion to traditional learning which characterized the conservative adherents to orthodox Jewry, known as *Mithnaggedhim*,[24] was very much less in evidence in Ḥasidic circles, where the joy of worship reigned supreme. In consequence, the cultural level of perhaps the majority of Ḥasidic communities was much inferior in the main to that obtaining amongst their orthodox opponents. Indeed, the ignorance and superstition attributed to the *Ḥasidhim* provide a constant target for the bitter satire of the *Maskilim*, who regarded that movement as one of the most serious obstacles to their plans for the widespread promotion of Enlightenment.[25] Their hostility to Ḥasidism, moreover, was sharpened further, because of the magnetic attraction which the sect exerted on many of the young men who, the *Maskilim* had hoped, could be won over to their own cause.[26] It is scarcely surprising, therefore, that the portrait of Ḥasidism reflected in these novels frequently descends to little more than the level of crude caricature.

Most indicative of the prevailing cultural conditions is the constantly repeated assertion that only a small percentage of Jews have any acquaintance with the language of the country in which they live![27] This single factor naturally served to reduce contacts between Jews and Gentiles to a minimum, and as such was regarded as an effective safeguard for the preservation of traditional Judaism. The orthodox, therefore, frowned upon the growing tendency for children to be taught the language of the state, while the teachers, themselves, were viewed with contempt.[28]

The *Maskilim*, however, endeavoured to foster such teaching by every means at their disposal, and fully supported the Russian government in its attempt to enforce the teaching of Russian by decree.[29] In consequence, the question is treated time and time again within the novels, while no opportunity of demonstrating the advantages accruing from such knowledge is neglected.[30]

The following snatch of conversation from *The Wanderer in the Paths of Life* may serve as an illuminating illustration of this aspect of Jewish life. The hero, Josef, after walking for six days and losing himself in a snowstorm at night, is finally offered the loan of a horse by a passing traveller. Only some time later, when they arrive at an inn, are they able to see one another, and the spectacle gives rise to mutual astonishment.

> ... When he saw me at the inn, he called out in amazement: 'Are you the man who was travelling with me?'
> 'Yes! Why are you so surprised?'
> 'A man like you, dressed in Ḥasidic clothes, speaking the language of the country fluently! That's something I never expected to see.'
> 'I know many Jews who speak it just as well'—I replied.
> 'I know that, too. I'm a Jew myself. But this is the first time I've seen a man dressed as a *Ḥasidh* speaking it.'—But I was even more surprised to hear that he was a Jew, for I had never expected to find a Jew dressed like a Gentile in these parts.

During the whole time I had spent with the *Mithnaggedhim*, I had never seen another instance of it. . . .[31]

The impression is confirmed by a subsequent remark that if Jews know two or three words of a language, they imagine that they speak it fluently.[32] In like manner, one of the heroes of Weisbrem's novel, *Between the Times*, endeavours to increase his prestige by talking a blood-curdling mixture of broken Polish and Russian.[33] Hence the exponents of Enlightenment enthusiastically welcomed the schools for Jewish children established by the Russian government,[34] while the orthodox bitterly resented the fact that Russian was taught in them at the expense of Hebrew.[35]

Among orthodox Jews, elementary education, which commenced in full rigour at the tender age of three or four, took place either in a private *Hedher*,[36] a public *Talmudh Torah*[37] or – in the case of wealthier parents – in the child's own home, under the guidance of a private *Melammedh*, who often resided with the family.[38] Parents regarded the education of their sons as a sacred duty, and no family, however poverty-stricken, would shirk the task. For the poorer children, who comprised the overwhelming majority, the physical conditions of schooling were quite dreadful. Lessons continued from morning till night, often in conditions of the utmost squalor.[39] When Josef, the hero of *The Wanderer in the Paths of Life*, is first brought to a *Hedher* he finds some ten children round the table in the *Melammedh's* house:

> . . . Some of them were studying Talmud and some the Bible, while one sat next to the teacher reading aloud in a sing-song voice, which blended with the notes produced by the teacher's wife, who was crooning by the side of her infant's cot. . . . But every now and again the teacher's voice drowned all the other noises, like a great clap of thunder blotting out the roar of surging waves.
>
> The sight of the teacher made me forget all the feelings of joy which I had experienced on seeing the house, for his appearance was terrifying. He was a short thin man, with sunken cheeks, and a long aquiline nose. His jet-black sidelocks dangled over his shoulders like ropes; but for all his years, his cheeks were covered only with sparse tufts of beard, for while deep in thought he would pluck the hairs out one by one— quite apart from those which his wife plucked out even without thinking! Clad in a skull-cap, as black and shiny as a greasy

cake, he wore a linen shirt—clearly not of the best material—unbuttoned at the neck, and revealing a chest covered with long, black hair. His linen trousers had once been white, but now they could boast a number of hues by virtue of the filth and dust that covered them, while his little son, who sometimes played on his knees, had contributed his share of stains by way of addition to his father's variegated splendour. . . .

When my uncle entered the house, the teacher jumped up and started running to and fro vainly searching for his shoes. But my uncle rescued him from his embarrassment by moving forward and saying: 'Here's a new pupil for you.' At that the teacher recovered his composure and resumed his seat. As we approached him, he stroked my cheek and asked: 'What have you learned, my son?' All the pupils gaped at me in envy. Never, since the long-forgotten day when they, too, had first arrived in school, had they heard such gentle words issuing from their teacher's mouth. . . .[40]

Josef, however, soon witnesses the kind of savage, senseless beating which formed the normal accompaniment to education, and which is so frequently portrayed, and condemned, within these novels.[41] The hard life of a poor schoolboy is poignantly described in Smolenskin's novel *The Inheritance*:

. . . I spent my childhood in tears and sorrow. Although I never had enough to eat at home, that did not upset me unduly, for I had never seen anyone living in luxury. My companions in the *Hedher*, like myself, were delighted to have a crust of bread; they too, had learned the meaning of sorrow in the home, and they, like me, were scarcely more than skin and bone. Our spirits were so depressed that even when we left the confines of the *Hedher*, where all day we had been used like prisoners of war, with shoulders hunched and heads bent forward, and where we straightened our backs only to receive the rod of chastisement—even then, when we hoped to find a few hours of rest and freedom and burst into song, the sound which escaped our lips was not the merry song of children unconscious of the toils and cares of life, but a noise of grief and lamentation; for we sang only to dispel our terror as we walked home in the pitch-black nights, splashing ourselves from head to foot as we waded through dirty, stagnant puddles, with our torn shoes disappearing every other minute into the mud, from which we had scarcely the strength to retrieve them; trembling with cold and fear lest we encounter evil spirits,[42] or peasants whom we dreaded even more. . . .[43]

The organization of the teaching year is outlined by Braudes for the benefit of such of his readers as have never been schooled in a *Ḥedher*, in order to explain the significance of the expression *Bên-ha-Zemannim* (between the terms):[44]

Do you still remember, dear reader, the expression *Bên-ha-Zemannim*? Can you still clearly recall the joy you experienced as a lad when that time came, and you pronounced the benediction: 'Blessed be He who has released me from the beatings of this *Melammedh*', even though you had no idea whether your next *Melammedh* might not beat you sevenfold and greatly increase your torments. . . If you have studied in a *Ḥedher*, you will surely remember all this. Even though you may well have forgotten everything else you learned there, you will certainly not have forgotten those beatings inflicted on you, and the hatred which you conceived for your teachers. So you will be fully aware of what the term *Bên ha-Zemannim* signifies. But for the benefit of those who have never studied in a *Ḥedher* and never had their faces smacked by their teachers in fierce anger, I will explain the expression.

Zeman (term) is the name which a Jew employs to denote a half-year, for a Jewish child is committed to the care of a *Melammedh* only for a half year at a time.[45] If the father is satisfied he will allow his son to remain for another term or two, but if the teacher has displeased the father, or the mother, or even the maid, the child will be sent to a different teacher after the end of term—for the teachers have an agreement not to take the food out of each other's mouth during term; nor will fathers readily consent to withdraw their sons during term, for the simple reason that a Jewish child, whose father has insisted on taking him away from a teacher before the end of term, will not be admitted to an other *Ḥedher*, and will be left without any instruction at all. Thus Jews will calculate the passage of time as follows: I studied for one term in this teacher's *Ḥedher*, two or three terms in someone else's *Ḥedher*, four or five terms in another, and so on. So the festivals of Passover and Tabernacles, in spring and autumn respectively, are known in Jewish parlance as *Bên ha-Zemannim*; namely: between the terms spent with one *Melammedh* and the next. That is the period for enlisting children for the *Ḥedher*. Teachers and pupils all roam the streets of the town, the former to muster their recruits and find out whether the number of the pupils will increase or diminish, and the latter to skip, jump and play, without fear of the teacher's rod. This is the time, too, when the teachers stir up strife, inciting fathers against other teachers, and *vice versa*, or exchange news, or ingratiate themselves with the mothers, for it is usually the mothers who decide the teacher's fate.[46]

The traditional system of education is severely criticised on numerous occasions within these novels, and no efforts are spared in pointing out its deleterious effect on the mind of the growing child. In outlining the boyhood of his hero, Samuel, Braudes describes how the child's questioning mind was continually finding difficulties in the Bible which embarrassed both his father and his teacher, for whom Holy Writ connoted unquestioning acceptance:

> This is the method of educating Jewish children, and these are the consequences: instead of allowing the child's feelings to unfold, deepening his capacities, encouraging his reasoning power to develop—instead of all these they tried to make the lad shut his eyes from earliest childhood, encouraged him to stifle his reason in spite of himself, to negate his feelings and to submit to a dreadful acceptance of whatever he heard from his teacher or anyone else, until his peace of mind was destroyed. His imagination got the better of him; the questions which arose in his mind of their own accord he regarded as evil spirits out to ensnare his soul, or the work of devils who planned to possess him once he had grown up—for such were the pronouncements of his teacher and even his father.[47]

To solve the problem, Samuel's father decides to send him to another teacher, so that he may begin the study of Talmud, which will allow him to give his questioning mind full vent:

> The Talmud and manner of its study impressed him deeply. It opened up a flood of difficulties and problems, thereby reawakening his spirit. At first he seemed to reel about as though intoxicated. He felt like a man on his first introduction to a great city with all its many streets and spacious squares which he has not yet learned to reconnoitre. But little by little Samuel became accustomed to the Talmud, and at the same time to the cries and gesticulations of the teacher (who in the course of his instruction would bellow at the top of his voice, stamp his feet, fling out his arms, and smack the boys' faces all indiscriminately—'teaching with every fibre of his body', as the townsfolk had it—all of which also made a deep impression on Samuel at first, adding astonishment to his mental bewilderment), and his mind began to probe and question this field

also. But whereas previously his father had rebuked and threatened him for raising difficulties now he heard his praises sung for doing exactly the same, and was delighted.[48]

Braudes proceeds to outline the effect on Samuel of studying such complex material, which a child can comprehend only superficially because the subject matter is so remote from his own limited experience. Such pedagogic insight provides a good example of the more restrained and consequently more convincing criticism advanced by the exponents of Enlightenment against the old system of education:

> The study of Talmud exerted two contradictory influences upon Samuel's tender and sensitive mind. On the one hand it gave his power of comprehension free rein, and on the other it bound it inextricably in fetters. He was given every freedom to make difficulties, to ask questions and sharpen his mind: but the tractates themselves remained only partially comprehensible. He was taught things, with whose subject matter he had only a theoretical and abstract acquaintance. In consequence, all the dialectic, all the obscurities and explanations, all the problems and solutions, and even all the difficulties which he invented for himself cannot be regarded as valid factors in the development of his mind and understanding. They served merely to confuse him, to afford him an entry into an uneasy world—a world of casuistry instead of knowledge, of bafflement in place of comprehension, a confusion of abstract notions without inner recognition or straight thinking.[49]

Nevertheless, the study of Talmud completely dominated traditional Jewish education, especially in the institution of higher education known as the *Yešibhah*, or *Bêth ha-Midhraš*. To study in a *Yešibhah* constituted the educational ambition of parent and child alike, and any intelligent lad would normally gravitate towards it.[50] Indeed, it is not unfair to state that the intellectual equipment of traditional Jewish life was forged almost exclusively upon the anvil of the *Yešibhah*. It was quite common for boys whose place of birth contained no *Yešibhah* to leave their homes even at the tender age of ten or eleven and sometimes travel great distances by foot in order to acquire education. The students, too, might easily move from one *Yešibhah* to another as the need arose, or if attracted by its fame and the renown of its teachers.

The institution was maintained by the local community, or

with the aid of funds collected from Jewish communities elsewhere, and instruction was given without charge. Because of the
prevailing poverty, most of the students were entirely without
means, and those not living at home slept in the *Yešibhah*, and depended for their meals on the local community[51] who performed
that service as an act of righteousness and charity.[52] In spite
of its defects,[53] therefore, the institution of the *Yešibhah* represents
an extraordinary example of the voluntary maintenance of a widespread system of higher education, available to every boy, no
matter how poor, with a modicum of intelligence and stamina.
Of its importance as a central prop in the framework of traditional Judaism there can be no doubt.

The novelists under review, Smolenskin and Braudes in particular, describe the *Yešibhah* and the part it plays in Jewish life on
numerous occasions, and dwell at length upon its strengths and
weaknesses, sometimes praising and criticising almost in the one
breath. Smolenskin, for example, while pointing out the intense
devotion of the Jewish people to the study of the *Torah*, which
supersedes all other intellectual ambitions, resorts to irony with
respect to the bright goal such study can attain in practical terms:

The *Torah*, the *Torah* alone constitutes the cornerstone of
all their thoughts, desires and ambitions. In that alone they
find honour and strength, peace and consolation. So all of
them, men and women, old and young alike diligently pursue
the word of God!
You must consider, reader, what is the driving force of a
Jewish boy? Is he interested in finding work that will provide
him with a livelihood? Does he feel the lofty urge to study in a
university and win renown there? Does he choose the battlefield in search of a hero's glory? Not at all! His sole desire is to
display his prowess in *Torah* and become well-versed in sacred
law. And should his ambitions actually be fulfilled, they will
seat him not on a royal throne, but on a dais as Rabbi and
mentor in Israel—a great and lofty honour!![54]

On the other hand, the extreme difficulty of obtaining office
as a Rabbi, and the more immediate practical possibilities which
motivate many of the students, are graphically outlined in the
following conversation between Josef, the hero of *The Wanderer
in the Paths of Life* and a fellow student who is initiating him into
the realities of life in the *Yešibhah*:

'But I want to study hard so that eventually I might know enough to be a Rabbi or teacher (in a *Yešibhah*).'[55]

'You—a Rabbi?'—he burst out laughing. 'You expect to become a teacher? Do you think it's easy to become a Rabbi? Even among great scholars only one in a hundred manages to obtain a Rabbinical office; and where can all those who have mastered the *Torah* find a sufficient number of towns for all of them to serve as Rabbis or teachers? Do you imagine that even all these most assiduous students[56] expect to become Rabbis or teachers, or are you teasing me?'

'But why do they study with such devotion if they do not expect to obtain a Rabbinical office?'

'They study so diligently to curry favour with the principal and the staff, so that they will be allotted good eating places,[57] and so that some rich man[58] will take them as a son-in-law . . .'[59]

The same novel contains a brief account of the system of instruction in the *Yešibhah*. It is, perhaps, a little curious that such a common term as *Šeʿur* should be explained as connoting the actual teaching period.[60] It would seem that Smolenskin envisaged readers unfamiliar with the *Yešibhah*, although in the Hebrew reading circles of his day such individuals must have been very rare. A similar phenomenon, however, may be found occasionally elsewhere within these novels.[61] The students were divided into a lower and more advanced class, membership of the latter being regarded as a highly coveted privilege.[62] For the greater part of the day the individual student studied alone:

At eight o'clock next morning after prayers and breakfast all the pupils sat down to study Talmud. The youth, who had befriended me, instead of chatting to me as on the previous day, proceeded to study with great concentration for some two hours, and I did likewise. After that we all sat in front of the teacher, who began to impart instruction. One of the students asked a question which the teacher answered. Seeing that questions were permissible I, too, raised a query, at which the teacher praised me openly, remarking that my question was valid. He then answered me with good grace. After sitting at the table in front of him for about an hour, we all returned to our respective places and spent approximately the same time revising and reflecting on what the teacher had said in order to understand his meaning properly. . . .[63]

Smolenskin also provides a lengthy and detailed description of the day to day life in a *Yešibhah*, and the activities and interests of the young students.[64] Many of the details, based on the author's personal experience, are so vivid that their authenticity can scarcely be held in serious doubt. The poverty of the scholars, and their manifold devices to eke out or increase their paltry resources, are of particular interest:

> . . . I returned to the *Yešibhah* and looked in vain for a text to study, for the numerous books were securely locked away in cupboards, to which only the principal and the overseer had access. The pupils were not given books, but purchased their own and brought them to the *Yešibhah* with them. Those who could not afford to buy a book paid their companions a few farthings to let them study with them.[65]

In similar vein Smolenskin describes how at nightfall the *Yešibhah* takes on the air of a market, with the students trading in food, buying and selling for coppers or on credit. Many of them persuade their patrons to give them bread and a few farthings instead of an evening meal, sometimes making do for supper with the bread, and sometimes even selling that in order to buy sweet pastries.[66] At the same time they gossip, fight, spin yarns, steal each other's food and quarrel over the position of the solitary candle on each table.[67] They are restrained only by the fear of the overseer and his vicious and indiscriminate beatings.[68] At night they sleep in the *Yešibhah* on benches and tables without any covering, and each in his own fixed place.[69] Every night, however, four boys are allotted to remain awake, one pair taking the first watch and the second the remainder of the night, so that the study of *Torah* may continue day and night without interruption.[70] Although this duty devolves upon each pupil once a month, some boys pay others a couple of coppers to do their turn. Josef at first finds great difficulty in sleeping because of the bugs and lice that swarm out of the cracks in the wooden benches and tables after dark![71]

With respect to the benches themselves, the following details are provided by Braudes as a prelude to a scene which describes a search in a *Yešibhah* for forbidden literature by obscurantist community officials:

> . . . The benches in these institutions have planks fixed to the sides reaching down to the floor, and lids on top. Every student who comes to study in a *Bêth ha-Midhraš* for the first

time takes possession of such a cupboard and secures it with a lock, and it remains at his disposal as long as he stays. Should one such locker prove too small to contain all his goods and necessaries he will also take the adjoining one and lock that too. This is the practice always followed by the 'poor students' ....[72]

As stated above,[73] such pupils as lived away from home depended for their meals on the charity of the local community. In the absence of such a system, the institution of the *Yešibhah* could never have served so wide a section of the population. As a voluntary contribution in the name of education, freely offered by a poverty-stricken community frequently at the cost of considerable self-sacrifice, it commands the warmest admiration. Of necessity, however, such a method engendered much suffering and humiliation for the pupils. Time and again the novelists deplore the unsatisfactory nature of the system of 'eating days', as it was called, and describe in great detail the unpleasant consequences which might ensue. Many of the pupils lived at starvation level and were forced to adopt all kinds of humiliating and undermining expedients; while the officials, whose recommendation could literally furnish or deny the meals for any particular student, enjoyed the kind of power which only too easily corrupts.[74] The following passage may serve by way of illustration:

These *Yešibhah* boys do not acquire their food and clothing in a normally dignified manner, but are forced to roam the town in search of sustenance. For such is the prevailing system. When a lad arrives in search of learning he must first ensure a supply of food. It makes no difference whether his intellectual capacity be suited for the study of *Torah* or not, he must go in search of 'days'! He trudges round from house to house with the plea: Would you be so kind as to provide a poor boy with a meal one day each week?

We already feed one *Yešibhah* boy here—they will tell him, and off he will go to another house. There they may let him eat his fill on that occasion, but can't provide him with a regular meal each week—and so on from one house to the next. Usually he will only knock on the doors of the poor, for the rich will only provide meals for such boys as bring a letter of recommendation from the principal or one of the managers of the *Yešibhah*. Eventually he will either fulfil his aim or he will become weary of the search and wait until some other pupil leaves the *Yešibhah* or finds a more attractive billet, thereby

הנדחת

ספור-אהבים נוסד על מעשה שהיה.

מאת

נחום מאיר שייקעװיטש

חלק ראשון

ווילנא

בשנת תרמ'ו לפ'ק

ПРЕСЛѢДУЕМАЯ

соч. Н. М. Шайкевича.

ВИЛЬНА.

Типографія Вдовы и братьевъ Роммъ.

Жмудскій переулокъ собст. домъ № 325/26 31.

1886.

Title-page of Sheikewitz's The Outcast
published in Vilna, 1886

allowing him to take his place in return for the promise of a few coppers. In this fashion the youngsters keep themselves alive, and it is not difficult to imagine that they entertain few scruples in resorting to flattery, slander or deceit if one of their companions is more favourably placed. . . . But still those who are sufficiently fortunate, even at the cost of such toil and humiliation, to find permanent meals for all seven days of the week are in a small minority. Some obtain meals for only six or five days each week, while many exist on four or even three. So that a lad who is provided with food every day of the week is regarded as the happiest in the land, and becomes the object of much envy. . . .[75]

The seamy side of life in a *Yešibhah* is described on a number of occasions,[76] but nowhere, perhaps, more effectively than in Braudes' novel, *Religion and Life*, where the author launches a fierce indictment not only of the physical plight of the poor students of Lithuania but also of the spiritual climate in which they live:

Hard and bitter is the fate of the poor students who dwell in these institutes of learning in Lithuania—hard indeed! Their lot is truly accursed, and the bread of affliction apportioned to them 'by days' as acts of charity is repugnant to any intelligent man. 'Whosoever is dependent upon another's table', the sages declare, 'lives in a darkened world.' But their mode of life is darker sevenfold. In shame they gnaw their humble crust, and eat their miserable fare in degradation. Nobody gives them a smile, speaks kindly to them or bothers to cheer them up. Even the servants and the charwomen despise them, while mistress and maid alike begrudge them their meagre repast. Everyone, in fact, looks down upon them. . . . And when they return to their abode, to the *Bêth ha-Midhraš*, there is no place to rest; nor can they sleep sweetly, lying on wooden benches without cushion, pillow or covering. They must make a pillow of their fists, and use their wretched clothes for covering. . . . Not that they are over-sensitive to poverty and want! Even at home they were scarcely spoiled! They have never been pampered from childhood; never in their lives have they eaten delicacies or worn fine clothing. Poverty has stalked their heels since the day of their birth, so that they have long come to terms with their own wretchedness. . . . . Their only consolation lies in their hope of better times when fortune will smile upon them; for soon the time will come when they will be in-

M

stalled with dignity as son-in-law to one of the townsfolk, and all their circumstances henceforward change for the better. . .

But their spiritual plight is harder and more bitter still, and in that respect they are very sensitive to the yoke they bear. Israel recognises no *saints*, and therefore the whole community consists of saints! There are no police or judges against religious profanation, and therefore every single individual regards himself as a policeman and a judge! . . . . There are no tyrants to enforce God's statutes and commandments, and so the whole people undertakes the task; all of them are zealots, officers and watchdogs to ensure that nobody infringes the code of the *Šulḥan he-ʿArukh*! . . .[77]

Admittedly, these watchdogs wield less authority over the merchants and solid householders, who stand in little awe of them. For when one says to the other 'Take the beam out of your eye', the second will answer 'Remove the mote from your own'; for each is aware of the other's shortcomings, and no one on earth is perfect. Consequently, not everyone is subjected to such careful scrutiny. Indeed the poor students alone are in the public view from one year's end to the other! They are the wretched victims of every zealot and tyrant. Since they live on the 'community purse', the entire population regards them as its stake in the 'world to come'. They represent a mere instrument for the merchants whose activities do not allow them to devote sufficient time to studying *Torah*, but who expect to derive some vicarious merit at their hands. So even the least of them lords it over the student. Any tailor or cobbler or anyone else, no matter how lowly or even corrupt, may set himself up as ruler, judge and watchdog over these poor students. . . . If an ordinary person sins, the townsfolk will gossip about it for a day or two—but then they will gloss it over, so that the sinner is quickly exculpated and his transgression quite forgotten. Very different is the case where the students of the *Bêth ha-Midhraš* are concerned. Even a 'mild transgression' which people usually brush aside; even a mere trifle which is normally overlooked; even the slightest matter which is not generally regarded as reprehensible—is gossiped about, chewed over and magnified out of all proportion by these 'authorities' until it is made to appear a major transgression. Woe to the student who is guilty of any such infringement! The whole populace will spit in his face; his 'eating days' will be taken away from him, and he will be expelled from the *Bêth ha-Midhraš* like a pestilence—nor will his sin ever be forgiven!

And so we see that the poor students of mediocre intellect,

or those who are carefully punctilious in public, or those who devote themselves entirely and sincerely to the study of God's *Torah*, or those who hypocritically assume an air of piety are not unduly affected by their humiliating status. Indeed, if they only eat at the tables of the well-to-do and fill their bellies, they are contented with their lot, and even laugh and joke. But those students who have become aware of Enlightenment, and begun to appreciate secular studies (in so far as their circumstances permit), but who are quite incapable of guile, are subjected to pressure in full ferocity. They are oppressed and tormented, and their spirit languishes in sorrow. . . .[78]

The positive sides of the *Yešibhah*, however, are also represented. Apart from the interest and companionship it afforded the growing Jewish boy,[79] the social function it performed in keeping lads from roaming wild in the streets,[80] and the continuity of Judaism which it safeguarded,[81] the important formative influences which it exerted on the minds of the better students are described by Smolenskin in glowing terms. In outlining the source of the intellectual and spiritual integrity which so distinguishes Simon, the hero of *The Joy of the Godless*, the author makes the following almost lyrical and certainly unequivocal pronouncement:

Who implanted within him such knowledge, and justice and sublimity of expression? Who kindled the divine spark in his soul to pursue truth with such devotion? Where else but in the *Yešibhah*? All praise and strength to you, O sacred institutions, the retreat and refuge of the remnant of Israel! It is from your gates that the chosen few still continue to emerge, who are destined to serve as a torch for their people and infuse the spirit of life into dry bones. Who knows but that the spirit of Israel might not have vanished completely from the face of the earth like a cloud; who knows but that the springs of truth might have been stopped up with the silt of nonsense and deceit brought by false teachers in such abundance and presented as jewels to all who would behold; who knows but that such falsehoods might have been implanted in the minds of the younger generation in the name of the Lord and his prophets? Except that this small and humble people aroused itself, and for all its lowliness succeeded in rescuing God's law from the midst of chaos—at a time when all justice, truth, righteousness and brotherly love had been rejected as the stumbling blocks of society by the philosophers of destruction with their perversions of God's word and their passionate desire to defile every avenue of faith.[82]

In this important appreciation of the *Yešibhah* Smolenskin contrasts its solid virtues with the feckless products of Enlightenment, the frivolous, selfish 'modern' teachers,[83] the cowardly advocates of assimilation, and particularly the graduates of the two Rabbinical seminaries (at Vilna and Zhitomir) established by the Russian government in 1847 and closed in 1873:[84]

> Whom, then, may we trust in the role of guardian of Israel's wisdom? The institutes which are called Rabbinical seminaries? You would be hard put to find anyone who either knows the *Torah* or is interested in it there. Does anyone go there in search of knowledge? There the attitude towards the years of study is like that of a hired worker waiting for his wages. They look forward eagerly to the time of their release; and as soon as a student has obtained his certificate of graduation, he abandons the study of *Torah* completely, henceforward despising both it and its admirers. For he regards it not as a crown of glory but merely as an instrument for earning a livelihood. And the teachers? Do they strive to implant a love of *Torah* and understanding in the minds of their pupils? Never! They, too, are more concerned with an elegant use of Russian than with knowledge, and with Greek lyrics than the Psalms of David. What hopes, then, can we entertain for the next generation, if those who have been designated the teachers of Israel know nothing of *Torah* except what income it will bring, and feel concerned not for the nation's spirit, but only that the place where they will be chosen to function as Rabbi may provide them with a comfortable and easy living?[85]

Elsewhere, however, Smolenskin adopts a much less critical attitude towards these Rabbinical seminaries and outlines their positive as well as their negative aspects.[86] In Braudes' novel, *Religion and Life*, on the other hand, the Rabbinical seminaries are consistently referred to as solid and respectable institutions, well worth attending,[87] and opposed only by religious bigots.[88] Braudes also supplies interesting data on the increasing difficulty of being accepted at the Vilna seminary, where large numbers of young Jews who have travelled great distances in order to study there are turned away daily and left utterly destitute.[89] The seminary at Zhitomir, however, is described as much easier of access. Although the standards are not inferior, entrance qualifications are less rigid, and the students have greater opportunity for earning a little money than in Vilna.[90] For Sheikewitz, too, the Rabbinical seminary clearly represents an admirable institution.[91]

Apart from the background of traditional education and culture, the novels are also deeply concerned with the problem of enlightenment in general, and the movement of Enlightenment known as *Haskalah* in particular. Although constituting one of the most significant elements to be found in these stories, this problem remains highly enigmatic. The difficulty arises from the ambivalence expressed by so many of the authors, and the variety of attitudes they display.[92] Without exception they must themselves be regarded as products, in greater measure, or in less, of the movement of Enlightenment—a fact to which the very act of writing a Hebrew novel bears ample testimony.[93] Indeed, with the significant exceptions of Smolenskin's *A Donkey's Burial* and Rabinowitz's *At the Crossroads*,[94] all the novels contain at least one hero who embodies the ideal of *Haskalah*. On the other hand, not only do some of the novelists attack even the basic concepts of *Haskalah* in most violent terms, but others—ostensibly staunch advocates of *Haskalah*—express severe criticism of many aspects of that movement. The treatment of the aims and methods of *Haskalah*, moreover, assumes a variety of forms, ranging from naïve acceptance to penetrating analysis.

The aspirations of the movement of Enlightenment in its classic form broadly embrace the following concepts: the dissemination of secular knowledge and European culture; the inculcation of a lofty, ethical attitude to life; the improvement of the political, social and economic position of the Jewish people; the encouragement of a discriminating use of the Hebrew language with an attendant refinement of taste, and the glorification of the Jewish past.[95] The aim was to mould a new type of Jew who would remain loyal to traditional Judaism, and would combine his faith with a full appreciation of European culture. As the ideal envisaged political emancipation and the integration of the Jewish people into the framework of European society, the movement also encouraged patriotism, especially in response to any alleviation of Jewish disabilities no matter how partial or ephemeral.[96]

Abramowitz, Braudes (in his *Religion and Life*), and most of the minor writers adopt extremely positive attitudes to the movement of *Haskalah*,[97] in the belief that Enlightenment will remedy

many of the evils of contemporary Jewish life. A strange dichotomy, however, may be perceived in the lofty, indeed grandiose
ideals upon which the theories of Enlightenment are based and
the pettiness of the practical forms in which Enlightenment
is expressed. The reading of secular books, the learning of
a foreign language,[98] the study of grammar, the adoption of
European-style clothing[99] represent the typical applications of
Haskalah. For all the nobility of sentiment and the broad humani-
tarianism which the heroes of these novels continually advocate,
there is little organic connection between aspiration in theory
and application in practice.

The difficulty was inherently environmental. Outside the large
towns, the Jewish communities of eastern Europe were close-
knit, self-contained and culturally insular. Their gentile contacts were largely with illiterate peasants, whom they tended to
despise. In the absence of immediate centres for imitation, such
as had confronted the Jews of western Europe on their emergence from the ghetto, the seeds of Enlightenment had to be imported from abroad where very different conditions prevailed.
Admittedly, the opening of the High Schools and Universities
to the Jews in Russia[100] gradually induced many of the exponents of Enlightenment to regard St Petersburg and Moscow
rather than Berlin and Paris as the centres for imitation. But in
either case the channels through which such influence might be
conveyed were so difficult to navigate and so very tortuous that
only a trickle of secular culture could be drawn through them.
'What connection can there be between European Enlightenment and Roumania?' Smolenskin shrewdly enquires. 'How can
we compare our brethren here to those in (western) Europe?'[101]

Some conception of the problem may be derived from such
passages in the novels as describe the means by which the ideas
of *Haskalah* were disseminated in eastern Europe. The new type of
secular learning was transmitted from one individual to another
usually in secrecy and in stealth, and in the teeth of orthodox
opposition. Indeed, the *Yeśibhah* itself, the very bulwark of
orthodoxy, proved the most vulnerable point of infiltration,
for its students were easily able to apply the long habits of
rigorous mental training to the acquisition of new disciplines:

I have seen many youngsters [Braudes writes] among those
who study Talmud and the Codes in the *Bêth ha-Midhraš* and

have a good command of Hebrew, reading the works of modern writers, and even acquiring foreign languages in secret—in spite of all the attempts of their elders to stem the 'waters of perdition', and raise barricades to prevent the spread of Enlightenment in their community. The elders labour in vain, and all their efforts are futile. They might just as well try to mend a breach in the cowshed once the wolf is inside.—The spirit of the times stirs within the youngster's breast; so what can any external guard or barricade avail? . . .

Reader, have you never seen a youth hiding something in his pocket on his way to the *Bêth ha-Midhraš*? Have you never noticed what seems to be a little book lying under the large Talmud open in front of him? Have you never plucked up courage to approach and see what sort of a book it is? Come, let me reveal his secret: *It will be some book of Haskalah in Hebrew, or a Russian text-book*. . . . Are you really surprised? In that case you are due for a much greater shock! Fully half of the students will have some similar work under the copies of the Talmud. . . . . The *Bêth ha-Midhraš* is destined to be the centre of learning in Israel, and so it will certainly teach secular knowledge and understanding to the young men who flock to its gates, without the elders even being aware of the fact.[102]

One or two individuals in a community, such as a teacher in a government school,[103] or an instructor in Russian in a *Yešibhah*[104] or simply private individuals[105] could serve to disseminate the ideas of *Haskalah* with surprising speed. Alternatively a private tutor,[106] a friend[107] or a chance acquaintance[108] could start a youth in the pursuit of secular knowledge. Weisbrem describes how the coming of the railway system[109] brought *Haskalah* in its wake, not always with favourable results.[110] Rabinowitz, again, outlines the role played by the travelling bookseller, and portrays his hero, Jehiel, buying a textbook on geometry, a Russian grammar, a manual of French conversation and a few stories. It is indicative of the author's attitude that although some of the books are defective, the hero still has to pay the full price of six roubles in the face of the bookseller's threat to denounce him as a heretic![111] Weisbrem also describes how *Haskalah* travelled from Russia to Poland,[112] while Braudes asserts that the ideas of Enlightenment were conveyed to Odessa by *Maskilim* from Brody in Galicia.[113] In the same novel, *The Two Extremes*, the author describes how Enlightenment first spread to Lithuania from the

neighbouring Prussia, and thence made its way via Galicia to
Volhynia and the Ukraine. In Lithuania, however, it adopted a
very serious attitude, in contrast to its superficial character in
the southern provinces. The older exponents of Enlightenment
maintained a rigorous orthodoxy, so that there was little conflict between them and the pietists. But the present generation,
even in Lithuania, have largely lost their ideals, and live only
for the moment.[114]

It is only to be expected that the spread of Enlightenment in so
haphazard, and frequently so furtive a manner should have produced unsatisfactory results. Even those novels which whole-
heartedly support the principles of *Haskalah* decry the superfici-
ality, frivolity and half-baked autodidacticism, which so often
passed for Enlightenment. It is significant that both Abramowitz
and Zobeizensky, whose advocacy of *Haskalah* is as wholehearted
as it is naïve, deplore the negative tendencies of the movement.[115] Braudes and Sheikewitz, whose approach to *Haskalah*,
while highly sympathetic, is more discerning, also denigrate the
consequences of a half-digested Enlightenment.[116] One of the
most revealing topics is the general onslaught which so many of
the novels launch against the practice of reading love stories,
which must frequently have represented the sole result of the
attempt by the *Maskilim* to foster a widespread interest in literature.[117]
   The most trenchant criticism of *Haskalah*, however, is to be
found in the novels of Smolenskin and Rabinowitz. It would be
incorrect to assume that these novelists did not appreciate the
positive aspects of *Haskalah*; indeed, they both express a deep
and perceptive understanding of the finer sides of that movement.[118] But the strength of their criticism stems from a penetrating grasp of the great gulf between the original ideals of the
movement of Enlightenment and its practical consequences.
Although Smolenskin severely criticises *Haskalah* in a number of
his novels,[119] his most devastating attacks are to be found in the
fourth part of *The Wanderer in the Paths of Life*.[120] Violently opposed to the theories of Moses Mendelssohn, from which *Haskalah* drew its inspiration, Smolenskin is equally critical of the fact
that the original ideal of the movement of Enlightenment to
effect a fusion of faith and reason has led only to the abandonment of faith coupled with the merest trappings of reason. But

even more serious, in his view, is the consequent decline in loyalty to the ancestral faith, the abandonment of traditional values and, particularly, the hollow and senseless imitation of the external and peripheral manifestations of European culture. For Smolenskin, the rapid spread of a false enlightenment had resulted in a generation losing its moorings, drifting aimlessly and unawares, on the perilous tides of assimilation and apathy. In the futile aping of western European culture, Smolenskin perceives the reason for the increase in antisemitism;[121] while the net result of *Haskalah*—and, incidentally, of the Hasidic movement—he equates with nihilism![122]

In his novel, *At the Crossroads*, Rabinowitz forcibly levels a similar indictment against *Haskalah* by showing the corrupting influence of its ideas on a pious and sincere young man, for whom Enlightenment ultimately spells disaster.[123] His first step on the slippery slope towards complete demoralization follows the purchase of a number of secular books:[124]

This was the first misfortune that befell him on the road to Enlightenment. But whereas his first mistake only cost him three roubles, for the future mistakes, which he continued to make with every step, he paid with his soul, his youthful vigour, the very marrow in his bones.[125]

The secular books serve only to make him waver in his traditional faith, thereby creating instead of solving his problems. Rabinowitz, however, makes a very interesting distinction between the negative and positive sides of *Haskalah*. The pious teacher, Judah, makes use of Jehiel's textbook on geometry—which the hero cannot be bothered to make the mental effort to understand—in order to elucidate some difficult Talmudic passages![126] Rabinowitz scathingly criticises the ease with which his hero picks up the terminology of *Haskalah* without knowing anything of its real content;[127] and he is equally devastating in his denunciation of Jehiel's blind worship of foreign languages: 'If he found that a certain author introduced a few foreign words into his book, he regarded him as a veritable Aristotle. . . .'[128] Again, the principle of 'the love of man' is taken by his hero to signify an unquestioning preference for Gentiles, however unworthy, over Jews.[129] One after the other, the ideas of Enlightenment, especially in their half-digested form, are trounced unmercifully.

The ambivalent attitude displayed towards the movement of Enlightenment naturally applies in equal measure to the exponents of that movement, the *Maskilim*. As stated above, the novels abound with characters that personify the finest ideals of *Haskalah*,[130] so much so that the highest form of recommendation is couched in the phrase: 'And he was a *Maskil* in every way'.[131] Nevertheless, even the staunchest advocates of Enlightenment deride the pseudo-*Maskilim* for their frivolity, indifference, hedonism and neglect of Hebrew.[132] 'Do you not know', Weisbrem remarks satirically, 'that the nobility and the *Maskilim* lie stinking in bed until noon?'[133] Sheikewitz berates their passion for composing worthless poetry,[134] while Jacob, the hero of *The Two Extremes*, which by and large expresses sober and moderate opinions, is surprised to find a young *Maskil* who is not a romantic, in spite of his familiarity with poetry, stories and novels romanticizing love.[135] Still more noteworthy is Braudes' tremendous attack, in *Religion and Life*, on the hypocrisy of what he calls the 'half-*Maskil*', and the devastating effect which such fathers exert on their children.[136]

Again, however, the most severe criticism against the exponents of Enlightenment is to be found in the works of Smolenskin and Rabinowitz. Neglect of Hebrew, laxity in morals, disloyalty to the Jewish people, and contempt for the traditional values of Judaism all occupy a leading place in Smolenskin's evaluation of the *Maskil's* creed![137] Particularly biting is his condemnation of their sycophantic admiration of gentile values. In one passage he describes them as apes[138] and in another as performing dogs![139] The strength of Rabinowitz's criticism, on the other hand, stems from his attributing to the *Maskilim* those very faults which they ascribe to their opponents:

> The *Maskilim* jeer at the Rabbis because of the many strange customs in the *Šulḥan 'Arukh*, but they do not see the mote in their own eye. How many absurd customs are to be found in the law of fashion which puts rigid fetters on all its adherents! Indeed, were they all to be collected together, their number would outstrip those of the *Šulḥan 'Arukh* of the orthodox. But they are handed on orally, and carried out punctiliously to the last detail, so that everyone who looks at them askance is dubbed despicable and loathsome—quite outside the pale.[140]

Similarly, the hero Jehiel brands the orthodox as fanatics, '. . . without realising that he, himself, is even more fanatical; but whereas their ardour is in the name of God, his ardour is in the name of *Haskalah*.[141] The effectiveness of Rabinowitz's satire may be seen from the following extract: 'She is a clever woman— Jehiel reflected after reading his wife's letter—Nature has endowed her with an unusually perceptive mind ("Nature"—not God, for Heaven forbid that a *Maskil* should believe in God).'[142] But perhaps the most poignant debunking of the aims of *Haskalah* appears towards the end of the novel:

> There is an idealist here, just like you, who for many years taught young Jews various languages, and wrote pleasant poems; but latterly his strength has failed, and he has become too weak to roam the streets in search of pupils. So now he lies on his sick-bed in hunger and thirst, and goes on writing poetry. . . .[143]

On the other hand there is no difference of opinion with respect to the blind obscurantism sometimes displayed by the orthodox opponents of *Haskalah*. The 'sin' of reading secular books, and the barbaric practice of destroying and burning them is roundly condemned on a number of occasions.[144] The most biting satire appears in Abramowitz's *Fathers and Sons*, where the bigoted Ephraim searches his son's bookshelves for 'forbidden' literature, one of the criteria being all books printed in short lines, with wide margins and vowelling points![145] The hero of Zobeizensky's novel, Israel, has his face slapped for defending Mendelssohn's commentary to the Pentateuch,[146] while the second part of Braudes' *The Two Extremes* closes with a most dramatic humiliation of a young man, who has been caught reading a book in Russian.[147] In bigoted circles, too, secular study is portrayed as being responsible for the deaths of women and children by way of Divine retribution.[148]

Reference has already been made to the overall neglect of the education of girls in orthodox circles.[149] On a number of occasions, however, the novels mention the fact that the daughters– in contrast to the sons–of pious *Ḥasidhim* and *Mithnaggedhim* were sometimes allowed a little secular education, for which reason they might be prone to despise their husbands whose education was entirely traditional.[150] The novelists strongly advocate the education of girls as well as boys, and are at pains to illustrate the healthy desire for learning shared by many of their heroines.[151] Braudes is particularly insistent on the importance of ensuring a good education—not forgetting handicrafts—for women,[152] and it is significant that the ideal school founded by the heroes of *Religion and Life* contains a department for girls.[153] Nevertheless, the evil results which may accrue from the spread of *Haskalah* amongst women, particularly in its more frivolous aspects, is pointed out in no uncertain terms.[154] It is significant, too, that although Smolenskin supports a modern education in the finer sense for women, he warns them against trying to compete with men.[155]

The overall picture which emerges from these novels, therefore, is highly tendentious. The novelists wielded a two-edged sword, with which they launched devastating attacks on many aspects of both the old position and the new trends in Jewish life. If the old generation is accused of folly, bigotry, superstition, ignorance and tyranny[156]—in a most powerful passage in Weisbrem's novel, *18 Coins*, one of the heroes bitterly complains that the old generation treats the new, as ladies their pet dogs[157]—the more disturbing characteristics of the new generation, especially its tendency to throw out the baby with the bath-water,[158] are no less stringently condemned.[159] On the other hand the solid virtues of traditional Jewish life and their importance for the preservation of Judaism and the Jewish people are frequently cited even by those authors who most stridently demand changes in the social, cultural and religious patterns of Jewish life in accordance with their estimate of changed conditions. That much of what they advocated with such passion appears misguided in the light of subsequent events is not, perhaps, surprising; but of the general sincerity of their intent and of their earnest desire to serve their people's cause there can be little doubt.

SEVEN

Aspects of Religion

The portrait of contemporary Jewish life reflected in the novels under review inevitably includes much information relative to religious conditions. The patterns of Jewish society in eastern Europe during the nineteenth century were largely conditioned by religious practice and belief. The very nature of Judaism, with its overriding emphasis on commandment and prohibition, necessarily dictated the forms of individual and public behaviour within a closely-knit society. Indeed, the life of an orthodox community was regulated in minute detail within the strict confines of Jewish law, reinforced by local custom. Any attempt to describe the contemporary Jewish scene, therefore, could scarcely have dispensed with frequent reference to some aspect of religious life, and it is only to be expected that religious questions frequently arise within the novels.

Again, the period with which these stories are mainly concerned was characterized by far-reaching changes in the structure of Jewish life in eastern Europe, brought about by both external and internal pressures. The alternating policies of repression and amelioration pursued by the Czarist government towards its Jewish subjects inevitably engendered corresponding reactions on the part of the Jewish population.[1] The violent emotions of fear, hatred, hope and disillusion, which these measures aroused in turn, were incompatible with any stability of outlook, and naturally gave rise to violent disagreements within the community with respect to the best means of coping with a situation so disturbingly in flux. Aggravated by the rapid growth of population and the consequent deterioration of an economic condition already chronic,[2] the Jewish position was further adversely affected by the three-sided battle waged with bitter antagonism within the community itself.

Even prior to the advent of the movement of Enlightenment, the unity of eastern European Jewry had been shattered by the growth of the Hasidic movement in the latter half of the eighteenth century.[3] Between the adherents of the vigorous new sect, the *Hasidhim*, and the staunch champions of the old orthodoxy, significantly connoted by the term *Mithnaggedhim* (Opponents), a fierce hostility of almost a century's standing had existed before the serious emergence of a third force in the shape of *Haskalah*. So bitter was the animosity prevailing between *Mithnaggedhim* and *Hasidhim* that members of the opposing sects would not consent either to eat at the same table or give each other their daughters in marriage; while desertion to the opposite camp was regarded as tantamount to leaving Judaism altogether.[4]

The appearance of the movement of Enlightenment in eastern Europe was viewed with hostility by *Mithnaggedhim* and *Hasidhim* alike. Both factions recognized the dangerous threat which the new movement represented to their views, and both opposed its spread with every means at their disposal.[5] Although initially loath to be drawn into serious conflict with the exponents of orthodox Judaism,[6] the *Maskilim* gradually became increasingly belligerent, partly because of the relentless hostility displayed by their opponents, and partly because of the growing radicalism of their own views. Against the movement of Hasidism, which was largely regarded as a conglomeration of base superstitions and blind fanaticism, the *Maskilim* maintained an overall attitude of unyielding animosity.[7]

The many descriptions of the religious scene to be found in these novels, therefore, are no less frequently tendentious than was the case with the portrait of social and cultural conditions outlined above.[8] The mere fact that so many of the authors deliberately advocate radical changes in Jewish society—while even those who are most critical of the ideas of *Haskalah*[9] must, themselves, be considered products of that movement in great measure—necessarily implies dissatisfaction with many aspects of the old patterns of Jewish life. But as that life was so inextricably bound up with traditional religious practice, it was virtually impossible to criticize the one without the other. Again, such authors as Braudes and Zobeizensky openly advocate religious reform;[10] and although the type of reform envisaged is very mild in comparison with the measures adopted by the Reform Movement in western Europe,[11] the proposals are advanced with passionate intensity in an atmosphere tense with conflict. Far from being able to discuss the questions dispassionately on their own merits, these novelists are seriously committed to the dissemination of their own views, and their approach to many aspects of Jewish religious practice is, of necessity, heavily weighted.

The same warning, then, is valid for the religious attitudes reflected within these novels as for the portraits of social and cultural conditions. Wherever the descriptions are deliberately tendentious or polemical, the views expressed must be regarded with due caution. Wherever, on the other hand, the background is described in incidental manner, or details of religious practice and local custom furnished almost unconsciously, considerably greater credence may be attached to the information to be derived. Not that the treatment of the traditional religious milieu is uniformly negative! On the contrary, most of the novels, particularly Braudes' *The Two Extremes* and Rabinowitz's *At the Crossroads*, contain numerous passages lauding the old traditional point of view, and expressing a sincere appreciation of the integrity of orthodox Judaism and its beneficial influence, particularly by contrast with the barren philosophy of a secular materialism. The frequent attacks on the negative consequences of 'Enlightenment' constitute at once an indictment of such of its exponents as have too easily surrendered the traditional values in the pursuit of chimerical fancies, abandoning the substance for the shadow, and also an affirmation of the intrinsic worth of the ancestral faith.

The attitude towards religion displayed by these novelists, therefore, frequently demonstrates the same ambivalence which characterizes so many aspects of their writing.[12] Their approach to Jews and Judaism embraces elements of both affection and dislike, sometimes approximating to a love-hate relationship, which throws much light upon the mental climate prevailing amongst some of the keenest and most sensitive observers of contemporary Jewry.[13] At times their strictures are so venomous that coming from the pen of any but a Jewish writer they would at once be classified as crude and blatant anti-semitic propaganda. On the other hand, the even more pronounced devotion to their people and loyalty to its cause, the compassion for its miserable plight, the obsessed preoccupation with its complex problems and above all, perhaps, the passionate and courageous love of the Hebrew language, as witnessed by the mere fact of writing novels in Hebrew, bear even ampler testimony to the depth and sincerity of their affection. In this respect the overall attitude displayed by most of these novelists to the fundamental concepts of Judaism is both positive and discerning. Their antagonism is reserved for what they considered to be meaningless excrescences, harmful misinterpretations and excessive stringencies in the application of religious law,[14] which had gradually crept into the religion due to the unnatural conditions of Jewish life, and which they believed must be purged if the religion were to remain healthy and dynamic.

Although the information relative to the religious life of east European Jewry in the nineteenth century is to be found scattered widely throughout the novels, the most thorough-going and consistent treatment occurs in the novels of Braudes and Rabinowitz. The former writer's *Religion and Life* and *The Two Extremes* and the latter's *At the Crossroads* together comprise a trio of considerable interest. While all three novels adopt a highly positive attitude towards traditional Judaism, they represent respectively the radical, moderate and orthodox points of view. Although the angle of differentiation is comparatively narrow, the difference of emphasis is significant, and lends itself to chronological analysis.

Religion and Life purports to be a realistic account of the struggle for religious reform, waged between the exponents of Enlightenment and the orthodox in Lithuania between the years 1869-71.[15] This battle, whose literary expression is preserved in the Hebrew literary journals of the time, revolved upon questions raised by the severe interpretation of religious law favoured by the Rabbis of Lithuania.[16] The passions generated by this controversy were out of all proportion to the proposals involved, so that the proponents and opponents of what amounted to very minor religious reforms abused each other in most virulent terms, and accused each other of heresy and obscurantism respectively. Braudes' own involvement in the conflict, and the fact that he composed his novel so soon after the struggle had reached its climax,[17] are doubtless responsible for the manifest bias which

שְׁתֵּי הַקְצָוֹת

רוֹמָן

מחיי היהודים בעת החֹהָה
בשני כרכים

מאת

ראובן אשר בן־יוסף ברודם.

(ראובן אבי־ב איש ווילנא.)

כרך ראשון

חוצאת בית מסחר הספרים של

אליעזר יצחק שפירא

ווארשא

תרמ"ח

Штеи Гакцовотъ.

г. е. Крайности,

романъ изъ современной жизни въ 2-ухъ частяхъ.

Р. А. Браудеса .

Изданіе книжнаго магазина Л. И. Шапиро Варшава 1885.

Title-page of the first edition of Braudes'
The Two Extremes, *published in Warsaw,* 1888

his story displays. The true *Maskilim*—and the qualification is important[18]—are described in glowing terms, while the orthodox Rabbis are portrayed as misguided bigots.

Braudes' second novel, *The Two Extremes*, however, reflects a rather different attitude. Published more than a decade later than *Religion and Life*, when the ardour of both reformers and orthodox had cooled before the chilling wind of wholesale desertions from Judaism and the bleak indifference to the tradition displayed by large sections of the younger generation, *The Two Extremes* is much more moderate and much less doctrinaire in its approach. In this novel the negative consequences of a false Enlightenment are afforded greater emphasis, while the warmth and stability of a pious community, despite its unprepossessing exterior and occasional manifestations of blind fanaticism, are described in highly appreciative terms. Braudes' ideal Jew in this novel is represented by a strictly orthodox yet secularly enlightened grandfather from Vilna, a survivor, in fact, of an earlier generation of pious *Maskilim*, whom the author obviously prefers to either of the two extremes—whether secular or religious—from which the story derives its title.[19] But the very fact that Braudes is forced to resort to a rapidly disappearing species, for an example worthy of emulation, is indicative of the scant prospect of success liable to accrue from his plea for a fusion of religion and enlightenment.

The change of attitude expressed in *The Two Extremes* is reflected more cogently still in Rabinowitz's *At the Crossroads*. Although it was published in 1887, a year before Braudes' novel, Rabinowitz condemns the evil consequences of *Haskalah* in far more definite and consistent terms.[20] By contrast, the virtues of orthodox religious practice and its stabilizing influence are stressed repeatedly. Rabinowitz maintains that the real need of the Jewish people is not for reform but rather for a strengthening of traditional religious knowledge. Although he concedes—via the medium of the idealist, Daniel[21]—that Enlightenment may confer certain benefits, such as by improving the economic conditions of the Jewish people or by cleansing the religion of any extraneous and harmful elements that may have crept in from time to time, he insists that *Haskalah* should never be regarded as a new ethical foundation for behaviour and belief, for such a function can be performed only by an authority that stands above criticism. He remains equally convinced that

N

all the precepts of Jewish religious law must be observed punctiliously.

From these three novels, therefore, it may be seen that, in spite of a shift of emphasis in an orthodox direction due to the increasingly distressing results of a growing secularism, a very positive attitude towards the fundamentals of Judaism is common to them all. The many passages of polemic and the scathing satire which these novels contain in great measure are directed not against Judaism as such, but against what the authors regarded as misguided attitudes towards it, or as unnatural accretions, base superstitions and ignorant fanaticism. As the particular target of their attack they select the hypocrite masquerading under the cloak of extreme orthodoxy,[22] or the unscrupulous businessman piously observing the ritual down to the last minute detail. Although frequently couched in bitter terms, their sallies may, on occasion, contain a genuine element of humour.[23]

The deep appreciation of Israel's tradition and the devout loyalty to Judaism which these novelists display may be illustrated from a chapter in Smolenskin's *The Wanderer in the Paths of Life*, devoted to the most solemn festival in the Jewish religious calendar—the Day of Atonement:

> For Israel that day is holy, a day of pardon and forgiveness, of exaltation, of mercy and loving-kindness, a day when the hearts of every Jew from one end of the earth to the other are united. That is the day appointed by the Lord who created a people to know his name and proclaim his glory amongst the nations for his own sake; in order that those who dwell in prosperity and in their pride and felicity have forgotten their Creator, their people and their faith, may remember and repent; and that those who are oppressed in hostile lands, and so ground into the dust beneath the foot of pride that they forget the Lord their Saviour, may also remember God and seek him.
>
> On that day Jews are aware that all their brethren scattered throughout the earth are likewise standing with their eyes devoutly raised to heaven, pouring out their plaint in identical prayer to the Lord God of Israel, the kind and merciful God who dwells with the oppressed and listens to the prayer of all that beseech him. The Jew does not confess to any priest for absolution from sin, nor does he seek to buy a dispensation for his transgressions. Instead, he speaks directly with his God,

his Creator and his Father, pouring out his plea before him and revealing all his sorrows. . . .

What a great day that is for Israel; a day that cleanses them of all sin. Could it be otherwise, when they have so steadfastly abstained the entire day from all life's pleasures, and their spirits have soared to the threshold of the Lord of all Creation, the King of all the earth, the source of all kindness and love? Shall they not be cleansed and forgiven, when each one of them on the previous day had forgiven all who have sinned against them? Shall they not be pardoned, after having come in search of pardon and to strengthen the bulwark of their faith against the assault of all the many currents of wickedness threatening to destroy it? . . .

That is the day when the children cluster about their merciful Father, to reveal to him their innermost thoughts. On that day their eyes shed tears like fountains, and on that day their minds are filled with dreadful recollections: terrible angels clad in black, storming against them these many days to scatter them; wrathful angels in the shape of evil priests slandering them for two thousand years. Yet, are the poor wretches' mouths filled with curses and imprecations? Do they call down the curse of God upon their persecutors? No! Only words of pardon and forgiveness pass their lips; and if only they could be certain that hatred had disappeared and that the wicked would no longer torment them, they would also forgive the transgressions of their enemies with all their hearts.

Israel! Though your sins abound like the sea, though your guilt be greater than the dust of the earth, you shall be forgiven. For the sacrifices which you have offered up on the altar of your God outweigh the number of your sins. Nor have you brought mere lambs and oxen as an offering. Your very children have been sacrificed. Therefore shall you be forgiven, and your persecutors bear the guilt.[24]

A similar reverence for the deep significance of the Sabbath in pious circles may be detected in Braudes' description of the effect of the Sabbath calm on Solomon, a wealthy but assimilated Jew, when he is invited for the Friday evening meal by a poor but very orthodox host:

How surprised he was on entering the house! How very moved he felt on first crossing that threshold! . . . He found himself in a humble Jewish house, belonging to a poor Jewish working man in a little town—yet how sparkling the house seemed now for the sanctification of the Sabbath. All signs of the man's trade had disappeared. The tools had vanished without trace, so that the house had taken on the same air as that of the rich Jeroham. This house, too, had been thoroughly cleaned, and stood all neat and tidy. This table, too, was covered with clean white linen, on which gleamed candlesticks with lighted candles. . . .

Both the man, his wife and his little sons and daughters were scrubbed and spruce, and dressed in fresh clean shirts and blouses. Everything on which his eye alighted within the house delighted him. He had already learned that the Sabbath was referred to as a 'bride' and now its owner seemed to him like a bridegroom straight from the wedding-canopy, while his wife and children resembled the guests who had come to share the bride and bridegroom's joy.[25]

Equally significant is the passionate avowal of faith made by Samuel, the hero of Braudes' *Religion and Life*.[26] Although Samuel is the principal champion of religious reform in this novel, all his proposals spring from a profound sense of historical and traditional continuity. In the following conversation he protests vehemently that his ideas have been misunderstood, and that his piety and sincerity have been impugned without cause:

'My dear friends!' Samuel replied. 'The words I uttered publicly in the Synagogue last Saturday before the congregation were pointed and severe, because they were aimed at resolving one particular detail, and meant particularly for the Rabbi who, I thought, would admit the truth of my remarks. But you heard the Rabbi's outburst, how he accused me of heresy and schism without even deigning to answer my point. That in itself upset me; but I was doubly grieved to learn in the afternoon that even those people who I had imagined would have understood my remarks and supported me— recognising the truth of what I said and hurrying to my aid— that even they who, far from harbouring any trace of bigotry or fanaticism, are pure of heart, suspected me of heretical and schismatic views. . . .'

'I never said any such thing,' Nahman replied, realising that Samuel's remarks referred to him. 'I merely pointed out the heretical flavour of the *words* you used. But I should be delighted if you would explain what you said and exonerate yourself completely. . . . .'

'I swear by God,' Samuel explained firmly, 'that as true as I am alive I have no truck with such things. I have no time for heretics, nor any sympathy for schismatics. With all my heart

I believe in the divine nature of both the written and the oral *Torah*. I believe that the *entire* written *Torah*, and the *principles* of the oral *Torah*, were given to Moses at Sinai. . . .'[27]

In the third part of the same novel Braudes emphasises even more strongly the sincerity of the young exponents of reform, and their ardent wish to strengthen Judaism by bringing it into conformity with the demands of life. Far from desiring to introduce alien elements into the religion, they are desperately anxious to cleanse it of all dross, and return to the dynamic principles of the *Talmud*:

> . . . All of them have taken as their standards the *Torah* and the Present Time, they have adopted both *Religion* and *Life* as their portents, using the *Talmud* as a plumb-line and *Wisdom* as a balance. They do not seek to create new concepts which their ancestors never imagined, nor to erect a new edifice such as the latter might have feared, nor to introduce alien plants into the Jewish vineyard—but purely to remove the thorns and thistles therefrom, to lighten a little the burden imposed in the later *Codes* which weigh upon the people heavy as sand, to strip away the unnecessary accretions added by the Rabbis in *recent times*, and to return to the method of the *Talmud*, to a real understanding of the oral *Torah*, which they revere as holy. . . .[28]

The loyalty to Judaism so frequently encountered in these novels is constantly emphasized by an intense preoccupation with the national past and a glorification of Israel's history. This devotion to the various manifestations of Judaism in previous ages constitutes a characteristic feature of the movement of Enlightenment in eastern Europe,[29] of which the following passage from Abramowitz's *Fathers and Sons* may serve as a typical illustration:

> 'My friend,' Simon exclaimed sadly, 'let me read to you something of Israel's history, something that you always enjoy hearing. Let me read to you about our people's greatness, its happiness and prosperity in its blessed land, the kindness of its kings and princes, the valour of its warriors, and the dignity of its priests and law-givers. . . . Let me read to you about the glory of the sons of Jacob, the wisdom of their sages, the understanding of their wise men, their splendid fabulists and poets in Babylonia, Persia, Spain and Italy. . . . Let me read you something of those who were devoted heart and soul to

their religion in perfect faith and absolute integrity, who gave up their lives for their religion, and gladly sacrificed themselves upon the altar in defiance of false priests. . . . Let me read you of those slaughtered sheep, our people, who poured out their souls unto death, who—in the lands of their enemies —are counted as transgressors, though innocent of guilt in word or deed.'[30]

This sense of historical continuity and identification with Israel's past naturally lends a strong flavour of nationalism, which may be encountered time and again within these novels. The sympathies of the authors are reflected in the deep concern displayed by so many of their heroes and heroines for the Jewish people, and the passionate loyalty and devotion to its cause which they so frequently display. The following passage, drawn from a chapter of Smolenskin's novel, *The Inheritance*, which describes the initiation of the hero, Zerahiah, into a Jewish fraternal society in Roumania, provides a typical example:

'Come here, my brother'—Eliakim declared—'from this day forward we are brethren, for only *brethren* assemble in this place, and everyone is addressed as brother.' 'Zerahiah, my brother, come here'—Zerahiah came forward, and after raising his hand in blessing over the new brother, Eliakim continued: 'My brethren! A new warrior has just come to swell our ranks, and I am happy to believe that he will prove faithful to us in body and soul when we go out to war. All of us are warriors, tried in battle in these bitter times! Who can be compared to our people Israel, who are engaged in eternal warfare and yet have always emerged victorious from all the battles waged against us? Israel has not embarked upon this warfare, for we seek peace, and desire only to dwell in harmony. But many nations have conspired against us to destroy us and obliterate our memory without success. And even though they sowed our land with salt, slaughtering the flower of our youth, killing suckling and sage alike, and scattering the surviving remnant to the winds like chaff, the nation still managed to revive. Attacked with slings and weapons of war, we took refuge in the *spirit*. Without plunging a sharp sword through the hearts of our enemies, without drinking the cup of vengeance or wading through blood, the nation has witnessed, nevertheless, a terrible revenge—an eternal revenge. Though all our enemies vanish like clouds and breathe their last in turn, a time still beckons when we shall rise again and live. Our peculiar quality resides in this ability to survive in spite of all efforts to destroy us, and repopulate the very places where they have buried us. Like the spirit of life Israel moves from one country to the next, and wherever we pass we quicken the spirit. Thus our ancient heritage has consisted in wreaking a beneficent revenge, for we bring advantage to our foes, and requite with good all those who harm us, by carrying light, righteousness, justice and integrity to those very places where we have been robbed of them. That has been our fate of old, and such will always be our destiny'.[31]

This nationalism is also, on occasion, expressed in terms of reverence for the ancient homeland. Even an olive brought from Palestine is sufficient to arouse astonishment and delight,[32] while a woman's passionate desire to settle in the land of Israel is described in the following terms:

'All day she remembers that I am in exile, and so she is always anxious to save money. She works the whole day long like any five servants, and refuses to employ any help. She doesn't spend a penny on clothes, but hoards her coppers one by one like an ant, without ever forgetting that we have two sons and a daughter. She has already saved enough to keep us in food, even if I can no longer find employment in this house. How, then, can I bring myself to blame her if, in the light of all this, she requests me not to squander money to no purpose? She supplies us with food in plenty, yet at the same time she denies herself even the slightest luxury for the sake of her husband and her children. Her sole demand is that I should remain steadfast in our faith, so that our children may not fall into evil ways; on that she is adamant. But her ultimate aim is to collect sufficient money for us to go to the land of Israel.'
—'To the land of Israel?!'—Zerahiah exclaimed in astonishment—'That's a fine ambition for you and your children! And what will your sons do there? Weep at the Wailing Wall and study the *Zohar*?'
—'Even if such were the case, I still would not regard it as so stupid as you think. What sort of a future lies in store for them here? In school they are beaten by the children and persecuted by the teachers; and when they grow up there will be no place for them. I doubt if their position would be any worse crying at the Wailing Wall but unmolested than living in comfort here at the risk of always having their faces slapped'—[33]

The speaker then affirms that if he could only find about another hundred like-minded persons, so that they might all have
a real chance of establishing themselves, he would willingly take
the plunge:

> If only there were others with me, so that we could live as a
> unit and found schools for our children, thereby blazing the
> trail for others to follow, then I would be more than glad to
> accede to my wife's ambition. . . .'[34]

It is significant that Rabinowitz, the most consistent suppor-
ter of traditional Judaism of all these novelists, specifically states
—through the mouth of one of his characters, Daniel—that he
agrees with Smolenskin that only a return to the land of Israel
can remedy the steady deterioration of the Jewish material position.[35] The importance of such statements uttered in the early
days of the nationalist revival for the growth of the Zionist movement scarcely requires reiteration.

The extremely positive attitude generally expressed in these
novels towards the virtues of traditional Judaism deserves adequate emphasis in view of the fierce criticism and biting satire
which the authors so frequently direct against what they considered to be the darker sides of traditional life. The unattractive
combination of religious fanaticism and stubborn obscurantism is
time and again exposed to the withering blast of their invective.
The following episode from Smolenskin's novel, *The Inheritance*,
describing the history of Eliakim the doctor, may serve as a forceful illustration of their approach. Eliakim acquired a taste for
secular learning in his childhood from a teacher imbued with
the spirit of *Haskalah*. As an antidote to such dangerous tendencies his parents married him while still a youth to a young woman who turns out to be a religious bigot:

> His wife embittered his life with her perpetual carping. She
> declared that he did not sufficiently prolong the benediction
> recited on washing the hands, and that such a prayer did not
> merit any breakfast. On one occasion, as she lay in ambush,
> she saw a sight which shocked her to the very core—peeping
> through the keyhole she observed her husband smoothing his
> hair with his hands on the Sabbath.[36] On another occasion
> she swore a most solemn oath that he had not recited the even-
> ing prayer on the festival of the Rejoicing of the Law. And
> there were innumerable other infringements of a similar kind.

For all of which the whole town regarded her as a 'saint'. Her father lavished praise upon her, while her mother, in particular, encouraged her constantly by saying: 'Watch your husband, my daughter; remember, his shame reflects on you, and your children will suffer for the sins of their father; think of his soul, my daughter, and of your own; if your husband goes to Gehenna, you will never enter Paradise.'—These and many similar lessons in living did she impart to her daughter every morning, and rejoiced to find her suggestions falling on attentive ears.[37]

Finally, Eliakim, who cannot tolerate the life of inactivity to which he finds himself condemned, goes abroad at the age of 25 to study. After ten years of poverty and suffering he finally qualifies as a doctor, and returns to his home-town, still strictly observant, in the hope of living with his wife in greater harmony. She refuses, however, to recognize his new status:

I was not wife to a doctor, my parents did not marry me to a doctor, nor did I choose a doctor. If, on account of my many sins, he has become a doctor, I shall go down to Sheol in sorrow; but I will not permit him to support me from his practice, nor, as long as I am alive, will I recognise his authority or allow him to educate my children in his ways. . . .[38]

She insists on maintaining her little shop to the complete neglect of her household:

. . . His wife remained in her shop all day, while the house was left in utter disorder and neglect. For she refused to exchange her filthy, stinking home for another, lest the new one look like a doctor's house. For such—she declared—were the ways of Satan and the powers of evil. At first he would incite her to change her dwelling, and then their style of dress,[39] and then their language and finally their very faith. But she would stand on guard at the gate, and block the path of the destroying angel. And indeed, she proved a faithful guardian, refusing to clean the house or courtyard, and allowing no one to remove the refuse and the heaps of dirt as though they were the true guardians of the faith.[40]

The unfortunate consequences which may result from an excess of piety are reflected in the final statements of the heroine of Sheikewitz's novel, *The Outcast*. Analysing the pressures which were inducing so many of the younger generation to abandon Judaism altogether, the heroine makes the following assertion:

... You only have to look about you properly to realise how many of you desert your faith each year and seek refuge in the protecting shadow of the dominant religion. And the reason is (if you will pardon the expression) that you are all behaving as though demented. The orthodox among you, in excessive zeal for the Lord, overburden your sons and daughters, and rigorously weigh them down with laws and customs inherited from the earliest Rabbis and all the generations of their disciples. But you are guilty of an even greater folly in seeking to dominate the mind and spirit of your offspring. You forget that people have different temperaments and that one man's meat is another's poison. And your children, weary of supporting the burden imposed by their parents, seek some avenue of escape. In so doing they not infrequently abandon their faith altogether.... [41]

The attack on excessive Rabbinical stringency, which constitutes the main theme of Braudes' *Religion and Life*, [42] and which expresses itself in a series of passionate demands for minor religious reform, is conducted simultaneously on a double plane. On the one hand the author accuses the Rabbis of stifling the spiritual life of the people with the severity of their interpretations and decisions; on the other hand he claims that such strictness is further worsening an economic situation already tragic, and increasing the overall hardship instead of alleviating it. Both aspects are equally apparent in the following terrible indictment which Braudes levels at the state of Lithuanian Jewry:

Do you know the land where poverty, hunger, want and general distress prevail, which lies desolate because of the lack of initiative and depression of its inhabitants? . . . . Do you know the people who dwell there sunk in lethargy like a rotting corpse, weary of life, slumbering from birth to death in stupor and devoid of vision? People who never notice the sun even when it shines at its brightest, and shut their eyes to the moon and stars? Whose sons are savages, and whose daughters are like animals without proper education? Who tremble at the sound of a falling leaf, and are terrified of demons, spirits, ghosts and anything else which cannot be seen or heard or comprehended? The only thing that does not frighten them is the burden of life itself, for they neither hesitate to take on the yoke of a wife and children, nor do they worry in the least about the problems of earning a livelihood or supporting a household—even though their ancestors were always homeless paupers, and they themselves are poverty-stricken, while their children will be equally oppressed and penniless. People upon whom the Rabbis have placed an iron yoke, taking the last morsel of food from their mouths and hedging them about with laws and restrictions, prohibitions and regulations, decrees and customs beyond all bearing. The Rabbis have so restricted every avenue of life, scarcely allowing the people to draw breath, that they have deadened their very spirit. And the people meekly bear the burden on their shoulders through blindness and fatigue, and have become a corpse among the living, without ever knowing that their Rabbis have overstepped the mark, broken the covenant of their *Torah*, and led them into the wilderness. People who hearken not to the spirit of the time, who do not stir to the clarion-call of Enlightenment, and who educate their sons as their fathers educated them, and thereby condemn the next generation equally to a living death. Do you know that land and that people?

Dear reader! That land is my homeland—*Lithuania*, and that people is my people—*Israel*!

And in that land, and with reference to that people, Nahman could say: 'But we do not yet know whether our generation needs reforms!. . .'

Were a man to come from western Europe, and with his own eyes see this backward people, their degradation, their level of culture, the education they give their sons and daughters, and their manner of life, without any doubt he would pose the question: Can reforms be of any avail? Is it still possible to reform them? Could even the third generation enter the society of men who are aware of life and all its manifestations? . . . Yet Nahman, the *Melammedh* from Minsk, could say to Samuel, for all the latter's long harangue during the 'Great Sabbath': 'We do not yet know whether our generation needs reform!'[43]

In similar vein Smolenskin attacks the use of the weapon of excommunication, the *Herem*, as crude and primitive persecution, even likening it in some respects to the Spanish Inquisition. In his powerful novel, *A Donkey's Burial*, he portrays the excommunication of the hero, Jacob Hayyim, for disclosing the nefarious practices of the leaders of the local community to the authorities:

The community leaders announced their verdict without fear or favour, and placed Jacob Hayyim under a great ban of excommunication. To the accompaniment of blasts on the

ram's horn, they declared him banished for ever from the community, and decreed that he should not be inscribed in the
roll of Israel nor bear its name. No Jew might engage him in
conversation or approach within four paces of him. Henceforward he was to be regarded as an abomination and a warning to the rebelliously inclined.

How dreadful is such a day of judgement! It is awe-inspir-
ing not merely for the believers, who blindly accept that it is
by divine decree that they must quake and tremble at the
sound of the ram's horn; it terrifies not merely those who are
afraid of excommunication, whether human or divine, and
similar punishments. But even the man who stands in no awe
of the ram's horn and the name of Satan, or of the punishment
of excommunication, experiences fear and terror. It is dreadful to watch people ally themselves with the evils of life to their
own hurt and that of their brethren—especially if the spectator is an Israelite who knows his people's history, and remembers their fate throughout the generations until the present
day. For how precarious is their position, with every eye glaring at them malevolently, and every tongue directed poison-
ously against them; with all their neighbours seeking only to
harm them, while even the best among them, who would
shrink from actually assaulting them, are nevertheless delighted
to witness their downfall—It is dreadful to see these judges
sitting round a table with angry faces, the black wax candles
burning without radiating light, and to hear the blast of the
ram's horn as though bringing bad tidings of a day of wrath.
Unconsciously the spectator will recall the assemblies of priests
convened to condemn poor Jewish victims to death by the
sword or by burning. And even if the difference between these
judges and the priestly tribunals is very great—for the former
condemn the spirit only, and leave the body alone, while the
latter consigned the body to the flames—nevertheless the mere
spectacle is enough to make the flesh creep, the spectacle of
men blithely assuming the right to condemn anyone who dis-
pleases them to satisfy their baser passions. And even the man
who previously had never believed in hell's torments, and the
demons and spirits entrusted with the task of drawing the
guilty soul through fire and water, might well begin to believe
in them from that day forward, and even imagine that he had
witnessed them himself. . . .[44]

In view of such passages it is not surprising that the novels, particularly Braudes' *Religion and Life*, contain many statements in

favour of religious reform. For Braudes, the chief target of the advocates of reform is represented by the *Šulḥan 'Arukh*,[45] against whose severities he directs the full weight of his attack:

> ... The young students in the *Bêth ha-Midhraš* enthusiastically adopted the ideas of reform and raised a commotion against the laws of the *Šulḥan 'Arukh*, demanding that many of its prohibitions be rescinded and that many of its severities, which had long lost their force, be alleviated. The camp of Israel resounded with the battle-cry: 'We want a new *Šulḥan 'Arukh*, one that is in line with the times: a *Šulḥan 'Arukh* which will not embitter our lives with unreasonable prohibitions, nor suck dry the very marrow from our bones. ...'[46]

The third part of *Religion and Life* supplies vivid details of the manner in which the reformers propagated their ideals, and how the orthodox combated their attempts. Apart from the widespread use of letters by both sides for disseminating their respective arguments,[47] and the formation of societies such as the *Maḥaziqê ha-Dath*[48] by the opponents of reform, the battle was largely waged through the literary journals of the period[49] and in pamphlets especially prepared for the campaign.[50] The main journal favoured by the exponents of reform was *Ha-Meliṣ*, although the less radical *Ha-Maggidh* also espoused their cause. For the orthodox, the journal *Ha-Lebhanon* performed a similar service.[51] One of the principal problems of resorting to such a medium, however, arose out of the difficulty of inducing supporters of the opposite camp to read the articles intended for their consumption. Braudes relates one episode in which a fanatical opponent of reform is induced to read the arguments of his antagonists:

> Rabbi Bezalzul was accustomed to study his lesson in Talmud every day in a certain *Klause*.[52] The beadle would set the tractate aside for him during his absence, and allow no one else to use it, declaring that it was being studied by the 'Rabbi'.
> But the bright young students at this *Klause* began to dip into secular books, works of criticism and research, and also to read the Hebrew journals, including *Ha-Meliṣ*. Intrigued by its articles devoted to *religious reform*, they gave the matter their closest attention, and read every book dealing with the subject. At the same time, a select number of the students received letters from Shraga with a copy of Samuel's missive, and after considerable reflection they decided to take up the cause, and

enter the frontline of the battle. All that was required was to find the right pretext for beginning the struggle with the Rabbis.

One day they took a copy of the journal *He-Haluṣ*,[53] and after cutting it into separate leaves, selected those dealing with the religious reform of things prohibited and permissible which were printed in Rabbinic script. Having erased the pagination to make them resemble odd leaves of sacred texts,[54] they inserted a few pages in the tractate reserved for the Rabbi at the place where he had left off the previous day. No one, not even the beadle, was aware of their action.

Next morning when the Rabbi came to study his lesson as usual, the beadle quickly brought his tractate, and the Rabbi opened it at the correct place—only to be confronted by a number of loose pages. As soon as he had glanced at them and identified them as apparently belonging to a proper book, for they were studded with quotations from Rabbinical sources, he read them through from beginning to end. The students, who were watching from a safe distance to see what he would make of them, noticed him twitching his face, screwing up his eyes, gesticulating with his finger and creasing his brow from time to time. He made no remark, however, and having finished reading them, returned to his Talmudic study as usual as though unaffected by what he had read.

As soon as the Rabbi had departed, the students removed the loose sheets, and inserted others in their place, before handing the tractate to the beadle. They continued the practice for several days.

'Where are these loose sheets from?' the Rabbi asked the beadle quietly on the second morning.

'I have no idea, Rabbi,' the beadle replied, and remained silent.

In the course of a few days, however, the Rabbi realized that this was no chance occurrence; for the previous day he had searched through the whole tractate without finding any loose sheets except those prepared for him, while the next day he discovered fresh ones. The realization that the pages had been planted deliberately—for he had already recognized them as heresy—was strengthened when he recalled the letter which he had received from the city of Naharayim. In consternation he summoned the beadle.

'Confess! To whom do these pages belong? Who put them in the tractate which I study every day?'—the Rabbi shouted at the beadle in threatening tones.

'I swear I don't know!' the beadle protested. And, indeed, he was quite ignorant of what had transpired.[55]

Subsequently the students openly challenged the Rabbi to answer the arguments contained in the article, only to bring down coals of fire upon their heads! It is of interest, however, that the demand for reform is not always aimed at the alleviation of the severities of religious law. On the contrary, Smolenskin criticises the ease with which a man may obtain a divorce and suggests that Rabbis who accept a fee for granting a divorce should be made liable to punishment. In that case, they would confine the grounds for divorce to cases of adultery, and thereby mitigate much needless suffering.[56] Even where an author is highly critical of certain aspects of orthodoxy and strongly advocates reform, he is equally at pains to warn against the dangers of irreligiosity.[57] Braudes, too, points out the dilemma which confronts the advocates of reform,[58] while Rabinowitz argues the case against reform with great cogency, pouring scorn on his hero's naïve belief that the mere publication of an article in a Hebrew journal will be sufficient to evoke a Rabbinical convention and initiate a programme of reform.[59] The perils to which the reformers exposed themselves may be adduced from the advice given to Samuel, the hero of *Religion and Life*, to study a profession which will secure his livelihood before attempting to propagate the ideas of reform.[60] Samuel, incidentally, makes the illuminating confession that his interest in reform was first stimulated by his reading about the work of Luther and the history of the French Revolution.[61]

Towards both the major divisions of eastern European Jewry, the *Mithnaggedhim* and the *Ḥasidhim*, the novels, in general, display a critical and at times fiercely satirical attitude. Mention has already been made of the manner in which the Ḥasidic faction is portrayed by the novelists under review.[62] But the *Mithnaggedhim* fare little better. Smolenskin, indeed, makes the following scathing indictment of both parties:

> Look at the *Mithnaggedh*, who fears not only God, but angels, ghosts and evil spirits; who night and day pores over dead books until his flesh withers and his dull eyes lose all spark of life; who lives only to fast and load himself down with the heavy burden of statutes and injunctions, and with the sorrow and lamentation of fast-days, as though for such things alone

God created man on earth. Behold, you will see before you
the image of the past, of death and of decay! Now turn your
gaze and look at the *Ḥasidh* by way of contrast–a lively man,
who banishes all the cares and worries of life from his heart,
and enjoys himself without a thought for the future, leaving
the morrow to look after itself; he will revel and sing, and whenever there is a celebration or a glass of wine, he is sure to be
there, and you will see him intent on the present, on what
exists now, on life! But you will not find him leading the life
of a sensible man, but rather that of a madman, without rhyme
or reason. His feelings make him dance like a goat and a glass
of wine will start him singing as though man were never born
to toil. . . .
    Both of these factions have led the people astray so that it takes
no heed of the future, and never asks itself such questions as:
What will happen to me in the end? Has salvation perished,
and is my hope of finding peace an illusion? Am I destined
to wander eternally? Must I wait for the end of the world to
put an end to my sorrows? . . .[63]

In another passage, after admitting that the *Ḥasidhim* do, at
least, support each other,[64] Smolenskin proceeds to launch an
onslaught on their opponents:

    The *Mithnaggedhim* are different. They thoroughly despise
the 'holy man', and bitterly mock at his nonsensical practices.
In their opinion no man can be considered holy during his
life-time. But once he has passed away, and all that is remembered of him is the book he has written, then both book and
writer are revered. Indeed, they regard all such books as holy,
no matter how trivial or vapid their content.[65] They pay no
heed to social organization, or think of helping one another.
Each one tramps alone to the synagogue every morning, and
then goes out in search of a livelihood (that is, if his wife is sick
or unsuccessful in business, for otherwise it is the woman who
is the bread-winner, while her husband spends his time in the
Bêth-Midhraš).[66] In the evening he returns to the Synagogue
to read a portion of the Talmud, the Mishnah, the *'Ēn Ya-
'aqobh*[67] or the *Šulḥan 'Arukh*. They are for ever diligently searching out every law and statute contained in the *Šulḥan 'Arukh*
and moreover, add to them any further laws they can themselves devise. For that reason they bitterly hate the *Ḥasidhim*,
who pay no regard to law and statute. . . .[68]

The loathing harboured by the *Mithnaggedhim* against the *Ḥasidhim* finds expression on a number of occasions in these novels.[69]

It is significant that in his novel, *The Two Extremes*, Braudes portrays a *Mithnaggedh*, whose son has become a *Ḥasidh*, as henceforward breaking off all contact with him and regarding him as dead.[70] This hostility applied even to the religious classic most favoured by the *Ḥasidhim*, the *Ẓohar*, which—according to Smolenskin—no *Mithnaggedh* would even deign to read.[71]

Both factions are continually satirized for their adherence to superstitious beliefs and old wives' tales, which incidentally afford many an interesting glimpse into current folklore and custom. The ancient belief that the deaths of innocent children are caused by somebody else's sin,[72] for example, is mentioned in variant and revealing forms. These deaths, on one occasion, are attributed to the 'new fangled' habits of the modern women such as dressing their hair and learning French,[73] while elsewhere the cause of death is purported to stem from somebody reading books in Russian![74] The superstitious belief in ghosts, witches, evil spirits and demons is frequently portrayed in the novels and would appear to have been widespread.[75] 'Never call children "dog" or "cat" at night,' one of Smolenskin's characters is made to declare, 'for there are devils with these names who come to destroy once they are invoked'.[76] In similar vein a dog barking at night is regarded as presaging evil.[77]

The *Yeshibhah*, in particular, is represented as a market for the exchange of old wives' tales, with the young students terrifying each other with stories of giants, witches and devils;[78] of the dead leaving their graves at night to pray in the Great Synagogue, or heal the sick with herbs,[79] or vex sinners;[80] or of evil spirits haunting the cemeteries[81] and frightening travellers at night.[82] These evil spirits, whose power is greater during the counting of the 'Omer,[83] are particularly prevalent at night in the women's gallery of the synagogue. Indeed, on only three nights during the year are they totally banished from it, namely at the New Year and the Day of Atonement.[84] Smolenskin relates the story of a man, who, finding himself alone in the synagogue at night, wishes he had some tobacco with him; whereupon a great red tongue with tobacco on its tip flickers out from the women's gallery in front of his very eyes![85] But the greatest peril consists in pronouncing the name of Lilith, the queen of the devils at night, even when not alone, and even in the synagogue.[86] Evil spirits are described as marrying and bearing offspring,[87] as well

o

as taking possession of unsuspecting individuals.[88] For the superstitiously inclined, Monday is regarded as unfavourable for business activities.[89]

Not unnaturally, popular remedies for healing the sick are associated with similar superstitious beliefs. The most common procedure described is the resort to some suitably qualified person – a gipsy-woman, witch or wonder-worker – to charm away the 'evil-eye' with the appropriate incantation.[90] Gipsy-women were also consulted, according to Smolenskin, not merely in cases of sickness, but even for general advice by men as well as women, though well aware that the practice is forbidden by Jewish law.[91] Curing by means of incantation, however, was also practised by pious and respected ladies:

... Apart from this, Sarah was recognised for her knowledge of incantations. No matter what the trouble—worms, toothache, a lost animal or anxiety over a child—Sarah knew the correct incantation; and many a person was prepared to testify that she had cured every sort of illness or affliction virtually with a touch of her hand.[92]

Similarly Sarah, in the capacity of midwife, recommends that salt be placed at the side of a newly born child to ward off the 'evil eye'.[93] The child is then swathed in a wrap containing a patch from the shirt of 'a man who has died at a ripe old age,' which the women have torn into shreds to sew into the garments of their small children, so that they, too, may enjoy long life.[94] Even the dead have a handful of earth from the holy land thrown into their graves as a defence against the ravages of worms.[95]

Among the miscellaneous superstitions mentioned is the belief that if *Mezuzoth*[96] affixed to the doorposts are not in order, fire will descend from heaven to consume the house and all its occupants.[97] Abramowitz refers to the custom of a man spending the night of *Hoša'na'Rabba'*[98] in study, snatching a furtive and frightened glance at the wall to see whether his head is casting a shadow, which is a sign that he will live throughout the coming year, whereas the absence of such a shadow portends his death.[99] Equally interesting is the idea related by Braudes that on the eve of the festival of Tabernacles the heavens open for a fraction of a second, and that anyone who recognizes the instant will have all his desires of that particular moment fulfilled.[100] On more than one occasion reference is made to the belief in a dead parent appearing in a dream either to give a message to her child, or take revenge on someone threatening her child.[101]

Rabinowitz, again, mentions the belief attributed to Rabbi Akiba, that by studying *Torah* a son may help his parents in the next world.[102] For the same reason the recitation of the *Qaddiš*, or memorial prayer, is explained as a means '. . . of raising your father's soul from the depths of hell to the heights of heaven'.[103] Conversely, in Manassewitz's novel the dying mother of the heroine, Miriam, declared that, although she is no longer able to help her daughter in this world, she will plead for her and shield her in heaven.[104] In Abramowitz's novel Sarah asks her husband to add another clause to her marriage-contract, bequeathing her a half of his share in the world to come.[105] In like manner Rabinowitz describes the wife of a poor teacher as contented '. . . because she firmly believed that God would amply reward her in the next world for allowing her husband to study the *Torah*'.[106]

Although the novelists are usually content to portray such customs and beliefs and allow the reader to draw his own conclusions, they occasionally indulge in direct unfavourable comment. Josef, the hero of *The Wanderer in the Paths of Life*, for example, bitterly complains that his teacher had instilled in him the fear that if he neglected his prayers for a single day he would die, instead of instructing him in the fundamental concepts of religion.[107] Samuel, the hero of *Religion and Life*, makes a still more forthright attack on the custom of throwing away all the water from a house where a death has occurred, as well as from the neighbouring houses, often at the expense of considerable hardship for the occupants. With all the appropriate references he explains the origins of the custom, and how inappropriate it can be for particular situations.[108] Of somewhat different order is the querulous complaint lodged by the hero of Zobeizensky's novel against the custom of performing the marriage ceremony in the courtyard of the synagogue instead of in the synagogue itself.[109]

On more than one occasion Smolenskin mentions the prescribed custom of leaving a corner of the table bare—except on Sabbaths and New Moons—in memory of the destruction of the Temple; for the same reason a portion of the wall is left unplastered and inscribed with the words *In memory of the destruction*.[110] He also outlines the practice of making mud candlesticks to supplement the normal candlesticks of brass for the festival of the Rejoicing of the Law: 'Mud and dust were rolled into spheres, in each of which a hole was pierced with the finger. Afterwards they were dried in the sun and used as candlesticks.'[111] Of the practices associated with the Day of Atonement,[112] the most vivid is to be found in Rabinowitz's novel *At the Crossroads*. '. . . During the afternoon service he would kneel before the "smiter", and joyfully suffer thirty-nine strokes. . . .'[113] But most interesting of all such practices, perhaps, are Smolenskin's descriptions of the annual feast organized by the burial society,[114] and the formula for a 'Donkey's burial' from which the novel derived its name:

> This register contains a list of all who have transgressed Israel's statutes, and who are due to be punished upon their death, for they will be given a *Donkey's burial*. But let not the reader fear that men are buried in graves belonging to donkeys, nor imagine that there is a cemetery maintained as a last resting place for those beasts. Far from it! The guilty are not buried *among donkeys*; but they (the members of the burial society) will not wash them, dress them in a shroud, bear them on their shoulders, or dig them a grave amongst their brethren. Instead they dump them fully dressed in a sack, cart them away and bury them outside the boundaries of the cemetery—to the lasting dishonour of the entire family.[115]

The action to be taken when inclement weather makes it impossible to recite the blessing over the new moon is described by Weisbrem with considerable humour in his novel *Between the Times*. After convening the leading members of the congregation, the Rabbi pronounces a day of fasting for the entire community; although in the event, a mere handful of citizens—even among those who attended the meeting and supported the measure—actually remember to fast.[116]

The infraction of, or negligence concerning, religious law and custom forms a constant theme within the novels.[117] In many of the large towns the standards of observance are described as very lax. Indeed, on learning that the Jewish inhabitants of Odessa smoke on the Sabbath and eat ritually unclean food, a pious Jew from Lithuania is so scandalized that he stuffs his fingers in his ears![118] In the small towns and villages, strict conformity to orthodox practice still held sway, and even the most minor departure from the accepted patterns of behaviour was viewed with the utmost disfavour. Frequent reference is made to the feelings of horror aroused in pious breasts by such infractions as wearing European-style clothes, shaving, leaving the head uncovered, carrying a handkerchief on the Sabbath, and reading secular books.[119]

The mere idea of even looking at a church[120] or visiting a theatre is described as abhorrent.[121] But the most serious censure is reserved for ritual infringements. The neglect of prayer naturally evokes hostility,[122] while Josef the hero of Smolenskin's *The Wanderer in the Paths of Life* is bitterly attacked because one of the fringes of his ritual garment the *Ṣiṣith*[123] is found to have only six threads instead of the prescribed eight.[124] But the abuse to which Josef is subjected on that score pales in comparison to the uproar that greets Benjamin, a member of a small Hasidic community, where he is accused of eating and drinking on a fast day.[125]

Of all such ritual transgressions, however, any violation of the dietary laws was regarded as particularly heinous, and is always condemned by the novelists. The underlying psychology is shrewdly outlined by Smolenskin in the following passage, where the hero is disgusted by the behaviour of his former master, a charlatan who had previously masqueraded as a pious wonder-worker, in ordering forbidden meat:

> I was very astonished at the sight, for even though I knew the man to be a scoundrel and a villain, I had never imagined that he would allow forbidden meat to pass his lips. For in common with all the Jews in my native land I had always regarded anyone who indulged in so nauseating a practice as guilty of a much greater crime than swindling or robbery. And even though I, too, had acquired the same habit for some time past,[126] I nevertheless regarded my own indulgence in a different light, for I had adopted European clothes and was versed in languages and secular knowledge. But that a man who dressed in traditional garb and was unable to read secular books should partake of gentile food appeared to me as a monstrous sin.[127]

The tendency to equate Enlightenment with a deliberate disregard for the dietary laws is frequently satarized with great bitterness in these novels, particularly by Rabinowitz, who portrays in a most contemptible light,[128] a Jewish doctor who openly

partakes of swine's flesh and presses others to do so. Conversely, one of Weisbrem's young heroes, an idealized *Maskil* of sterling character, is falsely accused of eating forbidden meat in a
villainous attempt to alienate his father's affection.[129] On the
other hand, the savage punishment inflicted for an infringement
of the dietary laws is no less scathingly attacked by Braudes in his
description of a man who has been put in the stocks because he
has been seen drinking tea in a gentile's house with his head uncovered.[130] In similar vein Smolenskin describes how a butcher,
who is discovered to have been selling ritually unclean meat
for ten years, is dragged through the town with an animal's
head tied round his neck while all the inhabitants pelt him with
dust. He is subsequently forbidden to sell meat for six months,
and told to atone for his sin by prayer and fasting.[131]

The slightest infringement of any religious law or custom, or
the merest suspicion of heterodox opinion was liable to evoke the
charge of *heretic* (*'Apiqores*) or heresy (*'Apiqorsuth*). These terms of
abuse were employed indiscriminately in condemnation of a
wide variety of offence ranging from open agnosticism—where
the application of the term is, indeed, justified—to such less
cogent reasons as the adoption of European dress,[132] the reading
of Hebrew books printed in Vilna,[133] and the disbelief in evil
spirits.[134] Altogether these expressions occur more than 270 times
within these novels, although it is significant that they are to be
found in Braudes' *Religion and Life* on more than 150 occasions,
while Sheikewitz's *The Outcast* accounts for a further 48. Several
of the stories, on the other hand, make no mention of the term.[135]
The full force of the weapon may be observed in the highly
dramatic scene in Braudes' novel in which Samuel and the local
Rabbi bitterly dispute the correct interpretation of religious
law, in synagogue before the entire congregation, until finally
the Rabbi accuses Samuel of heresy:

> 'Do you call that, too, an answer. . . .' Samuel began, but
> the Rabbi interrupted him.
> 'Answer?' the Rabbi rebuked him at the top of his voice.
> 'Oh, how mistaken I have been in answering you up till now.
> It is, indeed, an inspired and just law that forbids an Israelite
> to answer an *'Apiqores*. . . . .'
> 'Listen to me, O house of Israel!' Samuel began. . . .
> ''*Apiqores*!' The sound floated up to him from all the congre-
> gation.

''*Apiqores!*' Even the women were shouting it from behind the grills in the women's gallery.

Samuel was deeply perturbed. 'Even those whose battle I am fighting are persecuting me'—he thought bitterly. 'But no ... I shall not submit to the Rabbi's chastisement. I shall fight on, even for such fools as these.' But the voice of the Rabbi rose even stronger:

'What a sin I have committed in answering you. . . . I always regarded you as a scholar who enjoyed arguing with me over fine points of law. But now that I see that you are simply an '*Apiqores*, I have no further desire to answer the '*Apiqorsuth* you keep mouthing. It is forbidden even to listen. Get out of here, before you defile this holy place. . . . Not another word ... And never cross my threshold again. . . . It is forbidden even to look at you! It is forbidden to open the door to you!'[136]

The most heinous of all offences, however, was apostasy, and the problem of conversion to Christianity finds expression in almost all the novels,[137] but in particular in the stories of Smolenskin and Sheikewitz.[138]

Although many of the converts or intending converts described are motivated by material incentives—in order to obtain a residence permit,[139] for example, or a commission in the army,[140] or for the purposes of marriage,[141] or to escape a difficult situation[142]—the threat of conversion is sometimes used as the ultimate protest against real or imagined ill-treatment.[143] It is indicative of the author's attitude, however, that many of the converts and intending converts are subsequently stricken by remorse;[144] while a number of the heroines are characterized by their firm refusal to convert even in the face of heavy pressure.[145] The novels instance examples of threats and even force being employed in order to win converts to Christianity,[146] most notably in the case of a young girl of twelve kidnapped by her former nurse and imprisoned in an Italian nunnery.[147] On several occasions, however, Smolenskin portrays the more subtle methods employed by Christian missionaries, although the heroes concerned successfully withstand all such attempts to induce them to abandon their faith.[148] In view of the widespread abhorrence of apostasy which the novels portray, it is not surprising that Sheikewitz asserts on more than one occasion that Jews will afford a co-religionist every possible help in order to save him from conversion.[149] The same author bitterly upbraids the advocates both of ultra-orthodoxy and of extreme *Haskalah* as responsible for the large numbers of converts to Christianity.[150] Again, it is significant that the downfall of the arch-villain in Smolenskin's *The Wanderer in the Paths of Life* hinges upon the apostasy of his mother and grandfather.[151] On the other hand, in two of Smolenskin's novels a love affair between a Jewish hero and a gentile heroine ends happily with the bride embracing Judaism.[152]

Not unnaturally, the novels abound with ethical and moral reflections,[153] while the strong flavour of didacticism permeating these stories[154] is inevitably accompanied by an inclination to moralise at every conceivable opportunity.[155] Even Leinwand, whose novel *The Artful Villain* is crammed with cheap melodrama and absurd intrigue, feels constrained to include the following revealing observation:

> But I had better stop preaching at you, O house of Israel, for on this occasion I have entered the lists not as a moralist but as a writer of fiction. In the course of my story I have allowed myself to be carried away, but now I shall restrain my feelings and return to my tale.[156]

Of particular interest, however, are the not infrequent examples of heroes and heroines indulging in unethical behaviour, of which the most common type consists of listening through a keyhole, or from behind a door or through a wall to conversations not intended for their ears.[157] These practices cause even the authors some embarrassment, and on more than one occasion they attempt to justify the character's behaviour by pleading mitigating circumstances![158] In like manner one of the heroines in Braudes' *The Two Extremes* lies to her mother about the ownership of a Russian book without the slightest hesitation.[159] It is, perhaps, comforting to find that even such idealised paragons of virtue can occasionally succumb to human weakness![160]

The synagogue and its functionaries naturally play a not inconsiderable part in the novels under review, and on numerous occasions the authors describe their role in the structure of Jewish life. Apart from their primary function as places of worship, the synagogues of the small towns and villages were used to accommodate students and wayfarers, while strangers would be invited from the synagogue to share a meal with members of the congregation.[161] The courtyard of the synagogue which—according to Smolenskin—might consist of an insalubrious piece of wasteland,[162] was used for weddings, lamentations for the dead, and as the place where 'sinners' were punished.[163] Braudes maintains that in Lithuania, especially in the small towns, the synagogue provided a platform, from which the attention of the community could be drawn to a particular grievance; the individual concerned was permitted to interrupt the Sabbath service before the reading of the Law, and the service could not be resumed until the matter had been settled.[164] The same procedure was adopted for public announcements.[165]

Braudes, too, gives details of the different titles, allocated on a class basis, which were used in summoning members of the congregation to the reading of the Law;[166] while both Smolenskin and Weisbrem refer to synagogues frequented by people engaged in a specific trade.[167] Similarly the difference between a *Bêth-Tephillah* (House of Prayer) and a *Bêth ha-Midhraš* (House of Study) is defined on one occasion by the assertion that the former was patronized by tailors, cobblers and similar comparatively uneducated classes, while the latter was largely the preserve of the more scholarly or wealthier sections of the community.[168]

Although Braudes describes a synagogue, where the seats are bought or rented, and ownership indicated by a letter of the alphabet marked in red on a green circle at the top of the seat, the smaller synagogues, particularly those of the Ḥasidic sect, are described as remarkable for their utter lack of formality and, indeed, of even the slightest shadow of decorum.[169] Zobeizensky goes so far as to interrupt his narrative for several pages in order to deliver a diatribe against the manifold, disrespectful activities practised in the synagogue, as a prelude to his demand that the wedding ceremony should properly be performed there instead of in the courtyard, where the bride and bridegroom are often compelled to wallow in mud or deep snow during the winter months![170] On the other hand, Smolenskin is equally scathing about the large synagogues in Odessa, with their choirs, rented seats, and rules forbidding entry to non-members during the festivals. He satirically recounts the episode of a Rabbi involved in a tussle with a gentile beadle who has refused him permission to enter, while the warden of the congregation sides with the beadle.[171]

The novels contain numerous references to the portion of the synagogue reserved for women, which was situated on the

western side, and separated from the space reserved for the men
by a partition, which contained a number of grilles or windows
covered with a curtain.[172] Its topmost gallery was often closed
except on festivals,[173] and in consequence many superstitions were
centred on it.[174] The women's gallery sometimes housed a special
cupboard, to which were consigned worn-out prayer books and
other religious insignia, which were too holy to be destroyed.[175]
It was often used for secular and indeed frivolous activities,[176]
a fact which Abramowitz satirizes by claiming that even goats
and cows were permitted to roam there freely.[177]

With respect to the location of the synagogue, Braudes provides the following observation:

> No Lithuanian town lacks its 'Synagogue street' nor is there
> any town in which that street is not distinguished from all
> other streets by its particular character and flavour. Usually its
> distinction lies in its mud and filth, in its putrid atmosphere,
> and the stench which assails the nostrils of every passer-by.
> But the street is also distinguished for more elevated reasons.
> The synagogue and the house of study stand there conspic-
> uously; the most orthodox people in town live there—the
> teachers, beadles, cantors, and the Rabbi's house, too, is situ-
> ated there.[178]

The synagogue officials, however, are elsewhere described in
much harsher tones. Towards the cantors, Smolenskin maintains an attitude of overall animosity, and accuses them of pride,
conceit, venality, cynicism, hypocrisy and even immorality![179]
The choirboys, who often accompanied itinerant cantors from
town to town to eke out a meagre livelihood, fare scarcely better,
and are roundly upbraided for their irreligiosity and deceitful
practices.[180] Nor do the beadles receive more favourable treatment. Their ignorance, brutality and the abuse of their sometimes very considerable powers—such as, for example, their
authority to allocate 'eating-days'[181] or nominate conscripts[182]
—are severely criticised in the novels.[183]

The attitude towards the Rabbis, however, is by no means unequivocal. The most consistently unfavourable portrait of the
Rabbi occurs, not surprisingly, in Braudes' *Religion and Life*,
where the whole purpose of the novelist consists of an attack on
Rabbinical stringencies, often couched in highly satirical
terms.[184] Smolenskin, too, reserves some unpleasant comments for
them.[185] But, indeed, both authors, particularly the latter, sketch

a number of sympathetic portraits of Rabbis, emphasizing their piety, sincerity, moderation and essential kindness.[186] Weisbrem, too, includes a Rabbi of admirable character in his novel *Between the Times*,[187] while Rabinowitz compares the orthodox Rabbis most favourably with the 'enlightened' Rabbis appointed by the Russian government.[188] Again, Sheikewitz points out the unenviable lot of the Rabbi, and the many hardships to which he was frequently subjected.[189]

It is evident, therefore, that many aspects of the religious life of eastern European Jewry in the nineteenth century are reflected within these novels. The interest of the authors is wide-ranging, and embraces many facets of the religion in its corporate and individual manifestations. The ambivalent attitude expressed in so many of these novels arises from an overall sincere appreciation of the general principles of Judaism coupled with a highly critical approach to many of its details in practice. That the novelists were anxious to cleanse away what they considered to be its dross, and purge it of all unwholesome accretions and debasing superstitions can scarcely be doubted. But it is far less certain to what degree they sensed the winds of change, which were so soon to sweep away both dross and gold, both base accretion and solid core, breaking down the entire framework of traditional Jewish life in eastern Europe, and ultimately obliterating it almost without trace.

EIGHT

Conclusion

In the preceding chapters an attempt has been made to estimate the qualities of the Hebrew novel written in eastern
Europe between the years 1868-1888, and to describe the social,
cultural and religious facets of Jewish life which they reflect. The
dual purpose displayed in greater measure or in less by all the
novelists under review, in their desire to combine an attractive
tale with didactic ideas and social criticism, resulted in a hybrid
novel, whose major components are frequently at serious odds
with one another, and which at best are forced to nestle uncomfortably within a single framework. This awkward jostling of
fantasy and realism is further emphasized by the incongruity of
plot and setting. The violence which so many of the plots contain[1] in the shape of theft, abduction, arson, suicide and murder
stands out in striking contrast to the values and patterns of behaviour of the society which they purport to describe. This
strange paradox stems from the attempt to superimpose the flamboyant themes of the western European romantic novel upon
a background of Jewish life in eastern Europe which was characterized by sobriety, timidity and—in the case of the emotional
and passionate instincts—a rigid self-control and discipline.[2] The
environment and mental climate in which the Jews of eastern
Europe were reared and educated make any such wholesale recourse to the types of crime and violence depicted in these novels
quite unthinkable—a fact which largely explains the sense of the
grotesque so frequently engendered by these stories. Certainly,
the fact that so much of the action is manifestly out of character
with the setting from which it springs is largely responsible for
the unsatisfactory nature of these novels.

Both of the major elements in these stories, moreover, suffer from the inherent weaknesses previously outlined. The literary impact of the novels is inevitably weakened because of the many faults in plot construction, characterization and style. It is sufficient to recall the lack of any adequate literary tradition, the absence of a critical public, the over-hasty modes of composition, the compulsive didacticism and particularly the pathetically restricted linguistic resources, all of which detract from the literary value of these tales. On the other hand, the social aspects of the novels reflect the ambivalent attitude of many of the authors under review, the love-hate relationship which they display towards the Jewish people, and the simultaneous loyalty and revulsion which they evince in the face of the dreadful plight of the communities of eastern Europe. The genuine desire to ease their people's burden becomes all the more poignant in the light of their inability to suggest any but peripheral remedies, and of their helplessness in the face of problems of such magnitude.[3] In spite of their passionate involvement, and the deep sincerity which characterizes their strictures against the social abuses of their time, thereby lending a measure of power and conviction to their stories, the very ardour of their plea often tends to exaggerate and distort the picture of the society they portray, so that considerable caution must be exercised before accepting their depiction of Jewish life at its face value. For all the elements of realism, which may be detected so frequently within these novels, it is important to recall that the facts of the society they portray are presented through the prism of the various attitudes adopted by the novelists to their environment—attitudes which may be heavily weighted in accordance with a preconceived and highly prejudiced point of view. Indeed, in some respects their portraits —certainly the most virulent amongst them—shed more light at times upon their own states of mind than upon the state of the society they describe. Of their genuine intent to infuse a strain of realism into their stories, however, there can be no doubt.

Before proceeding, therefore, to evaluate the contribution of the novels, in the period under review, to the development of modern Hebrew literature, some attention should be devoted to the sources from which the authors drew the romantic and the realistic tendencies which together comprise these stories. In this respect even a cursory survey of the various influences to be detected in these tales yields abundant evidence of the hand of Abraham Mapu. As the first Hebrew novelist, Mapu's prestige stood very high, and his writings were held in the highest regard by his successors.[4] Indeed, it is scarcely an exaggeration to suggest that many of the leading Hebrew writers in the following generation developed their first interest in *belles-lettres* via the agency of Mapu's stories. The number of editions of Mapu's novels[5]—particularly *The Love of Zion*—which have appeared during the last one hundred years bears ample testimony to the appeal he has continued to exert on successive generations of readers.

In the course of this study, the influence of Abraham Mapu has already been indicated on a number of occasions.[6] It is even more significant, however, that the novels under review contain several specific references to Mapu's writings. In *The Wanderer in the Paths of Life*, for example, Smolenskin waxes eloquent on the benefits to be accrued from reading the works of Mapu, Lebensohn and Gordon, which 'delight the heart of everyone who reads them'.[7] In particular, he praises Mapu's first novel *The Love of Zion* and proceeds to dwell on Mapu's overriding superiority.[8] Sheikewitz, too, declares that Mapu's stories are read by all aspiring *Maskilim*;[9] while later in the story he justifies the inclusion of a dream in his novel by adding a satirical footnote to the effect that the practice is followed by some of the greatest Hebrew writers, and specifically mentions Mapu and Smolenskin.[10] Rabinowitz, on the other hand, who maintains a highly critical attitude towards *Haskalah* in general,[11] includes Mapu's novel *The Hypocrite* (and particularly Abramowitz's *Fathers and Sons*) amongst the works of fiction which exert a harmful influence on his hero.[12] When the latter gives a copy of *The Love of Zion* to his pious and devoted wife in the hope of arousing in her the concept of romantic love, he is deeply disappointed to find that the story leaves her quite unmoved.[13] In consolation, the hero conjures up in his mind a picture of 'the beautiful Elisheba whom Mapu had created out of his imagination'.[14] But even such satirical references only serve to emphasize the widespread popularity of Mapu's writings.

More specifically, the direct influence of Mapu's novel may be discerned time and time again in the stories under review. Josef, for example, the hero of *The Wanderer in the Paths of Life*, when arrested as a spy in France, is released by the intervention of the British Consul.[15] Similarly, one of the heroes of Mapu's *The Hypocrite* is rescued from a no less embarrassing situation by the British Consul at Damascus.[16] In *The Reward of the Righteous* the rumour of the hero's death by drowning[17] is paralleled by a similar incident in *The Hypocrite*;[18] while the three villainous teachers in *The Inheritance*[19] bear many points of resemblance to the trio of villains in Mapu's *The Love of Zion*.[20] In Weisbrem's *18 Coins* the midnight battle in which the heroes vanquish the villains[21] is very reminiscent of a similar midnight struggle in *The Hypocrite*,[22] while the heroes of both novels have just finished studying agriculture[23]—in accordance with the ideals of the exponents of Enlightenment.[24] Again, the planting of forged notes and the forging and interception of letters which occur respectively in the novels by Leinwand and Meinkin[25] are well-tried devices from Mapu's novels.[26] The murder and arson which occur in Zobeizensky's novel[27] have striking parallels in *The Love of Zion*,[28] while the heroes of both novels pour out their love for the heroines in a markedly similar manner. In Zobeizensky's novel, too, the high-flown language represents the closest attempt to imitate Mapu's style, although most of the minor novelists, at least, frequently insert passages clearly modelled on Mapu's use of language. Even the choice of such names as Zimri,[29] Nabal[30] and Reumah[31] to represent wicked characters, or Emil[32] for a young assimilated Jew who is no friend of his people, or Elisheba[33] for an enlightened heroine, are clearly borrowed from Mapu's stories. Again, the many attacks on hypocrites masquerading as pious men which these novels contain[34] closely follow the lines laid down by Mapu.

More importantly, however, Mapu represented one of the channels through which the influence of the French romantic novelists, particularly Eugène Sue and Alexandre Dumas, was conveyed into Hebrew literature. The violence, intrigue and crime, the exciting adventures and romantic love—all of which were so alien to the patterns of Jewish life in eastern Europe, yet which play so important a role in the stories under review—were transmitted from the French romantic novel into the Hebrew novel partly via the agency of Abraham Mapu.[35] A clearly recognizable chain of influence runs from Eugène Sue's *Mystères de Paris* through Mapu's *The Hypocrite* into the novels of Mapu's successors. This process of transmission supplies a key to the understanding of the grotesque superimposition of the flamboyant types of plot derived from the French novel on to a Jewish setting so unsuitable to receive them. The process naturally demanded the portrayal of Jewish villains and romantic heroes upon the somewhat sombre canvas of Jewish life in eastern Europe. But whereas the underworld of Paris constituted an admirable background for scenes of violence and intrigue, the resort to the Jewish community as the backcloth for similar complex adventures can only be regarded as a highly unsatisfactory substitute. The circumscribed horizons of Jewish life, and the severely limited scope of occupation which the Jews of eastern Europe might alone pursue, inevitably gave rise to a pettiness and narrowness of activity, which accord badly with the extravagant and wildly improbable plots of many of these stories.

It is, perhaps, for that reason that Braudes' novels, which carefully eschew the flamboyant intrigues to be found in the stories of most of his contemporaries, are in many ways the most successful. Certainly, the artificial and unconvincing nature of the principal heroes and villains of most of these novels stems largely from the lack of any organic connection between them and the society which provides the background for their activities.[36] Nevertheless, it is only fair to recall that the most improbable aspects of these stories were the ones which exerted the strongest appeal on a youth consistently starved of adventure and physical excitement.[37] In that respect, moreover, the relish displayed for violence and melodrama clearly demonstrates a need on the part of author and reader alike to compensate for the lack of aggression and activity in their own lives. The daring exploits and exciting episodes show marked escapist tendencies, and doubtless reflect an element of wish-fulfilment in the choice of theme and plot.

Mapu, however, derived an additional source of inspiration from Eugène Sue. The *Mystères de Paris* was regarded as a social novel, aimed against many of the abuses of contemporary society and fiercely critical in its approach. Mapu employed a similar technique in his novel of contemporary life, *The Hypocrite*, in which he sought to criticise what he considered to be the evils of Jewish life from the standpoint of a convinced exponent of Enlightenment. The criticisms expressed in *The Hypocrite*, however, are comparatively moderate, and Mapu's overall approach is cautious and restrained. Nevertheless, the social aspect of his long and rambling novel was equally transmitted to his succes-

sors, who proceeded to direct a much stronger and more withering blast of criticism against such evils as they saw besetting Jewish life. The developed social conscience of the authors under review may be discerned in the realist elements contained in their
stories, which form so stark a contrast to the romantic fancies
encountered in so many of the plots. The deleterious consequences resulting from this uncomfortable fusion of romantic
and realist elements have been previously demonstrated.[38]

The strong realist tendencies of these novels, however, drew
considerable support from another source—namely the Russian
critics of the Positivist School.[39] Partly from reading Russian literature in the original and partly via the agency of the penetrating
Hebrew critic A. U. Kovner,[40] the Hebrew authors of the period
came to look upon the writer's task as primarily that of a social
reformer. Literature was to be regarded as a force in life—an instrument for the propagation of ideas and the improvement of
society. The role of the writer, therefore, was only to be assumed
with all due seriousness and a fitting sense of responsibility.

The novels, themselves, contain ample evidence of such an
attitude, certainly as far as the more important authors are concerned. It is pertinent, for example, to recall the conception of
literature outlined by Braudes in his preface to the third part of
Religion and Life where the author emphasizes that the purpose
of literature is to increase the reader's awareness of life, and that
he has couched his chronicle in novel form only, as it were, to
sugar the pill. More specifically, the impact of Russian literature
on a number of the characters is described in detail.[41] Rachel,
for example, the heroine of *Religion and Life*, is portrayed as a firm
admirer of the Russian critic Pisarev:

> . . . The modern Russian authors greatly influenced her
> thought, and their ideas took deep root in her mind; she ad-
> mired the name 'Pisarev' enormously, and read with interest
> all the books and stories which he recommended.[42]

The following passage from the same story is equally revealing:

> Conversation between Samuel and Rachel was more like a
> discussion. Their views on life and *Haskalah* were very diffe-
> rent: Rachel had acquired her ideas and knowledge from
> *modern* Russian books, and they had exercised a powerful

P

influence on all her modes of thought and belief, so that she had become a realist; while Samuel was an *idealist* in word and deed. . . .[43]

The heroine of *The Two Extremes* undergoes a similar mental revolution:

> Since Shiphrah had learned Russian and begun to read the works of the modern writers, novelists and poets alike, which had set her thinking and given full play to her imagination— she had come to despise her companions, the young girls of her town, and found the idle gossip which occupied the young ladies of her own age utterly wearisome. In consequence she held herself aloof, feeling that it was better to read a book, or sit at home browsing through a novel, than to listen to the thousand empty phrases and sweet nothings with which the girls of Sukkoth amused themselves. . . .[44]

Rabinowitz, whose standpoint throughout his novel is severely critical of the impact of modern ideas upon young Jews who are not equipped to understand them properly, provides a negative confirmation of the growing interest in the new school of Russian literature by outlining the harmful influence exerted by the works of Pisarev and Dobrolyubov on his young hero.[45] Abramowitz, on the other hand, bitterly complains that Hebrew literature has fallen into dire straits because—unlike other literatures—it has no roots in the life of the people:

> Literature which is rooted in and grows out of the life and history of a people will in turn influence that life, forming a cycle of cause and effect, with both literature and the people reacting on each other. But Hebrew literature in our day, which has no contact with the people and its needs, and is unaffected by life, can exert no influence and is merely superfluous as far as life is concerned.[46]

This belief that it is the task of literature to perform a positive service for society is responsible for the bitterly satirical attacks upon such Hebrew writers as compile books metaphorically in a vacuum, or write poetry which is mere jingle without content.[47] Sheikewitz, for example, after including in his novel a particularly heinous jingle purportedly composed by Barukh Leib, a professional jester or *Badhehan*,[48] proceeds to vent his scorn on the uncritical composition and publication of Hebrew poetry:

I know that many of my readers will ask me angrily: Do we lack madmen who imagine themselves to be wonderful poets, and are constantly producing poems which are utterly worthless? Even many of our genuine *Maskilim*, the editors of weekly or monthly journals, are not ashamed to publish in their magazines poems such as these, which consist of mere sounds without the slightest spark of life. Nor is their language any better than that used by the *Badheḥan*, Barukh Leib.[49]

It is unfortunate that Sheikewitz almost immediately produces another poem - this time in all seriousness - which in itself is scarcely an improvement![50]

Apart from the clear traces of influence exerted by the French romantic novelists and the Russian realist critics, it is of interest to note the other authors whose names appear within these novels, and whose works may therefore be considered as part of the general literary background of the Hebrew writers of the period. Of Russian authors, mention is made of Pushkin and Lermontov,[51] Turgenev[52], Nekrasov[53] and Krylov.[54] German literature is represented by numerous references, mostly laudatory ,to Lessing's *Nathan der Weise*,[55] as well as to works by Goethe,[56] Schiller[57] and Berne.[58] There is also a fragment of Büchmann in translation, although the author's name is not mentioned.[59] Much of Smolenskin's *The Joy of the Godless*, indeed, consists of a long discussion devoted to such works by Goethe as *Werther, Hermann und Dorothea* and especially *Faust*, the latter being subjected to a detailed analysis and comparison with Shakespeare's *Hamlet*.[60]

Although Shakespeare is the only English author—apart from a number of philosophers referred to in Sirkis' *Esther*[61]—whose name is specifically mentioned in these novels, Smolenskin represents him as the greatest of all writers,[62] while one of his characters claims to have read all Shakespeare's plays and poetry.[63] It is of interest that when Miriam's father burns all her books in foreign languages, the number includes a Polish translation of *The Merchant of Venice*.[64] Braudes, too, warmly praises Shakespeare's great contribution to literature.[65] Smolenskin's stories, on occasion, also seem to bear strong traces of the influence of Dickens,[66] with whose works Smolenskin might well have been acquainted in German translation.[67] Of French authors, specific reference is made to Alexandre Dumas, Eugène Sue, Paul Pavel[68] and Victor Hugo,[69] while both Rousseau and Voltaire receive short shrift at Smolenskin's hands.[70] The latter also refers to Jewish boys who are acquainted with the Latin poets Horace and Virgil (as well as the Polish poet Mickiewitz),[71] while Braudes inserts a quotation from Plutarch's *Alexander of Macedon* in *Religion and Life*.[72]

This catalogue of foreign authors mentioned in the novels under review is not without interest from two points of view. On the one hand it illustrates the very serious attempts made by the exponents of Enlightenment to reach out into the various literatures of Europe. On the other hand, it serves as a poignant reminder of the comparatively narrow limitations of their general culture. Autodidacts as far as secular knowledge is concerned, and lacking the literary discipline which results from a systematic education, their acquaintance with the canons of European literature was fragmentary and uninformed. For the most part, therefore, they express themselves in a medium only partially grasped; and no matter how many of the techniques and literary devices they may have acquired, their compositions lack the inner cohesion of the mature and practised writer. The initial disability of having been first introduced to the very concept of literature at a comparatively advanced age proved too formidable a hurdle for any of them to overcome with complete success. When Jacob Hetzron, the hero of Braudes' *The Two Extremes* is made to ask the naïve but revealing question 'What is literature?'[73] his enquiry may almost be regarded as symbolizing the perplexity of his entire generation. All the novels under review represent, in some degree, an attempt to find an answer to that question. Some of the answers are nearer the mark than others, but all are lisped and stammered out and incomplete. They do, however, constitute a partial answer, and as such prepare the way for the more rounded and artistic novels of the subsequent period. In the development of modern Hebrew literature they represent not so much a great step as a clumsy but powerful lurch forward in the right direction.

It is against this background that the following brief estimates of the individual novels should be considered. Of all the novelists under review Smolenskin must certainly be granted pride of place by virtue of the number, range and power of his novels. His first and largest work, *The Wanderer in the Paths of Life* remains, perhaps, the most important. Picaresque and autobiographical in flavour, the story reflects the life of eastern European Jewry in the nineteenth century in extremely vivid colours. In spite of its crudities and exaggerations, its tortuous plot and melodramatic villainies, the kaleidoscopic nature of the work, together with the author's obvious sincerity and personal experience of the various facets of the life he describes, exert a considerable appeal even for the modern reader of more sophisticated tastes. Moreover, the hero Josef, represents one of the most serious attempts in all these novels to portray a real person of flesh and blood.[74] By the end of the third part, however, the story has worn itself out, so that part IV, written many years later,[75] has little organic connection with the rest of the novel. Completely different in outlook, the final part is important only for its penetrating analysis of, and proposed solutions for, the problems of Jewish life, motivated more by national feelings than by social, economic or political considerations.[76] The attempts to maintain the story, however, are fatuous, with the exception of the attractive little episode of the impertinent Halfon.[77] Nowhere else in Smolenskin's novels is the story-teller so completely ousted by the publicist.

To a lesser degree, the latter statement also applies to Smolenskin's second novel, *The Joy of the Godless*, whose flimsy and inconsequential plot serves only to house the long philosophical and critical discussions—or rather soliloquies—which comprise the core of the book. As a result, the overriding impression is one of lack of balance, the serious, almost Socratic dialogues contrasting strangely with the naïvety of the plot. There is some attempt at character analysis—an advance on Mapu in this respect—and occasional touches of humour, although both elements represent a mere shadow of Mendele's later achievement. More important, however, is Smolenskin's appreciation of the traditional values and ethical standards lurking behind the unprepossessing exterior of the Lithuanian *Melammedh*[78]—in striking contrast to the frivolous characteristics of the 'enlightened' young men whom he portrays. But the hero, Simon, who is supposed to personify the best of both worlds, is scarcely a sympathetic character.

Linguistically, the novel displays traces of a simpler and clearer mode of expression. Some of the conversations are quite lively, and the use of *Melisah*[79] is more restrained. But many of the epithets still consist of stock-phrases, while the gap between such writing and that of Mendele—let alone European literature—is all too wide. The personality of the author bursts through the novel at many points, displaying his vitality and power of thought. But the work manifests equally clear signs of carelessness, over-hasty and ill-considered writing, as well as an impatience, which has little in common with great artistry, and nothing in common with 'an infinite capacity for taking pains'. The lack of self-criticism, however, is partly offset by the author's sincerity, and by a spontaneity which exerts a considerable appeal.

Smolenskin's third novel, *A Donkey's Burial*, is equally uneven. The opening chapters are excellent, the plot original and the humour uproarious at times; but the same level is not maintained throughout the story in spite of the fairly consistent half-mocking style. The bitter social criticism which permeates the novel, the cutting satire and the inevitable untimely death of the hero detract from the interest of the narrative itself, while the final sanctification of the villainous Zebadiah is more effective as satire than as story. Here, again, there is the same invective against the leaders of the Jewish communities,[80] and the same criticism of the evils of Jewish life; but the author produces very moving arguments in extenuation. The characters develop little. Even the hero, in spite of his tendency to introspection, is neither convincing nor consistent. But Zebadiah, on the other hand, is far from being a mere melodramatic, double-dyed villain. Most of the characters suffer, however, from Smolenskin's fondness for exaggerated emotionalism. Apart from its social criticism, the point of the story is somewhat obscure. Certainly, the observation in the final paragraph that the novel demonstrates the power of love, and records the story of the stolen cakes,[81] can hardly be taken seriously in view of the style of writing. The novel does, indeed, contain many powerful passages, both in the humorous and the serious social episodes, and it supplies ample evidence of Smolenskin's fertile imagination. But the descriptions are still stock, and the limitations of language still painfully obvious.

Pride and Fall is by far the weakest of Smolenskin's novels. In spite of a promising beginning the framework of the story, consisting of a number of travellers each relating their histories to while away the voyage, is painfully naïve; while the clumsily contrived 'happy ending' with its *deus ex machina* in the shape of an inheritance to the tune of 15 million roubles is quite in keeping with the general low level. Some of the individual 'frame-stories' are well related, and contain many points of similarity with *The Wanderer in the Paths of Life*;[82] but the work can scarcely be regarded as a cohesive novel. There are a number of interesting attempts at characterization, but many of the people in the story are mere personifications of a single quality. Indeed, the very fact that some of them remain nameless throughout the story is indicative of their shadowy existence.

The fifth novel, *The Reward of the Righteous*, is of a very different order, although once more sadly uneven. The first part of the novel outstrips all the previous stories by far in its artistry, dramatic techniques, dramatic tension, and its serious attempts at characterization. Even the dialogue is more natural in parts. The main didactic themes—questions of marriage and education, particularly the education of girls—are handled skilfully without obtruding too awkwardly into the plot, which improves as it progresses. The second part of the story maintains the interest of the plot, and is also noteworthy for the ideas on nationalism which it contains, as well as a tremendous onslaught against the Poles for their treatment of the Jews. The power of Smolenskin's writing in this section is matched by the shrewd political realism which he expresses.[83] The third part of the novel, however, is interesting only as a further demonstration of Smolenskin's utter contempt for the Poles and their clergy, whereas the literary quality is very much inferior to the earlier parts of the work. Smolenskin, indeed, almost seems to have become bored with his plot, and to be making sporadic attempts to tie up the loose ends. Certainly, the third part of the novel is appallingly weak, and a great disappointment in view of the promise of the earlier parts.

Smolenskin's final novel *The Inheritance* again demonstrates his lack of self-criticism and the inability to maintain a constant high level throughout a long work. Here, again, the first part of the novel is even better than the corresponding section in *The Reward of the Righteous* in maturity, artistry, dialogue and conversation. The plot, moreover, is far more cleverly constructed and intrinsically gripping than in any other of his novels. After maintaining its very high level throughout the first section of the second part of the novel, it then quite suddenly loses cohesion and probability in a burst of melodramatic nonsense. Admittedly, the third part of the novel revives with the introduction of new characters, and contains one of the most skilful attempts at characterization to be found anywhere in the stories under review.[84]

But although the novel is brought to a close, it manifestly remains unfinished, with the main theme of 'the inheritance' left hanging in mid-air. The last chapter is extraordinarily improbable, and bears all the signs of a hasty attempt to reach a premature denouement—no doubt because of the author's deteriorating health. From many points of view, however, including those of plot, characters, dialogue, atmosphere and style, *The Inheritance* represents a great advance over any of Smolenskin's previous novels, and bears witness to the growing maturity of his art. Yet there is no marked linguistic development, and the gap between his writing and that of Abramowitz's later stories under the pseudonym of Mendele Mocher Sepharim remains very great.

Abramowitz's early novel *Fathers and Sons*, however, displays few signs of the mature artistry of his later works. On the contrary, *Fathers and Sons* is a poor novel, badly constructed. The plot is scrappy and haphazard, at times almost to the point of incomprehensibility, while the delineation of character is equally unsatisfactory. The nearest approach to a real attempt at characterization is Sarah—and, on the brief occasions when she appears, her maid.[85] Such interest as the novel contains lies primarily in the social ideas propounded in abundance; although even they appear naïve when compared to Smolenskin's more mature reflections. Three aspects of the novel, however, serve as pointers to the future artist—the very effective passages of natural description,[86] the flashes of humour and the brave though rarely successful attempt to produce colloquial conversation. Otherwise the novel is remarkable only as a yardstick, against which to measure its author's subsequent development.

Of all the major novelists in the period under review, Braudes displays the most developed sense of literature. In *Religion and Life* the presentation is straightforward and direct, and the narrative clear, concise and interesting. The issues are well-defined, the style comparatively natural, and both the characterization and the dialogue are competent within the linguistic limitations of the period. Even the didactic elements in the earlier parts of the story are introduced without too much irritable grating on the reader's susceptibilities. The novel is characterized by a neatness of plot construction, with the events portrayed in a natural and unforced sequence that bears witness to the author's considerable artistic skill. But even more significant is Braudes' handling of dramatic tensions, and the conflicts which they arouse in the minds of his principal characters. The novel, too, is almost entirely free from the crude melodrama[87] and wildly improbable devices to which most of his contemporaries are so unfortunately prone. In addition, *Religion and Life* conjures up a most vivid, even if heavily weighted, portrait of the cultural background and mental climate of Jewish communal life in Lithuania between the years 1869-1871. It is doubly unfortunate, therefore, that Braudes should have so deliberately neglected the literary aspect of his novel in the third part, which remains unfinished, in order to devote more and more attention to his didactic purposes. It is an ironic reflection on the period under review, that the one author who displays an innate sense of literature should have held its purely artistic aspects in such light regard.

Fortunately, in his second novel, *The Two Extremes* the artist takes precedence over the advocate of reform. This latter novel represents by far the most mature and well-constructed work in the entire period under review. Although the very title of the novel indicates the author's social purpose, which is to illustrate the harmful effects on Jewish life at both ends of the religious spectrum, and advocate a middle course combining orthodoxy and enlightenment, the didactic element is integrated into the main stream of the novel with great skill. As a result, far from obtruding painfully from the course of the narrative, the social purpose is treated as an organic element in the novel, which thereby achieves an inherent unity unrivalled in the other works of the period. The novel is remarkable for the delicate balance of its plot construction, in which the impact of each of the two contrasting environments upon a visitor from the other, and their gradual disillusionment after an initial enthusiastic acceptance is portrayed with insight and imagination. Here, again, the author demonstrates his intimate knowledge of both facets of Jewish life, and his estimation of their respective strengths and weaknesses is both sober and compelling. The principal demerit of the novel lies in its pitifully weak denouement based on a *deus ex machina* and a series of inevitable coincidences.[88] The final resolution is scarcely worthy of a novel, whose plot otherwise displays the signs of consummate artistry.

A survey of the remaining novels of the period again reveals a considerable diversity of literary merit.[89] Leinwand's *The Artful Villain*, for example, must be relegated to a lowly place even within so mediocre a collection.[90] Its tortuous, complex plot, by turns fantastic and utterly naïve, is full of tedious and needless repetition and pointless episodes. The heroes and villains with which the novel abounds are of the 'black and white' variety, as artificial and unconvincing as the contrived and highly euphuistic language which is maintained throughout the story with astonishing consistency. The one example of dramatic skill appears at the beginning of the second part of the story, which presupposes that the extraordinary plan outlined by the villains at the end of the first part has been put into operation, without any actual description of the event. This felicitous omission, however, is more than compensated by the final scene in court, where what virtually amounts to the whole of the highly complex plot is gratuitously repeated. It is of interest, however, that even in such a novel, the author attempts to propagate the ideals of *Haskalah*.[91]

A similar, strange insertion of serious elements within a puerile framework may be discerned in S. F. Meinkin's *The Love of the Righteous*.[92] Here, again, the plot is incredibly naïve, full of crude melodrama and 'cloak and dagger' incidents, which enfold a strange mixture of ill-related ingredients. The feeling of complete amateurism which this novel engenders is bolstered by the almost entire absence of punctuation throughout large sections of the story—a significant pointer to the literary background of the authoress. Yet even within such a pathetically weak tale of adventure and romance, there is the deadly serious theme of the kidnapping of a Jewish child to be brought up as a Catholic, on the model of the Mortara case.[93] Only in chapter fourteen does the story develop a certain swing, with a brave if crude attempt to describe a palace ball. Here, at least, the emotions of the heroine are described with considerable insight.

Zobeizensky's novel, *For Love of Ṣaddiqim*, however, represents by far the most extreme example of cheap melodramatic adventure to be found in all these novels. So fantastic are the vagaries of the plot, that even the author appears to have felt uneasy, and at one stage appends a footnote attempting to reconcile its wild improbabilities![94] The tedium is further increased by the numerous unnecessary repetitions within the story, as though the author were willing to credit the reader with no memory whatsoever. Yet even this novel is permeated with serious social criticism, while its outspoken patriotism and fervent defence of military service[95] divide its attitude sharply from that of any of the other novels of the period. As previously mentioned, the high-flown euphuistic style represents the closest attempt to imitate the writing of Mapu—in occasional passages not entirely without success.

Manassewitz's *The Parents' Sin* is primarily didactic in purpose. The central problem of the story—namely, the failure of parents to consult their daughters' wishes in the choice of a husband, often with disastrous results—was doubtless very real,[96] and therefore lends a certain air of conviction to the tale. The novel contains, moreover, some passages of more restrained and successful writing with touches of genuine pathos,[97] while the element of social criticism is quite effective. As a piece of literature, however, the novel is very poor. It contains a wide range of crude literary devices, including a liberal selection of absurd coincidences.[98] Worse still, however, is the author's slovenliness, and his apparent indifference to the details of his own plot. The construction is poor, the characterization sketchy in the extreme, while the description is limited and full of stock phrases. The style, too, frequently degenerates into unadulterated *Meliṣah*. Mercifully, it enjoys the merit of comparative brevity, being confined to a single part.

The same, unfortunately, cannot be said of Sheikewitz's *The Outcast*, which was devastatingly criticized by Frishmann for being dragged out over three complete parts.[99] The third section includes an interesting preface, in which the author warns all writers who have translated his Yiddish stories into Hebrew without acknowledgement to desist from the practice or face prosecution—an illuminating commentary on contemporary piracy. This novel, too, includes many passages of serious social criticism within a melodramatic adventure-story, crowded with fantastic episodes. Nevertheless, the story contains many moments of suspense and rapid action, which exercise a certain compelling power. The author makes good use of irony and satire—sometimes directed even against his readers, and on a number of occasions his tongue is manifestly in his cheek. He is very skilled in the *genre*, even if it is a poor one, and, quite obviously, at least a professional writer.

Rabinowitz's *At the Crossroads* is a novel of much greater consequence. Primarily interesting because of its forthright antagonism to the debasing effects of an only half-digested Enlightenment, the standpoint of the author represents, perhaps, a more mature evaluation of some of the forces at work in society than may be discovered in any of the novelists under review. But quite apart from any ideological interest, the literary qualities of the novel are of a comparatively high order. The plot is simple and well-constructed. Within the natural limitations of the language, the style is lively and the descriptions straightforward without too much recourse to *Meliṣah*. The characters are somewhat more developed than in many of these novels, and the author's literary sense makes his story pleasantly readable. It is unfortunate that the novel should have been marred by its fantastic ending. Having made his point, the author impatiently draws his tale to a close in a single paragraph by means of a melodramatic murder quite uncharacteristic of the story as a whole.[100]

With Sirkis' *Esther*, the literary level once more drops considerably. The story, itself, is trivial in the extreme. It neither hangs together properly, nor does it seem to be worth the telling. Even such themes as exist are handled in a puerile manner. The one redeeming literary feature is the interesting and unusual characterizations of Kemuel and Qalsi.[101] The story portrays strong national sympathies, and includes passages devoted to the author's philosophical views.[102] It also strongly advocates the emigration of Jews from eastern Europe to America. It may even attempt to express some sort of allegory, with the heroine Esther, and her desire for a new dress, respectively symbolizing the Jewish people and its urge for a new life. But in neither case is the point made manifest. The novel's complete oblivion is hardly surprising.

Weisbrem's stories, while resembling the majority of the novels under review as melodramatic, romantic tales of adventure with an admixture of social criticism, nevertheless contain a number

CONCLUSION237

of less usual features. Although *Between the Times* tends to run wild in its closing stages by resorting to a naïve denouement based on an absurd coincidence,[103] the novel includes some very attractive scenes portrayed with a wry sense of humour. Of these, the most noteworthy are the hero's attempts to disguise his Jewishness by launching into a bloodcurdling mixture of broken Polish and Russian,[104] the abortive fast ordained by the local community when inclement weather obviates the possibility of blessing the new moon,[105] and particularly the satirical attack on the elementary ignorance displayed by Zebulun the *Melammedh* in addressing a letter destined for Brazil.[106] The author's attitude towards the movement of Enlightenment, again, is less naïve than is the case with many of the novelists under review, and his hero, Gershon, is portrayed as the shiftless, unstable product of an empty and worthless Enlightenment, in contrast to the other hero, Jonathan, who represents the harmonious fusion of traditional and secular learning. The style, too, has a certain light-hearted flavour, which the author attempts to maintain in spite of many lapses into the more usual stilted and artificial language of the period.

Weisbrem's second novel, *18 Coins* differs only in its greater measure of both rapid action and serious social reflection. This novel, too, displays the author's skill in characterization,[107] as well as his considerable sense of humour. In spite of the element of *Melisah* and the occasional introduction of contrived and artificial phraseology, his writing is characterized by a certain ease of expression, which accords well with his light, lively and sometimes witty style. The ambivalent attitude to *Haskalah* is equally in evidence, while the Hasidic movement, as in most of the novels of the period,[108] becomes one of the principal targets for the author's satire. Like Sheikewitz, Weisbrem displays considerable skill in the handling of an inferior type of novel.

In the light of the foregoing brief evaluations, there is scarcely need to emphasize the fact that the novels under review are of far greater interest for the history of Hebrew literature than as works of art as such. Few modern readers, indeed, would be tempted to wade through them on aesthetic grounds alone. So manifestly do they bear the impress of a transitional stage, that the temptation to abandon them in favour of the more satisfying novels of the subsequent period is well-nigh irresistible. In an estimate of the importance of these novels, however, the fact that they constitute an indispensable stage of experimentation, from which later Hebrew novelists learned which ingredients could be utilized further and which of them must be rejected, by no means represents their sole merit. It is equally important to recognize the tremendous courage of the authors and their sheer devotion to the language in attempting to compose novels in Hebrew at all. In this respect the following quotation from Sheikewitz's *The Outcast* is most revealing:

> . . . Nevertheless I shall skip over these matters lest my reminiscences grow into a very large book, and no book-dealer would agree to publish it. . . . for fear lest the printing costs will not be covered by the income. After all, it is well known that the purchasers of Hebrew books amongst us are few in number; so much so that many of our writers have stopped composing their works in this lovely language, and have turned to colloquial Yiddish instead.[109]

No further testimony is required to the loyalty to Hebrew displayed by the authors under review, and their important role in keeping Hebrew literature alive throughout a difficult and discouraging period, thereby ensuring its subsequent renaissance.

Quite apart from their literary aspects, however, these novels deserve attention for the light they shed on the social, cultural and religious conditions of Jewish life in eastern Europe and particularly in Russia in the nineteenth century. In spite of the obvious prejudices and tendentious attitudes which colour many of the portraits of society reflected in these novels, they nevertheless provide most interesting illustrations of the problems and conflicts confronting the Jewish communities of that time, and afford many a penetrating glimpse into a society, which in the nineteenth century represented the most concentrated and vital centre of Jewry in the world. Even during the period under review the forces of change, which were to undermine the foundations of that society may be clearly discerned through the pages of these novels, and indeed received assistance from them in no small measure. Initially the novels served as a catalyst for the half-felt longings and groping ambitions of a questing generation. Today they mirror the traditional and cultural patterns of a society that has since been utterly and irrevocably destroyed.

NOTES

BIBLIOGRAPHY

INDEX

Notes

Abbreviations

The following abbreviated titles are used for the editions and Hebrew Titles of the novels under review, see above pp. 3f.

SM. 1.	P. Smolenskin,	*The Wanderer in the Paths of Life.*
SM. 2.	P. Smolenskin,	*The Joy of the Godless.*
SM. 3.	P. Smolenskin,	*A Donkey's Burial.*
SM. 4.	P. Smolenskin,	*Pride and Fall.*
SM. 5.	P. Smolenskin,	*The Reward of the Righteous.*
SM. 6.	P. Smolenskin,	*The Inheritance.*
ABR.	S. J. Abramowitz,	*Fathers and Sons.*
BRA. 1.	R. A. Braudes,	*Religion and Life.*
BRA. 2.	R. A. Braudes,	*The Two Extremes.*
LEIN.	J. Leinwand,	*The Artful Villain.*
MEIN.	S. F. Meinkin,	*The Love of the Righteous.*
ZOB.	B. I. Zobeizensky,	*For Love of Ṣaddiqim.*
MAN.	M. Manassewitz,	*The Parents' Sin.*
SHEIK.	N. M. Sheikewitz,	*The Outcast.*
RAB.	A. S. Rabinowitz,	*At the Crossroads.*
SIRK.	I. J. Sirkis,	*Esther.*
WEIS. 1.	I. Weisbrem,	*Between the Times.*
WEIS. 2.	I. Weisbrem,	*18 Coins.*
Klausner *History*.		J. Klausner, *Historiah šel ha-Siphruth ha-'Ibhrith ha-Ḥadhašah (A History of Modern Hebrew Literature)* 2nd. ed., Vols. 3-6, Jerusalem, 1953-58.

[Text references are in square brackets at the top of each page of Notes.]

Q

CHAPTER I

1. See below, ch. 6. For detailed studies of *Haskalah*, see e.g. J. S. Raisin, *The Haskalah Movement in Russia*, Philadelphia, 1913; A. Shohet, *Beginnings of the Haskalah among German Jewry* (Hebrew text) Jerusalem, 1960; J. Meisl, *Haskalah*, Berlin, 1919.

2. For a study of A. Mapu, see D. Patterson, *Abraham Mapu*, London, 1964, and Klausner, *History*, vol. 3, ch. 8, together with their respective bibliographies.

3. See below, chs. 2, 3, 4.

4. For a general survey of the literature of the period see, e.g. Klausner, *History*; P. Lahower, *Toledhoth ha-Siphruth ha-'Ibhrith ha-Hadhašah*, 7th ed., Tel Aviv, 1951; S. Halkin, *Modern Hebrew Literature, Trends and Values*, New York, 1950; N. Slouschz, *The Renascence of Hebrew Literature*, Philadelphia, 1909; S. Spiegel, *Hebrew Reborn*, London, 1931; M. Waxman, *A History of Jewish Literature*, vol. 3, rev. ed., New York-London, 1960.

5. See e.g. S. M. Dubnow, *History of the Jews in Russia and Poland*, translated by I. Friedlaender, Philadelphia, 1916-20, vol. 2; L. Greenberg, *The Jews in Russia*, New Haven, 1951.

6. See below, chs. 5, 6, 7.

7. Part 1, 1858, part 2, 1861, part 3, 1864, all in Vilna. The complete work in 5 parts was published posthumously in Warsaw in 1869. Of a fourth novel, *The Visionaries*, reputed to have run into no less than 10 parts, only a short fragment of 7 chapters is extant. See Klausner, *History*, vol. 3, pp. 313ff, where strong arguments are produced to the effect that only the first part was actually written.

8. In W. Zeitlin, *Bibliotheca Hebraica Post-Mendelssohniana*, Leipsig, 1891, p. 235, there is an entry in square brackets referring to a part 2 of the story published in Vilna in 1883. I have not, however, been able to locate a copy of part 2.

9. The name applied by members of the Hasidic sect to their holy men, literally 'righteous'. Cf. D. Patterson, 'The Portrait of the "Ṣaddik" in the Nineteenth-Century Hebrew Novel', in the *Journal of Semitic Studies*, vol. 8, No. 2, Autumn, 1963.

10. See below, pp. 148ff. For a full account of Abramowitsch's life and the relevant bibliography, see Klausner, *History*, vol. 6, pp. 315ff. Cf. Waxman, *op. cit.*

11. See below, ch. 6.

12. The area to which the Jews of Russia were confined. Cf. Dubnow, *op. cit.*

13. Klausner suggests that the first draft was modelled on the German story *Zwei Geschlechter* by Berta Friedrich, which appeared in 1863. See *History*, vol. 6, p. 422. The version of *Fathers and Sons* which Mendele included in the third volume of his collected works, Odessa, 1912, is quite different from that published in Odessa, 1868, namely the novel under review. For a detailed analysis of the plot of the final version see G. Shaked, 'Goral wa-'Alilah be-Yeṣiratho šel Mendele Mokher Sepharim', in *Sepher ha-Yobhel šel ha-Gimnasiah ha-'Ibhrith Birušalayim*, Jerusalem, 1962.

14. See below, p. 168.

15. This summary follows that given by Klausner, *History*, vol. 6, pp. 419ff, which although not strictly adhering to the sequence of events employed by Abramowitz, at least reduces the chaos to some order.

16. See below, pp. 148ff.

17. The influence of Eugène Sue's *Mystères de Paris* is manifest. See below, pp. 224f.

18. A translation of the scene may be found in D. Patterson, ' The Portrait of the Ṣaddik . . .' p. 171.

19. For a full account of Smolenskin's life and the relevant bibliography see Klausner, *History*, vol. 5, pp. 14ff. Cf. Waxman, *op. cit.*

20. See below, pp. 148ff.

21. For information on the *Yešibhah* (institute of higher education) see below pp. 172ff. For the system of 'eating days' see pp. 177ff.

22. See below, pp. 40f.

23. For information on the *Ḥedher* (private elementary school) see below, pp. 135f and pp. 168ff.

24. A symbolic name, equivalent to 'Darkville'. See below, p. 69, n. 8.

25. Cf. below, p. 144.

26. See below, pp. 82f.

27. Cf. below, p. 143.

28. Another symbolic name, signifying 'bereavement'. Cf. above, n. 24.

29. Cf. below, pp. 148ff.

30. Another symbolic name, signifying 'hypocrisy'. Cf. above, n. 24.

31. The orthodox opponents of Hasidism. See below, p. 190 and pp. 207ff.

32. Once more a symbolic name, with the sense of 'broken'. Cf. above, n. 24.

33. Smolenskin takes his hero severely to task for this misguided altruism. See below, pp. 67f.

34. See below, pp. 87ff.

35. See below, pp. 209ff.

36. Another symbolic name, signifying 'weakness'. Cf. above, n. 24.

37. See below, p. 212. The story is based on a real episode which occurred in Yaneve near Kovno where Smolenskin spent some time. Mr S. Goldsmith of London affirms that the grave of the victim was pointed out to him by local residents. It lay outside the boundary of the cemetery.

38. See below, pp. 167f.

39. See below, pp. 203f.

40. See below, pp. 215f.

41. See Klausner, *History*, vol. 5, p. 198, for evidence that Smolenskin's worst indictments were not without foundation.

42. Cf. e.g. *SM. 1*, pt. 3, pp. 22ff, with *SM. 4*, p. 211.

43. According to Klausner, Smolenskin was influenced in the composition of this story by L. Levanda's Russian novel *Hour of Crisis*, 1871-3. See Klausner, *History*, vol. 5, pp. 207f. The summary of this complex plot follows that given by Klausner, pp. 209ff.

44. See below, pp. 163ff.

45. This summary again follows that given by Klausner in his *History*, vol. 5, pp. 215ff.

46. Later in the story she is called Zipporah. See below, p. 41.

47. See Klausner, *History*, vol. 5, p. 215. Cf. below, pp. 198f.

48. This framework also affords Smolenskin the opportunity of propagating his nationalist ideas. See below, pp. 199f.

49. See below, pp. 59f and p. 122.

50. For the actual prototype of this character see Klausner, *History*, vol. 5, p. 216.

51. For a full account of his life together with the relevant bibliography see *ibid.*, vol. 5, pp. 345ff. Cf. Waxman, *op. cit.*

52. Cf. D. Patterson, 'Some Religious Attitudes Reflected in the Hebrew Novels of the Period of Enlightenment', in the

Bulletin of the John Rylands Library, vol. 42, No. 2, March 1960, pp. 399ff.

53. The best-known and most authoritative codification of Rabbinical Judaism, composed by J. Caro in the sixteenth century. See *The Jewish Encyclopaedia*, New York and London, 1901-6, vol. 3, p. 585.

54. See the *Mishnah, Yebhamoth. Yabham* signifies a man who is required to take to wife his brother's widow if his brother had died childless.

55. See below, pp. 214f.

56. See Klausner, *History*, vol. 5, p. 383.

57. See below, p. 119.

58. See *Sepher Zikkaron le-Sopherê Yisrael*, published by *Ha-'Asiph*, Warsaw, 1889, p. 58, and *Die Hebräische Publizistik in Wien* (B. Wachstein, I. Taglicht, A. Kristanspoller), Vienna, 1930.

59. A highly critical review of the novel by P. Smolenskin appeared in *Ha-Šaḥar*, 7th year, Vienna, 1875, pp. 607f.

60. See W. Zeitlin, *op. cit.*, p. 235.

61. See S. F. Foner, *Mi-Zikhronoth Yemê Yalduthi*, Warsaw, 1903. Unfortunately, in spite of the promise of the title, these memoirs are devoted solely to stories and episodes concerning Dvinsk, and yield scarcely any biographical information.

62. See below, p. 153.

63. See below, p. 52.

64. See above, n. 8.

65. In Zeitlin, *op. cit.*, p. 372, his name is spelled Sobeisensky.

66. See *Leksikon fun der Nayer Yiddischer Literatur*, vol. III, New York, 1960, p. 508, which draws upon information to be found in the *Leksikon fun der Yiddischer Literatur*, vol. 1, Vilna, 1928, p. 1015.

67. See *Ha-Meliṣ*, 1882, pp. 425f.

68. See below, pp. 150f.

69. See e.g. *Ha-Kerem*, Warsaw, 1887, and *Ha-Meliṣ*, 1900.

70. See *Ha-Do'ar*, vol. 8, No. 21, 23 March 1928, p. 332.

71. See below, pp. 38f.

72. Her second son simply disappears from the story, which is in any case full of careless inconsistencies.

73. Zeitlin, *op. cit.*, p. 342, spells his name Scheykewitsch. He is commonly known under the pseudonym *Šomer*.

74. For details of his life, see *Širê Šomer we-Zikhronothaw*, Jerusalem,

1952, and *Unser Vater Šomer*, compiled by his daughters and translated into Hebrew by A. Weisman under the title *'Abhinu Šomer*, Jerusalem, 1953.

75. Cf. below, pp. 169f.

76. See below, p. 235.

77. This episode is autobiographical. See *Širê Šomer we-Zikhronothaw*, *op. cit.*, p. 15.

78. This episode, too, is autobiographical; see *ibid.*, pp. 40f, 70, 86. On p. 70 Sheikewitz relates that his passion for the card-sharp's daughter was so acute that every time he saw her he would whisper a prayer to the effect that he might find favour in her sight; and in a footnote he adds that he has put the same words into the mouth of Jacob Rimmon in *The Outcast*, as well as endowing him with all the emotions which he, Sheikewitz, experienced at that time.

79. One of the symbolic names which abound in this story. It is more or less the equivalent of 'Dogsbody'. Cf. above, n. 24.

80. See below, p. 180.

81. See below, p. 215.

82. For a bibliography of his works, and of writings devoted to him see *Yadh La-Qore'*, year 1, nos. 3-4, April 1944, pp. 4ff, 9; and *Sepher Zikkaron le-Yobhel ha-Šibh'im šel A. S. Rabinowitz*, Tel-Aviv, 1924, pp. 13ff, 18ff.

83. See *ibid.*, p. 4. In a short autobiographical article in *Ha-'Areṣ*, 9 February 1934, on the occasion of his eightieth birthday, Rabinowitz gives Mapu's novel *The Love of Zion* as the source of his new interest. Cf. below, p. 222.

84. A public elementary school, see below, p. 168.

85. See below, pp. 51, 154.

86. Cf. below, p. 152.

87. See especially D. I. Birkowitz, *Ha-Ri'šonim Kibhnê-'Adham*, revised edition, Tel-Aviv, 1953, vol. 6, pp. 223-34.

88. See *Ha-Do'ar*, vol. 7, 14 Tishri, 1929, p. 635.

89. See *'Iggeroth Sopherim 'Ibhrim*, edited by M. Raisin, Brooklyn-New York, 1947, pp. 260-9.

90. See below, pp. 93f.

91. It is possible that the new dress is supposed to symbolise a new life for the Jewish people. See *SIRK.*, p. 106; and cf. below, p. 236.

92. See D. Patterson, 'Israel Weisbrem: A Forgotten Hebrew

Novelist of the Nineteenth Century', in the *Journal of Semitic Studies*, vol. 4, No. 1, January 1959, pp. 37ff. Although the plots of Weisbrem's novels may be found there, those which fall within the period under review have been included in this present study for the sake of completeness.

93. See below, pp. 71f and ch. 4.

CHAPTER 2

1. See above, ch. 1, n. 2.

2. See below, pp. 222ff.

3. See D. Patterson, 'The Hebrew Historical Novel', in *Sifrut*, vol. 1, London, 1955.

4. See below, chs. 3 and 4.

5. Even the European writers mentioned in the novels themselves provide evidence of a fairly wide acquaintance with general literature. See below, pp. 224ff.

6. *SM. 2*, ch. 20, and cf. ch. 17. N.B. Smolenskin's remark in his introduction (p. vii) that his reason for writing stories is to attract the reader, and thereby ensure that he pays attention to the literary criticism which they contain. Cf. below, p. 44.

7. See below, pp. 216f. Cf. H. James, *The Art of Fiction*, New York, 1948, p. 13.

8. Only with Abramowitz's later translations of his Yiddish novels into Hebrew, published under the pseudonym of *Mendele Mokher Sepharim*, was this fusion of story and lesson achieved.

9. See below, p. 131.

10. See below, p. 236.

11. See below, p. 235.

12. See Klausner, *History*, vol. 5, pp. 45ff.

13. See below, pp. 40f.

14. For a study of the problems involved in serialisation see K. Tillotson, *Novels of the Eighteen Forties*, Oxford, 1954.

15. Cf. *SM. 5*, pt. 3, pp. 52ff: *SM. 6*, pt. 2, pp. 178f. Even Braudes is occasionally constrained to remind the reader of what has previously occurred. Cf. *BRA. 1*, pt. 2, p. 16: *BRA. 2*, pt. 3, p. 297. Cf. also *SHEIK.*, pt. 2, p. 92: *ZOB.*, pt. 2, chs. 25, 26. In this connection E. M. Forster's warning is relevant: 'Every action or word in a plot ought to count; it ought to be economical and spare; even when complicated it should be organic

and free from dead matter. It may be difficult or easy, it may and should contain mysteries, but it ought not to mislead', *Aspects of the Novel*, London, 1927, p. 119. Particularly relevant, in this respect, is a footnote to *ZOB.*, pt. 2, p. 62, attempting to reconcile the fantastic improbabilities of the plot. Apparently even the author felt uneasy! Ch. 26 of the same novel, on the other hand, is full of unnecessary repetition, as though the author were unwilling to credit his reader with either intelligence or memory. Cf. below, p. 235.

16. E.g. *SM. 5*, pt. 3, ch. 8.

17. *SM. 1*, pp. ixf. For the dates of publication of *The Wanderer in the Paths of Life* see above, p. 3.

18. *SM. 6*, pt. 2, ch. 5 and p. 187 and editor's note. Cf. above, ch. 1, n. 46. Cf. A. S. Waldstein, *The Evolution of Modern Hebrew Literature*, New York, 1916, p. 58 footnote. Cf. also *SM. 1*, pt. 1, p. 215, where a quotation differs from its original form on p. 26; similarly, it is not clear whether the woman who suffers a public humiliation, pp. 127ff, is the same as the one described on p. 253; in *SM. 2*, ch. 13, Eve is described as having run away two months previously, which does not appear to fit into the sequence of events, see below, p. 50; on p. 234 it is strange that the old man should ask Simon to wait a few days when the trial is to take place on the same night; in *SM. 3* there is a contradiction on p. 98 and p. 99, and also a radical change in tone; in *SM. 5*, pt. 3, there is a change of rank from p. 140 to p. 141.

19. This is not, however, the case in his last novel, *The Inheritance*, probably due to the author's failing health. See Klausner, *History*, vol. 5, p. 169. Cf. above, p. 16.

20. See D. Patterson, *Abraham Mapu*, pp. 103f, and cf. below, p. 224.

21. Cf. below, pp. 221ff.

22. See above, pp. 5ff.

23. See below, pp. 171f.

24. One of Braudes' characters is made to ask the naive but revealing question: 'What is literature?' *BRA.* 2, pt. 1, pp. 55f. See D. Patterson, 'The Portrait of Ḥasidism in the Nineteenth-Century Hebrew Novel' in the *Journal of Semitic Studies*, vol. 5, No. 4, October 1960, p. 369. Cf. below, p. 228.

25. See below, ch. 5.

26. See below, p. 155.

27. See above, ch. 1, n. 12.

28. Again, the fanciful and highly improbable features of the plot are no more imaginative than many of the stories to be found in *Midhraš*, with which most students would be familiar, and considerably less far-fetched than much of the current folk-lore; see below, pp. 209ff.

29. See below, pp. 182f.

30. See below, p. 234.

31. See below, p. 131.

32. See above, pp. 17ff.

33. See *SM. 2*, chs. 17, 18, 20.

34. The whole plot of this novel is, in fact, light-hearted, as though even the author could not take it seriously. See e.g. the end of ch. 23 and the beginning of ch. 24. Cf. above, n. 6.

35. See below, pp. 184ff.

36. Cf. above, p. 38, and see, e.g. *SM. 1*, pt. 1, pp. 52f, 96ff, 159, 189ff, 219ff; pt. 2, chs. 3, 4, pp. 61ff, chs. 18, 28; pt. 3, chs. 6, 19: *SM. 2*, pp. 34ff, 93, chs. 13, 17, 18, 20 (cf. above, note 33) pp. 194ff: *SM. 3*, pp. 33ff, 94, 127ff, ch. 19: *SM. 4*, pp. 53, 215ff: *SM. 5*, pt. 1, p. 123; pt. 3, pp. 66ff: *SM.6*, pt. 2, pp. 31ff: *ABR.*, ch. 28: *BRA. 1*, pt. 1, pp. 28ff; pt. 2, pp. 76f, chs. 13, 15; pt. 3, chs. 1, 2 (and, indeed, large sections of the third part): *ZOB.*, pt. 2, chs. 17, 21: *MAN.*, pp. 6, 75f: *SHEIK.*, pt. 1, pp. 7f; pt. 2, p. 38: *RAB.*, pp. 28ff: *SIRK.*, pp. 116ff: *WEIS. 2*, pt. 2, p. 115. On innumerable occasions the narrative is interrupted to enable the author to indulge in philosophical or moral speculation sometimes at considerable length. This device is particularly noticeable at the beginnings of chapters, where it often serves as a bridge from a general to a particular situation. See below, p. 118.

37. See e.g. *SM. 1*, pt. 1, p. 53; pt. 2, pp. 9, 176; pt. 3, ch. 6, p. 158: *SM. 2*, chs. 13, 21: *SM. 4*, pp. 215ff: *SM. 6*, pt. 1, pp. 7f: *BRA. 1*, pt. 2, pp. 76ff: *BRA. 2*, pt. 4, pp. 320, 354: *LEIN.*, pt. 2, p. 68: *MAN.*, pp. 115f; *RAB.*, pp. 34, 58, 136: *SIRK.*, pp. 119ff: *WEIS. 1*, p. 17.

38. *SHEIK.*, pt. 1, p. 62. The phrase occurs constantly throughout these novels. Cf. below, pp. 105, 131f.

39. *SHEIK.*, pt. 2, p. 22. Cf. pp. 43f, and *SM. 2*, p. 106. Abramo-witz, too, deals with the plight of the Hebrew author; *ABR.*, pp. 15ff. For interesting criticism of Hebrew writers see *SM. 1*, pt. 4, chs. 9, 18: *SM. 5*, pt. 1, pp. 17f: *ABR.*, pp. 19, 56 and *SHEIK.*, pt. 1, pp. 61ff.

40. See below, pp. 123f.

41. *SM. 1*, pt. 1, pp. 135ff, 267. But see pt. 2, pp. 64, 266, and cf. D. Patterson, 'Some Religious Attitudes . . .', p. 409, n. 1.

42. *SM. 1*, pt. 1, pp. 268ff.

43. *Ibid.*, pp. 272f. But see below, p. 50. For comparable interruptions to the narrative due to Smolenskin's intervention see, e.g. *Ibid.*, pt. 2, p. 176: *SM. 2*, pp. 98, 194ff: *SM. 3*, pp. 16f, 37: *SM. 4*, pp. 30, 89: *SM. 5*, pt. 1, p. 145; pt. 2, p. 47; pt. 3, p. 109.

44. Braudes employs the terminology found in Exodus 26[11], where it is used with reference to the tabernacle.

45. *BRA. 1*, pt. 3, pp. 27ff; cf. pt. 1, p. 57: *BRA. 2*, pp. 100f. For a discussion of the religious implications of Braudes' *Religion and Life*, see below, pp. 192f and cf. D. Patterson, 'Some Religious Attitudes . . .', pp. 398ff.

46. *LEIN.*, pt. 1, pp. 27f; cf. *Ibid.*, p. 39.

47. See *SHEIK.*, pt. 1, p. 58; pt. 2, pp. 7f, 91f; pt. 3, pp. 105, 108. See above, p. 45, and below, pp. 61, 121, 222, 226.

48. *WEIS. 2*, pt. 1, p. 23.

49. *SIRK.*, p. 116. Cf. pp. 106, 119ff.

50. *Ibid.*, pp. 53, 54, 58. Cf. *SM. 5*, pt. 2, p. 97, where Smolenskin also addresses one of his characters directly. For remarks on the very numerous occasions upon which the authors of these novels resort to the practice of using the first person and addressing the reader directly, see below, pp. 123f.

51. Principally, ch. 12, chs. 17-19 (which comprise another frame-story!) and ch. 20.

52. The loose ends of the Manasseh story are finally tied in pt. 2, ch. 24, and pt. 3, chs. 28-32, which themselves form another frame-story!

53. Chs. 21 and 22.

54. See above, p. 13.

55. Chs. 9, 10, 15 and 22.

56. *SM. 5*, pt. 2, pp. 126-32. Cf. *SM. 1*, pt. 2, ch. 24. For a discussion on the role of letters in these stories, see below, pp. 61ff.

57. *SM. 6*, pt. 2, chs. 12 and 13.

58. *ABR.* pp. 82-9.

59. *Ibid.*, pp. 89-95.

60. *BRA. 1*, pt. 1, pp. 21-46.

61. *MAN.*, pp. 76ff. See below, pp. 152f. The novel contains a second frame-story, pp. 86ff.

62. *SHEIK.*, pt. 1, p. 71, to the end of pt. 1; pt. 2, pp. 16-91.

63. *Ibid.*, pt. 2, pp. 28ff.

64. *Ibid.*, pp. 91f.

65. Cf. *SM. 1*, pt. 3, chs. 29-33: *SM. 3*, ch. 10, pp. 190ff: *SM. 5*, pt. 2, chs. 3 and 5, pp. 94ff; pt. 3, pp. 121ff, 153ff: *SM. 6*, pt. 2, chs. 9 and 15, pp. 92, 135, 162ff, 176ff; pt. 3, pp. 311ff: *BRA. 1*, pt. 1, pp. 9ff, 21, 112ff; pt. 2, pp. 41, 45, 75f, 80ff: *BRA. 2*, pt. 3, p. 300: *MEIN.*, pt. 1, chs. 8 and 13, pp. 133ff: *LEIN.*, pt. 1, pp. 44ff, ch. 10: *SHEIK.*, pt. 1, pp. 71ff: *WEIS. 1*, pp. 96ff: *WEIS. 2*, pt. 2, pp. 134ff.

66. Cf. *SM. 5*, pt. 1, pp. 33ff; pt. 3, pp. 100ff: *SM. 6*, pt. 1, ch. 2: *BRA. 1*, pt. 1, pp. 46f: *BRA. 2*, pt. 2, pp. 149ff (but without completely interrupting the narrative as in Smolenskin).

67. *SM. 6*, pt. 2, ch. 14.

68. *BRA. 1*, pt. 1, ch. 8. This technique permeates *The Two Extremes*.

69. Ch. 7 and ch. 8 until p. 105. Cf. pp. 116-36.

70. E.g., *SM. 1*, pt. 1, pp. 159, 189f, 218ff, 247; pt. 2, p. 257: *SM. 2*, pp. 44, 79, 93, 114, 151: *SM. 3*, ch. 14: *SM. 4*, pp. 52, 74: *SM. 5*, pt. 3, pp. 66ff.

71. See above, pp. 39f.

72. Cf. *SM. 1*, pt. 2, chs. 20, 24; pt. 3, chs. 23, 28, 33; pt. 4, chs. 2, 13: *SM. 2*, chs. 14, 24: *SM. 4*, chs. 5, 10: *SM. 5*, pt. 2, chs. 9, 10, 11; pt. 3, ch. 6: *SM. 6*, pt. 1, ch. 13; pt. 2, ch. 21; pt. 3, chs. 1, 6, 8. Cf. above, p. 41.

73. *SM. 1*, p. 37.

74. *Ibid.*, p. 116; pt. 2, p. 270; pt. 3, pp. 250f.

75. *Ibid.*, pt. 2, p. 64; pt. 3, p. 250: *SM. 2*, pp. 91, 110: *SM. 4*, p. 166: *SM. 5*, pt. 1, pp. 113f, 140; pt. 2, pp. 101, 126; pt. 3, p. 109; *SM. 6*, pt. 1, pp. 144, 156.

76. *SM. 1*, pt. 1, p. 49.

77. *Ibid.*, p. 274. Cf. above, p. 45.

78. *BRA. 1*, pt. 1, p. 68; pt. 2, p. 41: *SIRK.*, p. 40: *SHEIK.*, pt. 3, p. 83.

79. *LEIN.*, pt. 1, p. 30.

80. *Ibid.*, pt. 2, p. 27.

81. *Ibid.*, pt. 1, p. 72.

82. *SM. 5*, pt. 1, ch. 10; pt. 2, chs. 3, 4, 5; pt. 3, ch. 1. Cf. *SHEIK.*, pt. 1, ch. 1.

83. E.g. *SM. 5*, pt. 2, ch. 3. Cf. *BRA. 1*, pt. 2, ch. 10.

84. For a discussion of the nature of such problems, see A. A. Mendilow, *Time and the Novel*, London, 1952.

85. Dov's unexpected appearance at the end of chapter 9 is convincingly explained, for example, at the end of chapter 10, and cf. pp. 58 and 109. Smolenskin, too, occasionally handles the time factor with no mean skill, e.g. *SM. 6*, pt. 1, ch. 1.

86. Cf. *SM. 1*, pt. 3, p. 120: *SM. 5*, pt. 3, p. 115: *ABR.*, p. 120: *ZOB.*, pt. 1, p. 60: *RAB.*, p. 98: *WEIS. 1*, p. 127.

87. Similar problems of co-ordination occur in *BRA. 2*, pt. 2, pp. 87, 139f: *WEIS. 1*, ch. 5: *WEIS. 2*, pt. 2, pp. 18f, 80.

88. *SM. 1*, pt. 1, p. 74.

89. *ABR.*, p. 120.

90. *ZOB.*, pt. 1, p. 60.

91. *MAN.*, ch. 4.

92. *RAB.*, chs. 3 and 4. See below, p. 154.

93. The novels by Braudes and Rabinowitz are, by and large, far more sober in their choice of themes. But see below, p. 52, n. 115.

94. Cf. *SM. 1*, pt. 1, chs. 1, 11, 13-25; pt. 2, chs. 20, 24; pt. 3, ch. 16: *SM. 2*, ch. 16; *SM. 3*, ch. 19: *SM. 5*, pt. 1, chs. 5, 9; pt. 3, chs. 1, 14: *SM. 6*, pt. 1, chs. 14, 18: *ABR.*, chs. 7, 30: *BRA. 1*, pt. 1, ch. 10; pt. 2, ch. 15; pt. 3, chs. 2, 3: *BRA. 2*, pt. 1, ch. 6; pt. 4, ch. 43: *LEIN.*, pt. 1, chs. 1, 14; pt. 2, chs. 4, 9: *SHEIK.*, pt. 1, ch. 18; pt. 2, ch. 9: *WEIS. 2*, pt. 1, ch. 8; pt. 2, ch. 15.

95. Cf. *SM. 1*, pt. 1, ch. 25; pt. 3, chs. 30, 31: *SM. 3*, ch. 18: *SM. 5*, pt. 2, ch. 9: *SM. 6*, pt. 1, ch. 1; pt. 3, ch. 4: *LEIN.*, pt. 1, chs. 2, 6, 17, 18, 19; pt. 2, chs. 7, 9, 13: *MAN.*, ch. 5: *SHEIK.*, pt. 2, ch. 13; pt. 3, chs. 2, 19: *WEIS. 2*, pt. 1, ch. 12.

96. *LEIN.*, pt. 1, chs. 2, 6, 15.

97. Cf. *SM. 1*, pt. 1, ch. 25; pt. 2, ch. 27; pt. 3, chs. 14, 15: *SM. 3*, chs. 11, 12: *SM. 4*, ch. 6: *SM. 5*, pt. 3, ch. 1: *SM. 6*, pt. 3, ch. 7: *BRA. 1*, pt. 2, ch. 4: *MEIN.*, ch. 4: *SHEIK.*, pt. 2, ch. 15.

98. Cf. *SM. 2*, ch. 13: *SM. 5*, pt. 3, ch. 2: *BRA. 2*, pt. 1, ch. 3: *LEIN.*, pt. 1, chs. 2, 7, 15; pt. 2, chs. 13, 14: *ZOB.*, pt. 2, chs. 18, 23, 26: *SHEIK.*, pt. 1, ch. 15; pt. 2, ch. 16; pt. 3, ch. 20.

99. *LEIN.*, pt. 2, chs. 13, 14. Cf. below, p. 234.

100. *Ibid.*, pt. 1, ch. 19; pt. 2, chs. 4, 5, 11.

101. Cf. *SM. 1*, pt. 2, ch. 19: *SM. 6*, pt. 1, ch. 1: *MEIN.*, chs. 8, 9,

10, 11, 18, 21: *MAN.*, chs. 5, 6: *SIRK.*, ch. 8: *WEIS. 2*, chs. 20, 23.

102. See C. Roth, *The History of the Jews in Italy*, Philadelphia, 1946, pp. 471f. Cf. below, pp. 215, 234.

103. *WEIS. 2*, pt. 2, chs. 20, 23.

104. *SIRK.*, ch. 8.

105. Cf. *SM. 1*, pt. 1, chs. 23, 25, 27; pt. 2, chs. 19, 20, 21, 24, 29; pt. 3, chs. 30, 32, 33; pt. 4, ch. 6: *SM. 3*, chs. 11, 20: *SM. 4*, chs. 6, 8, 10: *SM. 5*, pt. 3, ch. 12; *SM. 6*, pt. 1, chs. 1, 11, 13, 20; pt. 2, ch. 24; pt. 3, ch. 9: *LEIN.*, pt. 2, ch. 12: *MEIN.*, ch. 23.

106. Cf. *SM. 1*, pt. 1, ch. 25; pt. 2, chs. 19, 29; pt. 3, chs. 22, 33: *SM. 4*, ch. 8: *SM. 5*, pt. 2, chs. 4, 5; pt. 3, chs. 13, 19: *SM. 6*, pt. 1, ch. 12; pt. 2, chs. 4, 5, 9: *LEIN.*, pt. 1, chs. 7, 9, 18, 19: *MEIN.*, ch. 22: *MAN.*, ch. 5: *SHEIK.*, pt. 2, ch. 15; pt. 3, ch. 20: *RAB.*, chs. 9, 12: *WEIS. 2*, pt. 1, ch. 8.

107. Cf. *SM. 1*, pt. 3, chs. 18, 32, 33; pt. 4, ch. 6. (Joseph's release by the intervention of the British consul is very reminiscent of a similar episode in Mapu's *The Hypocrite*, pt. 4, ch. 8. Cf. D. Patterson, *Abraham Mapu*, p. 33, cf. below, pp. 222f): *SM. 5*, pt. 3, ch. 13: *SM. 6*, pt. 2, chs. 6, 7; pt. 3, ch. 9: *SHEIK.*, pt. 3, ch. 22.

108. Cf. *SM. 5*, pt. 3, ch. 13: *SM. 6*, pt. 2, ch. 8: *WEIS. 2*, pt. 2, chs. 22, 23. (See D. Patterson,' Israel Weisbrem . . .', p. 45, notes 6, 7.)

109. Cf. *SM. 4*, ch. 8: *SM. 5*, pt. 2, ch. 13: *SM. 6*, pt. 1, ch. 1: *MEIN.*, chs. 4, 24: *SHEIK.*, pt. 3, ch. 9.

110. Cf. *SM. 1*, pt. 2, ch. 22: *LEIN.*, pt. 1, ch. 10.

111. Cf. *SM. 1*, pt. 1, chs. 3, 4, 5, 6, 27; pt. 2, chs. 20, 21, 24; pt. 3, chs. 4, 27, 32; *SM. 2*, ch. 14; *SM. 3*, ch. 2: *SM. 4*, chs. 5, 8, 9: *ABR.*, chs. 6, 20: *LEIN.*, pt. 1, chs. 2, 15, 16, 17: *ZOB.*, pt. 1, ch. 1: *SHEIK.*, pt. 2, chs. 13, 17: *RAB.*, ch. 13: *WEIS. 1*, chs. 1, 2, 6: *WEIS. 2*, pt. 1, ch. 7.

112. *SM. 1*, pt. 1, ch. 27; pt. 3, chs. 30, 32: *SM. 5*, pt. 3, ch. 1: *BRA. 1*, pt. 3, chs. 2, 3, 6: *LEIN.*, pt. 1, chs. 10, 15, 16, 17, 18; pt. 2, ch. 7: *MEIN.*, chs. 22, 23: *ZOB.*, pt. 2, ch. 19: *SHEIK.*, pt. 2, chs. 11, 16: *RAB.*, ch. 13: *WEIS. 2*, pt. 1, ch. 9.

113. *SM. 1*, pt. 3, ch. 27.

114. *RAB.*, ch. 13.

115. *BRA. 1*, pt. 1, chs. 2, 3, 6.

116. *SHEIK.*, pt. 2, chs. 11, 16.

117. *SM. 4*, chs. 3, 6, 7: *SM. 5*, pt. 3, chs. 1, 9: *SM. 6*, pt. 2, ch. 22: *ABR.*, ch. 32: *LEIN.*, pt. 1, ch. 10: *ZOB.* pt. 1, ch. 1.

118. *WEIS. 2*, pt. 1, ch. 8.

119. *LEIN.*, pt. 1, ch. 16.

120. *WEIS. 2*, pt. 1, chs. 10, 11.

121. *SM. 2*, ch. 16: *SM. 3*, chs. 9, 10: *SM. 4*, ch. 5: *SM. 5*, pt. 3, ch. 1: *ABR.*, ch. 7: *LEIN.*, pt. 1, chs. 2, 19, 20; pt. 2, ch. 8: *WEIS. 2*, pt. 2, chs. 20, 23.

122. *ABR.*, ch. 7: *LEIN.*, pt. 1, ch. 20: *WEIS. 2*, pt. 2, chs. 20, 23. Cf. S. F. Meinkin, *Mi-Zikhronoth Yemê Yalduthi*, Warsaw, 1903, p. 9, where a similar incident is related.

123. *ABR.*, chs. 6, 7, 20: *LEIN.*, pt. 1, ch. 14; pt. 2, ch. 4. Most of these devices are to be found in Mapu's novels, which—in turn —leant heavily on Eugène Sue's *Mystères de Paris*. See below, pp. 220 and 223f.

124. *MAN.*, ch. 2.

125. *SM. 6*, pt. 1, ch. 20.

126. *SM. 1*, pt. 2, ch. 25: *SM. 5*, pt. 2, ch. 15: *SM. 6*, pt. 1, ch. 8; pt. 2, chs. 2, 23: *LEIN.*, pt. 2, ch. 5: *SIRK.*, ch. 8: *WEIS. 2*, pt. 2, ch. 23.

127. *SM. 2*, ch. 16.

128. *SM. 1*, pt. 2, ch. 24.

129. *SM. 1*, pt. 3, ch. 32: *SM. 2*, ch. 13: *SM. 3*, ch. 17: *SM. 4*, ch. 6: *SM. 5*, pt. 3, ch. 12: *SM. 6*, pt. 1, ch. 1; pt. 3, ch. 1: *LEIN.*, pt. 2, chs. 1, 2, 7, 14: *MEIN.*, ch. 10: *ZOB.*, pt. 1, ch. 13; pt. 2, chs. 16, 23: *RAB.*, ch. 13.

130. *SM. 1*, pt. 2, ch. 24: *SM. 6*, pt. 2, ch. 2.

131. *SM. 5*, pt. 2, ch. 13: *SM. 6*, pt. 2, chs. 23, 24: *BRA. 1*, pt. 1, ch. 3: *ZOB.*, pt. 2, chs. 16, 18: *WEIS. 2*, pt. 2, chs. 21, 22.

132. See *SM. 4*, ch. 5: *SM. 5*, pt. 2, ch. 13: *SM. 6*, pt. 2, chs. 23, 24: *ZOB.*, pt. 2, chs. 16, 18.

133. Cf. D. Patterson, *Abraham Mapu*, p. 33.

134. *SM. 5*, pt. 2, ch. 15; pt. 3, ch. 1. Cf. above, p. 14.

135. *MEIN.*, ch. 8. See above, n. 102.

136. Cf. *SM. 1*, pt. 1, chs. 18, 25; pt. 2, chs. 17, 22, 24, 29; pt. 3, ch. 38: *SM. 2*, chs. 13, 23: *SM. 3*, chs. 11, 14, 20, 21: *SM. 4*, chs. 5, 8, 10: *SM. 5*, pt. 1, ch. 11; pt. 2, chs. 11, 12, 14; pt. 3, chs. 2, 13, 21: *SM. 6*, pt. 1, chs. 3, 20; pt. 2, ch. 7; pt. 3, chs. 3, 7: *ABR.*, ch. 32: *BRA. 2*, pt. 1, ch. 20; pt. 2, ch. 25: *LEIN.*, pt. 1, ch. 18:

MEIN., chs. 18, 19, 24: *ZOB.*, pt. 1, chs. 3, 13: *MAN.*, ch. 2: *SHEIK.*, pt. 2, ch. 15; pt. 3, chs. 15, 19, 21: *SIRK.*, chs. 5,7, 8: *WEIS. 1*, chs. 6, 11: *WEIS. 2*, pt. 1, chs. 2, 3; pt. 2, ch. 18. See D. Patterson, 'Sickness and Death in the Hebrew Novel of the Haskalah' in *The Jewish Journal of Sociology*, vol. V, no. 1, June 1963.

137. Cf. *SM. 1*, pt. 1, chs. 1, 2, 25; pt. 2, chs. 14, 20, 24; pt. 3, chs. 21, 22, 24, 25, 37; pt. 4, chs. 7, 8: *SM. 4*, chs. 6, 8, 10: *SM. 5*, pt. 1, chs. 9, 11; pt. 2, chs. 7, 15: *SM. 6*, pt. 1, chs. 7, 8, 16; pt. 2, chs. 1, 2, 8, 10, 15, 17, 24; pt. 3, chs. 6, 9: *ABR.*, chs. 19, 31, 33: *BRA. 2*, pt. 3, chs. 1, 2, 32; pt. 4, ch. 43: *LEIN.*, pt. 1, chs. 7, 10, 16: *ZOB.*, pt. 1, chs. 8, 13; pt. 2, ch. 1; *MAN.*, chs. 2, 3, 4, 8: *SHEIK.*, pt. 1, ch. 11; pt. 2, ch. 8; pt. 3, chs. 1, 3, 20, 32: *RAB.*, chs. 4, 8: *SIRK.*, ch. 7: *WEIS. 1*, chs. 6, 9, 10: *WEIS. 2*, pt.1, chs. 2, 6, 7, 12; pt. 2, chs. 14, 18, 19, 22, 24.

138. *SM. 6*, pt. 3, ch. 9. Cf. below, notes 204-5.

139. *SM. 1*, pt. 2, ch. 29; pt. 3, ch. 32: *SM. 4*, ch. 11 (3): *LEIN.*, pt. 2, ch. 4.

140. *SM. 1*, pt. 1, chs. 23, 25; pt. 3, ch. 19 (where a character remarks that if his love is still disappointed in one year's time he will commit suicide as thousands do in London!): *SM. 2*, ch. 24: *BRA. 2*, pt. 4, ch. 41: *MEIN.*, chs. 20, 21, 22: *MAN.*, ch. 2: *SHEIK.*, pt. 2, ch. 10; pt. 3, chs. 21, 22.

141. *BRA. 2*, pt. 4, ch. 41.

142. Cf. *SM. 1*, pt. 1, chs. 1, 11, 23; pt. 2, chs. 14, 17, 21, 24; pt. 3, chs. 22, 24, 25, 38; pt. 4, ch. 24: *SM. 4*, chs. 5, 6, 7, 8: *SM. 5*, pt. 2, ch. 12; pt. 3, ch. 1: *SM. 6*, pt. 1, ch. 1; pt. 2, ch. 21: *ABR.*, chs. 33, 34: *BRA. 1*, pt. 1, chs. 2, 4; pt. 2, chs. 2, 6: *BRA. 2*, pt. 1, ch. 1: *LEIN.*, pt. 1, ch. 9; pt. 2, ch. 12: *MEIN.*, chs. 4, 7, 13, 22: *ZOB.*, pt. 1, chs. 1, 2, 3; pt. 2, chs. 18, 23, 24: *MAN.*, chs. 3 (eight deaths in one chapter!), 4, 8: *SHEIK.*, pt. 1, ch. 15; pt. 2, ch. 12; pt. 3, ch. 20: *RAB.*, chs. 9, 11: *SIRK.*, chs. 10, 11: *WEIS. 2*, chs. 8, 12; pt. 2, chs. 15, 16.

143. *SM. 1*, pt. 3, ch. 38.

144. See below, pp. 154f.

145. See below, p. 155.

146. See *Ibid.*

147. See below, pp. 141f.

148. Cf. *SM. 2*: *SM. 5* (a double wedding): *SM. 6* (a triple wedding!): *ABR.*, ch. 33: *BRA. 2*: *LEIN.* (a double wedding): *ZOB.*: *SHEIK.*: *WEIS. 1* (a double wedding): *WEIS. 2* (a double wedding).

149. Cf. *SM. 1*, pt. 3, ch. 22: *SM. 2*, chs. 6, 12, 14, 23: *SM. 3*, ch. 1: *SM. 4*, chs. 5, 19: *BRA. 1*, pt. 2, ch. 11: *BRA. 2*, pt. 1, ch. 4; pt. 3, ch. 27; pt. 4, chs. 39, 43.

150. *MAN.*, chs. 3, 5, 6, 7. Cf. above, pp. 25f.

151. *SM. 1*, pt. 1, p. 256. Cf. *ibid.*, pt. 2, ch. 24 for the cause of Dan's wish for revenge.

152. *Ibid.*, pt. 2, p. 257. Cf. *ibid.*, pt. 1, ch. 25; pt. 2, chs. 20, 24; pt. 3, ch. 25: *SM. 3*, chs. 14, 15, 17, 20, 21: *SM. 4*, chs. 5, 6 (this chapter is entitled 'Revenge'), 11: *LEIN.*, ch. 2: *SHEIK.*, pt. 2, ch. 18; pt. 3, chs. 15, 19: *WEIS. 1*, ch. 7.

153. Cf. Mishnah, *'Erubhin*.

154. *WEIS. 2*, pt. 2, chs. 21, 22. See D. Patterson, 'Israel Weisbrem . . .', pp. 46f.

155. Cf. below, p. 194.

156. *SM. 1*, pt. 3, chs. 28, 33.

157. *Ibid.*, ch. 24. Cf. *ibid.*, pt. 3, ch. 22. A similar incident occurs in Mapu's *The Hypocrite*, pt. IV, ch. 17. Cf. D. Patterson, *Abraham Mapu*, p. 33.

158. Cf. *SM. 1*, pt. 2, chs. 20, 24; pt. 3, ch. 25: *SM. 4*, chs. 5, 6, 7, 8: *SM. 5*, pt. 1, ch. 6; pt. 2, ch. 12; pt. 3, chs. 5, 8: *SM. 6*, pt. 3, ch. 9: *BRA. 2*, pt. 1, ch. 5: *SHEIK.*, pt. 3, ch. 19.

159. Cf. *BRA. 1*, pt. 1, p. 99; pt. 3, pp. 33ff, 45, 71: *BRA. 2*, pt. 1, pp. 73f, 189ff, 191, 196: *RAB.*, p. 152: *SIRK.*, pp. 95ff. Cf. above, p. 44.

160. *SM. 1*, pt. 1, p. 164.

161. *Ibid.*, p. 189. Cf. '. . . stamping his feet, clapping his hands and tearing his hair . . .', *ibid.*, pp. 213f.

162. *BRA. 1*, pt. 3, p. 71.

163. *SM. 4*, p. 187. Cf. *SM. 5*, pt. 2, p. 116.

164. E.g. *SM. 1*, pt. 1, pp. 16, 188: *SM. 2*, pp. 23, 228: *MAN.*, pp. 31, 43.

165. E.g. *SM. 1*, pt. 2, p. 154: *SM. 2*, p. 68.

166. Cf. *SM. 1*, pt. 1, p. 237: *SM. 2*, pp. 17, 44: *SM. 4*, p. 105: *SM. 5*, pt. 2, p. 116. See above, pp. 55f.

167. *LEIN.*, pt. 1, pp. 7f. Cf. p. 64. See below, pp. 74f.

168. *LEIN.*, pt. 2, ch. 12.

169. E.g., *ZOB.*, pt. 1, p. 60; pt. 2, pp. 50ff.

170. Cf. *MAN.*, pp. 31, 39ff, 42f, 73f: *SHEIK.*, pt. 1, p. 6; pt. 2, pp. 58, 100; pt. 3, p. 108: *WEIS. 2*, pt. 2, pp. 116, 190f, 200ff.

171. *MEIN.*, pp. 54f, 60, 66, 100, 113. Cf. *SM. 4*, p. 94.

172. *ABR.*, pp. 26f. See above, n. 123.

173. *ABR.*, pp. 29ff. See above, n. 122.

174. *ABR.*, pp. 135 ff.

175. See D. Patterson. 'The Portrait of Ḥasidism . . .', and 'The Portrait of the Ṣaddik . . .', See below, p. 207.

176. *SM.1*, pt. 2, p. 245.

177. *Ibid.*, p. 256. Cf. *ibid.*, pt. 1, pp. 198, 237, 255f; pt. 2, p. 230; pt. 3, p. 171.

178. Cf. *SM. 2*, pp. 96f, 122, 222: *SM. 3*, pp. 105, 159: *SM. 4*, pp. 94, 186f, 289: *SM. 5*, pt. 2, pp. 100, 122f; pt. 3, pp. 12ff, 111, 121: *SM. 6*, pt. 2, pp. 197, 200ff; pt. 3, pp. 316, 337, 363.

179. With the exception of those by Meinkin, Rabinowitz and Sirkis.

180. *BRA. 2*, pt. 4, pp. 350ff. See above, p. 20.

181. *BRA. 2*, pt. 4, p. 361.

182. *Ibid.*, pt. 1, p. 32.

183. *Ibid.*, pt. 2, ch. 1.

184. *ABR.*, pp. 93, 158f. Aryeh and Elkanah are, of course, identical; see above, p. 5.

185. *ZOB.*, pt. 2, p. 48. For other equally fantastic coincidences in this novel see *ibid.*, pp. 9, 27, 58, and especially p. 64. Coincidences of this type are found in wild profusion in the romantic German novel of the early nineteenth century.

186. *MAN.*, p. 89. See above, pp. 25f.

187. *SHEIK.*, pt. 3, p. 82. For other coincidences in this novel see pt. 2, p. 84; pt. 3, pp. 52, 96.

188. *WEIS. 1*, p. 59. See above, p. 31. For further examples of coincidence in Weisbrem's novels see D. Patterson, 'Israel Weisbrem . . .', p. 46.

189. *SM. 1*, pt. 1, p. 215.

190. *Ibid.*, p. 230.

191. *Ibid.*, pt. 3, p. 164.

192. *Ibid.*, pt. 4, p. 110.

193. E.g. *ibid.*, pt. 1, p. 207; pt. 2, p. 255; pt. 3, p. 216. For further remarkable coincidences in this novel see pp. 226f.

194. See above. p. 42. Cf. also *ZOB.*, pt. 2, p. 64.

195. *SM. 2*, p. 118: *SM. 4*, pp. 83, 109: *SM. 5*, pt. 2, pp. 61f; pt. 3, pp. 140ff.

R

196. *SM. 1*, pt. 3, pp. 26off.

197. *SM. 4*, pp. 29of.

198. *SM. 2*, pp. 8off. Cf. below, pp. 87, 156.

199. With the exception of Rabinowitz and Weisbrem.

200. Cf. *The Love of Zion*, chs. 3, 27: *The Guilt of Samaria*, pt. 1, chs. 5, 6, 8, 16; pt. 2, chs. 14, 20: *The Hypocrite*, pt. 2, chs. 2, 4, 9, 12, 14; pt. 3, chs. 2, 13; pt. 4, chs. 1, 6, 9, 10; pt. 5, ch. 6. See D. Patterson, *Abraham Mapu*, pp. 35f.

201. Cf. *SM. 1*, pt. 1, pp. 21, 40, 103f, 197, 217ff; pt. 2, pp. 127f, 233; pt. 3, pp. 81ff: *SM. 2*, pp. 46, 221: *SM. 6*, pt. 1, pp. 153f; pt. 2, pp. 26of. 33: *ABR.*, pp. 49ff, 109f, 128f: *BRA. 1*, pt. 1, p. 86: *LEIN.*, p. 24: *MEIN.*, pp. 74ff: *ZOB.*, pt. 1, p. 5: *MAN.*, pp. 26ff: *SHEIK.*, pt. 1, pp. 37f; pt. 2, pp. 7f; pt. 3, pp. 6, 102: *SIRK.*, pp. 20, 35, 40, 43, and cf. below, p. 211.

202. *SHEIK.*, pt. 2, p. 8. See above, n. 47.

203. *MAN.*, pp. 26ff. A similar incident occurs in *SHEIK.*, pt. 1, ch. 1.

204. *SM. 1*, pt. 1, pp. 21, 40, 103f, 217ff; pt. 2, pp. 127f, 233; pt. 3, pp. 81ff.

205. Cf. above, p. 53. Cf. W. Warrington, 'Dickens and the Psychology of Dreams', in *P.M.L.A.* LXIII, pp. 984-1006.

206. With the exception of those by Rabinowitz and Sirkis, the former containing only two examples, and the latter none.

207. *SM. 1*, pt. 1, pp. 16, 48, 113, 208f, 234ff, 245, 248, 266; pt. 2, pp. 151, 167ff, 189ff; pt. 3, pp. 75, 108, 116f, 217f, 233; pt. 4 (from ch. 2 onwards *in toto*): *SM. 3*, pp. 132f: *SM. 4*, pp. 69, 275, 291: *SM. 5*, pt. 2, pp. 117, 120, 126ff, 148; pt. 3, pp. 52, 61ff, 93ff, 128f: *SM. 6*, pt. 1, pp. 23, 25, 118, 131, 133, 238; pt. 2, p. 286; pt. 3, pp. 281, 324: *ABR.*, pp. 4f, 21ff, 36ff, 72, 76, 81ff, 96f, 116, 137f, 140, 146f, 155, 158: *BRA. 1*, pt. 1, pp. 28, 45, 124; pt. 2, pp. 16, 32f, 42, 61, 72, 8off; pt. 3, pp. 32, 59, 74ff, 81, 109, 127, 136, 193, 195ff: *BRA. 2*, pt. 1, pp. 32, 73f; pt. 2, pp. 139f, 146f, 153ff, 193; pt. 3, pp. 219f, 257, 265, 289, 291, 304, 306; pt. 4, pp. 316f, 323f: *LEIN.*, pt. 1, p. 31; pt. 2, pp. 3ff, 72f: *MEIN.*, pp. 28, 30, 54, 73, 104, 106, 110ff, 112ff, 117, 121, 138, 140, 148: *ZOB.*, pt. 1, pp. 48, 57f, 60, 62f; pt. 2, p. 62: *MAN.*, pp. 34ff, 55, 8of, 90, 102: *SHEIK.*, pt. 2, pp. 13, 70, 89; pt. 3, pp. 74, 94, 109: *RAB.*, pp. 77f: *WEIS. 1*, pp. 36, 39, 76ff, 85, 88f, 91f, 96ff, 98ff, 100ff, 118ff, 110ff, 114f, 121f: *WEIS. 2*, pt. 1, pp. 119, 161, 170, 173; pt. 2, pp. 22, 26, 125, 152f, 157f.

208. Cf. D. Patterson, *Abraham Mapu*, p. 36, and 'Epistolary Elements in the novels of Abraham Mapu'.

209. E.g. *SM. 1*, pt. 3, pp. 109, 116: *SM. 5*, pt. 3, pp. 93ff: *ZOB.*, pt. 1, pp. 57f, 62f; pt. 2, p. 28.

210. It is interesting that on two occasions he uses the actual letters P. S., *BRA. 1*, pt. 2, p. 83: *BRA. 2*, pt. 3, p. 220.

211. E.g. *BRA. 1*, pt. 2, pp. 80ff; pt. 3, pp. 32, 195ff.

212. *Ibid.*, pt. 3, p. 59.

213. *ABR.*, pp. 4f. Cf. *SM. 3*, p. 69: *BRA. 1*, pt. 3, p. 81: *BRA. 2*, pt. 3, p. 291.

214. See D. Patterson 'Israel Weisbrem . . .', p. 48. Cf. below, p. 116, n. 146.

215. See D. Patterson, 'Israel Weisbrem . . .', p. 49, n. 1.

216. E.g. *MEIN.*, pp. 110ff: *MAN.*, pp. 34ff: *SHEIK.*, pt. 2, p, 13: *WEIS. 1*, p. 88. Cf. below, pp. 108f.

217. See D. Patterson, 'Israel Weisbrem . . .', pp. 44f.

218. See below, p. 135.

219. E.g. *SM. 4*, pp. 52, 90, 292. Cf. *SM. 1*, pt. 4, p. 36: *SM. 5*, pt. 3, p. 94: *WEIS. 2*, pt. 1, p. 156; pt. 2, pp. 70, 162.

220. E.g. *SM. 1*, pt. 1, p. 248: *ZOB.*, pt. 2, p. 22.

221. *SM.1*, pt, 3, p. 178. See above, p. 52.

222. Cf. *SM.1*, pt. 4, p. 36: *SM. 4*, pt. 1, p. 3: *ZOB.*, pt. 2, p. 22: *SHEIK.*, pt. 3, p. 93. See below, p. 154.

223. See above, p. 44.

224. E.g. *SM. 1*, pt. 2, chs. 2, 17; pt. 3, chs. 4, 28; pt. 4, ch. 9: *SM. 3*, chs. 2, 3, 11, 19: *SM. 4*, ch. 6: *SM. 5*, pt. 1, chs. 6, 9, 10; pt. 2, ch. 14; pt. 3, chs. 1, 10: *SM. 6*, pt. 1, chs. 1, 2, 7, 10, 11, 13, 15, 17, 20; pt. 2, chs. 2, 3, 7, 12; pt. 3, chs. 1, 2, 7: *ABR.*, chs. 1, 11, 17: *BRA. 1*, pt. 1, chs. 3, 7, 10; pt. 2, ch. 6; pt, 3, chs. 8, 11, 12, 14, 16, 17: *BRA. 2*, pt. 2, chs. 12, 21, 24, 25; pt. 3, chs. 28, 33: *LEIN.*, pt. 2, ch. 1: *MAN.*, ch. 5: *SHEIK.*, pt. 2, ch. 11; pt. 3, ch. 4: *RAB.*, ch. 2: *SIRK.*, ch. 3: *WEIS. 1*, chs. 1, 3: *WEIS. 2*, pt. 1, ch. 5; pt. 2, ch. 21.

225. *BRA. 2*, pt. 1, p. 71.

226. *BRA. 1*, pt. 1, pp. 77f.

227. *SM. 1*, pt. 4, pp. 33-43.

228. *SM. 5*, pt. 3, p. 108. Cf. *SM. 1*, pt. 1, pp. 153ff, 159ff, 174f, 187f: *SM. 2*, p. 19: *SM. 5*, pt. 1, pp. 82, 140; pt. 2, pp. 100, 120: *SM. 6*, pt. 1, pp. 114f, 138, 209ff; pt. 3, pp. 284f, 311, 328:

BRA. 1, pt. 2, p. 27: *BRA. 2*, pt. 1, p. 37; pt. 3, p. 265; *LEIN.*, pt. 1, p. 9: *SHEIK.*, pt. 3, p. 52: *WEIS. 2*, pt. 1, p. 137; pt. 2, pp. 29, 147.

CHAPTER 3

1. Eccles. 7^{16}.

2. *SM. 1*, p. 219. For other instances of the authors directing advice towards their characters or analysing their motives or situation, see *ibid.*, chs. 11, 22: *SM. 3*. chs. 14, 17: *SM. 5*, pt. 1, ch. 7; pt. 2, ch. 9: *SM. 6*, pt. 1, ch. 7; pt. 2, chs. 6, 11; pt. 3, chs. 3, 6: *BRA. 1*, pt. 2, chs. 9, 10, 13; pt. 3, chs. 3, 20.

3. See D. Patterson, *Abraham Mapu*, pp. 56f.

4. *Ibid.*, pp. 61f. For a discussion on 'flat' and 'round' characters see E. M. Forster, *Aspects of the Novel*, London, 1927, p. 93. Cf. E. Muir, *The Structure of the Novel*, London, 1949, p. 142.

5. See below, p. 223.

6. See above, p. 44, and below, p. 185.

7. See above, p. 38, and below, chs. 5, 6, 7. Cf. F. R. Leavis, *The Great Tradition*, London, 1948, pp. 7ff.

8. Cf. *SM. 1*, pt. 1, p. 160: *SM. 3*, pp. 22, 143. Cf. *SM. 1*, pt. 1, pp. 33, 144; pt. 3, p. 96; pt. 4, pp. 33, 35: *SM. 3*, p. 32: *SM. 4*, pp. 3, 47, 229: *SM. 5*, pt. 1, pp. 43ff; pt. 3, p. 150: *SM. 6*, pt. 1, pp. 142, 144, 157, 166: *ABR.*, pp. 1, 26, 40, 57: *BRA. 1*, pt. 1, p. 11: *LEIN.*, pp. 3, 11: *MAN.*, p. 5: *SHEIK.*, pt. 1, p. 6; pt. 2, p. 18: *RAB.*, pp. 39, 43: *SIRK.*, pp. 70, 101: *WEIS. 1*, p. 28. Cf. above, ch. 1, n. 24.

9. See above, pp. 38, 44f.

10. See above, pp. 40f.

11. Cf. above, p. 69, n. 8.

12. Another symbolic name, signifying 'Horsey'.

13. *SM. 5*, pt. 1, pp. 43f.

14. *Ibid.*, pt. 3, p. 130. The technique of withholding characters' names for some time is quite common within these novels, but there is no comparable example of a major character being named only towards the end of the story.

15. Signifying, Delilah 'the deceiver'. Cf. above, p. 69, n. 8.

16. See *SM. 5*, pt. 3, chs. 1, 3, 5, 9, 14, 15.

17. Cf. above, p. 38.

18. See below, ch. 4. For information on some early attempts to

revive Hebrew as a spoken language see C. Rabin, '*Ibhrith Medhubbereth Liphnê 125 Šanah*, in the series *Lešonenu La-'Am*, Jerusalem, 1963.

19. See D. Patterson, *The Foundations of Modern Hebrew Literature*, London, 1961, *passim*.

20. See e.g. *SM. 1*, pt. 1, pp. 14, 159: *SM. 2*, pp. 3, 20ff, 52ff, 62: *SM. 4*, p. 9: *SM. 5*, pt. 1, pp. 8ff, 67f: *BRA. 1*, pt. 1, pp. 13f, 93: *LEIN.*, pp. 48, 92f: *ZOB.*, pt. 1, p. 27: *SIRK.*, p. 8: *WEIS. 2*, pt. 1, p. 68.

21. Here, as very frequently in these novels, the author feels constrained to supply a translation (usually into Yiddish) of a term or phrase the meaning of which is not clear in the Hebrew. See below, p. 104.

22. *SHEIK.*, pt. 1, pp. 46f. Cf. above, p. 46.

23. *SM. 2*, pp. 151f.

24. Pt. 2, pp. 12f.

25. Pt. 1, pp. 214f. Cf. also *SM. 1*, pt. 1, p. 29; pt. 2, pp. 72ff: *SM. 6*, pt. 2, pp. 13, 110f.

26. *ABR.*, pp. 103f.

27. *BRA. 1*, pt. 2, p. 75.

28. Pt. 2, pp. 61f.

29. *WEIS. 1*, p. 42. For remarks on Weisbrem's characterisations see D. Patterson, 'Israel Weisbrem . . .', pp. 49ff.

30. Cf. *SM. 1*, pt. 2, p. 267: *SM. 3*, p. 9: *SM. 6*, pt. 1, p. 168; pt. 2, pp. 110ff.

31. For information relative to Mendele's novels, originally written in Yiddish, but transmuted into Hebrew in the period following the one under review, see e.g. A. S. Waldstein, *The Evolution of Modern Hebrew Literature*, New York, 1916, ch. VII; S. Spiegel, *Hebrew Reborn*, New York, 1930, ch. X.

32. Cf. D. Patterson, 'Hebrew Drama', in the *Bulletin of the John Rylands Library*, vol. 43, No. 1, September 1960, pp. 91f.

33. See e.g. M. E. Chase, *Life and Language in the Old Testament*, London, 1956.

34. *LEIN.*, pt. 1, p. 6. Cf. pp. 14f, 34, 45, 68: *SHEIK.*, pt. 1, p. 17: *SIRK.*, pp. 9, 108f: *WEIS. 1*, pp. 3ff: *WEIS. 2*, pt. 1, p. 161.

35. *LEIN.*, pt. 2, p. 21.

36. *SM. 4*, p. 141. For further examples of artificial and stilted conversation, see *SM. 1*, pt. 1, pp. 15ff: *SM. 2*, p. 26: *SM. 3*.

p. 13: *SM. 4*, pp. 62ff: *SM. 5*, pt. 1, pp. 3ff, 59ff; pt. 2, p. 6: *ABR.*, pp. 27f: *BRA. 1*, pt. 2, p. 58: *BRA. 2*, pt. 3, p. 301.

37. E.g. *SM. 1*, pt. 3, p. 244: *SM. 5*, pt. 2, p. 12; pt. 3, pp. 163f: *SM. 6*, pt. 2, pp. 138, 146; pt. 3, p. 220: *BRA. 1*, pt. 1, p. 107; pt. 2, p. 42; pt. 8, p. 29: *BRA. 2*, pt. 1, p. 35; pt. 2, p. 106: *WEIS. 1*, p. 40.

38. *RAB.*, p. 18.

39. See *ABR.*, pp. 144ff. Cf. D. Patterson, 'Sickness and Death . . .', p. 91.

40. *ABR.*, pp. 154f. Cf. pp. 2ff, 34f, 44.

41. See below, pp. 173ff.

42. *SM. 1*, pt. 1, pp. 31ff; pt. 2, p. 32; pt. 3, pp. 55f. Cf. pt. 1, pp. 85ff; pt. 2, pp. 44, 155f; pt. 3, pp. 138ff.

43. See below, p. 156.

44. *SM. 2*, pp. 36, 83ff. Cf. p. 54 and ch. 19.

45. Cf. *SM. 3*, pp. 20, 55, 141ff, 163ff: *SM. 4*, pp. 9-20: *SM. 5*, pt. 1, pp. 74f; pt. 3, pp. 59f.

46. *SM. 6*, pt. 1, pp. 40, 212ff. Cf. pp. 160ff; pt. 3. pp. 236f.

47. Cf. *BRA. 1*, pt. 1, pp. 18f, 23; pt. 2, pp. 8ff; pt. 3, pp. 150ff: *BRA. 2*, pt. 1, pp. 23ff; pt. 2, pp. 115f.

48. See above, p. 44.

49. Cf. *SM. 1*, pt. 1, pp. 162ff; pt. 2, pp. 138ff: *SM. 2*, pp. 33ff, chs. 17, 18: *SM. 4*, pp. 42ff: *SM. 5*, pt. 2, pp. 33ff: *SM. 6*, pt. 2, pp. 49-62, 76ff, 113ff, 122ff: *ABR.*, pp. 24f: *BRA. 1*, pt. 2, pp. 55ff, 115ff: *ZOB.*, pt. 2, pp. 29ff.

50. *SM. 1*, pt. 1, p. 23: *SM. 2*, pp. 3, 17, 44, 78ff: *SM. 3*, p. 159: *SM. 5*, pt. 1, pp. 10ff, 64, 80ff, 87ff, 136ff, 143; pt. 3, pp. 130, 150: *SM. 6*, pt. 1, pp. 81ff, 86, 126; pt. 2, pp. 316f; pt. 3, pp. 218, 316, 320ff: *BRA. 1*, pt. 1, p. 35; pt. 2, pp. 40ff, 45, 74, 101ff, 120, 124: *LEIN.*, pt. 1, pp. 35f: *MEIN.*, pp. 31, 121, 122, 123: *ZOB.*, pt. 1, pp. 3f, 35, 36f, 47f, 49f, 56ff, 59f; pt. 2, p. 26.

51. *SM. 5*, pt. 3, p. 150.

52. *WEIS., 2*, pt. 1, p. 97. Cf. D. Patterson, 'Israel Weisbrem . . .', p. 52.

53. Cf. *SM. 1*, pt. 1, p. 33: *SM. 2*, pp. 235ff: *SM. 4*, pp. 84f: *SM. 5*, pt. 1, pp. 148ff; pt. 3, pp. 58f: *SM. 6*, pt. 1, pp. 29ff, 215ff; pt. 3, pp. 227, 231, 246. On one occasion Smolenskin facetiously intervenes to beg a character to stop using the same phrase over and over again! *SM. 4*, p. 89. See below, p. 87.

54. See Klausner, *History*, vol. 5, p. 380, and the shortened version

of *Religion and Life*, ed. by J. Frankel, Jerusalem-Tel-Aviv, 1947.
Cf. Lilienblum's autobiographical testament, *Ḥaṭṭo'th Ne'urim*,
Vienna, 1876. Cf. below, p. 196.

55. See below, p. 131.

56. See *The Jewish Encyclopaedia*, vol. 5, p. 589.

57. See *BRA.* 2, pt. 3, pp. 212, 215, 260.

58. *SM. 1*, pt. 2, ch. 13; pt. 3, ch. 13.

59. *Ibid.*, pt. 3, ch. 2.

60. *Ibid.*

61. *Ibid.*, pt. 3, chs. 13, 15.

62. *Ibid.*, ch. 20.

63. *Ibid.*, ch. 24.

64. *Ibid.*, ch. 38.

65. *Ibid.*, pt. 4, ch. 24.

66. *Ibid.*, pt. 3, ch. 19. See below, pp. 181, 191.

67. See Klausner, *History*, vol. 5, p. 188.

68. *SM. 1*, pt. 4, chs. 2, 14.

69. See above, pp. 11f.

70. *SM. 3*, ch. 8.

71. *Ibid.*, ch. 10.

72. *Ibid.*, ch. 11.

73. *Ibid.*, ch. 13.

74. *Ibid.*, ch. 15.

75. *Ibid.*, ch. 10. It is of interest that as in the case of Simon in *The Joy of the Godless* (see above, n. 2) Smolenskin also picks holes in the character of Jacob Hayyim, *SM. 3*, ch. 17. See also *SM. 6*, pt. 2, chs. 11, 15.

76. *SM. 6*, pt. 1, chs. 4, 6, 8, 9.

77. See above, n. 2.

78. *SM. 6*, pt. 2, chs. 14, 15.

79. *Ibid.*, ch. 21; pt. 3, ch. 13.

80. *Ibid.*, ch. 9.

81. See below, p. 184.

82. The same is largely true of the hero of Rabinowitz's *At the Crossroads* only in a reverse direction. See above, p. 44.

83. *SM. 1*, pt. 1, pp. 151ff.

84. *SM. 1*, pt. 3, chs. 13, 15, 16, 17. Cf. above, n. 61.

85. *SM. 6*, pt. 2, chs. 2, 4; pt. 3, chs. 1, 7.

86. *Ibid.*, pt. 3, ch. 7. For other shrewd psychological touches see
    SM. 1, pt. 1, pp. 33, 90, 92, 100; pt. 2, pp. 116, 127f, 154, 184:
    SM. 2, pp. 10f, 17, 72, 93: *SM. 3*, p. 188: *SM. 5*, pt. 1, p. 57:
    SM. 6, pt. 1, pp. 167f; pt. 3, p. 228: *BRA. 1*, pt. 1, pp. 23, 64,
    92.

87. More or less equivalent to the English idiom 'a fine one!' Cf.
    above, p. 69.

88. With the notable exception of Rabinowitz; see below, p. 155.

89. See below, pp. 154f.

90. See above, pp. 70f.

91. See below, p. 216.

92. See *SM. 6*, pt. 3, chs. 2, 8, 9.

93. At least not according to the description in pt. 2, ch. 2, although
    later she is described as pretty! *Ibid.*, ch. 6. Cf. Klausner,
    History, vol. 5, p. 384.

94. *BRA. 1*, pt. 2, chs. 2, 6, 9, 10, 13; pt. 3, chs. 11, 12.

95. Cf. above, p. 80.

96. *SM. 1*, pt. 1, p. 95. Cf. below, pp. 151f.

97. An ethical work by Elijah de Vidas, first published in Venice,
    1578.

98. See above, ch. 1, n. 53.

99. *SM. 1*, pt. 2, pp. 273f. Cf. below, p. 201.

100. *SM. 1*, pt. 2, p. 279.

101. Cf. above, p. 11.

102. *SM. 2*, ch. 24.

103. *Ibid.*, chs. 19, 23, 24. Cf. above, n. 53.

104. See below, pp. 180f.

105. Cf. above, p. 69, n. 8.

106. See below, pp. 214f.

107. See below, pp. 153f.

108. *SM. 2*, pp. 235ff.

109. Cf. below, p. 141.

110. See above, p. 69, n. 8.

111. *SM. 2*, p. 23.

112. E.g. *SM. 1*, pt. 1, chs. 2, 6, 10; pt. 2, ch. 27; pt. 4, ch. 9: *SM. 2*,
     chs. 1, 14: *SM. 3*, chs. 1, 2, 16: *SM. 4*, chs. 3, 5, 6: *SM. 5*, pt. 1,
     chs. 8, 11; pt. 2, ch. 14: *SM. 6*, pt. 1, ch. 2; pt. 2, chs. 12, 18, 19.

113. Cf. *SM. 2*, ch. 14. Cf. below, n. 134.

114. For this type of stock description, cf. above, p. 72.

115. See below, pp. 140f.

116. Once more a symbolic name, representing 'division' or 'strife'. Cf. above, p. 69, n. 8.

117. See below, pp. 172f.

118. Mediaeval philosophical texts composed respectively by Maimonides, Judah ha-Levi, Bahya Ibn Paquda and J. Albo. See e.g. I. Husik, *A History of Mediaeval Jewish Philosophy*, Philadelphia, 1946.

119. For other examples of nicknames in these novels see *SM. 1*, pt. 2, pp. 33, 73, 77: *SM. 2*, pp. 82, 211: *SM. 3*, pp. 8, 10, 11, 15, 60: *SM. 4*, p. 207: *SM. 5*, pt. 1, pp. 72, 91: *ABR.*, p. 73: *BRA. 1*, pt. 1, pp. 102, 104; pt. 2, p. 12: *BRA. 2*, pt. 2, pp. 92, 94; pt. 3, p. 277: *SHEIK.*, pt. 1, p. 25: *WEIS. 1*, pp. 45, 50.

120. By Moses ben Joshua of Narbonne. See e.g. *The Jewish Encyclopaedia*, vol. 9, p. 71.

121. See below, p. 187.

122. *BRA. 1*, pt. 1, pp. 93f.

123. *BRA. 2*, pt. 3, p. 278.

124. See above, n. 87.

125. For the conflict between the orthodox and the exponents of 'Enlightenment', see below, ch. 6.

126. *BRA. 1*, pt. 2, ch. 4. Cf. pt. 3, chs. 2, 13, 14, 15, 19.

127. *Ibid.*, pt. 1, ch. 10; pt. 3, chs. 9, 11.

128. *WEIS. 2*, pt. 2, pp. 71f. See D. Patterson. 'Israel Weisbrem . . .', p. 50.

129. *SIRK.*, p. 12.

130. *Ibid.*, pp. 23f. For further skilful characterisations, cf. *SHEIK.*, pt. 3, ch. 4: *RAB.*, chs. 1, 2, 6, 7, 10, 11: *WEIS. 1*, chs. 3, 9: *WEIS. 2*, pt. 1, chs. 6, 10, 12.

131. See below, pp. 141f.

132. See *WEIS. 2*, pt. 1, chs. 1, 11; pt. 2, chs. 16, 17, 21. Cf. *SM. 3*, ch. 1: *SM. 5*, pt. 1, ch. 7; pt. 2, ch. 8.

133. *BRA. 1*, pt. 1, chs. 5, 6, 10, 12; pt. 2, chs. 9, 16; pt. 3, chs. 9, 10.

134. Only too frequently characters are described simply by such titles as 'an old man'; e.g. *SM. 1*, pt. 3, ch. 4. Cf. above, n. 113.

CHAPTER 4

1. See above, pp. 34 and 71 ff.

2. See above, ch. 1, n. 1.

3. See Klausner, *History*, vol. 1, pp. 9f. Cf. Waxman, *op. cit.*

4. For a brief outline of this important factor see D. Patterson, *The Foundations of Modern Hebrew Literature.*

5. The constant appeals for refined expression, themselves couched in clumsy and highly artificial snatches of conversation, constitute a revealing, if ironical commentary on the linguistic dilemma confronting the novelists in the period of *Haskalah.*

6. See below, pp. 171 ff.

7. The subject has been treated by Mr. B. Shahevitch in a paper 'The Nature of Melitza', delivered at the Third World Congress of Jewish Studies in Jerusalem on 28 July, 1961, the gist of which may be seen in the synopsis of lectures for the Hebrew Literature Section, pp. xviif.

8. See above, ch. 1, n. 2.

9. See above, p. 79.

10. See above, pp. 97f.

11. In the following section only a few characteristic examples out of hundreds have been utilised. For a fuller account see D. Patterson, 'Some Linguistic Aspects of the Nineteenth-Century Hebrew Novel' in the *Journal of Semitic Studies*, vol. 7, No. 2, Autumn, 1962. See also the examples quoted in D. Patterson, 'Israel Weisbrem . . .', pp. 52f.

12. *SM. 2*, p. 98.

13. *SM. 1*, pt. 1, p. 160.

14. *Ibid.*, pt. 3, p. 95.

15. *SM. 5*, pt. 3, p. 140.

16. *Ibid.*, p. 13.

17. *SM. 6*, pt. 1, p. 171.

18. *RAB.*, p. 30.

19. *SM. 1*, pt. 2, p. 39.

20. *SM. 6*, pt. 2, p. 171.

21. *SM. 1*, pt. 3, p. 105.

22. *WEIS. 1*, p. 91.

23. *Ibid.*, p. 121.

24. *BRA. 1*, pt. 3, pp. 42, 59. This is the term at present in use in modern Hebrew.

25. *BRA. 2*, pt. 3, p. 220.

26. *Ibid.*, pt. 1, p. 44.

27. *BRA. 1*, pt. 3, p. 32.

28. *BRA. 2*, pt. 2, p. 193.

29. *WEIS. 1*, p. 91.

30. *SM. 2*, p. 98: *WEIS.* 1, p. 11.

31. *SM. 4*, p. 170.

32. *SM. 6*, pt. 1, p. 39; pt. 2, p. 79: *LEIN.*, pt. 1, p. 3.

33. *SM. 1*, pt. 4, p. 43: *MEIN.*, p. 149.

34. *BRA. 2*, pt. 1, pp. 7, 8; pt. 3, p. 304: *LEIN.*, pt. 2, p. 13: *MEIN.*, p. 149: *SIRK.*, p. 116: *WEIS. 1*, pp. 10, 63. This phrase is clearly modelled on the French, and is still acceptable in modern Hebrew.

35. *SIRK.*, pp. 116, 124: *WEIS. 1*, p. 63. The word is derived from a root meaning 'to travel'. Cf. below, n. 105.

36. Cf. D. Patterson, 'Israel Weisbrem . . .', p. 53, n. 3.

37. *BRA. 2*, pt. 2, p. 81: *SIRK.*, p. 49.

38. *SM. 1*, pt. 2, p. 253: *BRA. 2*, pt. 2, p. 81.

39. *ABR.*, p. 160.

40. *BRA. 1*, pt. 3, p. 180.

41. *SM. 4*, p. 185.

42. *LEIN.*, pt. 2, p. 30.

43. *SM. 1*, pt. 4, p. 111.

44. *WEIS. 1*, p. 45.

45. *RAB.*, p. 139.

46. *SM. 6*, pt. 2, p. 108.

47. *SIRK.*, p. 96.

48. *SM. 2*, pt. 2, p. 53: *SM.* 3, p. 38.

49. *SM. 5*, pt. 3, p. 129.

50. *SM. 6*, pt. 1, p. 181.

51. *ABR.*, pp. 13, 112. Literally, 'the house of the male cooks.'

52. *SM.1*, pt. 1, p. 21: *SM. 2*, pp. 4, 86: *BRA. 2*, pt. 1, p. 73: *SIRK.*, p. 46. Literally, 'the house of the female cooks'.

53. *MEIN.*, p. 15: *RAB.*, pp. 12, 17: *SIRK.*, p. 3. Literally, 'the room of the female cooks'.

54. *SM. 3*, p. 115: *MEIN.*, p. 15: *WEIS. 1*, p. 39.

55. *SM. 3*, p. 36.

56. See above, ch. 3, n. 21.

57. *SM. 1*, pt. 4, p. 100.

58. *BRA. 1*, pt. 2, p. 12.

59. *BRA. 2*, pt. 1, p. 7.

60. *Ibid.*, p. 12.

61. *LEIN.*, pt. 1, p. 48.

62. *MEIN.*, p. 7.

63. *RAB.*, p. 63.

64. *SM. 1*, pt. 4, p. 64.

65. *MEIN.*, p. 33.

66. *Ibid.*, p. 56.

67. *RAB.*, p. 111.

68. *Ibid.*, p. 116.

69. *LEIN.*, pt. 2, p. 9.

70. *WEIS. 2*, pt. 1, p. 183; pt. 2, p. 31.

71. *Ibid.*, pp. 131, 133.

72. As here, too, the references run into thousands, and as the subject is treated in greater detail in the article referred to above in note 11, only a number of characteristic examples are mentioned here, without detailed reference.

73. See D. Patterson, *Abraham Mapu*, p. 75.

74. See *ibid.*, pp. 88f.

75. See below, ch. 6.

76. *SM. 1*, pt. 1, p. 35. Cf. Eccles. 1^{18}.

77. *Ibid.*, p. 71. Cf. *BRA. 1*, pt. 2, p. 7. Cf. 1 Sam. 9^2.

78. *Ibid.*, pt. 3, p. 108. Cf. Ex. 4^{13}.

79. *SM. 2*, p. 30. Cf. Is. 36^6.

80. *Ibid.*, p. 70. Cf. Ruth 2^7.

81. *SM. 3*, p. 18. Cf. Ps. 137^8.

82. *SM. 4*, p. 281. Cf. *BRA. 1*, pt. 1, p. 57. Cf. Eccles. 1^8.

83. *ABR.*, pp. 22f. Cf. Ruth 1^{19-20}.

84. *Ibid.*, p. 51. Cf. Gen. 49^{12}.

85. *BRA. 1*, pt. 1, p. 64. Cf. 1 Sam. 9^{14}.

86. *Ibid.*, pt. 2, p. 106. Cf. Is. 66⁶.

87. *Ibid.*, pt. 3, p. 56. Cf. *WEIS. 1*, p. 55. Cf. Is. 40²⁸.

88. *BRA. 2*, p. 16. Cf. 1 Sam. 10¹¹.

89. *SHEIK.*, pt. 1, p. 12. Cf. Cant. 3².

90. *WEIS. 2*, pt. 2, pp. 2, 204. Cf. Eccles. 1¹³.

91. *ABR.*, p. 88. Cf. Jonah 4¹¹.

92. See above, p. 100.

93. Cf. *SM. 1*, pt. 2, pp. 88, 136f: *ABR.*, p. 19: *BRA. 1*, pt. 3, p. 208. Here, again the influence of Mapu is very clear; cf. D. Patterson, *Abraham Mapu*, pp. 88f.

94. *SM. 1*, pt. 1, p. 90. Cf. *SM. 3*, p. 192: *RAB.*, p. 11.

95. *Ibid.*, p. 96.

96. *SM. 2*, pp. 7f. Cf. *SM. 5*, pt. 3, p. 90.

97. *Ibid.*, p. 29.

98. *Ibid.*, p. 111.

99. *SM. 4*, p. 58.

100. *SM. 5*, pt. 3, p. 19. Cf. *SM. 6*, pt. 2, p. 261.

101. *SM. 6*, pt. 1, p. 1.

102. *BRA. 1*, pt. 2, p. 41. Cf. pt. 3, p. 42.

103. *MAN.*, p. 32.

104. *Ibid.*, p. 53.

105. *ZOB.*, pt. 1, p. 61. Presumably 'a train'! Cf. above, p. 103.

106. Used as a term of respect, not kinship.

107. *WEIS. 1*, p. 39. Cf. above, p. 62.

108. See e.g. *MAN.*, p. 58: *ZOB.*, p. 15: *MEIN.*, pp. 104ff; *LEIN.*, pt. 1, pp. 18f, 23, 51.

109. *ABR.*, ch. 3.

110. *Ibid.*, pp. 17f. Cf. Sheikewitz's indictment of the poetry composed by *Maskilim*, *SHEIK.*, pt. 1, p. 63. See below, pp. 186, 226.

111. A common epithet for *Meliṣah* in the literature of *Haskalah*, roughly equivalent to the term *Muse*.

112. *ABR.*, p. 19. These criteria were used by Abramowitz with devastating effect in his *Mišpaṭ Šalom*, Vilna, 1860, an attack on E. Zweifel's *Minnim we-ʿUggabh*, Vilna, 1858. Cf. below, p. 226.

113. See above, p. 97.

114. See above, p. 44.

115. See above, pp. 63f.

116. See above, pp. 84ff.

117. See below, pp. 190, 207f.

118. See below, p. 146.

119. See below, pp. 168ff.

120. See below, pp. 140f.

121. *ABR.*, pp. 75f.

122. See below, pp. 148ff.

123. *SM. 1*, pt. 1, ch. 4.

124. *Ibid.*, pt. 2, ch. 31.

125. *Ibid.*, pt. 2, ch. 2.

126. *Ibid.*, pt. 3, ch. 4. See D. Patterson, 'The Portrait of Hasidism . . .', pp. 368f.

127. *SM. 2*, p. 34.

128. *Ibid.*, ch. 7.

129. See below, pp. 22f.

130. See below, p. 9.

131. *SM. 6*, pt. 2, ch. 2.

132. *Ibid.*, ch. 19. Cf. below, p. 145.

133. *SM. 6*, pt. 2, ch. 20.

134. *Ibid.*, chs. 14, 15.

135. *BRA. 1*, pt. 2, p. 115. Cf. pt. 1, chs. 7, 10; pt. 3, chs. 1, 4, 5.

136. The tendency to use the term 'nature' (*Ha-Ṭebha‘*) instead of God is bitingly satirised by Rabinowitz in *At the Crossroads. RAB.*, p. 78. See below, p. 187.

137. *SHEIK.*, pt. 3, pp. 106f.

138. See above, p. 45.

139. *SM. 1*, pt. 4, chs. 3, 4, 5, 6.

140. *SM. 5*, pt. 2, ch. 17. For the part played by the Jews in the first Polish revolt, 1830-31, see Jacob Halevi-Levin's memoirs, *Ha-Yehudhim we-ha-Meredh ha-Polani*, ed. by N. M. Gelber, Jerusalem, 1953.

141. *SM. 6*, pt. 2, ch. 19. Cf. *SM. 1*, pt. 4, ch. 19.

142. *SM. 6*, pt. 2, ch. 20.

143. *SM. 4*, chs. 3, 10.

144. *SIRK.*, pp. 119ff. Cf. above, pp. 30f, and below, p. 236.

145. *BRA. 1*, pt. 3, pp. 201ff, and see author's footnote.

146. *ABR.*, chs. 1, 10, 11,32: *BRA. 1*, pt. 1, chs. 3, 5, 7, 10; pt. 2, chs. 2, 6, 11; pt. 3, chs. 4, 6, 20: *BRA. 2*, pt. 1, ch. 2; pt. 4, ch. 38: *MEIN.*, pt. 1, chs. 7, 16: *SHEIK.*, pt. 1, chs. 2, 9: *RAB.*, chs. 3, 13: *WEIS. 1*, chs. 3, 9: *WEIS. 2*, pt. 1, ch. 4; pt. 2, chs. 15, 21. Cf. S. Werses, "Iyyunim ba-Mibhneh šel "Megalleh Ṭemirin" u-"Bhoḥan Ṣaddiq" ' in *Tarbiṣ*, vol. 31, No. 4, 1962. Cf. above, p. 62.

147. *SM. 2*, p. 53.

148. *Ibid.*, p. 18.

149. *Ibid.*, p. 129.

150. *Ibid.*, p. 138. Cf. also *ibid.*, p. 167: *SM. 1*, pt. 3, p. 249: *SM. 5*, pt. 1, pp. 83, 123; pt. 2, p. 41: *SM. 6*, pt. 3, p. 331.

151. *BRA. 2*, pt. 1, p. 63. Cf. *ibid.*, p. 29; pt. 2, p. 160: *BRA. 1*, pt. 1, p. 92; pt. 2, p. 96; pt. 3, p. 66.

152. Cf. *SM. 1*, pt. 1, pp. 162ff: *SM. 2*, pp. 132ff: *ABR.* ch. 3: *BRA. 2*, pt. 1, p. 52.

153. *BRA. 2*, pt. 2, pp. 178ff.

154. *BRA. 1*, pt. 3, pp. 155ff. See below, pp. 225f. Cf. D. S. Mirsky, *A History of Russian Literature*, London, 1927, p. 279.

155. *SM. 1*, pt. 1, chs. 3, 5, 8, 22; pt. 2, chs. 1, 13, 20, 27; pt. 3, chs. 1, 6, 17; pt. 4, chs. 2, 6, 7, 22: *SM. 2*, chs. 10, 11, 17, 18, 24: *SM. 3*, chs. 1, 4, 11, 13: *SM. 4*, chs. 1, 4, 5, 9: *SM. 5*, pt. 1, chs. 3, 7; pt. 2, chs. 1, 3; pt. 3, ch. 11: *SM. 6*, pt. 1, ch. 15; pt. 2, chs. 1, 4, 19, 21, 22; pt. 3, ch. 9. Cf. above, ch. 2, n. 36.

156. E.g. *SM. 1*, pt. 1, ch. 8.

157. Cf. above, pp. 63f.

158. Cf. *BRA. 1*, pt. 2, chs. 1, 6, 13: *RAB.*, ch. 13: *SIRK.*, chs. 2, 10.

159. Cf. *SM. 1*, pt. 1, pp. 124, 138, 162ff, 181, 186, 208f, 255; pt. 2, pp. 167ff, 252, 256f; pt. 3, pp. 164ff: *SM. 2*, pp. 3, 17, 33, 203, 239ff: *SM. 4*, pp. 130ff: *SM. 5*, pt. 1, pp. 8off, 136ff; pt. 3, pp. 66ff: *SM. 6*, pt. 1, pp. 81ff, 204f; pt. 2, pp. 45f; pt. 3, pp. 297, 306, 316: *BRA. 1*, pt. 1, pp. 53f, 87; pt. 2, pp. 34, 40ff, 77, 121: *BRA. 2*, pt. 1, p. 48; pt. 2, p. 144; pt. 3, pp. 216f; pt. 4, p. 329: *LEIN.*, pt. 1, p. 43: *MAN.*, p. 30: *SHEIK.*, pt. 2, p. 98; pt. 3, p. 90.

160. *BRA. 2*, pt. 3, p. 217.

161. Cf. *SM. 3*, p. 102: *SM. 5*, pt. 1, pp. 116ff; pt. 2, p. 111; pt. 3, chs. 8, 13, 18, 19, 20: *SM. 6*, pt. 1, pp. 1ff, 102, 158f, 18of, 224, 226, 250; pt. 2, pp. 277f, 304, 64, 177, 191, 204; pt. 3, p.292: *BRA. 1*, pt. 1, pp. 46f, 49, 108, 11of, 118; pt. 2, pp. 13, 23f, 86,

109f; pt. 3, pp. 11, 13f, 24, 28, 145, 165: *BRA. 2*, pt. 3, pp. 215, 240, 308.

162. E.g. *SM. 1*, pt. 1, pp. 16ff, 108ff; pt. 2, p. 289: *SM. 2*, pp. 206f: *SM. 5*, pt. 2, p. 66: *BRA. 1*, pt. 1, p. 26.

163. *MAN.*, ch. 4: *SIRK.*, ch. 11.

164. *SM. 1*, pt. 1, p. 169.

165. *SM. 2*, p. 32.

166. *Ibid.*, p. 33.

167. *SM. 4*, p. 1.

168. *SM. 6*, pt. 3, p. 253.

169. *BRA. 1*, pt. 3, pp. 29, 53.

170. *SM. 1*, pt. 1, p. 199. For further examples of metaphorical style see *ibid.*, pp. 230f; pt. 2, pp. 63f, 95, 138f, 158; pt. 3, p. 190: *SM. 2*, pp. 29, 42, 105, 151, 194: *SM. 3*, pp. 121f, 131f: *SM. 5*, pt. 2, pp. 17, 24, 64f; pt. 3, p. 5: *SM. 6*, pt. 1, pp. 123f, 134: *BRA. 1*, pt. 1, pp. 24, 50ff: *BRA. 2*, pt. 1, p. 50; pt. 3, p. 294: *MAN.*, p. 30: *SIRK.*, p. 122.

171. See D. Patterson, *Abraham Mapu*, p. 40.

172. *SM. 5*, pt. 2, pp. 136ff.

173. *SM. 1*, pt. 1, pp. 40, 111, 113; pt. 2, pp. 194f; pt. 3, pp. 9, 169: *SM. 2*, pp. 30, 92, 160, 194: *SM. 4*, p. 86: *SM. 5*, pt. 1, pp. 41, 65: *SM. 6*, pt. 1, p. 111.

174. E.g. compare the description of a lily withering in the sun, *SM. 2*, p. 30, with the same theme in Mapu's *The Love of Zion*, ch. 4. A similar description also appears in *SM. 3*, p. 17.

175. *SM. 2*, p. 30. Cf. *BRA. 2*, pt. 1, p. 51, and A. Mapu, *The Love of Zion*, ch. 4.

176. *SM. 1*, pt. 4, p. 12.

177. *BRA. 1*, pt. 2, pp. 81, 87, 90, 122; pt. 3, pp. 84, 124, 157: *BRA. 2*, pt. 2, pp. 7f, 10; pt. 2, pp. 176, 183f, 214.

178. *BRA. 1*, pt. 2, pp. 81, 86f: *BRA. 2*, pt. 1, p. 7; pt. 3, p. 214.

179. *LEIN.*, pt. 1, pp. 3f; pt. 2, p. 119: *MEIN.*, p. 9: *ZOB.*, pt. 1, p. 67; pt. 2, pp. 21, 25, 34, 49: *RAB.*, p. 33: *SIRK.*, pp. 3, 85ff, 111: *WEIS. 2*, pt. 1, pp. 117f.

180. *SHEIK.*, pt. 1, p. 17. Cf. above, p. 46.

181. *SHEIK.*, pt. 1, p. 34.

182. *ABR.*, pp. 6, 12, 20, 22, 26, 72, 79f, 89ff, 99f, 118f, 152f, 159.

183. *Ibid.*, p. 80.

184. *Ibid.*, pp. 72, 89ff.

185. *Ibid.*, pp. 47ff, 152f.

186. *Ibid.*, pp. 4, 35, 41, 48f, 87f.

187. *Cf. SM. 1*, pt. 1, pp. 57, 161; pt. 2, pp. 18, 98ff, 239; pt. 4, pp. 37, 40ff: *SM. 2*, pp. 4, 15, 19f, 21f, 24, 49f, 79ff, 99f, 108f, 152, 220: *SM. 3*, pp. 15, 66, 101f, 139ff: *SM. 4*, pp. 2ff: *SM. 5*, pt. 2, p. 140: *SM. 6*, pt. 1, pp. 29ff.

188. *SM. 2*, p. 270.

189. *MAN.*, p. 65.

190. *RAB.*, pp. 15, 44f, 46, 110.

191. *SIRK.*, pp. 21, 72.

192. Cf. *WEIS. 1*, pp. 25f, 28ff, 113ff: *WEIS. 2*, pt. 1, p. 23. See D. Patterson, 'Israel Weisbrem . . .', pp. 47, 54.

193. Cf. *SM. 1*, pt. 1, pp. 52, 99, 116f, 122f, 128, 132ff, 272f; pt. 2, pp. 20f, 27ff, 81, 202, 274, 278f, 281; pt. 4, pp. 86f: *SM. 2*, pp. 6, 92f, 98, 106, 202: *SM. 3*, pp. 7ff, 44, 47f, 49ff, 83ff, 125ff, 173, 196: *SM. 4*, pp. 1, 4, 24ff: *SM. 5*, pt. 1, p. 34; pt. 2, pp. 62, 99; pt. 3, pp. 26, 155: *SM. 6*, pt. 1, pp. 5, 224, 227; pt. 2, p. 12. See below, p. 130.

194. *SM. 4*, pp. 24ff.

195. *SM. 5*, pt. 1, p. 34; pt. 3, p. 26.

196. *BRA. 1*, pt. 1, pp. 118ff; pt. 2, pp. 46f, 98, 110f: *RAB.*, pp. 6, 40, 63: *WEIS. 1*, pp. 4, 8f, 24ff, 27, 34, 38, 40, 64: *WEIS. 2*, pt. 1, pp. 8of.

197. *WEIS. 1*, pp. 33f. Cf. below, p. 212.

198. The following figures must be regarded as the minimum number, as each passage often contains numerous individual examples.

199. *SM. 2*, pp. 3, 16, 17, 20, 25, 62, 71, 72, 75, 93, 98, 106, 107, 125, 201, 206, 219, 222, 224, 229.

200. *SM. 3*, pp. 7, 8, 9, 10, 16, 17, 18, 24, 32, 36, 37, 38, 44, 60, 61, 83, 192.

201. *SM. 4*, pp. 1, 4, 9, 25, 30, 56, 89, 279, 280, 282.

202. *SM. 5*, pt. 1, pp. 33, 34, 41f, 55, 56, 66, 68, 71, 83, 86, 92, 100, 101, 102, 105, 106, 117, 139f, 145; pt. 2, pp. 40ff, 47, 49, 77, 101, 110, 111f; pt. 3, pp. 7, 98, 107, 115, 122, 135, 149.

203. *SM. 6*, pt. 1, pp. 26, 27, 29, 35, 38, 92, 95, 111, 135, 136, 138, 156, 158, 167, 173, 178f, 180f, 187, 209, 225, 226, 242; pt. 2, pp. 272, 278, 280, 288, 296, 306, 311f, 324, 327, 92, 106, 162,

s

177, 192, 194, 201, 202, 204; pt. 3, pp. 212, 222, 229, 253, 255, 259, 307, 308, 311, 319, 322, 330f, 360.

204. *ABR.*, pp. 7, 21, 25, 26, 31, 33, 63, 64, 73, 74, 80, 105, 106, 115, 118, 139, 149.

205. *BRA. 1*, pt. 1, pp. 21f, 40, 45, 46, 47, 49, 57, 66, 69, 99, 105, 108, 110, 111, 118, 122, 124; pt. 2, pp. 5, 6, 12, 13, 15, 21, 22, 23, 24, 27, 34, 41, 46ff, 68, 76ff, 80ff, 83, 86ff, 98, 110; pt. 3, pp. 5ff, 9, 10, 11, 12, 13, 14, 15, 16, 19, 23, 24, 25, 27, 28, 29, 30, 47, 48, 59, 60, 62, 63, 66ff, 87, 129, 130, 131, 180, 183, 196, 202.

206. *BRA. 2*, pt. 1, pp. 22, 28, 49, 50, 70; pt. 2, pp. 84, 116, 161, 162, 198; pt. 3, pp. 232, 245ff, 277, 288, 296, 299, 311, 314ff.

207. *LEIN.*, pt. 1, pp. 3, 5, 6, 16, 27, 31, 39, 40, 61, 93, 101, 102; pt. 2, pp. 18, 20, 30, 41, 67, 74, 75, 77, 87, 113, 114, 119.

208. *MEIN.*, pp. 7, 8, 9, 10, 20, 34, 42, 84, 85, 89, 133.

209. *ZOB.*, pt. 1, pp. 9, 19, 36, 42f, 46, 59, 63, 65; pt. 2, pp. 20, 23, 36.

210. *RAB.*, pp. 7, 29, 30, 46, 63, 107, 108, 128, 151.

211. *SIRK.*, pp. 11, 13, 24, 25, 32, 33, 42, 53, 54, 67, 68, 82, 83, 86, 102, 105, 106, 116, 117, 118, 119, 120, 121, 122.

212. *WEIS. 1*, pp. 10, 26, 79, 84: *WEIS. 2*, pt. 1, pp. 23, 35, 38, 47, 73, 94, 96, 105, 149; pt. 2, p. 134. Cf. D. Patterson, 'Israel Weisbrem . . .', p. 54.

213. *SM. 1*, pt. 1, pp. 13, 24, 28, 59, 61, 77, 78, 108, 109, 110, 122, 123, 135, 136, 272, 273; pt. 2, pp. 20, 25, 26, 27, 176, 274.

214. *SM. 2*, pp. 16, 25, 44, 52, 71, 75, 76, 92, 93, 106, 107, 201f, 220, 222, 224.

215. *SM. 3*, pp. 9, 15, 32, 36, 37, 44, 47, 126, 128, 135, 166, 173, 190.

216. *SM. 4*, pp. 3, 89.

217. *SM. 5*, pt. 1, pp. 67, 68, 91, 92, 116ff; pt. 2, pp. 5, 113; pt. 3, pp. 52, 54, 118.

218. *SM. 6*, pt. 1, p. 39; pt. 2. pp. 194, 202, 203, 295, 311, 319; pt. 3, p. 253.

219. *ABR.*, pp. 9, 13, 26, 30, 31, 33, 46, 63, 64, 73, 74, 76, 96, 106, 139, 142.

220. *BRA. 1*, pt. 1, pp. 29, 43, 57, 60, 69, 99, 104, 105, 108, 110, 111, 118, 119, 122; pt. 2, pp. 6, 7, 11, 15, 16, 27, 32, 41, 46, 47, 66, 76ff, 80ff, 83, 86, 98, 105, 110; pt. 3, pp. 5ff, 10, 14, 16, 29, 30, 48, 60, 84, 85, 127, 131, 180.

221. *BRA. 2*, pt. 1, pp. 11, 28, 74; pt. 2, pp. 79, 179; pt. 3, 225, 246, 247, 278, 297, 299; pt. 4, pp. 311, 316.

222. *LEIN.*, pt. 1, pp. 4, 5, 12, 16, 27, 28, 30, 39, 40, 72, 73, 74, 93, 102, 104; pt. 2, pp. 18, 20, 30, 33, 41, 43, 55, 59, 60, 61, 62, 67, 74, 77, 80, 87, 113, 114, 119.

223. *MEIN.*, pp. 7, 8, 15, 59, 64, 87, 88, 92, 106, 133.

224. *ZOB.*, pt. 1, pp. 9, 43; pt. 2, pp. 7, 20, 23, 38, 62, 71.

225. *MAN.*, pp. 12, 19, 70.

226. *SHEIK.*, pt. 1, pp. 6, 7, 8, 9, 12, 18, 19, 24, 25, 26, 27, 28, 29, 34, 42, 47, 48, 58, 61, 62; pt. 2, pp. 8, 12, 91, 92, 96, 98; pt. 3, pp. 6, 14, 30, 57, 64, 73, 83, 90, 105, 108, 110.

227. *RAB.*, pp. 12, 116, 128, 129, 152.

228. *SIRK.*, pp. 8, 11, 13, 24, 25, 26, 28, 31, 40, 42, 45, 53, 54, 56, 58, 72, 105, 106, 119, 120.

229. *WEIS. 2*, pt. 1, pp. 38, 47, 105, 149: *WEIS. 1*, 11, 79.

CHAPTER 5

1. For the influence of the social ideas propagated by the positivist Russian literary critics on the Hebrew writers of the period see above, pp. 117f, and below, pp. 225f.

2. Cf. *SHEIK.*, pt. 1, p. 62: *SIRK.*, pp. 116ff. See above, p. 45.

3. Largely due to the enormous expansion of the Jewish population in eastern Europe during the nineteenth century. Cf. A. Ruppin, *The Jews of the Modern World*, London, 1934, pp. 104f. For a vivid portrait of the period under review see *A Jewish Bard*, being the Biography of Eliakum Zunser (in Yiddish and English), New York, 1905; and P. Wengeroff, *Memoiren einer Grossmutter*, Berlin, 1908-10.

4. *SM. 2*, p. 162.

5. *Ibid.*, p. 206.

6. *BRA. 1*, pt. 2, p. 119. See also *ibid.*, pp. 109ff, and pt. 1, pp. 99ff.

7. *BRA. 2*, pt. 4, pp. 311f.

8. *SM. 1*, pt. 1, p. 43. A similar troupe of wandering beggars plays a major role in S. J. Abramowitz's Yiddish Novel, *Fishke der Krumer* (1869); translated into English by G. Stillman, New York-London, 1960.

9. *SM. 6*, pt. 2, pp. 265f. For a brief account of the oppression of the Jews in Roumania see Klausner, *History*, Vol. 5, pp. 77ff. Smolenskin had undertaken a widespread tour of Roumania in the year 1874 on behalf of the Executive Committee for the Jews of Roumania in Vienna; see *ibid.*, pp. 79ff.

10. *SHEIK.*, pt. 3, pp. 27f.

11. *LEIN.*, pt. 2, p. 77.

12. *SM. 4*, pp. 130ff.

13. *SM. 2*, p. 155.

14. *Ibid.*, pp. 158f.

15. *SM. 3*, p. 93.

16. See *SM. 5*, pt. 1, p. 6: *BRA. 1*, pt. 1, p. 27.

17. See *SM. 2*, p. 5, where the price of meat is quoted as ten kopeks for half a litre. Cf. *SM. 6*, pt. 1, p. 162, where a rapacious tax-farmer is accused of raising the price of meat from twelve to twenty kopeks for a pound. Abramowitz devoted a Yiddish drama, *Die Takseh*, Zhitomir, 1869, to the subject. See Klausner, *History*, vol. 6, pp. 349ff.

18. Cf. *BRA. 1*, pt. 1, p. 12.

19. *Ibid.*, p. 13, and cf. *SM. 2*, p. 5.

20. *SM. 1*, pt. 1, pp. 28f; cf. pt. 3, p. 17.

21. *MAN.*, p. 96.

22. *BRA. 1*, pt. 2, p. 35.

23. *RAB.*, p. 127. Apparently a misprint for M, as Moscow is probably intended. Cf. Rabinowitz's memoirs in *Sepher Zikkaron le-Yobhel ha-Šibh'im šel A. S. Rabinowitz*, Tel-Aviv, 1924, pp. 7f.

24. *RAB.*, p. 129f, and cf. *SM. 6*, pt. 2, p. 108f.

25. *SM. 6*, pt. 1, pp. 87f.

26. *RAB.*, p. 12.

27. *SM. 5*, pt. 1, p. 7.

28. *SM. 1*, pt. 4, pp. 58ff and 74f: *SM. 3*, p. 94: *SM. 6*, pt. 2, p. 55.

29. See above, p. 135 and n. 17. See also *SM. 1*, pt. 2, pp. 242ff: *BRA. 1*, pt. 1, p. 69: *SHEIK.*, pt. 2, p. 24.

30. Cf. *SM. 1*, pt. 3, p. 197.

31. Cf. *BRA. 2*, pt. 2, p. 82. See also *ibid.*, pt. 1, p. 18.

32. Cf. *ibid.*, pt. 2, p. 94.

33. Cf. *SM. 6*, pt. 1, p. 28: *BRA. 2*, pt. 1, p. 38; pt. 2, p. 83: *SIRK*, p. 12.

34. *Ibid.*

35. *SHEIK.*, pt. 1, p. 49.

36. *LEIN.*, pt. 2, p. 62.

37. *Ibid.*, p. 61.

38. *Ibid.*, pt. 1, p. 9.

39. Cf. *RAB.*, p. 106.

40. *MAN.*, p. 5.

41. See *WEIS. 2*, pt. 1, p. 87. Cf. below, p. 183.

42. A teacher of elementary Hebrew to young children. See below, pp. 140f.

43. *WEIS. 1*, p. 28; and cf. p. 45.

44. *RAB.*, p. 30.

45. See S. M. Dubnow, *History of the Jews in Russia and Poland*, vol. 2.

46. *SM. 3*, p. 95.

47. *SM. 6*, pt. 1, p. 12.

48. *WEIS. 2*, pt. 1, pp. 84f.

49. Specifically religious functionaries, such as Rabbis and Cantors, are treated below, pp. 218f.

50. Cf. *WEIS. 1*, p. 28. For a vivid account of brutal treatment see *The Autobiography of Solomon Maimon*, London, 1954, p. 31, and S. Levin's autobiographical *Childhood in Exile*, London, 1929, pp. 45ff. See below, p. 169.

51. Cf. above, p. 136.

52. Cf. *SM. 4*, p. 56; and see, e.g., D. Patterson, *Abraham Mapu*, p. 17.

53. See *SM. 6*, pt. 1, pp. 82ff. Cf. *SM. 3*, pp. 33f, 38, 68.

54. *BRA. 1*, p. 22. See also *ibid.*, pp. 51f, 59f; pt. 2, p. 62, p. 110.

55. Cf. *BRA. 1*, pt. 2, pp. 70f and 102. See below, p. 207.

56. Cf. *SM. 2*, pp. 12, 25, 41, 55, 62, 202: *SM. 6*, pt. 1, pp. 82f. Cf. above, pp. 89f.

57. Cf. *SM. 5*, pt. 2, p. 101.

58. E.g. Zalman Yentis in *BRA. 1*, Jekutiel in *WEIS. 2*, and Samson in *SM. 5*. See above, pp. 94f.

59. Cf. *RAB.*, p. 16.

60. According to Smolenskin, 2 per cent to 3 per cent, *SM. 6*, pt. 1, p. 130.

61. Cf. *LEIN.*, p. 50.

62. Braudes appends the following footnote: 'The title *Naghidh* is given by the Jews of Russia to a moderately well-off man, who occupies a position midway between a rich man—who is called

a *Gebhir*—and a *Ba'al Bayith*—a man who earns a comfortable living.'

63. *BRA. 1*, pt. 1, p. 118f.

64. Pt. 1, pp. 6of. See below, pp. 226f. Cf. *SM. 5*, pt. 1, p. 91.

65. Cf. *SM. 1*, pt. 4, p. 33: *SM. 5*, pt. 2, p. 139.

66. See *SHEIK.*, pt. 1, p. 60 and footnote.

67. *BRA. 1*, pt. 1, p. 100. The word used for bootpolish is *Gir*, which Braudes explains in a footnote as *Schuhwachs*, supporting his usage with a reference to *Beṣah*, 15a. According to Sheikewitz, polishing of shoes is a characteristic of the young exponents of enlightenment, *SHEIK.*, pt. 1, p. 87; Smolenskin mentions a soap-maker, *SM. 1*, pt. 3, p. 95.

68. *LEIN.*, p. 6.

69. *SM. 6*, pt. 1, p. 52, and particularly *RAB.*, p. 51. Abramowitz later wrote under the pseudonym 'Mendele the Bookseller'. Cf. above, p. 4.

70. *SHEIK.*, pt. 2, p. 20f.

71. *Ibid.*, p. 30f.

72. *SM. 4*, p. 67.

73. *SHEIK.*, pt. 2, pp. 21f, 43f. Cf. *ABR.*, pp. 15ff.

74. *WEIS. 1*, p. 112. Cf. D. Patterson, 'Israel Weisbrem . . .', pp. 44f.

75. *ZOB.*, pp. 23f.

76. *SHEIK.*, pt. 3, p. 70.

77. *Ibid.*, p. 62.

78. *LEIN.*, p. 102.

79. For the measures adopted by Nicholas I relative to his Jewish subjects see S. M. Dubnow, *op. cit.*, vol. 2, chs. XIII, XIV, XVII.

80. See below, pp. 148ff.

81. *SM. 2*, p. 101.

82. *SM. 1*, pt. 1, pp. 120ff. Cf. *ibid.*, p. 253. See above, ch. 2, n. 18.

83. Cf. *SM. 1*, pt. 1, p. 132.

84. See *BRA. 1*, pt. 1, pp. 99f and footnote, and see below, p. 214. For further attacks on community leaders see *SM. 1*, pt. 1, pp. 94, 270; pt. 2, pp. 10, 30, 182: *SM. 3*, pp. 48, 176f: *SM. 6*, pt. 1, pp. 17f: *BRA. 1*, pt. 3, pp. 147, 154: *SHEIK.*, pt. 1, p. 9. For a sympathetic portrait of a community leader see e.g. *SM. 3*, pp. 93ff, 116.

85. See *SM. 1*, pt. 1, pp. 107f: *SM. 4*, p. 70. Cf. *SM. 2*, p. 72: *SM. 4*, p. 79: *MAN.*, p. 56: *ZOB.*, p. 7.

86. *SM. 3*, pp. 128f. Cf. *SM. 1*, pt. 1, p. 123.

87. See below, pp. 172f.

88. See e.g., *SM. 1*, pt. 1, pp. 44, 157: *SM. 6*, pt. 1, p. 88: *BRA. 1*, pt. 3, p. 143.

89. See below, pp. 172ff.

90. *SM. 1*, pt. 2, pp. 69f.

91. See *SM. 1*, pt. 2, pp. 178ff. See above, n. 45.

92. See below, pp. 215f.

93. Cf. *SM. 1*, pt. 2, p. 178; pt. 3, p. 200: *ABR.*, p. 74: *BRA. 2*, pt. 1, p. 12.

94. *SM. 1*, pt. 2, p. 180. For details of the plan to establish schools for Jews see S. M. Dubnow, *op. cit.*, vol. 2, pp. 50ff.

95. *SM. 1*, pt. 2, pp. 36f. Cf. *SM. 3*, p. 66: *SM. 5*, pt. 1, p. 108. Cf. above, pp. 111f.

96. *SM. 6*, pt. 2, p. 115.

97. *SM. 1*, pt. 2, p. 294.

98. *Ibid.*, p. 295.

99. *ABR.*, p. 104.

100. *BRA. 2*, pt. 2, p. 152.

101. *Ibid.*, p. 95.

102. *Ibid.*, pt. 1, p. 11: *SM. 1*, pt. 2, p. 181.

103. *BRA. 1*, pt. 3, p. 39.

104. Cf. *RAB.*, p. 97; and see S. M. Dubnow, *op. cit.*, vol. 2, ch. XVIII.

105. Cf. *SM. 1*, pt. 2, p. 239.

106. Cf. *BRA. 1*, pt. 3, pp. 144, 154.

107. Cf. *ibid.*, p. 115.

108. Cf. *ibid.*, pp. 97 and 103; and see above, p. 141. Smolenskin, however, is much less happy about the consequences of Enlightenment. See *SM. 1*, pt. 4, pp. 118ff.

109. *ABR.*, p. 40.

110. Cf. *RAB.*, pp. 106. and 131: *SHEIK.*, pt. 3, pp. 66f.

111. The cost of an official stamp on such a travel permit is quoted as one rouble and thirty kopeks. *RAB.*, p. 133.

112. *Ibid.*, p. 129.

113. Cf. *BRA. 1*, pt. 1, p. 100.

114. *SM. 3*, p. 87.

115. Cf. *SM. 1*, pt. 1, pp. 227, 248.

116. *Ibid.*, pt. 2, p. 36. See above, pp. 111f.

117. *Ibid.*, pt. 1, p. 251; pt. 3, p. 116: *LEIN.* p. 99.

118. *RAB.*, p. 133.

119. *SM. 3*, p. 94. See above, p. 135.

120. *SM. 6*, pt. 2, p. 199.

121. Cf. *LEIN.*, pt. 2, p. 6.

122. *SM. 3*, p. 160.

123. See S. M. Dubnow, *op. cit.*, vol. 2, pp. 18ff, 145ff, and cf. *ABR.*, p. 90: *SM. 1*, pt. 2, p. 181: *BRA. 1*, p. 101.

124. *BRA. 1*, pt. 1, p. 101. Cf. *SM. 1*, pt. 2, p. 232, and pt. 4, p. 33, where the Austrian Empire is described as a haven for such fugitives: *SM. 4*, pp. 6, 129: *SM. 5*, p. 46: *SM. 6*, pt. 1, p. 208: *RAB.*, p. 106.

125. *SM. 1*, pt. 2, p. 302.

126. *ZOB.*, pt. 1, p. 50.

127. *SM. 1*, pt. 2, p. 21.

128. *SM. 1*, pt. 2, p. 182: *SM. 3*, pp. 85, 147.

129. Cf. *SM. 1*, pt. 2, pp. 181ff.

130. In *Fathers and Sons* a father prefers to send his son, aged eleven, abroad even without friends or money for fear of his safety. *ABR.*, p. 90. See also *SM. 1*, pt. 1, p. 107.

131. Cf. *SM. 1*, pt. 1, pp. 10, 107: *SM. 3*, pp. 18, 31, 40, 48: *SM. 6*, pt. 1, p. 16: *ABR.*, p. 74: *SHEIK.*, pt. 1, p. 9. See above, p. 143.

132. Cf. *SM. 1*, pt. 1, p. 107; pt. 2, pp. 74ff, 104, 130ff, 165, 206: *SM. 3*, pp. 8, 146f: *SM. 6*, pt. 2, p. 115: *BRA. 1*, pt. 1, p. 101.

133. The figure of fifty roubles is mentioned, *SM. 1*, pt. 2, p. 125: *SM. 3*, p. 58.

134. See S. M. Dubnow, *op. cit.*, vol. 2, p. 19.

135. *SM. 1*, pt. 1, pp. 108ff. Cf. the description of the Russian writer Alexander Hertzen quoted by Dubnow, *op. cit.*, vol. 2, pp. 24f.

136. *ZOB.*, pt. 1, pp. 58f. Cf. below, p. 181.

137. *ZOB.*, p. 56.

138. *Ibid.*, p. 49. Cf. p. 59.

139. *Ibid.*, pt. 2, pp. 5ff.

140. *Ibid.*, p. 47.

141. *SHEIK.*, pt. 1, p. 41.

142. *ABR.*, p. 107. Cf. *ibid.*, p. 48. It is significant that Abramowitz states that he intends introducing extracts from his heroine's diary to show that women, too, have understanding. *Ibid.*, p. 106; cf. *SM. 1*, pt. 1, p. 95: *SM. 2*, p. 237: *BRA. 2*, pt. 2, p. 130. Cf. below, pp. 187f.

143. Cf. *SM. 2*, pp. 17, 42, 220, 222.

144. Cf. *SM. 1*, pp. 2, 27f: *SM. 2*, p. 42: *SM. 4*, p. 56: *SM. 5*, pt. 1, p. 117: *SM. 6*, pt. 1, p. 24: *BRA. 2*, pt. 2, p. 108. For information relative to the education of women see below, pp. 166 and 187f.

145. Cf. *SM. 5*, pt. 1, p. 117: *RAB.*, pp. 38, 208.

146. Cf. *RAB.*, p. 31.

147. Cf. *SM. 1*, pt. 2, p. 73: *SM. 2*, p. 101: *SM. 3*, p. 21: *SM. 4*, p. 54: *BRA. 1*, pt. 1, p. 106; *MAN.*, pp. 75f. Also see above, p. 142. Contrast Smolenskin's criticism of young men who have begun to seek rich brides instead of brides of good family, *SM. 2*, p. 34.

148. Cf. Especially *BRA. 1*, pt. 1, pp. 32, 44: *MAN.*, pp. 9, 21ff: *MEIN.*, p. 26.

149. *ABR.*, pp. 113f. Cf. *Ibid.*, p. 11: *SM. 1*, pp. 15, 220: *SM. 4*, p. 86: *SM. 5*, p. 154: *BRA. 1*, pt. 1, pp. 30ff; pt. 3, p. 99: *BRA. 2*, pt. 2, pp. 118, 152f: *SIRK.*, p. 16: *SHEIK.*, pt. 1, p. 43: *MEIN.*, p. 26. Smolenskin describes the scandal which would arise if a young man attempted to marry a girl without her parents' consent. Indeed, no Rabbi, who knew the circumstances, would perform the ceremony. *SM. 1*, p. 28.

150. Cf. *BRA. 1*, pt. 1, p. 106: *SHEIK.*, pt. 1, p. 47.

151. *BRA. 2*, pt. 1, p. 36; Jewish law, however, ensured that an orphan girl could not be forced into a marriage against her will. Cf. *BRA. 1*, pt. 1, p. 108.

152. Cf. *SM. 1*, pt. 2, pp. 256, 291; pt. 3, pp. 60, 73, 139: *SM. 2*, p. 206: *SM. 5*, p. 30.

153. Cf. *SM. 1*, pt. 3, p. 22: *SM. 2*, p. 236: *SM. 3*, p. 64. Cf. D. Patterson, 'The Portrait of Ḥasidism . . .', p.367.

154. Cf. *SM. 2*, p. 237: *SM. 3*, p. 109, and especially *SM. 4*, pp. 54ff. Contrast, however, *BRA. 1*, pt. 2, p. 24.

155. See above, pp. 145f. Even then it was certainly no innovation. See *The Autobiography of Solomon Maimon*, p. 59.

156. Cf. *SM. 1*, pt. 2, p. 180: *SM. 5*, pt. 1, p. 23; pt. 2, p. 143: *BRA. 1*, pt. 2, p. 77: *WEIS. 2*, pt, 1, p. 154. Braudes also illustrates the tragic plight of divorced women who cannot remarry because of some technical error in the bill of divorce. *BRA. 1*, pt. 3, p. 95. The same point was stressed by J. L. Gordon in his long poem *Qoṣo šel Yodh*.

157. Cf. *BRA. 1*, p. 27: *MAN.*, p. 47: *RAB.*, p. 26.

158. Cf. *SM. 2*, pp. 34ff. The son-in-law regarded this maintenance as a right. Cf. *BRA. 1*, pt. 1, p. 40.

159. Cf. *SM. 2*, p. 238: *SM. 3*, p. 8: *SM. 4*, p. 3: *SM. 5*, p. 96: *BRA. 1*, p. 27: *ZOB.*, pt. 2, p. 22: *MAN.*, p. 47: *SHEIK.*, pt. 1, p. 81; pt. 3, p. 93: *RAB.*, pp. 26, 31.

160. Cf. *MAN.*, p. 50: *RAB.*, p. 26. Cf. above, p. 143, n. 85.

161. Cf. *SHEIK.*, pt. 1, pp. 77f.

162. Cf. *SM. 2*, p. 6: *SM. 4*, pp. 234f.

163. Cf. *SM. 1*, p. 6: *WEIS. 1*, p. 5: *WEIS. 2*, pt. 1, pp. 21f; pt. 2, p. 95: *RAB.*, p. 108.

164. *BRA. 2*, pt. 2, pp. 318ff; cf. *SM. 1*, pt. 2, p. 274: *SM. 4*, p. 240: *WEIS. 2*, pt. 1, p. 25. For a woman's hair to be seen was considered sinful. Cf. *BRA. 1*, pt. 1, p. 102.

165. Cf. *SM. 2*, pp. 52ff: *RAB.*, pp. 28f.

166. See above, p. 54.

167. Cf. *SM. 1*, pt. 3, pp. 147, 155.

168. Cf. *SM. 2*, p. 48: *SM. 3*, p. 21: *ABR.*, p. 56: *BRA. 1*, pt. 1, p. 124: *BRA. 2*, pt. 1, p. 28.

169. Cf. *SM. 1*, pt. 1, pp. 59f; pt. 3, pp. 133f: *SM. 2*, pp. 3, 14, 53: *SM. 3*, p. 60: *SM. 4*, pp. 58ff, 255f, 262f: *SM. 5*, pt. 1, pp. 15ff; pt. 2, p. 47; pt. 3, p. 38. *ABR.*, p. 70: *BRA. 1*, pt. 1, pp. 36f, 90ff: *BRA. 2*, pt. 2, pp. 105ff, 121f: *MEIN.*, p. 33: *MAN.*, p. 113: *SHEIK.*, pt. 1, pp. 32, 35: *WEIS. 2*, pt. 1, pp. 93f.

170. *SM. 2*, pp. 76ff, 130ff, 148: *SM. 3*, pp. 108ff.

171. *SM. 4*, pp. 157f: *BRA. 1*, pp. 91ff, 128.

172. Cf. *BRA. 2*, pt. 2, p. 139: *LEIN.*, pt. 1, pp. 42, 47f; pt. 2, pp. 25f, 120: *ZOB.*, pt. 1, pp. 35f, 41: *WEIS. 2*, pt. 1, pp. 69f; pt. 2, pp. 109ff.

173. *RAB.*, pp. 28f. Cf. *BRA. 2*, pt. 1, p. 53, where the hero learns of love and the language of love from reading Russian novels, and models his behaviour towards the heroine on the rules he finds there. Similarly in Weisbrem's *Between the Times*, the hero at first indignantly rejects the suggestion that he should abandon

his beloved in order to woo a wealthier lady with the remark
that such things are never done in the love stories of *Haskalah!*
WEIS. 1, p. 50. Cf. D. Patterson, 'Israel Weisbrem . . .', p. 48.

174. *SHEIK.*, pt. 1, p. 64, and cf. above, p. 144. See also *ABR.*, p.
156, although the kiss is omitted from the later edition of this
novel! Cf. also *BRA. 1*, pt. 1, p. 73: *BRA. 2*, pt. 2, p. 174; pt. 3,
p. 272: *ZOB.*, pt. 2, p. 40: *SHEIK.*, pt. 3, p. 102: *SIRK.*, pp. 65,
92.

175. Cf. *BRA. 1*, pt. 3, p. 209. Cf. D. Patterson, 'Sickness and
Death . . .', p. 87.

176. *LEIN.*, pt. 2, p. 27.

177. *RAB.*, pp. 28f. See also *ibid.*, pp. 34, 89, 113. See below, p. 184.

178. *SM. 2*, pp. 83ff.

CHAPTER 6

1. See above, ch. 1, n. 1.

2. See below, pp. 168ff.

3. Cf. the title of Abramowitz's first novel, *Fathers and Sons*.

4. See e.g. *BRA. 1*, pt. 2, p. 11, footnote.

5. Cf. D. Pattterson, *Abraham Mapu*, pp. 88ff.

6. See above, pp. 138ff, and below, p. 181.

7. See J. Klausner, *Yoserim u-Bhonim*, vol. 1, Tel-Aviv, 1925,
p. 188, and see below, p. 184. Cf. D. Patterson, *Abraham Mapu*,
p. 95.

8. See above, note 3, and cf. *SM. 1*, pt. 4, p. 107: *SM. 4*, p. 164:
SM. 5, pt. 1, pp. 84, 89ff, 102ff; pt. 2, pp. 12ff, 42, 108f: *BRA. 1*,
pt. 1, pp. 29, 42ff, 111; pt. 2, pp. 22ff: *SHEIK.*, pt. 1, p. 15:
WEIS. 2, pt. 1, pp. 6of, 140f.

9. See below, pp. 186ff.

10. It was considered unusual for Jews of eastern Europe to speak
any language other than Yiddish. See below, pp. 167f.

11. *BRA. 1*, pt. 1, pp. 42f. And see below, p. 167. The opposition
of the orthodox to secular education is also manifested in their
bitter hostility to the schools for Jewish children established
by the Russian government. See S. M. Dubnow, *op. cit.*, vol. 2,
pp. 53 ff. Cf. above, p. 111, and *ABR.*, p. 75: *BRA. 1*, pt. 1,
p. 111; pt. 2, p. 67. For a description of the type of school
favoured by the exponents of Enlightenment including a
section for girls, see *ibid.*, pp. 83ff, 87f.

12. *SM. 1*, pt. 4, p. 107.

13. *SM. 5*, pt. 1, pp. 102f.

14. *Ibid.*, p. 90.

15. *Ibid.*

16. *Ibid.*, pt. 2, pp. 12-29.

17. *Ibid.*, p. 17.

18. *Ibid.*, pp. 108f.

19. *Ibid.*, p. 25. For very sober remarks on the conflict between the generations see also *SM. 1*, pt. 4, ch. 18.

20. Smolenskin remarks that books are to be found in every Jewish house, even if the master cannot read them. *SM. 5*, pt. 1, p. 67.

21. See above, pp. 151f.

22. See above, p. 140, and see below, pp. 171f.

23. See below, pp. 187f.

24. See below, pp. 207f.

25. See D. Patterson, 'The Portrait of Ḥasidism . . .', and 'The Portrait of the Ṣaddik . . .'.

26. See S. Werses, 'Ha-Ḥasidhuth Be-'Êinê Siphruth ha-Haskalah' in *Moladh*, vol. 18, No. 144-5, August-September 1960.

27. E.g. *SM. 1*, pt. 3, pp. 95, 159: *SM. 3*, p. 69. See above, n. 10.

28. *SM. 3*, p. 69.

29. See above, p. 145.

30. Cf. *SM. 1*, pt. 2, pp. 121, 124; pt. 3, p. 95: *SM. 3*, pp. 66, 71, 96, 164, 185: *ABR.*, pp. 71, 107: *BRA. 1*, pt. 1, p. 69: *MAN.*, p. 16: *WEIS. 2*, pt. 1, pp. 54f. See below, p. 182.

31. *SM. 1*, pt. 3, pp. 95f. See below, p. 182.

32. *SM. 1*, pt. 3, p. 159.

33. *WEIS. 1*, pp. 41ff. See D. Patterson, 'Israel Weisbrem . . .', p. 54. Cf. *SHEIK.*, pt. 2, p. 31, and *SM. 2*, p. 93.

34. See S. M. Dubnow, *op. cit.*, vol. 2, pp. 136f.

35. Cf. *BRA. 1*, pt. 2, p. 67. Cf. above, n. 10.

36. For a picture of the *Ḥedher* from an orthodox point of view see A. M. Lipschitz, *Kethabhim*, vol. 1, Jerusalem, 1947, pp. 305-366.

37. Cf. *SM. 4*, pp. 203ff.

38. See above, pp. 140f.

39. See above, p. 140.

40. *SM. 1*, pt. 1, pp. 29f. Cf. N. Slouschz, *The Renascence of Hebrew Literature*, Philadelphia, 1909, pp. 254f.

41. *Ibid.*, p. 32. Cf. *SM. 4*, pp. 203ff: *ABR.*, 102: *SHEIK.*, pt. 1, p. 10: *WEIS. 1*, pp. 8ff, 98ff: *WEIS. 2*, pt. 1, pp. 52f, 85. See above, ch. 5, n. 50.

42. See below, pp. 209ff.

43. *SM. 6*, pt. 2, p. 114.

44. Cf. the title of Weisbrem's first novel, p. 4 above.

45. According to Braudes the teaching term lasted five months. Cf. *BRA. 1*, pt. 2, p. 47, but see next note. The break between the two terms was also referred to as *Ḥol ha-Moʿedh* (the half-festive days intervening between the first and last days of Passover and Tabernacles), *ibid.*, p. 95. The end of term was marked by *Šabbath ha-Gadhol* (The Sabbath preceding Passover), *ibid.*, p. 47. After *Šabbath Berešith* (The Sabbath following Tabernacles) the boys also studied at night, *SM. 5*, pt. 1, p. 157.

46. *BRA. 1*, pt. 2, pp. 98f. Smolenskin gives the same overall picture, but describes the terms as lasting six months each, and that during the breaks between them, called *Bên ha-Zemannim*, the teachers give instruction only until noon, and spend the afternoon going from house to house in search of pupils for the following term, *SM. 3*, p. 173. For the hard life of the *Melammedh* see above, pp. 140f.

47. *BRA. 1*, pt. 1. p. 24.

48. *Ibid.*

49. *Ibid.*, p. 25.

50. The number of would-be students, however, often exceeded the places available in a *Yešibhah*. Cf. *SM. 1*, pt. 2, p. 16: *SM. 5*, pt. 1, p. 3.

51. See below, pp. 176f.

52. Cf. *SM. 1*, pt. 2, p. 85. For a study of Smolenskin's views on education see N. Peniel, *Ha-Ḥinnukh ha-ʿIbhri be-Yeṣiratho šel Peretz Smolenskin*, Tel-Aviv, 1957.

53. See below.

54. *SM. 1*, pt. 2, p. 27.

55. Unlike the elementary teacher, the instructors in a *Yešibhah* and especially its principal commanded great respect. They are usually portrayed very sympathetically in these novels, although on more than one occasion Smolenskin accuses such a principal of venality. *Ibid.*, pt. 1, p. 146; pt. 2, pp. 20f. It transpires, however, in one case that he has been appointed on govern-

ment order because he can speak Russian. *Ibid.*, p. 39; later, moreover, even he is described as a decent man, although no saint! *Ibid.*, p. 64.

56. The assiduous student or *Mathmidh* devoted himself entirely and unsparingly to study. See *ibid.*, pp. 35ff. Cf. H. N. Bialik's poem *Ha-Mathmidh*. According to Smolenskin, most boys at the *Yeŝibhah* studied seriously for only a few hours each day. *SM. 1*, pt. 2, p. 59.

57. See below, pp. 176f.

58. See above, p. 152, n. 147.

59. *SM. 1*, pt. 2, p. 40. Cf. *SM. 2*, p. 205.

60. *Ibid.*, p. 65.

61. Cf. above, p. 170, and *SM. 3*, p. 87. See also D. Patterson, 'Israel Weisbrem . . .', p. 58.

62. *SM. 1*, pt. 2, p. 61.Smolenskin also informs us that whereas the older boys are called by their own names, the younger ones— except those born in the town which houses the *Yeŝibhah*—are referred to by the name of their place of origin. *Ibid.*, pp. 68f. Cf. *BRA. 1*, pt. 2, p. 21. Cf. above, p. 80, where the name Ha-Birzi is of this type.

63. *SM. 1*, pt. 2, pp. 64f.

64. *Ibid.*, chapters 5-13 *passim*. For an extract in English translation see N. Slouschz, *op. cit.*, pp. 256-60.

65. *SM. 1*, pt. 2, p. 31.

66. *Ibid.*, pp. 42ff.

67. *Ibid.*

68. *Ibid.*, p. 47. Cf. p. 15, and *SM. 5*, pt. 2, p. 30. To be allowed to study in the overseer's closet was regarded as a great privilege. Cf. *ibid.*, pt. 1, p. 86.

69. *SM. 1*, pt. 2, p. 48.

70. *Ibid.*, p. 49. Cf. *BRA. 1*, pt. 3, p. 48, footnote.

71. *SM. 1*, pt. 2, p. 49.

72. *BRA. 1*, pt. 3, p. 48.

73. See above, p. 173.

74. Cf. *BRA. 1*, pt. 3, p. 58.

75. *SM. 1*, pt. 2, pp. 24f. Cf. *ibid.*, p. 11; pt. 3, p. 98: *SM. 2*, pp. 211ff: *SM. 3*, p. 7: *BRA. 1*, pt. 1, pp. 27, 67: *MAN.*, pp. 6, 19, 78, and particularly *RAB.*, pp. 15ff.

76. Cf. *SM. 1*, pt. 1, p. 146; pt. 2, pp. 57f: *SM. 2*, p. 202.

77. See above, ch. 1, n. 53.

78. *BRA. 1*, pt. 3, pp. 46f. Cf. *SM. 3*, pp. 121ff.

79. Cf. *SM. 1*, pt. 2, p. 61.

80. *Ibid.*, pt. 1, p. 56.

81. *SM. 5*, pt. 2, pp. 11f.

82. *SM. 2*, pp. 202f. Cf. H. N. Bialik's poems *Ha-Mathmidh* and '*Al Saph Bêth ha-Midhraš*. Cf. N. Slouschz, *op. cit.*, p. 261.

83. *SM. 2*, p. 202. Cf. above, pp. 89f.

84. See S. M. Dubnow, *op. cit.*, vol. 2, pp. 58f, 174ff.

85. *SM. 2*, p. 204. Cf. pp. 216f. Rabinowitz adopts a similar view, *RAB.*, p. 136.

86. *SM. 4*, pp. 230ff, 239ff, 249.

87. *BRA. 1*, pt. 1, pp. 44, 70; pt. 2, pp. 22, 127.

88. *Ibid.*, pt. 1, p. 121.

89. *Ibid.*, pt. 3, pp. 168f.

90. *Ibid.*, p. 177.

91. *SHEIK.*, pt. 1, p. 15; pt. 2, p. 91.

92. See above, p. 159.

93. In 'unenlightened' circles the concept of *belles lettres* scarcely existed. Cf. D. Patterson, 'The Portrait of Ḥasidism', p. 369; and see below, p. 228.

94. Even Rabinowitz includes a short but important description of an idealised *Maskil*. See D. Patterson, 'Some Religious Attitudes . . .', p. 407. Cf. below, pp. 187 and 193.

95. See D. Patterson, *Abraham Mapu*, p. 86, and cf. above, p. 159.

96. See above, pp. 150f. Cf. *ZOB.*, pt. 1, pp. 52f; pt. 2, p. 18. See also *ABR.*, pp. 22, 120f (omitted in revised edition), and p. 133: *SM. 1*, pt. 2, p. 239: *SM. 3*, p. 93: *SM. 6*, pt. 2, p. 39.

97. Cf. *ABR.*, pp. 7f, 120ff: *BRA. 1*, pt. 3, pp. 7, 125: *BRA. 2*, pt. 1, pp. 51ff; pt. 2, pp. 110, 118ff; pt. 4, pp. 313ff: *LEIN.*, pt. 1, p. 119; pt. 2, pp. 4, 11, 114: *ZOB.*, pt. 1, pp. 12ff; pt. 2, pp. 29ff: *MAN.*, pp. 14, 17f: *SHEIK.*, pt. 2, pp. 45ff: *WEIS. 2*, pp. 124f. (Cf. D. Patterson, 'Israel Weisbrem . . .', pp. 55f).

98. These novels abound with references to the acquisition or use of foreign languages, including of course the language of the country in which each particular community lived (cf. above, pp. 167f). See above, p. 167, n. 30 and cf. *SM. 1*, pt. 1, pp. 118, 184; pt. 2, p. 149; pt. 3, pp. 111, 119: *SM. 2*, pp. 47 ,53, 93, 212, 215f: *SM. 4*, pp. 233, 273: *SM. 5*, pt. 1, pp. 24f, 31; pt. 2,

p. 88: *SM. 6*, pt. 1, pp. 52, 128; pt. 2, pp. 53ff: *ABR.*, p. 107: *BRA. 1*, pt. 1, p. 42; pt. 3, pp. 54ff: *BRA. 2*, pt. 1, pp. 17f; pt. 2, pp. 29, 43, 67, 104, 117; pt. 3, p. 205; pt. 4, p. 330: *ZOB.*, pt. 1, pp. 14f: *MAN.*, pp. 12, 17, 30: *SHEIK.*, pt. 2, pp. 31, 36f, 42, 48: *RAB.*, pp. 65, 90, 110: *WEIS. 1*, pp. 19, 40ff, 80f, 110, 125: *WEIS. 2*, p. 54. The main languages are French, German, Polish and Russian; but Latin and sometimes Greek are also mentioned, *SM. 1*, pt. 2, p. 149: *SM. 2*, p. 215: *SM. 5*, pt. 1, p. 22: *SM. 6*, pt. 2, p. 155 (where the study of Latin and Greek is criticised); cf. D. Patterson, *Abraham Mapu*, p. 16.

99. See above, pp. 167f and cf. *SM. 1*, pt. 1, p. 119; pt. 2, p. 244: *SM. 2*, pp. 50f: *SM. 5*, pt. 1, p. 12; pt. 2, p. 80: *BRA. 1*, pt. 2, pp. 40, 70; pt. 3, p. 84: *LEIN.*, pt. 2, p. 62: *SHEIK.*, pt. 1, p. 87: *RAB.*, p. 63: *WEIS. 1*, p. 42, p. 111.

100. See S. M. Dubnow, *op. cit.*, vol. 2, p. 209.

101. *SM. 6*, pt. 2, p. 55. Cf. Braudes' observation that it is essential for a *Maskil* to be acquainted with the new ideas circulating in Russian literature, *BRA. 1*, pt. 3, p. 156. Cf. below, pp. 225f.

102. *BRA. 1*, pt. 1, p. 111. Cf. *SM. 1*, pt. 2, p. 89.

103. *BRA. 1*, pt. 1, p. 111.

104. *Ibid.*, pt. 3, p. 164. Cf. above, p. 145.

105. *BRA. 1*, pt. 1, p. 103.

106. Cf. *LEIN.*, pt. 2, p. 11.

107. Cf. *SHEIK.*, pt. 2, pp. 45ff.

108. *BRA. 2*, pt. 2, pp. 118ff.

109. Cf. above, p. 139.

110. *WEIS. 1*, pp. 10ff.

111. *RAB.*, pp. 52f.

112. *WEIS. 2*, pt. 1, p. 79.

113. *BRA. 2*, pt. 1, p. 12.

114. *Ibid.*, pt. 4, pp. 313ff.

115. Cf. *ABR.*, p. 24: *ZOB.*, pt. 1, pp. 26, 32ff; pt. 2, pp. 19, 38. See above, pp. 159f.

116. Cf. *BRA. 1*, pt. 1, p. 67: *BRA. 2*, pt. 2, p. 77: *SHEIK.*, pt. 2, pp. 79ff. It is indicative of Braudes' more subtle attitude to *Haskalah* in his novel *The Two Extremes* that Solomon, one of his heroes, while reflecting on how a pious and God-fearing man can be so unscrupulous in business, comes to the conclusion that neither *Haskalah* with its emphasis on ethical behaviour, nor religion with its stress on man's relation to God are suffi-

cient to make men overcome their evil inclinations. *BRA. 2,* pt. 2, p. 110.

117. This in spite of the fact that the *Maskilim* were anxious to stimulate the emotional life of the Jew. Cf. above, pp. 154f. See *SM. 2,* pp. 53, 60: *SM. 3,* p. 60: *SM. 4,* pp. 59, 255: *SM. 5,* pt. 1, pp. 15f: *SM. 6,* p. 69: *ABR.,* pp. 55f: *BRA. 2,* pt. 1, p. 53; pt. 2, pp. 114, 137; pt. 3, pp. 213, 260, 281: *ZOB.,* pt. 1, p. 57; pt. 2, p. 49: *SHEIK,* pt. 1, p. 19; pt. 2, p. 59 (but see pt. 3, pp. 105 and 107): *SIRK.,* p. 52: *WEIS. 1,* p. 50, and particularly *RAB.,* pp. 28f, 112f and 116: 'After the period of mourning was over, he fell on his knees before Jeanette and begged her to make him happy by becoming his spouse. She answered not a word, but stretched out her arms to him etc—as the reader may find in all the love stories where the entire procedure has been described so many times that nothing remains for us to add.'

118. See e.g. *SM. 2,* p. 215: *SM. 4,* pp. 130ff: *SM. 5,* pp. 45, 57: *RAB.,* p. 148.

119. Cf. *SM. 4,* pp. 82, 121ff: *SM. 5,* pt. 1, pp. 18ff: *SM. 6,* pt. 1, pp. 9f, 26, 83, 88; pt. 2, pp. 115f.

120. Cf. *SM. 1,* pt. 4, pp. 54ff, 59ff, 68ff, 73ff, 97ff, 114ff.

121. *Ibid.,* p. 118.

122. *Ibid.,* pp. 99ff. Cf. *SM. 6,* pt. 2, p. 267.

123. See D. Patterson, 'Some Religious attitudes . . .', p. 406.

124. See above, p. 183.

125. *RAB.,* p. 53. See above, p. 183, for discrepancy in price.

126. *RAB.,* pp. 54f.

127. *Ibid.,* pp. 61f.

128. *Ibid.,* p. 80.

129. *Ibid.,* p. 81.

130. See above, p. 181, and cf. pp. 79f. Cf. S. Halkin, *Modern Hebrew Literature,* New York, 1950, p. 52.

131. See *BRA. 1,* pt. 1, p. 69; pt. 2, p. 11. Cf. D. Patterson, *Abraham Mapu,* pp. 90f. Note, however, Braudes' satirical variant: 'Solomon was a *Maskil* in every way, and all the girls of Odessa loved him.' *BRA. 2,* pt. 2, p. 80.

132. Cf. *ABR.,* pp. 15ff, 152: *BRA. 2,* pt. 2, pp. 77, 158f, 133ff, 161ff: *MAN.,* p. 40: *SHEIK.,* pt. 1, p. 87: *WEIS. 1,* pp. 25f: *WEIS 2,* pt. 1, pp. 79, 115f; pt. 2, pp. 53f. Cf. D. Patterson, 'Israel Weisbrem . . .', pp. 54ff.

T

133. *WEIS. 1*, p. 65. Cf. above, p. 160.

134. *SHEIK.*, pt. 1, pp. 62f. Cf. below, pp. 226f.

135. *BRA. 2*, pt. 3, pp. 281f.

136. *BRA. 1*, pt. 2, pp. 22ff. Isolated *Maskilim* in bigoted communities frequently pretended to be orthodox. Cf. *ibid.*, p. 175; pt. 3, p. 68. For an interesting illustration of the loathing which the orthodox might entertain for a *Maskil*, see *SM. 5*, pt. 1, p. 94.

137. See *SM. 1*, pt. 4, pp. 75f, 78ff, 98, 118 (although in the latter case, he does admit grudgingly that their number may contain two or three men of sense!): *SM. 2*, pp. 195, 202: *SM. 5*, pt. 2, pp. 23, 130, and see below, p. 188.

138. *SM. 1*, pt. 4, p. 118.

139. *SM. 6*, pt. 1, p. 58.

140. *RAB.*, p. 28, footnote.

141. *Ibid.*, p. 85.

142. *Ibid.*, p. 78. Cf. above, ch. 4, n. 136.

143. *RAB.*, p. 143. See above, n. 94.

144. *SM. 1*, pt. 2, p. 142: *SM. 2*, p. 236: *ABR.*, p. 46 (where a typesetter's note, explaining that an heretical *Sepher Torah* should be burned, mentions a Pentateuch with (Mendelssohn's) commentary which was, in fact, burned. A fire was kindled in the *Bêth-ha-Midhraš* and the participants lit candles: then each took a leaf and burned it in the flame until the book was consumed): *BRA. 1*, pt. 1, p. 94; pt. 3, pp. 22, 57f: *ẒOB.*, pt. 1, p. 24; pt. 2, p. 43: *WEIS. 1*, p. 12. Cf. below, p. 227.

145. *ABR.*, ch. 10, and see *ibid.*, pp. 4f and 37f.

146. *ẒOB.*, pt. 1, pp. 19f.

147. See also *BRA. 2*, pt. 2, p. 190.

148. *SM. 1*, p. 126: *SM. 2*, p. 6: *SM. 4*, p. 198: *BRA. 2*, pt. 2, pp. 109, 198. Cf. *WEIS. 1*, p. 28, and see D. Patterson, 'Israel Weisbrem ...', p. 51; see also D. Patterson, 'The Portrait of Hasidism ...', p. 371. See below, p. 209.

149. See above, pp. 151f. Cf. *ABR.*, p. 68: *SM. 5*, pt. 1, p. 103: *BRA. 2*, pt. 2, p. 148: *SHEIK.*, pt. 1, p. 6: *SIRK.*, p. 48: *WEIS. 1*, pp. 15ff.

150. See *SM. 5*, pt. 1, pp. 119ff: *SM. 6*, pt. 1, pp. 128f: *ABR.*, p. 9: *BRA. 1*, pt. 2, p. 27: *WEIS. 2*, pt. 1, pp. 7f. Cf. D. Patterson, 'Israel Weisbrem ...', p. 55.

151. Cf. *Ibid.*, and see e.g. *SM. 4*, pp. 57, 63ff: *SM. 5*, pt. 1, p. 120:

BRA. 1, pt. 3, p. 146: *SHEIK.*, pt. 1, pp. 14f: *WEIS. 2*, pt. 1, p. 70.

152. Cf. *BRA. 1*, pt. 2, pp. 12, 89. Cf. A. Mapu, *The Hypocrite*, pt. 3, ch. 11, and D. Patterson, *Abraham Mapu*, p. 95.

153. *BRA. 1*, pt. 3, pp. 83ff, 87f.

154. *SM. 1*, pt. 4, pp. 79f, 90ff; *BRA. 2*, pt. 2, pp. 109, 133ff, 146: *RAB.*, pp. 108ff, 116ff.

155. *SM. 1*, pt. 4, p. 64.

156. Cf. *SM. 1*, pt. 1, p. 137: *SM. 2*, pp. 48, 50: *SM. 4*, pp. 53, 225ff *SM. 5*, pt. 1, pp.157 f: *ABR.*, pp. 150f, 154, 158: *BRA. 1*, pt. 1 p. 24: pt. 2, pp. 23, 77: *ZOB.*, pt. 2, pp. 29f: *WEIS. 1*, pp. 112ff (see D. Patterson, 'Israel Weisbrem . . .', pp. 44f): *WEIS. 2*, pt. 1, pp. 150ff.

157. *WEIS. 2*, pt. 1, pp. 140f.

158. *SM. 5*, pt. 2, p. 58.

159. Cf. *SM. 2*, pp. 20ff, 164ff, 194ff, 198ff: *SM. 3*, pp. 35ff: *SM. 4*, p. 82: *SM. 5*, pt. 2, pp. 33ff: *SM. 6*, pt. 2, pp. 124ff: *BRA. 1*, pt. 1, p. 67: *LEIN.*, pt. 1, pp. 61ff, 101f; pt. 2, p. 41: *ZOB.*, pt. 1, pp. 32ff; pt. 2, p. 38: *SHEIK.*, pt. 1, p. 63; pt. 3, p. 106: *WEIS. 1*, p. 65. Cf. above, p. 186, n. 137.

CHAPTER 7

1. See S. M. Dubnow, *op. cit.*, vol. 2.

2. See above, pp. 132ff.

3. See e.g. S. Horodetsky, *Ha-Ḥasidhuth we-ha-Ḥasidhim*, Berlin, 1923; G. G. Scholem, *Major Trends in Jewish Mysticism*, 3rd ed., London, 1955.

4. Cf. D. Patterson, 'The Portrait of Ḥasidism . . .', pp. 374f. Cf. below, pp. 208f.

5. Cf. above, p. 158. Cf. *SM. 5*, pt. 1, p. 94.

6. Cf. *BRA. 2*, pt. 4, p. 314.

7. See D. Patterson, 'The Portrait of Ḥasidism . . .', and 'The Portrait of the Ṣaddik . . .'.

8. Cf. above, pp. 130f, 160.

9. Cf. above, p. 181.

10. See below, pp. 202f, 204f, 207.

11. See e.g. D. Philipson, *The Reform Movement in Judaism*, 2nd. ed., New York, 1930.

12. See above, pp. 81, 130, 181.

13. Cf. *SM. 1*, pt. 2, pp. 295f, 312ff; pt. 3, pp. 123ff; pt. 4, p. 18: *SM. 4*, pp. 24ff, 122f, 130ff: *SM. 5*, pt. 1, pp. 38ff: *ABR.*, pp. 123f: *BRA. 1*, pt. 3, p. 66: *BRA. 2*, pt. 3, pp. 246f: *MEIN*, p. 17.

14. See D. Patterson, 'Some Religious Attitudes . . .', pp. 401f.

15. *BRA. 1*, pt. 1, pp. 7f.

16. For a detailed study of this literary war see G. Katznelson, *Ha-Milḥamah ha-Siphruthith bên ha-Ḥaredhim we-ha-Maskilim*, Tel-Aviv, 1954. Cf. D. Patterson, 'Some Religious Attitudes . . .', pp. 398ff.

17. Cf. Klausner, *History*, vol. 5, p. 352.

18. See above, p. 186.

19. Cf. D. Patterson, 'Some Religious Attitudes . . .', p. 405.

20. See *ibid.*, pp. 406f, and cf. above, pp. 184f, 186f.

21. *RAB.*, pp. 146ff. Cf. above, ch. 6, n. 94, and p. 187.

22. This pattern was laid down by Abraham Mapu in his long novel '*Ayiṭ Ṣabhu'a* (The Hypocrite), and imitated constantly. Cf. *SM. 6*, pt. 1, pp. 17ff: *ABR.*, p. 32: *BRA. 1*, pt. 1, p. 105; pt. 3, p. 120: *LEIN.*, pt. 1, p. 63: *SHEIK.*, pt. 1, pp. 44f. See below, p. 223.

23. Cf. *WEIS. 2*, pt. 2, pp. 178ff, and see D. Patterson, 'Israel Weisbrem . . .', pp. 46f. Cf. *BRA. 2*, pt. 2, pp. 100, 110: *SHEIK.*, pt. 1, pp. 9f, 12.

24. *SM. 1*, pt. 2, pp. 297ff. Cf. pt. 1, p. 217.

25. *BRA. 2*, pt. 3, pp. 250ff. Cf. p. 253; pt. 2, pp. 77, 84f: *BRA. 1*, pt. 1, p. 68: *SM. 5*, pt. 1, pp. 65f: *ABR.*, pp. 123f: *ZOB.*, pt. 1, pp. 50f.

26. Samuel is modelled on M. L. Lilienblum one of the principal protagonists of the struggle for reform waged in Lithuania, 1869-71, mentioned above. Cf. above, p. 80, n. 54.

27. *BRA. 1*, pt. 2, p. 50.

28. *Ibid.*, pt. 3, p. 29.

29. Cf. above, p. 181. The historical romances of the first Hebrew novelist, Abraham Mapu, namely '*Ahabhath Ṣiyyon* (*The Love of Zion*), and '*Ašmath Šomron* (*The Guilt of Samaria*), represent clear examples of this tendency.

30. *ABR.*, p. 124. Cf. *SM. 5*, pt. 2, pp. 110ff.

31. *SM. 6*, pt. 2, pp. 49ff. Cf. *ibid.*, pp. 58ff: *SM. 2*, p. 79: *SM. 5*, pt. 1, pp. 16ff; pt. 2, ch. 3; pt. 3, p. 63: *BRA. 1*, pt. 1, pp. 54, 91: *LEIN.*, pt. 1, p. 63: *SHEIK.*, pt. 1, p. 28; pt. 3, p. 107: *SIRK.*,

p. 116. Cf. J. Heller, 'Mišnatho šel Smolenskin be-Yahadhuth', in *Metsudah*, December 1943, pp. 153-8.

32. *SM. 1*, pt. 2, pp. 96f. Cf. below, ch. 8, n. 76.

33. *SM. 6*, pt. 2, p. 158.

34. *Ibid.*, p. 159. Cf. *SM. 1*, pt. 1, p. 36: *SM. 5*, pt. 2, pp. 131ff: *WEIS. 2*, pt. 1, pp. 124f. (Cf. D. Patterson, 'Israel Weisbrem . . .', p. 56.)

35. *RAB.*, p. 150. Cf. D. Patterson, 'Some Religious Attitudes . . .', p. 407.

36. Cf. *SM. 3*, p. 148: '. . . after two men had testified to seeing him carrying a comb in his pocket on the Sabbath, all the leaders of the community concluded that it was their duty to keep him at a distance, and perhaps even to banish him from the town.' Cf. below, pp. 212f.

37. *SM. 6*, pt. 2, pp. 30f.

38. *Ibid.*, p. 33.

39. The wearing of 'short clothes' in European style was one of the hallmarks of a *Maskil*. Cf. above, p. 182.

40. *SM. 6*, pt. 2, p. 34. Cf. *SM. 1*, pt. 2, pp. 273ff.

41. *SHEIK.*, pt. 3, p. 106. The author proceeds to lay equal blame on the *Maskilim*. Cf. *ABR.*, pp. 25, 36f. Cf. below, pp. 215f.

42. See above, pp. 192f. For a very different picture of orthodox life, see J. H. Lipschitz, *Toledhoth Yiṣhaq*, Warsaw, 1896, *Maḥaziqê ha-Dath*, Pietrokow, 1903 and *Ẓikheron Yaʿaqobh*, Kovno-Sloboda, 1924-30.

43. *BRA. 1*, pt. 2, pp. 108f. Cf. pt. 1, p. 13; pt. 2, pp. 15f, 35f, 37ff, 40f, 48f; pt. 3, p. 117ff.

44. *SM. 3*, pp. 99f. Cf. pp. 24ff, 47f, 113, 116, 165.

45. See above, ch. 1, n. 53.

46. *BRA. 1*, pt. 3, p. 63.

47. *BRA. 1*, pt. 3, pp. 59f, 195f. Cf. pt. 2, pp. 17, 82.

48. Cf. *Ibid.*, pt. 3, ch. 14.

49. *Ibid.*, ch. 19. Cf. G. Katznelson, *op. cit.*

50. *BRA. 1*, pt. 3, p. 201.

51. Cf. D. Patterson, 'Some Religious Attitudes . . .', pp. 398f.

52. Braudes appends a footnote explaining that almost every *Bêth Midhraš* and *Yešibhah* in Ayalon (Vilna) was so called. *BRA. 1*, pt. 3, p. 69.

53. A literary annual founded in 1852. See *'Aḥi'asaph*, Warsaw, 1923, p. 242.

54. See Braudes' footnote, *BRA. 1*, pt. 3, p. 69.

55. *Ibid.*, pp. 69f.

56. *SM. 2*, pp. 37f.

57. *ZOB.*, pt. 2, pp. 36ff.

58. *BRA. 1*, pt. 2, p. 17.

59. *RAB.*, pp. 58ff.

60. *BRA. 1*, pt. 2, p. 102. Cf. above, p. 141.

61. *BRA. 1*, pt. 1, p. 45.

62. See above, p. 166, n. 25.

63. *SM. 1*, pt. 3, pp. 52f. Cf. D. Patterson, 'The Portrait of Ḥasidism . . .', p. 372. Cf. *SM. 1*, pt. 2, pp. 243f; pt. 3, pp. 130f.

64. Cf. D. Patterson, 'The Portrait of Ḥasidism . . .', p. 374, n. 11.

65. Cf. *SM. 1*, pt. 3, p. 29: 'I went to the bookcase for a book, and was astonished to see how few there were. It is quite the reverse in the synagogues of the *Mithnaggedhim*, the *Guardians of the Torah*, for whom bookcases crammed with all sorts of books—copies of the Talmud, Midhraš, Scripture and ancient commentaries—constitute their chief pride and joy. Not that they are read, for no one will dare to glance into them lest his faith be shaken, or lest anyone see him and regard him as an atheist.'

66. See above, p. 152.

67. An Aggadic collection of the sixteenth century by Jacob Ibn Ḥabib. See *The Jewish Encyclopaedia*, vol. 6, p. 124.

68. *SM. 1*, pt. 2, p. 244.

69. Cf. *Ibid.*, pt. 1, p. 194; pt. 3, pp. 52f, 130f: *SM. 3*, p. 86: *SM. 4*, p. 208: *WEIS. 2*, pt. 1, p. 4. See above, p. 190.

70. *BRA. 2*, pt. 2, pp. 151ff. Cf. above, p. 190.

71. *SM. 4*, p. 208.

72. Cf. *SM. 1*, pt. 1, pp. 124, 126, 143: *SM. 3*, p. 126: *BRA. 2*, pt. 2, p. 198: *SHEIK.*, pt. 2, p. 69: *WEIS. 1*, p. 28. Cf. above, p. 187.

73. *SM. 2*, p. 6.

74. *BRA. 2*, pt. 3, p. 233. Cf. *WEIS. 1*, p. 28, where the bigoted Zebulun blames the arrival of a number of teachers of grammar for the inclement weather which has made it impossible to recite the blessing over the new moon. See above, p. 187, n. 148.

75. Cf. *SM. 1*, pt. 1, pp. 53, 75, 96; pt. 2, pp. 43, 51ff; pt. 3, pp. 52,

69: *SM. 2*, p. 202: *SM. 3*, pp. 38, 43, 49f, 64f: *SM. 5*, pt. 1, pp. 33f; pt. 2, p. 144: *SM. 6*, pt. 2, p. 168: *BRA. 1*, pt. 1, p. 24; pt.3, p. 93: *RAB.*, p. 84: *WEIS. 1*, p. 45. And see especially *ABR.*, pp. 45f and footnote.

76. *SM. 1*, pt. 1, p. 75.

77. *Ibid.*, p. 96.

78. *Ibid.*, p. 43.

79. *Ibid.*, and pt. 2, pp. 51f.

80. *SM. 2*, p. 202.

81. *SM. 3*, pp. 64f. Cf. *SIRK.*, p. 84: '. . . For if a corpse is not guarded by a living person, evil spirits will crowd into the body. . . .'

82. *Ibid.*, and see especially the tale of the enchanted butcher, *SM. 1*, pt. 2, pp. 53ff.

83. *Ibid.*, p. 54. The seven weeks between Passover and the Feast of Weeks.

84. *SM. 3*, p. 43. Cf. *SM. 5*, pt. 1, pp. 33f.

85. *SM. 1*, pt. 2, pp. 52f. The same incident is mentioned in *SM. 3*, p. 38.

86. *SM. 1*, pt. 2, pp. 51f.

87. *SM. 5*, pt. 1, p. 33.

88. *SM. 4*, p. 77: *SM. 5*, pt. 1, p. 158; pt. 2, p. 144: *SM. 6*, pt. 2, p. 168.

89. *SM. 3*, p. 64.

90. Cf. *SM. 3*, p. 112: *SM. 5*, pt. 1, pp. 93f, 157f: *ABR.*, p. 45. (In a footnote to p. 46 the author states that these superstitions are actually held by the people.) Cf. *SM. 1*, pt. 1, p. 142: *BRA. 2*, pt. 2, pp. 187f: *SHEIK.*, pt. 2, p. 40: *RAB.*, p. 84: *WEIS. 1*, p. 45.

91. *SM. 2*, p. 155.

92. *RAB.*, p. 13.

93. *Ibid.*, p. 37.

94. *Ibid.*

95. *SM. 1*, pt. 2, p. 100.

96. See *The Jewish Encyclopaedia*, vol. 8, p. 531.

97. *SM. 1*, pt. 2, p. 196. Cf. *SM. 2*, p. 152.

98. See e.g. M. Friedlander, *The Jewish Religion*, 4th ed., London, 1931, pp. 397f.

99. *ABR.*, p. 6. Cf. *BRA. 2*, p. 183.

100. *BRA. 2*, pt. 2, p. 184. Cf. A. Mapu, *Kol Kithbhê Abraham Mapu*, Tel-Aviv, 1950, p. 364.

101. *SHEIK.*, pt. 1, p. 38: *SIRK.*, pp. 20ff, 40.

102. *RAB.*, p. 10. Cf. Oesterley and Box, *The Literature of Rabbinical and Mediaeval Judaism*, London, 1920, p. 184.

103. *SM. 1*, pt. 1, p. 18; cf. *SM. 2*, p. 5. Rabinowitz portrays a daughter reciting the prayer, *RAB.*, pp. 105, 116.

104. *MAN.*, p. 53.

105. *ABR.*, p. 114.

106. *RAB.*, p. 7.

107. *SM. 1*, pt. 1, p. 111.

108. *BRA. 1*, pt. 2, pp. 35ff. See also D. Patterson, 'Some Religious Attitudes . . .', p. 401.

109. *ZOB.*, pt. 2, pp. 36ff. See below, p. 217.

110. *SM. 1*, pt. 1, p. 130; pt. 2, pp. 277f.

111. *Ibid.*, p. 274.

112. *Ibid.*, pp. 285f, 292:   *RAB.*, pp. 107f.

113. *Ibid.*, p. 107. Cf. *ABR.*, p. 47.

114. *SM. 3*, p. 25. Cf. Z. Schneour, *Noah Pandre's Village*, translated by J. Leftwich, London, 1938.

115. *SM. 3*, p. 47. Cf. Jeremiah, 22^{19}. For a further reference to *A Donkey's Burial*, see *SM. 6*, pt. 1, p. 17.

116. *WEIS. 1*, pp. 27ff, 35. Cf. D. Patterson, 'Israel Weisbrem . . .', pp. 50f. See above, pp. 122f.

117. Rabinowitz's novel *At The Crossroads* is, indeed, devoted to the theme. See above, pp. 28ff, and cf. D. Patterson, 'Some Religious Attitudes . . .', pp. 406f.

118. *SM. 2*, p. 153. Cf. *BRA. 1*, pt. 1, p. 82; pt. 2, p. 116: *BRA. 2*, pt. 2, p. 136.

119. Cf. *SM. 1*, pt. 1, p. 138; pt. 2, p. 187: *SM. 3*, pp. 69f: *BRA. 1*, pt. 1, pp. 102f. See also above, pp. 200f.

120. *SM. 1*, pt. 2, pp. 9f.

121. *BRA. 2*, pt. 1, p. 22.

122. Cf. *SM. 1*, pt. 1, p. 138.

123. See Numbers 15^{38}ff, and cf. M. Friedlander, *op. cit.*, pp. 329ff.

124. *SM. 1*, pt. 1, p. 89.

125. *BRA. 2*, pt. 3, p. 278.

126. See *SM. 1*, pt. 3, p. 176.

127. *Ibid.*, p. 192. For a similar reaction see *SM. 3*, pp. 145f. Cf. also *ibid.*, pp. 37, 82, 174f: *SM. 4*, p. 173.

128. See above, note 117, and cf. *RAB.*, pp. 77, 81, 100. Cf. *SM. 5*, pt. 1, pp. 93f: *SHEIK.*, pt. 3, p. 85: *WEIS. 1*, pp. 43, 64.

129. *WEIS. 2*, pt. 1, p. 170.

130. *BRA. 1*, pt. 1, pp. 99f. Cf. above, p. 143, n. 84.

131. *SM. 1*, pt. 2, pp. 200f.

132. Cf. *BRA. 1*, pt. 1, p. 110.

133. *SM. 1*, pt. 1, p. 10. Cf. *ABR.*, pp. 4 and 40, where the pseudonym Yabhne'el is used to denote Vilna.

134. *SM. 1*, pt. 2, p. 51.

135. The distribution of the terms by novels is as follows: *SM. 1* (16); *SM. 2* (5); *SM. 3* (5); *SM. 4* (4); *SM. 5* (5); *SM. 6* (5); *BRA. 1* (154); *BRA. 2* (16); *ZOB.* (8); *SHEIK.* (48); *RAB.* (6); *WEIS. 2* (1).

136. *BRA. 1*, pt. 1, p. 83.

137. The theme does not occur in the novels by Abramowitz, Manassewitz, nor—more surprisingly in view of the subject-matter—in Braudes' stories.

138. Cf. *SM. 1*, pt. 1, pp. 188, 241; pt. 2, pp. 207, 232f; pt. 3, pp. 202, 205, 217, 221, 231ff, 236ff: *SM. 3*, p. 196: *SM. 4*, pp. 124f, 128, 136: *SM. 5*, pt. 1, p. 63; pt. 2, pp. 77, 120f; pt. 3, pp. 25, 164: *SM. 6*, pt. 2, pp. 291f; pt. 3, pp. 313, 365: *LEIN.*, p. 71: *MEIN.*, p. 56: *ZOB.*, pp. 47, 67: *SHEIK.*, pt. 2, pp. 58, 60; pt. 3, pp. 36, 44, 47, 88ff, 94f, 106, 109: *RAB.*, pp. 143, 158: *SIRK.*, pp. 64, 92: *WEIS. 1*, p. 56: *WEIS. 2*, pt. 1, p. 162.

139. *RAB.*, p. 143.

140. *ZOB.*, pt. 2, p. 47. It is typical of the author's patriotism that this action is not criticised. Cf. above, pp. 150f. Even the converted officer's mother reconciles herself to the situation, *ZOB.*, pt. 2, p. 67.

141. Cf. *SM. 5*, pt. 2, p. 120: *LEIN.*, p. 71: *SHEIK.*, pt. 2, p. 58; pt. 3, p. 90: *SIRK.*, p. 64.

142. *SM. 1*, pt. 2, pp. 232f; pt. 3, p. 202: *SM. 4*, p. 128.

143. Cf. *SM. 1*, pt. 1, p. 188: *SM. 3*, p. 196.

144. Cf. *SM. 1*, pt. 1, p. 241; pt. 3, p. 217: *SM. 4*, p. 136: *SHEIK.*, pt. 2, p. 58; pt. 3, p. 109. Smolenskin maintains, however, that a watch was kept on converts, who could not reconvert without emigrating, *SM. 1*, pt. 3, p. 205.

145. Cf. *SM. 5*, pt. 2, pp. 120f: *SHEIK*, pt. 3, p. 36: *WEIS. 1*, p. 56.

146. Cf. *SM. 5*, pt. 1, p. 63; pt. 2, p. 291; pt. 3, p. 25: *SHEIK.*, pt. 3, p. 44.

147. *MEIN.*, p. 56. The episode is clearly modelled on the famous Mortara case. Cf. above, ch. 2, n. 102.

148. *SM. 1*, pt. 2, pp. 207f; pt. 3, pp. 231ff, 236ff. Cf. *SM. 5*, pt. 2, p. 77.

149. *SHEIK.*, pt. 2, p. 60; pt. 3, p. 47.

150. *Ibid.*, pt. 3, p. 106. Cf. above, p. 202.

151. *SM. 1*, pt. 3, ch. 33.

152. *SM. 5*, pt. 3, p. 164: *SM. 6*, pt. 3, p. 365.

153. See e.g. *SM. 1*, pt. 2, pp. 33ff; pt. 3, pp. 58, 124ff: *SM. 2*, pp. 123, 156, 163, 165, 235: *SM. 4*, pp. 3ff: *SM. 5*, pt. 2, pp. 64ff: *SM. 6*, pt. 3, p. 292: *LEIN.*, pt. 2, p. 21: *ZOB.*, pt. 2, p. 21: *SHEIK.*, pt. 1, p. 52.

154. See above, pp. 38f.

155. See e.g. *SM. 1*, pt. 1, pp. 73, 98ff, 254f; pt. 2, pp. 92, 197; pt. 3, pp. 113f: *SM. 2*, pp. 10, 31, 73, 76, 135, 176, 194ff: *SM. 6*, pt. 1, p. 235: *MEIN.*, pp. 39f, 41: *SHEIK.*, pt. 1, p. 12.

156. *LEIN.*, pt. 1, p. 102.

157. *SM. 6*, pt. 2, p. 74: *BRA. 1*, pt. 3, pp. 109, 116: *LEIN.*, pt. 2, p. 85: *SIRK.*, p. 52.

158. *SM. 5*, pt. 3, pp. 106f: *LEIN.*, pt. 1, pp. 36, 40.

159. *BRA. 2*, pt. 2, p. 107.

160. A similar phenomenon may be observed in the novels of Abraham Mapu. See D. Patterson, *Abraham Mapu*, p. 93.

161. *SM. 1*, pt. 1, pp. 84, 137.

162. *Ibid.*, p. 122.

163. *Ibid.*: *SM. 3*, p. 125. Braudes recalls the time when every large synagogue had its own stocks near its entrance for the punishment of transgressors, *BRA. 1*, pt. 1, p. 99, and see above, p. 214, n. 130.

164. *BRA. 1*, pt. 1, p. 74 and footnote. Cf. D. Patterson, 'Some Religious Attitudes . . .', p. 401.

165. *BRA. 1*, pt. 1, p. 63.

166. *Ibid.*, p. 99.

167. *SM. 1*, pt. 2, p. 216: *WEIS. 1*, p. 45.

168. *SM. 1*, pt. 1, p. 129.

169. *BRA.* 2, pt. 2, p. 93, and especially *SM.* 1, pt. 3, pp. 28ff. Cf. D. Patterson 'The Portrait of Ḥasidism . . .', pp. 368f.

170. *ZOB.*, pt. 2, pp. 36ff. See above, p. 211.

171. *SM.* 1, pt. 1, pp. 130ff. See also *SM.* 3, pp. 168f.

172. *BRA.* 1, pt. 1, p. 78: *BRA.* 2, pt. 3, p. 298.

173. *SM.* 1, pt. 2, p. 53: *SM.* 3, p. 43.

174. See above, p. 209.

175. *ABR.*, p. 46.

176. Cf. *ZOB.*, p. 38.

177. *ABR.*, p. 47.

178. *BRA.* 1, pt. 1, p. 46.

179. *SM.* 1, pt. 1, pp. 111, 134, 160, 257ff, 261f.

180. *Ibid.*, pp. 100ff, 263.

181. See above, pp. 176f.

182. Cf. *ABR.*, pp. 73f.

183. For the various functions of the beadle see *SM.* 1, pt. 2, pp. 45f: *SM.* 2, pp. 36f: *SM.* 3, pp. 126f, 177: *ABR.*, pp. 47f, 83: *BRA.* 1, pt. 1, p. 100; pt. 3, p. 58: *SIRK.*, pp. 69ff: *RAB.*, p. 22; and see above, pp. 205ff.

184. Cf. above, pp. 192, 202f. See *BRA.* 1, pt. 3, pp. 60ff, 77ff, 129, 131, 137, 197f, 205f, 208. Cf. *BRA.* 2, pt. 2, p. 176, for an attack on Rabbinical stringencies, unusual in *The Two Extremes.*

185. *SM.* 1, pt. 2, p. 84: *SM.* 2, pp. 35ff, 279f, and see above, p. 207.

186. Cf. *SM.* 2, pp. 210, 212: *SM.* 4, pp. 161ff: *BRA.* 1, pt. 3, pp. 54ff, 184f.

187. *WEIS.* 1, pp. 12, 14, 37, 109, 124. See above, n. 116.

188. *RAB.*, pp. 134f, 140. See S. M. Dubnow, *op. cit.*, vol. 2, p. 176.

189. *SHEIK.*, pt. 1, p. 92.

CHAPTER 8

1. See above, p. 53.

2. In criticising the Yiddish novel of the period, the famous Yiddish writer Shalom Aleichem notes the same phenomenon in the contemporary Yiddish story. See Shalom Aleichem, *Šomer's Mišpaṭ*, Berdichev, 1888, and cf. A. R. Malakhi, *Massoth u-Rešimoth*, New York, 1937, pp. 34-44.

3. Smolenskin specifically states the fact that all Hebrew writers in

Russia display their helplessness in the face of the great problems confronting the Jews. *SM. 1*, pt. 4, p. 89.

4. Cf. the praise of Mapu by P. Smolenskin quoted by R. Brainin in his *Abraham Mapu*, Piotrokow, 1900, pp. 51f.

5. See Klausner, *History*, vol. 3, pp. 333f, and D. Patterson, *Abraham Mapu*, p. 4.

6. See above, ch. 2, pp. 38, 42, 53, 58, 61(2), and ns. 107, 123, 157, 200; ch. 3, pp. 68f; ch. 4, pp. 101f, 105, 120, 121, and n. 93; ch. 6, n. 152; ch. 7, ns. 22, 29, 160.

7. *SM. 1*, pt. 1, p. 162.

8. *Ibid.*, and p. 164.

9. *SHEIK.*, pt. 1, p. 87.

10. *Ibid.*, pt. 2, p. 6.

11. See above, pp. 184f.

12. *RAB.*, pp. 51f. But see above, ch. 1, n. 83.

13. *RAB.*, p. 86.

14. *Ibid.*, p. 89. Elisheba is one of the heroines of Mapu's social novel, *The Hypocrite*.

15. *SM. 1*, pt. 4, p. 20.

16. A. Mapu, *The Hypocrite*, pt. 4, ch. 8.

17. *SM. 5*, pt. 3, ch. 4.

18. Pt. 2, ch. 9.

19. *SM. 6*, pt. 1, ch. 11; cf. *LEIN.*, pt. 1, ch. 20.

20. *The Love of Zion*, ch. 16.

21. *WEIS. 2*, pt. 2, ch. 23.

22. Pt. 3, ch. 12.

23. *WEIS. 2*, pt. 1, ch. 7; *The Hypocrite*, pt. 1, ch. 1. Cf. *MAN.*, ch. 1.

24. See J. Raisin, *op. cit.*, pp. 140ff.

25. *LEIN.*, pt. 1, ch. 12: *MEIN.*, ch. 20.

26. See D. Patterson, *Abraham Mapu*, p. 36.

27. *ZOB.*, pt. 2, ch. 16.

28. Chs. 2, 11, 21, 24.

29. *SM. 6*, pt. 1, ch. 14. Cf. J. Rabinowitz, 'Peretz Smolenskin' in *Sepher Smolenskin*, ed. by S. Breiman, Jerusalem, 1952.

30. *LEIN.*, pt. 1, ch. 19.

31. *SHEIK.*, pt. 1, ch. 15.

32. *SM. 5*, pt. 1, ch. 3.

33. *WEIS. 2*, pt. 1, ch. 8.

34. See above, p. 194.

35. For the influence of the French romantic novelists on Mapu, see S. Sha'anan, *'Iyyunim be-Siphruth ha-'Haskalah'*, Merhavia, 1952. Sue's *Mystères de Paris*, 1842, was translated into Hebrew during the years 1857-60 by Kalman Schulman. See D. Patterson, *Abraham Mapu*, pp. 102ff.

36. See above, pp. 66f.

37. See above, pp. 42f.

38. See above, pp. 38f.

39. For the main currents of contemporary Russian thought see e.g. R. Hare, *Pioneers of Russian Social Thought*, London, etc., 1951; E. Lampert, *Studies in Rebellion*, London, 1957; S. R. Tomkins, *The Russian Intelligentsia*, Oklahoma, 1957.

40. See *Kol Kithbhê A. U. Kovner*, Tel-Aviv, 1947. Cf. S. Breiman, 'A. U. Kovner and his Place in the History of Hebrew Criticism', in *Metsudah*, 1954, pp. 416-57 (Hebrew text).

41. Cf. above, pp. 117f.

42. *BRA. 1*, pt. 2, p. 13. Cf. above, ch. 6, n. 101.

43. *BRA. 1*, p. 66.

44. *BRA. 2*, pt. 2, pp. 178f.

45. *RAB.*, p. 91.

46. *ABR.*, p. 17. Cf. above, pp. 109f.

47. Cf. *ABR.*, pp. 60f., 125f: *SM. 1*, pt. 4, pp. 41, 75, 78ff: *SM. 5*, pt. 1, p. 91: *RAB.*, pp. 90f: *SHEIK.*, pt. 1, pp. 62f; pt. 3, pp 16f.

48. See above, p. 142.

49. *SHEIK.*, pt. 1, p. 62f. Cf. *SM. 1*, pt. 4, ch. 9.

50. *SHEIK.*, p. 64, and cf. above, p. 46, ch. 4, n. 110, and p. 186, n. 134.

51. *SM. 3*, pp. 154f.

52. *BRA. 1*, pt. 2, p. 19.

53. *BRA. 2*, pt. 2, p. 103.

54. *ABR.*, p. 107: *BRA. 2*, pt. 2, p. 13: *SHEIK.*, pt. 1, p. 63.

55. *SM. 2*, pp. 150, 164ff (adversely critical), 191f, 196: *ABR.*, pp. 110f: *BRA. 1*, pt. 2, pp. 17f, 128: *BRA. 2*, pt. 4, p. 366.

56. *SM. 2*, pp. 130ff, 149 (adversely critical), 151, 165ff, 173: *SM. 5*, pt. 2, p. 42.

57. *MEIN.*, p. 21: *MAN.*, p. 30.

58. *BRA. 1*, pt. 1, pp. 38, 41f, 92.

59. *Ibid.*, pt. 2, p. 82.

60. For Smolenskin's criticism of the Hebrew translation of Faust by M. Letteris, which was published under the title of *Ben-Abuyah*, see his article *Biqqoreth Tihyeh*, Odessa, 1867. Cf. also *SM. 5*, pt. 1, pp. 41f.

61. *SIRK.*, pp, 34, 119.

62. *SM. 2*, p. 166.

63. *Ibid.*

64. *SM. 5*, pt. 2, p. 76. See above, p. 187, n. 144.

65. *BRA. 1*, pt. 3, p. 7.

66. Cf. *SM. 1*, pt. 2, ch. 12; pt. 3, ch. 30: *SM. 6*, pt. 1, ch. 17.

67. See E. N. Gummer, *Dickens' Works in Germany, 1837-1937*, Oxford, 1940. Although Klausner argues that Smolenskin knew sufficient English to read English books. See Klausner, *History*, vol. 5, pp. 30f.

68. *SM. 2*, p. 132, all in unflattering terms.

69. *SIRK.*, p. 68.

70. *SM. 1*, pt. 4, p. 98: *SM. 2*, p. 149.

71. *SM. 5*, pt. 1, p. 50. Cf. *Ibid.*, pp. 21f.

72. *BRA. 1*, pt. 1, p. 56.

73. See *BRA. 2*, pt. 1, pp. 51f. See above, p. 42, n. 24, and p. 181, n. 93.

74. See above, pp. 80f.

75. See above, pp. 3, 41.

76. For Smolenskin's nationalism, see J. Klausner's article in *Sepher Smolenskin*, ed. S. Breiman. Cf. above, pp. 198ff.

77. See above, p. 64.

78. See above, pp. 87ff.

79. See above, pp. 107f.

80. See above, p. 143.

81. It is an example of Smolenskin's carelessness that they are here called *Lebhibhoth*, whereas in the early part of the story they are always *Tuphinim*.

82. *Pride and Fall*, in fact contains an important discussion on *The Wanderer in the Paths of Life*. See *SM. 4*, pp. 190-6.

83. See *SM. 5*, pt. 2, pp. 133ff.

84. See *SM. 6*, pt. 3, ch. 7, for the character sketch of Palti. Cf. above, p. 83.

85. See above, pp. 77f.

86. See above, p. 121.

87. See above, pp. 44, 56.

88. See above, p. 20.

89. The remaining novels are here reviewed in the chronological order of their publication.

90. A gentle but devastating review of this novel by Smolenskin appeared in *Ha-Šaḥar*, Vienna, 1876, pp. 607f.

91. See above, p. 39.

92. See above, p. 22.

93. See above, p. 52, n. 102.

94. *ZOB.*, pt. 2, p. 62.

95. See above, pp. 150f.

96. See above, p. 153.

97. See above, p. 120.

98. See above, pp. 25f, 60.

99. In *Ha-Yom*, 2nd year (1887), Nos., 257/8. The article was reprinted in *Kol Kithbhê David Frishmann*, vol. 5, Warsaw-New York, 1930, pp. 24-36. See above, n. 2. For Sheikewitz's defence against his critics see *SHEIK.*, pt. 3, p. 105, and cf. D. Sedan's introduction to *Širê Šomer we-Zikhronothaw*.

100. Cf. above, p. 44.

101. See above, pp. 93f.

102. See above, pp. 30f.

103. See above, pp. 31f, 60.

104. *WEIS. 1*, ch. 4. See above, p. 168.

105. See above, pp. 122f.

106. See D. Patterson, 'Israel Weisbrem . . .', pp. 44f.

107. See above, pp. 92f, and D. Patterson, 'Israel Weisbrem . . .', pp. 46f.

108. See above, ch. 6, n. 25.

109. *SHEIK.*, pt. 3, p. 57.

Bibliography

(*For bibliographical details of the novels utilised for this study, see above pp. 3f. For studies on S. J. Abramowitz, P. Smolenskin and R. A. Braudes, see ch. 1, notes 10, 19 and 51.*)

'Aḥi'asaph, Warsaw, 1923.

Ha-'Areṣ, 9 February 1934.

AUERBACH, E., *Mimesis*, trans. by W. Track, Princeton, 1953.

BENNETT, E. K., *A History of the German Novelle from Goethe to Thomas Mann*, 2nd ed. revised and continued by H. M. Waidson, Cambridge, 1961.

BIRKOWITZ, D. I., *Ha-Ri'šonim Ki-Bhnê-'Adham*, rev. ed., Vol. 6, Tel-Aviv, 1953.

BLACK, F. G., *The Epistolary Novel in the Late Eighteenth Century*, Eugene, 1940.

BRAININ, R., *Abraham Mapu*, Piotrokow, 1900.

BREIMAN, S., 'A. U. Kovner and his Place in the History of Hebrew Criticism', in *Metsudah*, 1954. (Hebrew Text.)

BREIMAN, S., ed., *Sepher Smolenskin*, Jerusalem, 1952.

CHASE, M. E., *Life and Language in the Old Testament*, London, 1956.

DALZIEL, M., *Popular Fiction 100 Years Ago*, London, 1957.

DAVIDSON, I., *Parody in Jewish Literature*, New York, 1907.

DOBRÉE, B., *Modern Prose Style*, Oxford, 1934.

Ha-Do'ar, Vol. 7, 14 Tishri, 1929.

DUBNOW, M., *History of the Jews in Russia and Poland*, translated by I. Friedlaender, Philadelphia, 1916-20.

EHRENZELLER, H., *Studien zur Romanvorrede*, Berne, 1955.

ELKOSHI, G., ed., *Letters from P. Smolenskin to J. L. Gordon*, Jerusalem, 1960.

FICHMAN, J., *'Alluphê ha-Haskalah*, Tel-Aviv, 1952.

FICHMAN, J., *'Anšê Besorah*, Tel-Aviv, 1938.

FONER, S. F., *Mi-Zikhronoth Yemê Yalduthi*, Warsaw, 1903.

FORSTER, E. M., *Aspects of the Novel*, London, 1927.

FRIEDLANDER, M., *The Jewish Religion*, 4th ed., London, 1931.

FRISHMANN, D., *Kol Kithbhê David Frishmann*, Vol. 5, Warsaw-New York, 1930.

GRABO, C. H., *The Technique of the Novel*, Scribner's, U.S.A., 1928.

GREENBERG, L., *The Jews in Russia*, New Haven, 1951.

GUMMER, E. N., *Dickens' Works in Germany 1837-1937*, Oxford, 1940.

HALEVI-LEVIN, J., *Ha-Yehudhim we-ha-Meredh ha-Polani*, ed. by M. Gelber, Jerusalem, 1953.

HALEVI-ZWEIK, Y. *Musag ha-Yahadhuth bi-Thequphath ha-Haskalah*, Tel-Aviv, 1955.

HALKIN, S., *Modern Hebrew Literature, Trends and Values*, New York, 1950.

HARE, J., *Pioneers of Russian Social Thought*, London, etc., 1951.

HELLER, J., 'Mišnatho šel Smolenskin be-Yahadhuth', in *Metsudah*, December, 1943.

HORODETSKY, S., *Ha-Ḥasidhuth we-ha-Ḥasidhim*, Berlin, 1923.

HOUSE, H., *The Dickens World*, 2nd ed., London, 1942.

HUSIK, I., *A History of Mediaeval Jewish Philosophy*, Philadelphia, 1946.

JAMES, H., *The Art of Fiction*, New York, 1948.

KATZNELSON, G., *Ha-Milḥamah ha-Siphruthith bên ha-Ḥaredhim we-ha-Maskilim*, Tel-Aviv, 1954.

Ha-Kerem, Warsaw, 1887.

KLAUSNER, J., *Hisṭoriah šel ha-Siphruth ha-'Ibhrith ha-Ḥadhašah*, 2nd ed., Vols. 3-6, Jerusalem, 1953-58.

KLAUSNER, J., 'Peretz ben Moshe Smolenskin—'Abhi ha-Ra'yon ha-Le'umi ha-'Ibhri', in *Sepher Smolenskin*, ed. by S. Breiman, Jerusalem, 1952.

KLAUSNER, J., *Yoserim U-Bhonim*, Vol. 1, Tel-Aviv, 1925.

KLAUSNER, J. A., *Ha-Nobhilah ba-Siphruth ha-'Ibhrith*, Tel-Aviv, 1947.

KLAUSNER, J. A., 'The First Hebrew Faust', in *German Life and Letters*, New Series, Vol. X, July, 1957, No. 4.

KOVNER, A. U., *Kol Kithbhê A. U. Kovner*, Tel Aviv, 1947.

LAHOWER, P., *Meḥqarim we-Nisyonoth*, Warsaw, 1925.

LAHOWER, P., *Toledoth ha-Siphruth ha-'Ibhrith ha-Ḥadhašah*, 7th ed., Tel-Aviv, 1951.

LAMPERT, E., *Studies in Rebellion*, London, 1957.

LANDAU, J. L., *Short Lectures on Modern Hebrew Literature*, London, 1938.

LEAVIS, F. R., *The Great Tradition*, London, 1948.

Leksikon fun der Nayer Yiddischer Literatur, Vol. 3, New York, 1960.

Leksikon fun der Yiddischer Literatur, Vol. 1, Vilna, 1928.

LEVIN, S. *Childhood in Exile*, London, 1929.

LIDDELL, R., *A Treatise on the Novel*, London, 1949.

LILIENBLUM, M. L., *Ḥaṭṭo'th Ne'urim*, Vienna, 1876.

LIPSCHITZ, A. M., *Kethabhim*, Vol. 1, Jerusalem, 1947.

LIPSCHITZ, J. H., *Toledhoth Yiṣḥaq*, Warsaw, 1896.

LIPSCHITZ, J. H., *Maḥaziqê ha-Dath*, Pietrokow, 1903.

LIPSCHITZ, J. H., *Zikheron Ya'aqobh*, Kovno-Sloboda, 1924-30.

U

LUBBOCK, P., *The Craft of Fiction*, London, 1921.

MAIMON, S., *The Autobiography of Solomon Maimon*, translated by J. Clark Murray, London, 1954.

MALAKHI, A. R., *Massoth u-Rešimoth*, New York, 1937.

MAPU, A., *Kol Kithbhê Abraham Mapu*, Tel-Aviv, 1950.

MEISL, J., *Haskalah*, Berlin, 1919.

Ha-Meliṣ, 1882, 1900.

MENDILOW, A. A., *Time and the Novel*, London, 1952.

MIRSKY, D. S., *A History of Russian Literature*, London, 1927.

MUIR, E., *The Structure of the Novel*, London, 1949.

MIDDLETON MURRY, J., *The Problem of Style*, Oxford, 1922.

OESTERLEY and BOX, *The Literature of Rabbinical and Mediaeval Judaism*, London, 1920.

PARES, B., *A History of Russia*, London, 1926.

PATTERSON, D., 'Israel Weisbrem: A Forgotten Hebrew Novelist of the Nineteenth Century', in the *Journal of Semitic Studies*, Vol. 4, No. 1, January 1959.

PATTERSON, D., 'Some Religious Attitudes Reflected in the Hebrew Novels of the Period of Enlightenment', in the *Bulletin of the John Rylands Library*, Vol. 42, No. 2, March 1960.

PATTERSON, D., 'Hebrew Drama', in the *Bulletin of the John Rylands Library*, Vol. 43, No. 1, September 1960.

PATTERSON, D., 'The Portrait of Ḥasidism in the Nineteenth Century Hebrew Novel', in the *Journal of Semitic Studies*, Vol. 5, No. 4, October 1960.

PATTERSON, D., *The Foundations of Modern Hebrew Literature*, London, 1961.

PATTERSON, D., 'Some Linguistic Aspects of the Nineteenth-Century Hebrew Novel', in the *Journal of Semitic Studies*, Vol. 7, No. 2, Autumn 1962.

PATTERSON, D., 'Sickness and Death in the Hebrew Novel of the Haskalah', in *The Jewish Journal of Sociology*, Vol. V. No. 1, June 1963.

PATTERSON, D., 'The Portrait of the "Ṣaddik" in the Nineteenth-Century Hebrew Novel', in the *Journal of Semitic Studies*, Vol. 8, No. 2, Autumn 1963.

PATTERSON, D., *Abraham Mapu, The Creator of the Modern Hebrew Novel*, London, 1964.

PATTERSON, D., 'Epistolary Elements in the Novels of Abraham Mapu', in the *Annual of the Leeds University Oriental Society*, Vol. IV, 1964.

PENIEL, N., *Ha-Ḥinnukh ha-'Ibhri be-Yeṣiratho šel Peretz Smolenskin*, Tel Aviv, 1957.

PHILIPSON, D., *Max Lilienthal*, New York, 1915.

PHILIPSON, D., *The Reform Movement in Judaism*, 2nd ed., New York, 1930.

RABIN, C., ''Ibhrith Medhubbereth Liphnê 125 Šanah', in the series *Lešonenu La-'Am*, Jerusalem, 1963.

RABINOWITZ, A. S., *Haphṭarah*, Tel-Aviv, 1928.

RABINOWITZ, J., 'Peretz Smolenskin', in *Sepher Smolenskin*, ed. by S. Breiman, Jerusalem, 1952.

RABNITSKY, I. H. *Dor we-Sopheraw*, Tel-Aviv, 1927.

RAISIN, J. S., *The Haskalah Movement in Russia*, Philadelphia, 1913.

RAISIN, M., ed., *'Iggeroth Sopherim 'Ibhrim*, Brooklyn-New York, 1947.

REIDER, J., 'Negative Tendencies in Modern Hebrew Literature', in *Hebrew Union College Annual*, Jubilee Volume, Cincinnati, 1925.

RICHARDS, I. A., *The Philosophy of Rhetoric*, New York, 1950.

ROBACK, A. A., *The Story of Yiddish Literature*, New York, 1940.

ROTH, C., *The History of the Jews in Italy*, Philadelphia, 1946.

RUPPIN, A., *The Jews in the Modern World*, London, 1934.

SACHER, H. M., *The Course of Modern Jewish History*, London, 1958.

SAMUEL, M., *The World of Sholom Aleichem*, New York, 1943.

SCHNEOUR, Z., *Noah Pandre's Village*, translated by J. Leftwich, London, 1938.

SCHOLEM, G. G., *Major Trends in Jewish Mysticism*, 3rd ed., London, 1955.

Sepher Zikkaron le-Sopherê Yisrael, published by *Ha-'Asiph*, Warsaw, 1889.

Sepher Zikkaron le-Yobhel ha-Šibh'im šel A. S. Rabinowitz, Tel-Aviv, 1924.

SHA'ANAN, A., *'Iyyunim be-Siphruth ha-'Haskalah'*, Merhavia, 1952.

SHAKED, G., 'Goral wa-'Alilah be-Yeṣiratho šel Mendele Mokher Sepharim', in *Sepher ha-Yobhel šel ha-Gimnasiah ha-'Ibhrith Biru-šalayim*, Jerusalem, 1962.

SHALOM ALEICHEM, *Šomer's Mišpaṭ*, Berdichev, 1888.

ṢITRON, S. L., *Mapu u-Smolenskin we-Sippurêhem*, Cracow, 1889.

ṢITRON, S. L., *Yoṣerê ha-Siphruth ha-'Ibhrith ha-Ḥadhašah*, Vilna, 1922.

Širê Šomer we-Zikhronothaw, Jerusalem, 1952.

SLOUSCHZ, N., *The Renascence of Hebrew Literature*, Philadelphia, 1909.

SOKOLOW, N., *Hibbath Zion*, Jerusalem, 1935.

SPICEHANDLER, E., 'Joshua Heschel Schorr: Maskil and East European Reformist', in the *Hebrew Union College Annual*, Vol. XXXI, 1960.

SPIEGEL, S., *Hebrew Reborn*, London, 1931.

STREIT, S., *Ba-'Aloth ha-Šaḥar*, Tel-Aviv, 1927.

TILLOTSON, K., *Novels of the Eighteen Forties*, Oxford, 1954.

U*

TOMKINS, S. R., *The Russian Intelligentsia*, Oklahoma, 1957.

Unser Vater Šomer (translated by A. Weisman under the title *'Abhinu Šomer*), Jerusalem, 1953.

VERNADSKY, G., *A History of Russia*, 3rd ed., New Haven, 1953.

WACHSTEIN, B., etc., *Die Hebräische Publizistik in Wien*, Vienna, 1930.

WALDSTEIN, A. S., *The Evolution of Modern Hebrew Literature*, New York, 1916.

WAXMAN, M., *A History of Jewish Literature*, Vol. 3, rev. ed., New York-London, 1960.

WENGEROFF, P., *Memoiren einer Grossmutter*, Berlin, 1908-10.

WERSES, S., ' 'Iyyunim ba-Mibhneh šel "Megalleh Ṭemirin" u-"Bhoḥan Ṣaddiq" ' in *Tarbiṣ*, Vol. 31, No. 4, 1962.

WERSES, S., 'Ha-Ḥasidhuth be-'Ênê Siphruth ha-Haskalah', in *Moladh*, Vol. 18, No. 144-5, August-September, 1960.

WIENER, L., *The History of Yiddish Literature in the Nineteenth Century*, London, 1899.

Yad la-Qore', year 1, nos. 3-4, April, 1944.

ZBOROWSKI, M., and HERZOG, E., *Life is with People*, New York, 1952.

ZEITLIN, W., *Bibliotheca Hebraica Post-Mendelssohniana*, Leipsig, 1891.

ZUNSER, E., *A Jewish Bard*, New York, 1905.

Select Supplementary Bibliography

A comprehensive survey of the bibliography of *HASKALAH* may be found in the following works by S. WERSES:

Trends and Forms in the Literature of Haskalah (Hebrew), Jerusalem, 1990, pp. 356–412.
'New and old studies in the literature and the era of *Haskalah*' (Hebrew) in *Madda'ê ha-Yahadhuth*, 36, pp. 43–72, 1996.
'New and old studies in the literature and the era of *Haskalah*, additions and supplements' (Hebrew) in *Madda'ê ha-Yahadhuth*, 37, pp. 31–38, 1997.

ABERBACH, D., *Realism, Caricature and Bias: The Fiction of Mendele Mocher Sefarim*, Oxford, 1993.
ALTER, R., *The Invention of Hebrew Prose: Modern Fiction and the Language of Realism*, Seattle, 1988.
BEN-YEHUDA, E., *A Dream Come True*, translated by T. Muraoka, ed. by G. Mandel, Boulder, 1993.
BRAUDES, R.A., *Ha-Dath we-ha-Ḥayyim (Religion and Life)*, ed. by G. Shaked, Jerusalem, 1974.
BRAUDES, R.A., *Setê ha-Qesawoth (The Two Extremes)*, ed. by B-A. Feingold, Jerusalem, 1989.
CROWN, A.D., trans., *The World of Israel Weissbrem*, Boulder, 1993.
FEIERBERG, M.Z., *Whither? And Other Stories*, translated by H. Halkin, Philadelphia, 1973.
FRANKEL, J., *Prophecy and Politics: Socialism, Nationalism, and the Russian Jews, 1862–1917*, Cambridge, 1981.
GLINERT, L., ed., *Hebrew in Ashkenaz*, New York, 1993.
HABERER, E.E., *Jews and Revolution in Nineteenth-Century Russia*, Cambridge, 1995.
KLIER, J.D., *Imperial Russia's Jewish Question, 1855–1881*, Cambridge, 1995.
LEDERHENDLER, E., *The Road to Modern Jewish Politics: Political Tradition and Political Reconstruction in the Jewish Community of Tsarist Russia*, New York and Oxford, 1989.
LÖWE, H-D., *The Tsars and the Jews: Reform, Reaction and Anti-Semitism in Imperial Russia, 1772–1917*, Chur, 1993.

MAOZ, R., *Villainy in the Novels of Peretz Smolenskin,* unpublished doctoral thesis, Oxford, 1989.

MINTZ, A., *Banished From Their Father's Table: Loss of Faith and Hebrew Autobiography,* Bloomington, 1989.

MIRON, D., *A Traveller Disguised,* New York, 1973.

PATTERSON, D., 'The influence of Hebrew literature on the growth of Jewish nationalism in the nineteenth century', in R. Sussex and J.C. Eade, eds., *Culture and Nationalism in Nineteenth Century Eastern Europe,* Columbus, 1985.

PATTERSON, D., *A Phoenix in Fetters: Studies in Nineteenth and Early Twentieth Century Hebrew Fiction,* Savage, 1988 [1990].

ROGGER, H., *Jewish Politics and Right-Wing Politics in Imperial Russia,* London, 1986.

SHAKED, G., *Ha-Sipporeth ha-'Ibhrith, 1880–1970,* vol. 1., Tel-Aviv, 1977.

SMOLENSKIN, P., *Qebhurath Ḥamor (A Donkey's Burial),* edited by D. Weinfeld, Jerusalem, 1968.

STANISLAWSKI, M., *'For Whom Do I Toil?' J.L. Gordon and The Crisis of Russian Jewry,* New York, 1988.

VITAL, D., *The Origins of Zionism,* Oxford, 1975.

ZIPPERSTEIN, S.J., *The Jews of Odessa: A Cultural History, 1794–1881,* Stanford, 1985.

Index

Where references are given to notes, the page number is that *on* which the note is printed, not *from* which the reference emanates

Chanuka: A Moment Kindled In Time

James Kaufman

(*Baruch atah adonai . . .*)
 The blessing echoes down the hall
 into rooms furnished with time and history,
 and sleeping children snugly rolled up
 like Torah scrolls that will carry the message
 from room to room.

 Walls absorbed in memory—reminiscing,
 each side sharing what the other was missing.
 Windows looking both ways absorbed in circumspection,
 two sides, two views in one conception.

(*asher kidshanu b'mitzvotav . . .*)
 Lingering by the room's doorposts,
 the blessing commands a pause
 hearkening descendants and ancestors
 halt at a moment kindled in time,
 and share what the other is missing,
 two directions pausing at a common destiny.

(. . .*l'hadlik nair shel chanuka*)
 The festival flames bring light to shadowed rooms,
 revealing history to those who strike the match
 to elevate a moment in time
 where descendants become ancestors
 and Jews are windows
 seeing two directions: backwards and forwards,
 becoming two reflections: of our people then and of ourselves now
 and all converging in one connection: sleeping children snugly rolled

      up like Torah scrolls carrying
      the message from room to room.

JAMES KAUFMAN serves Temple Beth Hillel, North Hollywood, California.

Paste —

Robert Hammel is _not_ free

dinner tonight .

Map. The Pale of Settlement *to which the Jews of Russia were* *confined. This area of* 362,000 *square miles comprised* 20% *of the* *entire European Russia and* 4% *of the entire Russian area. It contained* *the districts of:* 1. *Bessarabia,* 2. *Chernigov,* 3. *Ekatorinoslav,* 4. *Grodno,* 5. *Kalisch,* 6. *Kherson,* 7. *Kielce,* 8. *Kiev,* 9. *Kovno,* 10. *Lomza,* 11. *Lublin,* 12. *Minsk,* 13. *Mohilev,* 14. *Piotrokow,* 15. *Plosk,* 16. *Podolia,* 17. *Poltava,* 18. *Radom,* 19. *Suwalki,* 20. *Syedletz,* 21. *Taurida,* 22. *Vilna,* 23. *Vitebsk,* 24. *Volhynia,* 25. *Warsaw*

About the Author

DAVID PATTERSON is the Emeritus President of the Oxford Centre for Hebrew and Jewish Studies, and an Emeritus Fellow of St. Cross College, Oxford.